ALICE TO THE LIGH

Also by Juliet Dusinberre and from the same publishers

SHAKESPEARE AND THE NATURE OF WOMEN

VIRGINIA WOOLF'S RENAISSANCE: Woman Reader or
Common Reader?

Alice to the Lighthouse

Children's Books and Radical Experiments in Art

Juliet Dusinberre
M. C. Bradbrook Fellow in English
Girton College
Cambridge

Published in Great Britain by
MACMILLAN PRESS LTD
Houndmills, Basingstoke, Hampshire RG21 6XS and London
Companies and representatives throughout the world

A catalogue record for this book is available from the British Library.

ISBN 0–333–75984–2 hardcover
ISBN 0–333–65850–7 paperback

Published in the United States of America by
ST. MARTIN'S PRESS, INC.,
Scholarly and Reference Division,
175 Fifth Avenue, New York, N.Y. 10010

ISBN 0–312–22057–X

Library of Congress Cataloging-in-Publication Data
Dusinberre, Juliet.
Alice to the lighthouse : children's books and radical experiments
in art / Juliet Dusinberre.
p.   cm.
Includes bibliographical references and index.
ISBN 0–312–22057–X (pbk. : alk. paper)
1. Children's literature, English—History and criticism.
2. English literature—20th century—History and criticism.
3. Children's literature, American—History and criticism.
4. American literature—20th century—History and criticism.
5. Children—Books and reading—History—20th century.
6. Literature, Experimental—History and criticism.   7. Woolf,
Virginia, 1882–1941—Technique.   8. Carroll, Lewis, 1832–1898–
–Influence.   I. Title.
PR990.D87   1999
820.9'9282'0904—dc21   98–44053
                                                        CIP

© Juliet Dusinberre 1987, 1999

First published 1987
Reissued (with alterations) 1999

This book is printed on paper suitable for recycling and made from fully managed and
sustained forest sources.

10   9   8   7   6   5   4   3   2   1
08   07   06   05   04   03   02   01   00   99

Printed and bound in Great Britain by Antony Rowe Ltd, Chippenham, Wiltshire

For Edward and Martin

*'I will plant a lighthouse here, a
head of Sweet Alice.'*

Virginia Woolf, *The Waves*

Contents

List of Illustrations

Small illustrations appear inset in the text as follows:

from *Alice's Adventures in Wonderland* on pp. 37, 55, 162, 187, 193;
from *Through the Looking-Glass* on pp. 2, 36, 70, 71, 142, 179, 180,
    278;
from the *Strand Magazine* on p. 40;
from John Bunyan, *The Pilgrim's Progress* on p. 53.

Acknowledgements

I do not think that this book would have been written if I had not been elected to a Research Fellowship at Clare Hall, Cambridge. I owe an incalculable debt to its President and Fellows, matched only by my obligations to Girton College for unstinting support both financially and in the generous granting of sabbatical leave. I would like to express my thanks especially to Michael Lapidge and Jill Mann, and to Gillian Beer, whose learning and enthusiasm have sustained me at every stage of the work.

Professor Quentin Bell was unfailingly patient and precise in responding to my questions about Virginia Woolf. I acknowledge with thanks his permission to quote from the holograph drafts of *To the Lighthouse* and *The Waves*, from the essay on *Robinson Crusoe* which is in the same notebook as *To the Lighthouse*, and from the earlier typescript of *The Voyage Out*; as well as to reprint two photographs from Stella Duckworth's Album, a photograph of the holograph of the final page of *The Waves*, and a page decorated by Vanessa Bell from the Hogarth Press limited edition of *Kew Gardens* (1927). All of these materials are in the Henry W. and Albert A. Berg Collection of English and American Literature in the New York Public Library and I am most grateful to the Curator, Dr Lola Szladits, and the staff of the Collection for making its resources available to me.

I was fortunate to be able to talk to Mrs Pamela Diamand about her father, Roger Fry, only three weeks before her sudden death in August 1985. Her daughter, Mrs Annabel Cole, together with the co-executrix of Mrs Diamand's estate, have graciously permitted me to use quotations from Roger Fry's letters to his family, from his unpublished papers, and from the unpublished Fellowship dissertation, all in the King's College Archive, Cambridge. I would like to record my appreciation of the willingness of the archivist, Dr Michael Halls, to offer me his expert knowledge of his collection, and for his permission to quote from the correspondence between Roger Fry and Goldsworthy Lowes Dickinson, which he is editing.

I am very grateful for the generous help I have received in the preparation of this book. Dr J. C. Rathmell gave judicious criticism of the complete draft of the manuscript, as did Brian Alderson, editor of F. J. Harvey Darton's *Children's Books in England* (reissued in 1982). Dr Susan James advised me on the sections on phenomenology, with particular reference to William James and Bergson; Dr Eric Warner made many constructive suggestions about the presentation of material, and shared with me his own knowledge of Virginia Woolf scholarship. Needless to say, any waywardness which remains is my own. Dr Barbara Rosen and Dr Francelia Butler both gave help and encouragement when I started working in the field of children's literature.

I would like to thank the Curator and staff of the Beinecke Rare Book and Manuscript Library, Yale University, for furthering my work in the Stevenson Collection of books and manuscripts; and to acknowledge the permission of the Yale University Library to quote from unpublished letters of Robert Louis Stevenson, from drafts for *A Child's Garden of Verses*, and from unpublished notes.

I am much indebted to the courteous service provided by Mrs Gaskell and the staff of the Girton College Library, and particularly for access to the children's books in its Gamble collection; to the English Faculty Library, and to Janice Fairholm and the staff of Cambridge University Library; to all those who have helped me at the University of Warwick main library and at its Westwood branch; to the staff of the British Library; to Duncan Haldane and Anne Hobbs at the Victoria and Albert Museum; and to Elizabeth Newlands at J. M. Dent and Sons Ltd. The late Miss Aline Burch, secretary of Leonard Woolf, generously bequeathed me her Hogarth Press books.

Excerpts from *The Waves* by Virginia Woolf, copyright 1931 by Harcourt Brace Jovanovich, Inc., renewed 1959 by Leonard Woolf; from *To the Lighthouse* by Virginia Woolf, copyright 1927 by Harcourt Brace Jovanovich, Inc., renewed 1955 by Leonard Woolf; and from *The Voyage Out* by Virginia Woolf, copyright 1920 by George H. Doran and Company, renewed 1948 by Leonard Woolf, are all reprinted by permission of Harcourt Brace Jovanovich, Inc., and by permission of the author's estate and the Hogarth Press. Excerpts from *My Ántonia* by Willa Cather, published by Virago Press Ltd 1980, copyright © by Willa Cather 1918 and renewed 1951 by the executors of the estate of Willa Cather are reprinted by permission of the Virago Press Ltd; and the same excerpts from *My Ántonia* by

Willa Cather, copyright 1918, 1936, 1946 by Willa Sibert Cather, copyright 1954 by Edith Lewis, copyright © renewed 1977 by Walter Havighurst, are reprinted by permission of Houghton Mifflin Company. Dr Brian Crozier has given me permission to refer to material in his valuable unpublished Cambridge PhD thesis 'Notions of Childhood in London Theatre, 1880–1905' (1981). Some of the discussion in this book of Flora Thompson's *Lark Rise to Candleford* appeared in an expanded and somewhat different form in my article 'The Child's Eye and the Adult's Voice: Flora Thompson's *Lark Rise to Candleford*', *Review of English Studies*, n.s. xxxv, no. 137 (Feb 1984) 61–70, published in Oxford at the Clarendon Press.

I am grateful to the Syndics of Cambridge University Library for permission to reproduce illustrations from G. H. Payne, *The Child in Human Progress* (1916), from Gertrude Jekyll, *Children and Gardens* (1908), from Mark Twain, *Huckleberry Finn* (1884) and from R. L. Stevenson, *A Child's Garden of Verses* (1896), illustrated by C. Robinson. The British Library has given me permission to reproduce the picture of a death-bed scene from *Froggy's Little Brother* by Brenda (1875), and of a doll's funeral from *Aunt Sally's Life* by Mrs Gatty (1865). The cartoon by George Price is reproduced with acknowledgements to the *New Yorker Art and Artists Album* (1970) and Tate Gallery Publications, *A Child of Six Could Do It* (Exhibition catalogue, 1973). The *Punch* cartoon 'Our Decadents' (1894) is also reproduced from this catalogue. The line drawing from *Heidi* by Johanna Spyri, illustrated by Vincent O. Cohen (1950) in the Children's Illustrated Classics series, is reproduced by kind permission of J. M. Dent and Sons Ltd. The Gresham Press has permitted me to reproduce a line drawing from its facsimile edition (1978) of Bunyan, *The Pilgrim's Progress*. I am extremely grateful for the help I have received from R. S. Pile at Primavera Cambridge Ltd, and from the Pallas Gallery (Moxton Square, London).

I would like to thank Mrs Clare Price for much hard work and good humour in the preparation of the manuscript; Mrs Mary Caswell for help in the early stages of the project; and Mrs Jean Smith at Girton College for speedy relief at moments of crisis. Aspects of the venture would have been impossible without John and Thea Stainer, Mrs Pam Grainger, and the hospitality in the USA of Pat and Gerald Pollack and of Jane and Henry Turner, to all of whom most grateful thanks. My uncle, Robert Cecil, kindly allowed me to share his work on death in Victorian children's books; Pauline

Stainer's interest spurred me on; and my mother-in-law, Charlotte Snelson, recalled American childhood reading for my benefit.

Many of the books discussed here were read aloud to me by my grandmother, Marjorie Cecil, whose gifts were only surpassed by those of her daughter, my own mother, Thea Stainer. In reading aloud to my own children, I hear only their voices.

To Bill, what can be said? Perfect indexer, proof-reader, cook? Well, not really. But here it is at last, and thank you for everything.

J.A.D.

Preface to the 1999 Reissue

Since the publication of *Alice to the Lighthouse* in 1987 the field of children's literature has steadily gained ground as a serious academic study and many sophisticated and stimulating books have appeared since this book was published. My particular project was to demonstrate the symbiotic relation between children's books and adult writing, and the close connections between the ways in which a society views children and the books it produces for them to read. The generation of children for whom Carroll's Alice replaced Bunyan's Christian suddenly had access to fictions in which the pious child was itself exposed as a fiction of the adult world.

When the Ramsay children in Virginia Woolf's *To the Lighthouse* sit at Mrs Ramsay's famous dinner table while she serves out Böeuf en Daube, they make their presence felt by a process of silent disruption. They are not assimilable to the aesthetic moulding of guests at which Mrs Ramsay is adept. A spirit of satire, risibility and irreverence augurs the eventual collapse of the Victorian world the Ramsays embody, even at its most triumphant moment. The brood of children who seem to confirm the creativity and durability of that Victorian family scene are the new generation who witness and partake in its destruction, as Virginia Woolf herself did. Woolf recalled later the painful contradictions of wanting to laugh when everyone cried at her mother's deathbed. The same spirit of irreverent dissociation surrounds Rachel Vinrace in Woolf's first novel, *The Voyage Out*, as she listens to the academic gossip of the men on the Euphrosene, a boat whose name mocks the poems published by Virginia Woolf's new Bloomsbury circle of Cambridge friends, a volume she satirised (in an unpublished review) for its melancholia and condescension towards the reader.

If one had to choose one characteristic which distinguished writing for children during the century before Virginia Woolf's birth in 1882, it would be condescension to the reader. The stance of the adult writer towards the child reader seldom deviated from the aim of spiritual, moral and educational improvement. The author's right to dictate to the reader was a given of children's books until the advent of Louis Carroll's Alice in *Alice's Adventures in Wonderland* (1865) and *Through the Looking*-Glass (1871). Carroll declared of his book that he had no special 'meaning' in mind when he wrote it: he was content for it to mean what the reader wanted. This abrogation of authorial control became one among many ways in which the *Alice* books set the scene for changes in the relation of writer and reader, later mirrored in adult fiction.

Lewis Carroll's Alice seems to have had two immediate and radically contrasted forbears. At one extreme walks Dickens's little Nell on her earthly pilgrimage, a figure closely associated with that of Bunyan's Christian, towards a death which became immediately legendary across the English-speaking world as a tear-jerker. At the other extreme stands Charlotte Brontë's Jane Eyre, stoutly asserting to Mr Brocklehurst that the way to avoid going to hell is to stay well and not die. In Carroll's work you can run very fast and stay in one place, or start the race at any point; if Alice is going anywhere, it is not on a pilgrimage, but across a chess-board to become a Queen. Like Jane Eyre, she is solid and intransigent. When Carroll makes her the sturdy and irrepressible critic of the world around her, suppressing laughter, astonishment, pity and disdain, like the children at Mrs Ramsay's dinner-table, he at the same time undermines the language and conventions of fiction itself. It is not just the book which may mean anything the reader likes. In *Alice in Wonderland* (as it quickly became in general speaking) words themselves slip away from the control of the speaker. The medium has its own ludic life:

'When *I* use a word,' Humpty Dumpty said, in rather a scornful tone, 'it means just what I choose it to mean – neither more or less.'

'The question is,' said Alice, 'whether you *can* make words mean so many different things.'

'The question is,' said Humpty Dumpty, 'which is to be master – that's all.'

The question of mastery over language, structure, vision, morals, characters and readers was to become the central concern not only of children's authors, but of many adult writers – Virginia Woolf, Henry James, Joyce – in the shift of consciousness at the turn of the twentieth century usually loosely christened 'modernism'. In that radical revisioning of narrative, which had parallels both in music and in the visual art of the Post-Impressionists championed by Roger Fry, children's books after *Alice* play a part which has been ignored because they are perceived by the critical establishment as belonging to a separate sub-culture which has never been allowed a place in the discussion of high culture.

Robert Louis Stevenson, a friend of Virginia Woolf's father, Leslie Stephen (editor of the *Cornhill Magazine*), remembered the tedium of Sundays dedicated to imbibing the saccharine sentiments and instruction of Maria Louisa Charlesworth's *Ministering Children* (1854). When he wrote *Treasure Island* he dispensed with the dominant third person narrator and spun a yarn in which children could escape from their subjection to the author as well as to adults. In her first published words – the note which she wrote for Maitland's biography of her father – Virginia Woolf recalled Leslie Stephen's reading *Treasure Island* aloud to the Stephen children. She said of her father's treatment of his children:

> My impression as a child always was that my father was not very much older than we were. He used to take us to sail our boats in the Round Pond, and with his own hands fitted one out with masts and sails after the pattern of a Cornish lugger; and we knew that his interest was no 'grown-up' pretence; it was as genuine as our own; so there was a perfectly equal companionship between us.[1]

The invented world of the Cornish lugger in which children and adults could be equal is Stevenson's, not only in *Treasure Island* (1883) and *A Child's Garden of Verses* (1885), but in his influential and widely-quoted essay on 'Child's Play', published in 1878, in which he attacked the tyranny with which adults had tried to control the child's perceptions of reality. Children are not truth-tellers, but fantasists, where adults are constrained by their own inability to pretend. The children in E. Nesbit's *The Story of the Treasure Seekers* (1899) stomach cold mutton by pretending that 'it was a savoury stew made of red deer that Edward shot. So then they were the Children of the New Forest, and the mutton tasted much better'. The attack on realism for its insistence on empirical truth becomes central to Virginia Woolf's own rebellion against the fiction of Arnold Bennett and John Galsworthy in the famous essay

'Mr Bennett and Mrs Brown'. In repudiating a rigid demarcation between the real and the unreal, Woolf remains true to the child's vision which she recognised when her father played with herself and her siblings. Sadly, Leslie Stephen ceased to play when his wife died, creating instead an overpowering myth of loss from which Viriginia Woolf only escaped by writing her 'elegy' novel, *To the Lighthouse.*

Virginia Woolf's wicked wit and irreverent spirit were both relished and feared by her friends. When the Stephen children conversed with other children about the nature of Good Friday Vanessa recalls that Virginia had to be banished, shrieking with laughter, though Quentin Bell's recollection of the story is that when asked about the meaning of Christmas Virginia replied that it celebrated the Crucifixion of our Lord. Scepticism was natural in the children of Leslie Stephen who had lost his faith and become an atheist, but Virginia's irreverence embraced not only the Deity, but the sacred cows of the entire male world and its authority structures.

The after-life of Virginia Woolf has suffered as much from distortion as the after-life of her own mother suffered at the hands of Leslie Stephen's lugubrious indulgence of his grief, enshrined in the *Mausoleum book* he wrote for his children. Even within her own life-time Woolf felt herself to be defined as an invalidish Bloomsbury aesthete, a lady-novelist, a category she despised as vehemently as George Eliot had done. Her rediscovery by the late twentieth-century women's movement and by feminist scholars has sometimes painted instead a portrait of a dauntingly earnest Virginia Woolf. The testimony of her friends, as well as of her diaries, letters and critical essays, especially in the two volumes of *The Common Reader*, provides an antidote to the high-culture image of the demanding and remote author of *The Waves*, giving her the more approachable face of someone with the common touch, a quality few people even now are willing to allow to her. The laughter which she struggled to conceal at her mother's death-bed for the pompous rituals of demise, she was to carry with her into her own adult life. When her friend Jacques Raverat, the painter, died, she wrote: 'I do not any longer feel inclined to doff the cap to death. I like to go out of the room talking, with an unfinished casual sentence on my lips.' The same casualness surrounds the celebrated confining of Mrs Ramsay's death to brackets. But just as Virginia felt that her father played with his children as though he were a child himself, so she held on to her childish refusal to be dominated by the text in which he rewrote his wife's life and death, not only on the page but in actual living. Her rebellion has its roots in Carroll's *Alice* books with their death jokes, as well as in many later children's books.

In 1935 Walter de la Mare reflected on the Victorian tradition of pathetic child deaths, mentioning *Eric, Misunderstood, Uncle Tom's Cabin* and *Bleak House*. Brenda's *Froggy's Little Brother* (1875), was certainly also a top favourite in the necrophiliac stakes. The menacing sentimentality imposed by the author on the child reader has complex roots in Victorian culture. The revolt of writers against it began in children's books, and two of the leading heroes in the attack were the creations not of British writers, but of Mark Twain in *The Adventures of Tom Sawyer* (1876) and *The Adventures of Huckleberry Finn* (1884). If the death of Beth in Louisa May Alcott's *Good Wives* was composed, however touchingly, in the old style, the staged funeral service in *Tom Sawyer* – rudely disrupted by the 'dead' boys themselves – strikes a new note.

An irreverent view not only of death itself, but of its sanctified topos in children's books, characterises Frances Hodgson Burnett's *The Secret Garden* (1911), in which the pampered invalid Colin Craven is rescued from adult morbidity by Mary Lennox, whose literalness and solidity hark back to Carroll's Alice. *The Secret Garden* was the more remarkable for following the very different *In the Closed Room* (1904), in which the author transparently uses the traditional children's book mode of death narrative to lament the loss of her own son, Lionel. But seven years later Burnett ruthlessly cast off the shackles of her own authorial dictatorship, as Virginia Woolf herself was to do when she closed the book on Mrs Ramsay's world at the end of the first section of *To the Lighthouse*, and portrayed not death but survival.

The recovery of the literal was for Woolf another form of protest against the false celebration of the literary which she associated with Victorianism, where everything acquired symbolic and moral significance. She claimed that the lighthouse was not a symbol, but just a lighthouse. Woolf annexed into writing Roger Fry's conviction that painters must paint only what they see, and that what matters is not ethical and narrative significance, but design, colour and medium. Woolf attacked E. M. Forster for writing about the novel without saying anything about its medium, words. Her own sense of words as a medium comparable to paint, with a life and texture of their own, also looks back to the virtuosity with which words in *Alice in Wonderland* and *Through the Looking-Glass* assert their independence from the world of meaning. Roger Fry wrote to Woolf that like Henry James she used 'language as a medium of art', making 'the very texture of the words have a meaning and quality really almost apart from what you are talking about'.² This way of writing is part of the modernist revolt against Victorian preaching, pioneered by a number of children's writers following Lewis Carroll, among whom one of the most prominent is E. Nesbit.

The germ of *Alice to the Lighthouse* lay in a sudden recognition of the irreverence of E. Nesbit's books, an irreverence often identified with the child narrator, Oswald Bastable. That distinctive mood conjured up Virginia Woolf, the anarchic, devastatingly comic Virginia Woolf who has been largely written out of literary history. In Nesbit's hand the cardinal sin is not moral, but aesthetic: not bad children, but bad writing. Writing becomes what it was to Woolf, a form of play.

For Nesbit there is no contradiction between the literal and the fantastic. The rejection of realism is for her a repudiation of tired fictions imposed by adults on an unwilling child reader. In their fantastic adventures her children are literal children not literary ones. The turning-away from allegory to a more solid vision of childhood was part of a whole cultural movement in which children were allowed to be part of a Darwinian world, recovering a relation to animals rather than angels. *Alice to the Lighthouse* ends with a comparison of Willa Cather and Laura Ingalls Wilder, which shows Wilder capturing an authentic childish vision of a literal landscape which Willa Cather wanted to portray in her depiction of pioneer life, but which involved for the adult writer a problematic casting-off of powerful literary traditions. Laura Ingalls Wilder, writing for children, has the freer hand. Charlotte M. Yonge had declared in a critical essay written in 1869, four years after the publication of *Alice's Adventures in Wonderland*, that Lewis Carroll had injected the traditional fairy tale with solidity, the literal rather than the literary. In that shift of consciousness lay emancipation for the child in the book, as well as for the child reader. For Mr Ramsay in *To the Lighthouse* an outing in a boat was a 'passage to that fabled land where our brightest hopes are extinguished, our frail barks founder in darkness', but for his son James and his daughter Cam it was just a boat with someone rowing, who might, like Alice, catch a crab: 'A dear little crab!' thought Alice. 'I should like that'. Virginia Woolf, who has suffered from being passed off as too 'literary' for comfort, rejected her father's literary world because its metaphors were exhausted by over-use. When she asserted, to an audience of schoolchildren, that the reader must be the author's writer and accomplice, she proposed a new contract which had been pioneered in children's books written after *Alice*. In this new relationship the child was not a tool fashioned to relieve adult guilt and cultural weariness, but an independent resistant being, for whom adults were ridiculous.

The absence of a deliberately pointed moral, and of linear direction in narrative, the abdication of the author as preacher, and the use of words as play, all of which were pioneered in children's books in the latter half of the nineteenth century, feed into the work of Virginia Woolf and her generation of writers. *Alice to the Lighthouse* charts the passage of a whole culture from *Alice's Adventures in Wonderland* and *Through the Looking-Glass* through Freud and Fröebel, Sully and Roger Fry, towards Virginia Woolf's *To the Lighthouse*.

Juliet Dusinberre

NOTES

1 'Note by one of his daughters', in Frederick William Maitland, *The Life and Letters of Leslie Stephen* (London: Duckworth, 1906), p. 474.
2 Quoted in Frances Spalding, *Roger Fry* (1980), p. 212.

1
Children's Books, Childhood and Modernism

In 1932 the centenary of Lewis Carroll's birth was celebrated with plenty of treacle from the treacle well. Simultaneously the new journal *Scrutiny*, edited by the Leavises, carried in its first issue an attack on Virginia Woolf, whose novel *The Waves* had just been published. The lectures which Roger Fry gave during the 1932 exhibition of French painting at Burlington House appeared in book form under the title *Characteristics of French Art*.[1] Kenneth Grahame, author of *The Golden Age* (1895), *Dream Days* (1899) and *The Wind in the Willows* (1908),[2] a man born the year Darwin's *Origin of Species* was published – in 1859 – died. The lighthouse beam which illumined these events might have flashed momentarily across the Atlantic on another first work, the childhood memories cast in the form of a children's book, of a woman born in a pioneer family two years after the official publication of *Alice's Adventures in Wonderland* in 1865, Laura Ingalls Wilder, author of *Little House in the Big Woods*. 1865 had witnessed an audacious new venture in Carroll's children's book,[3] just as 1932 saw Woolf at her most daring after the brilliant success of *To the Lighthouse* five years earlier.

This is a study in interaction between children's books and adult books, between children and adults, between theories and images. It seeks to relate *Alice* not only to a whole generation of children who became adults with the new century, but to a generation of thought and writing. By the time of Carroll's death in 1898 *Alice* had supplanted *The Pilgrim's Progress* in the popular imagination.[4] How did this affect the culture which produced Virginia Woolf and what did she owe to those transmutations of thought and feeling in which the two *Alice* books played a central part?

The essay which Woolf wrote on Carroll in 1939 is pinched in its praise. He was a man in whom childhood lodged 'whole and entire. . . . As he grew older . . . this hard block of pure childhood starved the mature man of nourishment.' She concludes, with a peculiar

1

mixture of asperity and admiration, that 'the two Alices are not books for children; they are the only books in which we become children'.[5] But she had not always been so solemn and censorious, either about Carroll or about becoming a child. In September 1921 she wrote in her diary: 'Clive came suddenly into view yesterday, in white flannel trousers, and open flannel shirt. He seemed bursting through; and his neck a series of rings of fat, like the Chess Queen's body. A dowager would hide this with a dog collar.'[6] Both Carroll's Chess Queens in *Through the Looking-Glass* are represented by Tenniel as clad in Michelin tyres, and, whether or not Virginia Woolf saw in her mind's eye the White Queen bursting out of the wood to be tidied up by Alice, the irreverent comparison suggests an imagination peopled with Carrollean figures. She and her sister, Vanessa Bell, nicknamed Roger Fry 'the White Knight', the character in which he appeared at Angelica Bell's eleventh birthday party in which everyone had to dress up for *Alice in Wonderland*, Leonard appearing as the Carpenter and Virginia as the March Hare 'and mad at that'.[7] Carroll's books ran in the bloodstream of that generation.

Woolf's first novel, *The Voyage Out*, gravitates towards *Alice in Wonderland* in many different ways. Her two greatest works, *To the Lighthouse* and *The Waves*, evoke and encapsulate childhood as she claimed Lewis Carroll had done.[8] She referred to her own need for a childish vision, to the old 'childish passion' for reading, to her love for her sister as 'the old childish feeling that we were in league together against the world'.[9] Peter Coveney writes that 'her mind very often displays the consciousness of the child when she was not in fact writing of children'.[10] She admired Proust's exploration of that same country so much that she felt alarmed that his voice would

1   The White Knight (frontispiece to *Through the Looking-Glass*)

inhibit her own.[11] Both Woolf and Proust, whose novel, *Du côté de chez Swann* was published in 1913, two years before *The Voyage Out*, drew their consciousness of childhood not only from their own memory but from a cultural context which placed the child at the centre of many different forms of awareness.

Roger Fry, who had played the White Knight so convincingly, lamented the dissolution of English Romantic painting into Victorian sentimentality, demanding of the painter William Etty: 'What has brought a man like Etty to the level of this insipid and puerile stuff? A mawkish sentimental drivel is all that remains of our imaginative invention. . . . Under the influence of that sentimentality Etty loses all his qualities as a painter. There is no consistency either in tone or colour; everything has become slimy and slippery and without body.' He adds a footnote: 'Perhaps we must reckon *Alice in Wonderland* and *The Rose and the Ring* as the only jewels that we have picked out of that mud.'[12] The art critic who was to introduce an astonished England to the Post-Impressionists in 1910, the date which Virginia Woolf assigned to the beginning of the modern movement in art and literature, preserved two children's books from the detritus of the past as solitary solid objects worth collecting from the ooze of time. Fry seems to have recognised in those two books something of the spirit which he associated with contemporary French art, in particular with Cézanne. Carroll becomes part of an aesthetic which involves not only Virginia Woolf's insistence on words as the medium of writing in the same way that paint is the medium of the artist, but her insistence too on literary form as the creation of both space and pattern. Fry locates in *Alice and Wonderland* a new way of seeing which would set free from the burdens of spiritual significance writers as different as Woolf and Willa Cather, Nesbit and Laura Ingalls Wilder, but which involves each of them in a disinheriting of Bunyan and the traditions which he represented. For Fry the children's story – Carroll's fantasy for the Liddells and Thackeray's Twelfth Night revel for his daughters – contains the germs of a radical redirection of Victorian culture.

In Roger Fry's criticism the word 'art' encompasses both painting and writing. He saw no eccentricity in talking about children's books as though they were included in an aesthetic which affected painters and writers of adult novels.[13] For him, as for most of his generation, Jacqueline Rose's suggestion of some '*necessary* relation' between childhood and modernism would not have needed emphasis.[14] In the late nineteenth and early twentieth centuries children's books and writing about children provided the soil from which *Sons and Lovers, A la recherche du temps perdu, A Portrait of the Artist as a Young Man*, Willa Cather's *O Pioneers!* and *My Ántonia, The Voyage Out, To the Lighthouse* and *The Waves* all sprang. To name these novels is perhaps misleading, for the argument is not that children's books created books about children, but that cultural change was both reflected and pioneered in the books which children read. Radical experiments in the arts in the early modern period began in the books which Lewis Carroll and his successors wrote for children.[15]

I CLASSIFYING THE CHILD

Writers at the turn of the century continually noted what they considered to be a new cult of childhood. Max Beerbohm in two reviews of the play of *Peter Pan* in the *Saturday Review* of 1905 laments the growth of public sentimentality about childhood and sees it as something distinct from Carroll's own practice in the *Alice* books: 'Twenty years ago it was quite different. The cult for children did not exist then. Children were not regarded as specimens of a race apart – specimens to be carefully preserved, and dotingly dilated on. They were simply regarded as adults in the making. . . . Child-lovers there were, as now. But they were very few in number, and dared not proclaim their cult.'[16] Many modern writers have agreed with Beerbohm's dating of a child-cult and with his disapproval of its character, from Peter Green, biographer of Kenneth Grahame, to George Boas, author of *The Cult of Childhood* (1966), and Peter Coveney, whose book *The Image of Childhood* (1967) provides a survey of many different elements which contributed to the 'cult' in both literary and social history. For all these historians the mood of the 1890s is escapist: 'Children become the ideal symbol of their elders' glutinous yearning for purity.'[17] If for some writers the aesthetic movement represents the greenery-yallery phase of the once invigorating forces of Romanticism, *Peter Pan* suggested sentiments which made Beerbohm fear that the writer of a good old-fashioned pantomime such as he urges on Barrie 'may not find, in this generation, anyone so bold as to imply that children are not perfect'.[18]

When the psychologist James Sully's book *Studies of Childhood* appeared in 1895, its reviewer in the journal *Mind*, Alice Woods, referred to the popular conviction that 'it is only during the decadence of Art that childhood is represented', mentioning a critic who accused Sully's work of being part of that degeneracy. But the tenor of Woods's review is the reverse of treacly. Sully's work is 'the first careful attempt that has been made in England to study childhood on a large scale'.[19] *Sensation and Intuition* had appeared more than twenty years earlier in 1874. Some of Sully's essays were printed in the *Cornhill* in the late seventies at the time that Leslie Stephen, who became a lifelong friend, brought out Robert Louis Stevenson's 'Child's Play'.[20] Sully's pioneering work on psychology and education, *Outlines of Psychology*, was published in 1884. His interest in the development of children owed much to Darwin and Herbert Spencer as well as to Preyer's *The Mind of the Child* (1881). The new book, *Studies of Childhood*, was based in part on personal experience of children's behaviour. In the upsurge of interest which followed the success of Grahame's *The Golden Age* (1895) Sully adapted his own work for a popular market under the title *Children's Ways* (1897). In so doing he pandered to the taste for sentiment and literary highlighting of childhood moments which Beerbohm disliked, and which he himself, somewhat inconsistently, criticised fiercely in Alice Meynell's collection of essays, *The Children*, which he reviewed in the *Fortnightly Review* alongside *The Golden Age*.[21] If his revised version of *Studies of Childhood*, with the new chapter-headings 'The Young Pretender' and 'Mysteries of Dolldom', makes his complaints sound like the pot calling the kettle black, his twenty-one-year record of pioneer psychology gave him some right to demand that Meynell back her remarks about children with some awareness of new research. When the Swedish reformer Ellen Key observed in *The Century of the Child* (1909) that 'an absolutely novel factor in our times is the study of the psychology of the child, and the system of education that has developed from it',[22] she was thinking not of Freud, whose essay 'Infantile Sexuality' appeared in 1905, but of his nineteenth-century predecessors, among whom were not only Darwin and Preyer, but Sully himself, and earlier, and in many ways more influential, Froebel.

Froebel's ideas began to be well known in England in the 1850s. The first English kindergarten was established in 1851, the year before Froebel's death,[23] and his theories were explained and popularised during the fifties by the Baroness Marenholtz-Bülow, who did a lecture tour in England, and whose readable account of

Froebel's main convictions was published in 1879 under the title *Child and Child-Nature*. Froebel himself had gained much from Pestalozzi and had worked with him at Yverdon, but he thought Pestalozzi's curriculum too narrow.[24]

Much educational theory, whatever its period, starts with some form of classification. Rousseau classified the child as by nature uncorrupted. Foucault argues that the late eighteenth century demonstrates a shift from taxonomy, systems of classification, to the idea of organic growth.[25] Froebel's mentor, Pestalozzi, aimed to discover and apply what he called 'the principle of the organic'.[26] Both men were strongly influenced by Rousseau. Froebel's original interests had been in biology. He was acquainted with Batsch, the founder of the Natural History Society, to which Goethe belonged. E. R. Murray, who in 1914 claimed Froebel as a pioneer of modern psychology, points out that he was 'pre-Darwinian in time . . . but post-Darwinian in many of his beliefs'. She quotes Froebel's observations that it would be difficult 'to define where the purely physical ends and the purely intellectual begins'.[27] The name of his nursery, *Kindergarten*, encapsulated his belief that education is a process of growth and development, a leading out of nature under the skill of an 'intelligent gardener'. For each child the discovery of Nature is a rediscovery of the parable of Eden.[28] It is no coincidence that Stevenson's influential *A Child's Garden of Verses* (1885) echoes both name and idea, for the child in the poems plays, as F. J. Harvey Darton pointed out in 1932, 'in an ordinary English garden, not Paradise'.[29] The garden's secularity is as marked as it is in the equally celebrated work by Frances Hodgson Burnett, *The Secret Garden* (1911), which shows two children escaping from the claustrophobic interior of a Victorian mansion full of outdated notions of child-rearing, and thriving in a garden with as much vigour as the plants which they tend. For Froebel the child is an organism, like any other natural species.

The *System of Infant Gardens* was one of the earliest of Froebel's works to be translated into English, in 1855,[30] ten years before the publication of *Alice in Wonderland*. In *Through the Looking-Glass* an old system of classification is contrasted with a newer one. The first occasion is when the Pigeon fears that its eggs have been stolen:

'Serpent!' screamed the Pigeon.
'I'm *not* a serpent!' said Alice indignantly.
'Let me alone.' . . .

'Well! *What* are you?' said the Pigeon. 'I can see you're trying to invent something!'

'I – I'm a little girl,' said Alice, rather doubtfully, as she remembered the number of changes she had gone through, that day.

'A likely story indeed!' said the Pigeon in a tone of the deepest contempt. 'I've seen a good many little girls in my time but never *one* with such a neck as that. No, no! You're a serpent; and there's no use denying it. I suppose you'll be telling me next that you never tasted an egg!'

'I have tasted eggs, certainly,' said Alice, who was a very truthful child; 'but little girls eat eggs quite as much as serpents do, you know.'

'I don't believe it,' said the Pigeon; 'but if they do, why, then they're a kind of serpent: that's all I can say.' (*AW*, 76)

The child is bewildered by a system of classification of which she is a part but over which she exerts no control. The classification of little girls as serpents has a well-documented theological history. An alternative system surfaces in the encounter between Alice and the Fawn in the wood where things have no names. They become fast friends:

So they walked on together through the wood, Alice with her arms clasped lovingly round the soft neck of the Fawn, till they came out into another open field, and here the Fawn gave a sudden bound into the air, and shook itself free from Alice's arms. 'I'm a Fawn!' it cried out in a voice of delight. 'And, dear me! you're a human child!' A sudden look of alarm came into its beautiful brown eyes, and in another moment it had darted away at full speed. (*L-G*, 227)

The child and the animal are happy and at ease together until the system of classification forces them asunder. On the second occasion the Sheep's query about whether Alice is a child or a teetotum (spinning top) is part of the same categorising principle.

Froebel, in seeing the child as both seed and egg, embryo in mind and body, for whom education must be a process of developing from within, not instructing from without, anticipated both Darwin and Freud. Freud wrote in *Totem and Taboo*, first published in 1913: 'Children show no trace of the arrogance which urges civilized men

2 Children and animals: (a) Alice and the Fawn (from *Through the Looking-Glass*); (b) Heidi and a Goat (from *Heidi*, by Johanna Spyri)

to draw a hard-and-fast line between their own nature and that of
other animals. Children have no scruples over allowing animals to
rank as their full equals. Uninhibited as they are in the avowal of
their bodily needs, they no doubt feel themselves more akin to
animals than to their elders, who may well be a puzzle to them.'[31] As
early as 1826 Froebel had written: 'We give room and time to young
plants and animals, well knowing that they will develop and grow
according to the laws inherent in them. . . . Why does man,
wandering through gardens and fields, meadows and groves, fail to
open his mind, and refuse to listen to the lesson which nature
silently teaches?' For Froebel the education of the child meant first
and foremost the observation of the inner laws of its being, just as
the nurturing of plants and animals required not only a general
understanding of biological process, but a particular understanding
of each individual species.[32]

II   CHILDHOOD AND PHENOMENOLOGY

Murray argued in 1914 that, although Froebel lacked William
James's range of philosophical concepts, many of his ideas about the
child's consciousness, instincts and relation to the world he
perceives anticipate the early phenomenology of William James.[33]

Froebel, as his championing of the cube and the ball as playthings
demonstrates,[34] saw education as a process of interaction between
the child and the world of objects, which he experiences through his
senses: 'As the new-born child, like a ripe grain of seed dropped
from the mother plant has life in itself, and as it spontaneously
develops life in *progressive connection with the common life whole*; so
activity and action are the first phenomena of his awakening life.'
Everything that the child is given to play with must help him 'freely
to express what is in him and to bring the phenomena of the outer
world nearer to him. . . . Each new phenomenon is a discovery in
the child's small and yet rich world.'[35] His exploration of things
through tearing, breaking and biting[36] may be continued into
drawing and a discovery of what the Froebel specialist Ebenezer
Cooke, Vanessa Stephen's first art-master, called the 'language of
line'. Froebel observed that the child's discovery of 'linear
phenomena directs his attention to the linear properties of
surrounding objects'.[37] Froebel's statement about the 'close welling
or flowing into one another of the Physical and Psychical' prefigures

the relation between mind and body which William James formulates in *The Principles of Psychology* (1890), in which the chapter entitled 'The Stream of Thought' influenced Virginia Woolf and her contemporaries.

Froebel's focusing on the senses leads, as it was to do in the work of William James, Roger Fry[38] and Woolf, to an evocation of rhythm. Bülow declared that for Froebel 'rhythm is one of the great fundamental principles of all that is expressed in the motion of the spheres, the flight of birds, the course of the deer, in the excitement of the dance, and the whole wide harmony of creation and of human genius'. For the child 'body and soul at the beginning of life may be said to be one'. It 'must first have taken in from the outward world a series of impressions, images, and ideas, before thoughts will germinate in its mind'.[39] When Virginia Woolf revised the first draft of *The Waves* she set out a plan in her notebook, dated 15 June 1930:

> *Part One*
> Childhood in the garden.
> The gradual wakening: No breaks if possible.
> The beginning with pure sensations.
> . . .
> And there must be the separate experiences
> of each of the children: The rhythm of the
> waves must be kept going all the time.

Two days earlier she had written that 'each child wakes and sees something a globe: an object'.[40] The representation of childhood is envisaged in terms of 'pure sensations', interaction, separateness and rhythm, all of which are central to Froebel's theory, just as the idea of line as visual experience of the phenomenological world was central to the practice and aesthetic theory of Vanessa Bell and Roger Fry.

If Virginia Woolf did not, unlike her sister, have any direct access to Froebel's views,[41] she might have imbibed them from the work of William James, Sully, Stevenson and Pater. When Rachel and Terence Hewet in *The Voyage Out* think of the children they will have they 'sketch an outline of the ideal education – how their daughter should be required from infancy to gaze at a large square of cardboard, painted blue, to suggest thoughts of infinity',[42] which suggests that Woolf knew about Froebel's ideas, and also perhaps that she was a little tired of hearing about them. Bülow had written

that the parent or teacher must consider 'the fitness of the things set
before the child, to enable it the more easily to take in form, size,
number, colour, sound etc.'.[43] Pater observed in *Plato and Platonism*
that 'wherever people have been inclined to lay stress on the
colouring, for instance, cheerful or otherwise, of the walls of the
room where children learn to read, as though that had something to
do with colouring of their minds; or the possible moral effect of the
beautiful ancient buildings of some of our own schools and colleges;
on the building of character, in any way, through the eye and ear;
there the spirit of Plato has been understood to be'.[44] That spirit was
also Froebel's.

In 'The Child in the House', an autobiographical fragment, Pater
had described his own 'process of brain-building' in which the child
Florian responds to the world of objects and sensations as
passionately as Proust was later to do. Pater's description of the red
hawthorn in flower anticipates Proust's in the Méséglise way in *Du
côté de chez Swann*. Pater's Florian recalls:

> Lo! within, a great red hawthorn, in full flower . . . a plumage of
> tender, crimson fire and of the heart of the dry wood. The
> perfume of the tree had now and again reached him, in the
> currents of the wind. . . . Always afterwards, summer by
> summer, as the flowers came on, the blossom of the red hawthorn
> still seemed to him absolutely the reddest of all things. . . . Then,
> for the first time, he seemed to experience a passionateness in his
> relation to fair outward objects . . . a revelation to him . . . of
> beautiful physical things, a kind of tyranny of the senses over
> him.[45]

It is easy to assign such an experience to either Keats or Freud, or to
an uneasy marriage of the two. But as an analysis of 'brain-building'
it is nearer to Froebel than to either of them, and looks forward to
William James's determination to describe the realities of subjective
consciousness.[46] Froebel had claimed that 'from the outer world the
child's soul collects a store of images which must stamp themselves
upon it, and grow into ideas before the first signs of spontaneous
mental activity can show themselves outwardly',[47] just as Sully had
described the 'historical and genetic' preoccupations of modern
psychology.[48] Roger Fry's earliest work in art history, the
unpublished and unsuccessful Fellowship dissertation 'On the
Laws of Phenomenology and their Application to Greek Painting'

(1889), defined phenomenology as a 'science which deals with the impressions made on us by external objects in their entirety',[49] showing that the principles associated with Brentano and William James in the late eighties and early nineties were already known and understood in England before James's work was published.

Froebel's conviction of the 'necessary continuity between the life of childhood and that of manhood'[50] underpinned all the investigations of the early phenomenologists.[51] Sully declared that the psychologist's aim was to 'get at this baby's consciousness so as to understand what is passing there' in order to 'find his way through the intricacies of adult consciousness'.[52] For Henri Bergson adult passion was a return to the intense perceptions which Pater evokes in 'The Child in the House': 'How do you become aware of a deep passion, once it has taken hold of you, if not by perceiving that the same objects no longer impress you in the same manner? All your sensations and all your ideas seem to brighten up: it is like childhood back again.'[53] James wrote of the past that 'the things in the room here which I survey, and those in my distant home of which I think, the things of this minute and those of my long-vanished boyhood, influence and decide me alike, with a reality which my experience of them directly feels. They both make up my real world.'[54] James's refusal to separate mind and body, child and adult consciousness, looks back, whether consciously or not, to Froebel's educational theory.

Froebel's concentration on the significance of play in the child's development anticipates Stevenson's essay 'Child's Play', published by Leslie Stephen in the *Cornhill Magazine* in 1878, a work which influenced Sully's psychology as much as it affected Kenneth Grahame's evocation of childhood in *The Golden Age*. Froebel's ideas formed part of a debate about the relation between the child and the artist. Children's play was seen to provide a paradigm for artistic creation. Stevenson's essay popularised – although he remained clear about the extent to which the artist moves on from the child – ideas which the German poet Schiller had formulated as early as 1795 in his essay 'On Simple [Naïve] and Sentimental Poetry'. Herbert Spencer, Sully and even writers for children such as Matthew Browne [William Brighty Rands] in *Lilliput Lectures* (1871),[55] pointed out that not only can the playing child reveal aspects of the creative process, but that art itself must always remain to some extent a form of play, a belief which conditions the world of Fry, Virginia Woolf and Joyce.

Roger Fry admired the playful spirit of Chinese art and connected it with a consciousness which had not separated itself from children and animals: 'Whilst their fun is sometimes almost childishly naïve and exuberant, their gravity is never altogether untouched by humour. . . . Since, the Chinese might argue, the world does not revolve round us as its centre, we need not take either the world or ourselves too seriously. We can afford to play. We can play with the offspring of our imagination.'[56] Virginia Woolf wrote of the importance for the writer of 'the play side' and cannot have been unconscious of the pun in her description of *The Waves* as a 'play-poem'.[57] In an analysis of the disjunction between the new generation and the old, José Ortega y Gasset declared in 1931 that 'so far as the old are concerned the lack of seriousness in the new art is a defect which is quite enough to render it negligible: while in the view of the young that very lack of seriousness counts as the supreme value of art'. His formulation that 'art, in the consciousness of the new race, becomes philistinism or not-art as soon as it is taken seriously'[58] defines the revolt of Virginia Woolf's generation against high Victorian culture, just as *Alice in Wonderland* expresses the protest of Carroll's generation against the burden of Evangelical earnestness.

Schiller, who had suggested connections between the child and the artist, shared Rousseau's idealism about children; both men influenced Wordsworth, whose 'Intimations of Immortality' must be almost the most quoted text of the nineteenth century, appearing with wearisome regularity every time children are mentioned. For Wordsworth childhood was both real and symbolic, both experience and myth, as Pater pointed out in *Appreciations* (1874) when he described Wordsworth's 'regrets for a half-ideal childhood, when the relics of Paradise still clung about the soul – a childhood, as it seemed, full of the fruits of old age, lost for all, in a degree, in the passing away of the youth of the world, lost for each one, over again, in the passing away of actual youth'.[59] The fable of the paradise within, of childhood retraceable in every man, is certainly present in Froebel's thought. But his mood is much less elegiac. Schiller wrote that the child moves us because 'all is *disposition* and *destination*; in us, all is the state of a *completed*, *finished* thing, and the completion always remains infinitely below the destination'.[60] Virginia Woolf gives this perception to Bernard when as adults the characters in *The Waves* reunite over dinner: 'We saw for a moment laid out among us the body of the complete human being whom we have failed to be, but at the same time, cannot forget. All that we might have been we saw; all that we had missed, and we grudged for a moment the other's claim, as children when the cake is cut, the one cake, the only cake, watch their slice diminishing.'[61] If in one part of Woolf's imagination lies Schiller's lost paradise, in another resides Grahame's *The Golden Age*, in which the absence of one of the children, who has gone away to school, is lamented in the same image: 'From out the frosted cake of our existence Fate had cut an irreplaceable segment. Turn which way we would the void was present.'[62] The language of childish hunger and childish greed makes the child's consciousness not a thing of the past, but a living reality in the remembering adult's present, as Froebel had insisted that childhood must always be. In *Centuries of Meditation*, first published in 1909, the seventeenth-century poet Thomas Traherne wrote of childhood in terms which anticipated the Romantics: 'Certainly Adam in Paradise had not more sweet and curious apprehensions of the world, than I when I was child.'[63] The same year witnessed Ellen Key's bracing demand that parents should educate themselves not in the myth but in the living realities of childhood, the sciences of basic psychology and hygiene. That word, which falls like a cold shower on the plants of Paradise, had been part of an ongoing debate for at least a quarter of a century before Key's book appeared.

III   EDUCATING THE PARENT

One of the most radical aspects of Froebel's teaching was its stress on the need for parents and teachers to know more about the principles which govern child development, both mental and physical. The climate of opinion which he helped to form, in which adults must admit ignorance, may lie behind the new anxiety which Linda Pollock finds parents expressing in nineteenth-century diaries about their competence in their role.[64] Marenholtz-Bülow wrote in 1879 that 'the laws of development of the infant mind are . . . still veiled in obscurity'.[65] The laws of the infant body, with many children still dying in infancy, were hardly less so. By the turn of the century the Froebel journal *Child Life* still felt the need to exhort readers in an article challengingly entitled 'The Child as the Director of the Parent's Education': 'Let us look for a moment at the normal disqualifications of the average parent. First, we have to deal with the utter ignorance of what may be termed common-sense psychology, and also of common-sense physiology, which is of more importance in education than is generally supposed. Then there is the sheer inability to answer truthfully and rationally the natural questions of an intelligent child.' This protest against parental ignorance punctuates a period which has been accused of using children as a pretext for wallowing in nostalgia. The writer asserts abrasively: 'In the first stage of the parent's education it is therefore necessary to make a very diligent study of child nature, including the best which has been written by experts and people with direct vision on this matter.'[66] She or he points out that an enormous number of books are already available for the instruction of the parent, particularly in America, where Ellen Key's work was welcomed by reformers such as Charlotte Perkins Gillman, whose own study of children, in suggesting that obedience was a thing of the past, caused even the *Child Life* reviewer a moment's pause.[67] That parents should obey had become a nursery joke at least by the time of Kate Greenaway's *Little Folks Painting Book* (1879), in which 'You are Old, Father William' is rewritten: the picture for the child to colour shows Father William reined in by a very young man.[68] In an unusually serious vein Stevenson enquired in a short meditation entitled 'Parent and Child': 'What do we owe our parents? No man can *owe* love; none can *owe* obedience. We owe, I think, chiefly pity.'[69] In the 1880s Roger Fry, in his first undergraduate paper to the Cambridge Apostles,[70] entitled 'Shall We Obey?', attacked parents for insisting on obedience. He complained that parents rated obedience above honesty and love and made no distinction between 'that which is wrong in itself and that which is only inconvenient or inopportune'. However, Fry's light-hearted report of the event to his mother belies any easy stereotype about the repressiveness of his own Quaker upbringing: 'The sort of answer I gave you have probably had enough experience of my views to guess.'[71]

It would be wrong to suggest that the contributors to *Child Life* were too clinical to share Kenneth Grahame's passionate conviction that 'children are not merely people; they are the only really living people that have been left to us in an over-weary world'.[72] The *Child Life* reviewer of *Peter Pan* liked Barrie's play much better than Beerbohm did, seeing in it a celebration of a time when 'we were absolutely ourselves; it is then that we were original. No convention had moulded us to its type. We could surprise. We said wonderful things that no one had ever said before; we had something of genius about us.'[73] This eulogy is followed by the inevitable quotation from Wordsworth about the prison-house and fading into the common light of day. But by 1905 interest in genius was more genetic in focus than it had been when Schiller observed the genius of the young child a century earlier.

The movement to reinstate the body as the centre of all experience stimulated enquiry into the transmission of genius from one generation to the next. Galton's *Hereditary Genius*, originally published in 1869, was revised in 1892,[74] one year after the appearance of Lombroso's *The Man of Genius*, a work which argues the close connections between genius and insanity. Both books must have been arresting reading for Leslie Stephen who, in an essay on Robert Louis Stevenson, spoke of the 'invincible boyishness so often noticed as characteristic of genius. . . . The mental processes in the man of genius are still vital instead of being automatic.'[75] Lombroso discussed the case of the child Mozart in his book at a time when London was hospitable to a number of child prodigies, both in the theatre and in music. The child actress Vera Beringer made her name in the stage version of *Little Lord Fauntleroy* in 1888.[76] Galton's observation that genius often seems to enter the male line through the mother, which Ellen Key refers to in *The Century of the Child*, connects both writers with the development of the eugenics movement, which Key describes as one of 'the great consequences of Darwinism, that Darwin himself did not see'. Key shared Nietzsche's conviction 'that man as he now is, is only a bridge, only a transition between the animal and the "superman"'.[77] The holocaust gives this aspect of Key's thought an eerie and sinister ring. But the eugenics movement is important in the history of childhood because it focused attention on the health and welfare of mothers and children. The journal *The Child*, founded in the autumn of 1910, gave as much space to physical health and medical matters as the earlier *Child Life* had given to educational theory, and the happier aspects of eugenics are evident in the pioneering of special education for disabled or retarded children. The journal's inaugural editorial announced resoundingly: 'The race marches forward on the feet of little children. The child of today will be the citizen of to-morrow.'[78]

When she presented Froebel's ideas to the British public, Baroness Marenholtz-Bülow emphasised, as Froebel himself constantly did, the importance of the mother's role in the education of the child: 'With the elevation of child-nature, the elevation of woman and her veritable emancipation are closely bound up.'[79] The interdependence of women's rights and children's rights is still today part of a radical platform,[80] as it was in the nineteenth century. Sully points to the need for educated women to take part in research which involves the observation of young children, and shows cognisance of a new generation of women capable of such work. Girton College was founded in 1869, one year before the first universal Education Act, which has been used as a landmark for identifying the emergence of the modern concept of childhood. While that precise date is a convenience rather than a reality for the cultural historian, reforms relating to children coincided with the increased impact of feminism after 1870. William Stead's exposure of child prostitution occurred in 1885; the Children's Charter of four years later was followed in 1894 by the Prevention of Cruelty to Children Act (seventy-two years later than the legal protection afforded to animals).[81] Reformers stressed that the bringing-up of children required the knowledge and skill of both parents, but particularly of mothers, because their contact with their children was more prolonged. The insistence of Froebel's followers on the need for more understanding of the child's nature generated new insight into the relation between mind and body in the healthy child. Johanna Spyri's emphasis in *Heidi* (1885) on the health-giving properties of mountain air and fresh milk for the invalid Clara goes hand in hand with the belief that Clara began to walk because when she fed the goats she experienced the pleasures of independence, of caring for something else, instead of always being cared for.[82]

The argument for birth control in the last quarter of the nineteenth century was both biological – a demand made on behalf of the health of mother and child – and directed towards emotional needs: 'a new view of the married woman's rights to independent self-development'. Although many feminists maintained a low profile on the issue of birth control, perhaps through fear of discrediting their own cause by connecting it with the Besant–Bradlaugh trial of 1877, campaigners stressed the impossibility of a mother's finding in herself sufficient mental and physical energy to rear a dozen or more children.[83] The photograph of the Strachey family in Michael Holroyd's biography of Lytton Strachey can only be contemplated calmly if one forfeits imaginative insight into the practical problems of nurturing such strings of Stracheys. Lytton was the eleventh of thirteen children, born between 1860 and 1887, three of whom died in infancy. The loving attention to each child's physical and mental growth which Froebel posits is out of the question thirteen times over in twenty-seven years, as Holroyd's description of the gloom and disharmony in the Strachey family home amply demonstrates.[84]

The growth of social anthropology at the turn of the century contributed to a new awareness of family power structures by depicting their dependence on cultural patterns which varied from society to society. Westermarck's observation in *The Origin and Development of Moral Ideas* (1906) that in European societies 'parents are . . . considered to possess in some measure proprietary rights over their offspring, being their originators and maintainers; and in various cases, it seems, the father is also regarded as their owner because he is the owner of their mother',[85] drew attention to the fact that the ordering of family relations in the English Protestant system was not necessarily ordained by God for Adam. Whether or not God was dead, as Nietzsche and later Ellen Key robustly claimed, Adam was now hanging from the Tree of Knowledge by his tail. When G. H. Payne published in 1916 his pioneering work *The Child in Human Progress*, which Lloyd DeMause describes as the first history of childhood[86] – although it is more a study of the place of children in the family structures of many primitive societies – he printed many beautiful photographs of our ape ancestors, looking more carefree than Victorian parents, but as recognisably that species as the creatures in *Alice in Wonderland* are. Payne's thesis locates man's moral evolution in the maternal instinct, which he believes to be the only human impulse not governed by self-interest: 'The moral idea is born, legitimately enough, out of the altruistic maternal affection.' Quoting Ellen Key he declares that 'in this, the "century of the child", there is a great conception of humanity, and even of children's rights'.[87] He stresses the enlarged Darwinian timespan of human history and connects human customs with the rearing habits of animals and birds. Like Westermarck, whose later book *Ethical Relativity* (reviewed by James Smith in the second issue of *Scrutiny* in September 1932) incorporated Einstein's theory into the study of societies, Payne saw the subjection of women and children as closely linked in the history of social structures.

Photography, tellingly invoked as evidence in Payne's book, has been seen as feeding the sentimental excesses of the cult of childhood,[88] but it was also capable of a more objective function. *The*

Child in Human Progress carries – ironically, considering its title – a photograph of a child in a New York cruelty case who had been attacked with a pair of scissors.[89] Dr Barnado used the camera to expose child neglect. As Peter Fuller points out in an essay in *Changing Childhood*: 'The camera has the capacity to reveal where childhood is being contradicted or denied.'[90] Photography made available, to adapt Foucault's argument, perceptions which had been veiled before its advent. Philippe Ariès in *Centuries of Childhood* bases his assumptions about attitudes to childhood to some extent on the infrequency with which children were painted, but this ignores an economic dimension in the whole debate. The family album became popular in Victorian households where the painting of a portrait would have been much too expensive.[91] The artist costs more than the machine just as the good teacher costs more than the computer. Carroll's own photography may sometimes seem sentimental to a modern eye, but his attitude to it was not sentimental, as the poem 'Hiawatha's Photography', in which the family group comes out as a disaster – described in a parody of Longfellow – shows. 'A Photographer's Day Out' describes a family sitting:

> PICTURE 3. – 17th sitting. Placed the baby in profile. After waiting till the usual kicking had subsided, uncovered the lens. The little wretch instantly threw its head back, luckily only an inch, as it was stopped by the nurses's nose, establishing the infant's claim to 'first blood' (to use a sporting phrase). This, of course, gave *two* eyes to the result, something that might be called a nose, and an unnaturally wide mouth. Called it a full-face accordingly.

The three daughters of the household look in the photograph as if they have just taken a dose of noxious medicine: 'Of course, I kept this view of the subject to myself, and merely said that "it reminded me of a picture of the three Graces", but the sentence ended in an involuntary groan, which I had the greatest difficulty in converting into a cough.'[92] Carroll's descriptions of Alice's variations in size derive partly from his intuition into children's feelings – he would have approved of Ogden Nash's 'Epistle to the Olympians': 'Whisper in accents mild / The proper size for a child'[93] – and partly from his photographic experience of the ability of the camera to play tricks with size, as evinced in many of the photographic entries in the *Strand Magazine* in the 1890s. If the camera speaks at the turn of

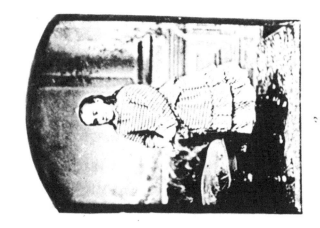

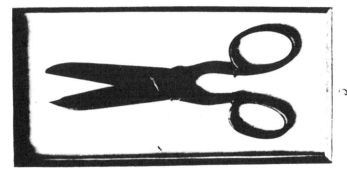

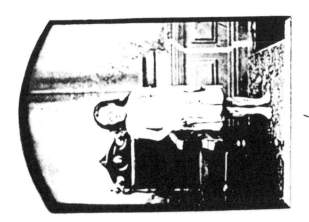

3   Mary Ellen and the Scissors with which She was Beaten (from G. H. Payne, *The Child in Human Progress*)

the century to adult nostalgia for childhood, it also projects new ways of looking at the child.

IV   CHILDREN AND POST-IMPRESSIONIST PAINTING

When Roger Fry observed that both the Pre-Raphaelites and the Impressionists 'yielded to, or were inspired by, a simple physiological delight in brilliance and purity of colour, approaching in this respect to the position of the Primitives, though arriving at it from the very opposite pole',[94] he began to notice the analogues between adult and child art. He found in children a capacity to observe without interpreting, which he believed that the Post-Impressionists, and particularly Cézanne, recaptured: 'We learn to read the prophetic message, and, for the sake of economy, to neglect all else. Children have not learned it fully, and so they look at things with some passion. Even the grown man keeps something of his unbiological, disinterested vision with regard to a few things. He still looks at flowers, and does not merely see them.'[95] Pater's Florian had gazed at the red hawthorn bush with exactly that intensity of pure perception. Modernist art, like Froebel's educational theory, tried to re-embody the child's unity of perception, his lack of prudery and inhibition. Fry's description of the outrage which greeted Manet's *Déjeuner sur l'herbe*, with its nude woman picnicking not, as in Giorgione, in the safe conventional confines of the classical landscape, but on the banks of the Seine, is in tune with Ellen Key's protest against prudery in art.[96] The adult wish to return to the uninhibited sensuality of the child created the artistic climate for D. H. Lawrence, whose first novel, *The White Peacock*, was published in 1911, two years after *The Century of the Child*.

The public outcry against Fry's first exhibition of Post-Impressionist art at the Grafton gallery in 1910 derived from the sense that this was not art at all. The paintings were dismissed as comparable to the drawings of children. George Melly suggests in his essay 'Jokes about Modern Art' that Manet, Matisse, Duchamps, Epstein, Picasso and Van Gogh shocked the public 'because much of the tension they help to release is of sexual origin'.[97] Freud believed that jokes create relief from sexual repression, and Melly's view is perhaps supported by the laughter of the public which so exasperated Fry: 'Before asking the artists to mend their morals, we

"You are silent. Am I to assume that you do *not* have a child who can do every bit as well?"

4   George Price, cartoon (from George Melly and J. R. Glaves-Smith, *A Child of Six Could Do It*)

have some right to ask our censors to look a little more to their manners.' He wrote in 1920 that he 'tried in vain to explain what appeared to me so clear, that the modern movement was essentially a return to the ideas of formal design which had been almost lost in the fervid pursuit of naturalistic representation'.[98] Virginia Woolf was equally surprised by the violence of the reaction: 'Why all the Duchesses are insulted by the post-impressionists, a modest sample set of painters, innocent even of indecency, I can't conceive. However, one mustn't say that they are like other pictures, only better, because that makes everyone angry.'[99] The absence of restraint particularly in the use of colour seemed to flaunt sensuality exactly as Vanessa Bell flaunted it in her Bloomsbury lifestyle.

Van Gogh's *Sunflowers* was painted in 1888, the year Brentano gave his first lecture on 'descriptive and genetic psychology', the recording of the phenomena of consciousness as perceived through the senses. Fry wrote of Van Gogh that the painter's 'feeling was mainly due to this almost physiological response. His reaction was far more nervous than mental, by which I mean that it was rather the lower than the higher nerve centres that were involved in his response. His reaction to colour, as to so much else, is elementary and childlike.' Artists felt that Van Gogh made available to them a new world of visual perception. Fry describes his impact as José Ortega y Gasset described the effect of the new culture in dividing the young from the old. He was 'the most overpowering revelation to the rising generation. [His painting] destroyed in them the prestige of a culture which preached the doctrine that all real works of art were already enshrined in museums, and that the best that could be hoped for from the modern artist was the multiplication of skilful pastiches.'[100] For the older generation Van Gogh's art flouted tradition and so was not art at all.

Although Fry was excited by Van Gogh's painting he found it too childlike and primitive. He certainly believed that Western art could learn much from studying the designs of the Negro and the Bushman. He shared Gauguin's 'love of savage art with its naïve assertion of the individual object', and admired negro sculpture for its realisation of volume in space. But he felt that primitive drawings evinced, like those of children, a preoccupation with 'symbols of concepts. In a child's drawing of a face a circle symbolizes the mask, two dots the eyes, and two lines the nose and mouth.' The true artist must 'discover what things look like to an unbiased eye'.[101] He wrote in 'An Essay in Aesthetics' in the *New Quarterly* in 1909 that

OUR DECADENTS.

Fliphutt (the famous young Art-Critic). "ULLO! WHAT'S THIS PENCIL SKETCH I'VE JUST FOUND ON THIS EASEL!"

Our Artist. "OH, IT'S BY FLUMPKIN—THE IMPRESSIONIST FELLOW ALL YOU YOUNG CHAPS ARE SO ENTHUSIASTIC ABOUT YOU KNOW. CLEVER, AIN'T IT!"

Fliphutt. "CLEVER! WHY, IT'S DIVINE! SUCH FRESHNESS, SUCH NAÏVETÉ! SUCH A SPLENDID SCORN OF MERE CONVENTIONAL TECHNIQUE! SUCH A——"

Our Artist. "ULLO, OLD MAN! A THOUSAND PARDONS! THAT'S THE WRONG THING YOU'VE GOT HOLD OF! THAT'S JUST A SCRIBBLE BY THIS LITTLE SCAMP OF A GRANDSON OF MINE. HIS FIRST ATTEMPT! NOT VERY PROMISING, I FEAR: BUT HE'S ONLY FOUR."

5   Cartoon from *Punch*, July 1894 (from George Melly and J. R. Glaves-Smith, *A Child of Six Could Do It*)

'children, if left to themselves, never, I believe, copy what they see, never, as we say, "draw from nature", but express, with a delightful freedom and sincerity, the mental images which make up their own imaginative lives.' He felt that Van Gogh worked 'as a child who has never been taught works, with a feverish haste to get the image which obsesses him externalised in paint'. The likeness of his drawings to a child's made him a less great painter, in Fry's view, than Cézanne, whose childlike perception of colour progressed to a 'profoundly meditated colour structure'.[102] He did not believe that the painter owed anything except the freshness of his perceptions to the condition of childhood, a freshness which Fry found in Lewis Carroll's *Alice*. The statement that a man painted like a child was usually for him a form of adverse criticism, as when he commented that the painter Claude demonstrates 'naïvetés which may or may not be intentional: sometimes they have the happiest effect, at others they seem not childlike but childish. . . . There is, in fact, a real excuse for Ruskin's exaggerated paradox that Claude's drawings look like the work of a child of ten.' He had no romantic notions about untaught genius, and regretted that Cézanne assimilated Baroque design through instinct rather than formal training.[103] Nevertheless, he was in 1917 excited by the children's drawings which Marion Richardson, a Dudley schoolteacher, exhibited at the Omega Club[104] and wrote to his daughter Pamela that he planned to 'do a book on children's drawings with illustrations', and had already begun it. All that survives of the project is an unpublished draft, in which Fry argues that the way forward in art is through the expressiveness and lack of reverence for tradition of the untaught child.[105]

In Fry's aesthetic the real primitive is not child or Negro, but the great British public, whose philistinism testifies to the truth of Wilfrid Trotter's thesis of the herd instinct. Fry concludes his book on Cézanne by comparing the painter with Flaubert: 'They are both protagonists in the thrilling epic of individual prowess against the herd which marks the history of French art in the nineteenth century.'[106] Nineteenth-century artists were 'a band of heroic Ishmaelites with no secure place in the social system, with nothing to support them in the unequal struggle but a dim sense of a new idea, the idea of the freedom of art from all trammels and tyrannies'. To the Victorians art was 'useless frivolity, . . . a mere survival of mere primitive states of evolution'. By the time of the Post-Impressionist exhibition he scented change in the world of art, but not of society: 'The revolution in art seems to be out of all proportion to any corresponding change in thought and feeling.'[107] But Fry underestimated the interdependence of the artist with his own culture. The impetus which had led men to study the relation between the child and primitive man, as well as between the child and Primitive painting, was part of a wider canvas of change than he himself could identify, however precisely he observed the revolution in perception in his own part of the picture.

Fry believed, like Froebel, that rhythm is the central force in man's spiritual life, creating a unity between sensations and intellect. He wrote of the 'extraordinary power an artist shows of holding together in a single rhythmic scheme such an immense number of small and often closely repetitive movements'. Part of this activity he saw as subconscious: 'Perfect rhythmic continuity and coherence is only attainable by human beings when their activity is at least partially unconscious.' He declared that 'I sometimes think that painting is as much based on giving us the orientation of our spirits in space as music is our orientation in time.' All these aesthetic principles are central to Virginia Woolf's stress on her own rhythm as a writer, on the 'process of elimination and concentration'[108] (Fry on Cézanne), and on the refusal to separate mind from body.

When M. C. Bradbrook remarked in *Scrutiny* that 'Mrs Woolf never, as is so frequently asserted, attempts to reproduce the process of thinking', the novelist was stung by the criticism, seeing in it an accusation of moral and intellectual evasion.[109] Her anti-intellectual and anti-logical stance derived from a renegotiation of the relation between mind and body, which placed her in the same sphere as not only Roger Fry but also Froebel, Darwin, Sully, Nietzsche, William James, Ellen Key, Freud, Husserl and José Ortega y Gasset. Fry shared Freud's conviction that Darwin's resituating of man in the animal kingdom created a revolution in perception comparable to that set in motion by Copernicus in the sixteenth century.[110] In both cases art responds to man's new knowledge that he is not the centre of the universe, and cannot afford to separate himself either from animals, or from the condition of childhood in which the human being displays naturally his affinity to them.

V CHILD SEXUALITY

Froebel's rejection of dualism in the adult as well as in the developing child helped to create the intellectual environment for Freud's theory of infantile sexuality. Froebel does not talk at all about infant sexuality. But his ideas about the body allow a child to enjoy his physical nature as spontaneously as an animal. Why shouldn't Alice and the Fawn walk together? The educationalist had urged that repressed passions 'will only break forth with greater ferocity when free scope is allowed them, like a tiger escaping from its cage. . . . Education is emancipation – the setting free of the bound-up forces of the body and soul.'[111] Stephen Kern has argued that Freud exaggerated his own claim to originality and that 'child sexuality was indeed a "burning question" by 1901 – four years before the appearance of Freud's *Three Essays*'. Only the theory of polymorphous perversity, by which the 'individual is able to enjoy sexual pleasure almost anywhere in his body', was new. Freud himself had at first held the more common view that any infant sexuality was pathological, which he modified in 1905 so that only 'compulsive masturbation and pre-pubertal intercourse' remained in that category. But Kern points to the views of many psychologists that 'children have some special physical sensitivity that adults do not'.[112] The pioneer of that position was Froebel.

Ariès is not alone in a view of cultural history which locates change at a particular point – the late eighteenth century – and connects it centrally with the writings of one man, Rousseau. Julia Kristeva suggests that Rousseau and Freud represent two points in time at which the world turned for renewal to the child.[113] Such a view, though theoretically neat, is historically misleading.[114] Complex continuities connect Rousseau's *Emile* (1761) with Locke's *Thoughts concerning Education* (1693), a work in which Rousseau found his own repudiation of the fabulous, itself an orthodox tenet of Puritan thought. Rousseau's educational ideals arise out of a universe in which man is a moral being divided against himself.[115] Between Freud, with his view of child sexuality as a constituent of normal psychic and physical development, and Rousseau, lies almost a century and a half in which the child becomes part of a larger investigation by Froebel, Darwin and many others, into embryology.[116]

Froebel's interest, which derives in part from Rousseau, is centred on the developing child and his negotiation of his world. To see

Freud as the main initiator of that concern is to recognise a truth as partial as that which would claim for Darwin sole rights over the theory of evolution. When Froebel writes of the importance of the child's contact with the mother's breast, not only is his theoretical position the same as Freud's, but, in the identifying of the soft ball as ideal plaything, he anticipates Winnicott's theory of transitional objects.[117]

Peter Fuller has suggested that the sentimental aspects of the late Victorian cult of childhood mask the shock of a new realisation that children have a knowledge of the body which adults must recover in their sexual lives.[118] Freud's understanding of adult sexuality begins in an observation of the child's pleasure in his own body.[119] In *The History of Sexuality* (1981) Foucault points out that 'it was in the relationship of psychiatrist to the child that the sexuality of adults themselves was called into question'.[120] Although the advent of psychiatry may be seen as an extension of the power of the family over the child,[121] it also undermined parental power, as Foucault suggests, by providing an alternative to religion. Foucault identifies the confessional aspects of psychoanalytic techniques. Freud's theories do allow him a kind of godhead at a time when religion no longer dominated children's lives as it had done earlier in the nineteenth century. Fuller's suggestion that adults took refuge in a fantasy of childish innocence and ignorance at a time when both appeared to have no basis in reality uncovers the anxiety caused by a new awareness of the physical and emotional drives present in young children. But this consciousness was not as new as such a chronology might suggest.

Victorian readers could have read in translation as early as 1862 Tolstoy's evocation of child sexuality in the first two volumes of his autobiographical novel, *Childhood* and *Boyhood*, which appeared, with the addition of the third volume, *Youth*, in a new English translation in 1889. Tolstoy describes the physical excitement of the child Nikolai at the beauty and proximity of Katya. The 1889 translation reads: 'Her little shoulder was within two fingers' length of my lips. I no longer looked at the worm: I stared and stared at Katenka's shoulder, and kissed it with all my might. She did not turn around, but I noticed that her cheeks crimsoned up to her very ears.'[122] The earlier translation edits the moment so that the child's sexual interest is underplayed: 'Her shoulder was just then close to my lips. I looked at it and kissed it.'[123] The greater accuracy and explicitness of the later translation suggests a readership ready for

Freud's theory of infant sexuality, as well as the truth of Freud's own admission that many of his discoveries had been anticipated by creative writers.[124]

When writers observed in the 1890s the emergence of books *about* children rather than *for* them,[125] they had somewhere in mind the exploits of Cedric Erroll. In an essay in the Froebel journal *Child Life* in 1905 Catherine Ponton Slater lamented that Frances Hodgson Burnett's *Little Lord Fauntleroy* (1885) had replaced the more stalwart creations of Maria Edgeworth in the early part of the century.[126]

Adults at the turn of the century read eagerly many books which would now be considered for children, although some of them were not originally written for a child readership.[127] Virginia Woolf[128] noted in her diary on 25 January 1905 that Gerald Duckworth had taken the family to *Peter Pan* in order to give her a birthday treat. She praised the play for its wit and imaginativeness although she also recognised Barrie's sentimentality.[129] She was twenty-three. It does not seem to have occurred to her that this was a childish outing. But nor should the occasion be read as evidence that *Peter Pan* was an adult entertainment. Barrie wrote in his dedication to the published edition that he had to insert into the original a warning to children not to try to fly unless they had been sprinkled with fairy dust: 'So many children having gone home and tried it from their beds . . . need surgical attention.'[130] Whatever the ambiguities in *Peter Pan*, no child can resist the flying.[131] In writing about the spirit of youth Barrie, at least as playwright, largely appealed to that spirit in children as well as in adults.

Burnett's hero seems to have appealed to both adults and children. Zangwill wrote that his bank-manager had read *Little Lord Fauntleroy* ten times.[132] Henry James pointed out that although Stevenson's *Kidnapped* was originally published in a 'boy's paper', there 'would have been a kind of perverse humility in his keeping up the fiction that a production so literary . . . is addressed to immature minds'.[133] James envied the fame and popularity of his neighbour, Frances Hodgson Burnett. He would hardly have been gratified to find Dorothy Richardson's heroine in *Pilgrimage* recommending to a man who prefers history to novels that 'he should read, as Anglo-American history, first *Little Lord Fauntleroy* and then *The Ambassadors*'.[134] But although Burnett's child hero became a cult figure, whose velvet suit and 'large Vandyke collar of rich lace' adorned the windows of London tailors, the book's popularity went deeper than its commercial image might imply. The

Paris magazine which labelled it *subversif*[135] observed the persistent criticism of adult values from the standpoint of the child which underpins Burnett's later books, *A Little Princess* (1905) and *The Secret Garden* (1911). In celebrating the intense feelings of a mother for her child, Burnett developed ideas already present in such books as Mary Molesworth's *Carrots*. But Burnett's keener writing carves out a place for a new emotion in fiction.

In *Sons and Lovers*, published in 1913, two years after Frances Hodgson Burnett's *The Secret Garden* (in which Burnett, herself originally a North Country woman, uses the intimate 'tha' which Lawrence gives to his Nottinghamshire community) the author depicts in Mrs Morel a passion for her first child, William, which draws not only on the emotions which animate *Little Lord Fauntleroy*, but also on the public interest in them which that book created. Like Burnett, Mrs Morel, alienated from her husband, finds in her son the satisfaction of her own emotional intensity, but to see the mother-and-child relation in either book as a simple Freudian transference is to misread the understanding of the woman's feelings which both writers evince.

The first description of William in *Sons and Lovers* recalls the golden child of Burnett's story:

> The boy was small and frail at first, but he came on quickly. He was a beautiful child, with dark gold ringlets, and dark-blue eyes which changed gradually to clear grey. His mother loved him passionately. He came just when her own bitterness of disillusion was hardest to bear; when her faith in life was shaken, and her soul felt dreary and lonely. She made much of the child, and the father was jealous.

If this is the Oedipus complex it is Jocasta's version of it. A major crisis is sparked off by Morel's shearing of the golden curls:

> Against the chimney-piece, sat Morel, rather timid; and standing between his legs, the child – cropped like a sheep with such an odd round poll – looking, wondering at her; and on a newspaper spread out upon the hearthrug, a myriad of crescent-shaped curls, like the petals of a marigold scattered in the reddening firelight.
>
> Mrs Morel stood still. It was her first baby. She went very white, and was unable to speak.

The moment of transition from baby to child, which is so poignant to the mother, can only lose its real impact by being psychoanalysed. The cutting of the hair – Morel says that she was trying to make a girl of William and she comes to admit that it would have been necessary – is the cutting of a physical cord between mother and baby: 'The act had caused something momentous to take place in her soul. She remembered the scene all her life, as one in which she had suffered most intensely.' There is nothing to match the intensity of that scene in Burnett's book. But nevertheless it grows from a space which Burnett created in *Little Lord Fauntleroy* for a mother's fantasies:

> William was only one year old, and his mother was proud of him, he was so pretty. She was not well off now, but her sisters kept the boy in clothes. Then, with his little white hat curled with an ostrich feather, and his white coat, he was a joy to her, the twining wisps of hair clustering round his head.

Like Cedric in the Vandyke suit, he is knight, courtier and woodcutter turned fairy prince. Mrs Ramsay's feelings about her children in Virginia Woolf's *To the Lighthouse* (1927) tap the same area of the fabulous, as the novelist probably realised when she worried that Lawrence and she were trying to do too much the same thing, and resented his preaching.

When, in *Sons and Lovers*, Paul Morel is born, his mother's emotion is different, but the same impulse is there: 'The thought of being the mother of men was warming to her heart. She looked at the child. It had blue eyes, and a lot of fair hair, and was bonny.'[136] It is impossible now to read those lines from a pre-Freudian consciousness, as Lawrence himself was no doubt well aware, any more than a present-day audience can now listen innocently to Peter Pan's wish to be a devoted son to the disappointed Wendy.[137] But, whereas Barrie seems to skate over the real repudiation of sexuality implicit in *Peter Pan*, Lawrence, like Burnett, perceives in the mother's love for the child a return to a polymorphous capacity to experience passion through the whole body, a capacity which Freud saw in the child but did not notice in the mother. Lawrence annexes into the adult novel emotions first explored in books about children which were the offshoot of a fashion created in large part not only by women as Slater claims in her attack on Burnett, but also by Stevenson in his essay 'Child's Play' (1878).

The feelings of parents about children are not likely to interest child readers, although they have a central place in the adult novel. Virginia Woolf wrote of Madame de Sévigné's letters – read by Proust's grandmother on the train journey to Balbec in *Du côté de chez Swann* – that in the present age the seventeenth-century letter-writer who enumerates her child's doings in such loving detail would 'probably have been one of the great novelists'.[138] Sir Lawrence Jones writes in *A Victorian Boyhood* (1955) of his childhood antipathy to Blake's 'Nurse's Song': 'Their own voices heard on the green can have no pathetic or tender overtones for children.' He explains: 'The children that interest children are not "the little ones" of loving mothers and nurses, or Wordsworth's anaemic little girls; they are the rowdy boys in Louisa Alcott's *Little Men* or the brave treasure-seekers of E. Nesbit. *Songs of Innocence* are far removed from the spirit of lusty combative childhood; and it would be doing a service to Blake and Wordsworth to keep them hidden away from infant philistines.'[139] Many writers in the late nineteenth century analysed in books which children certainly read – whether or not they were originally intended for a child readership – the complicated emotions of adults towards children. But children also have complicated emotions, as the research of Freud and other psychologists demonstrated. Books about children in exploring new areas of feeling between adult and child became significant in changing society's view of that relationship. Virginia Woolf recorded in her diary in July 1926 a remark of H. G. Wells's that 'we are happier perhaps – children are certainly more at ease with their parents'.[140]

The children's book is open to the accusation that the adult uses the child as part of an adult exploitative discourse.[141] But the Marxist view that childhood could be dispensed with is as much a cultural myth, proposed in defiance of the biological fact of children's size,[142] as Barrie's lingering in a state which for psychological health he should have taken with him into adult consciousness. The only real freedom for adults and for children lies in the recognition of the myths by which a society orders its vision of the real and the ideal. When the late nineteenth century found that its researches into origin and development focused attention on the child, it simultaneously produced for those children a literature which revealed as clearly as possible adult hopes for the new generation. This will always be the case because children do not write their own books and their books are bought for them by teachers and parents. But it also means that in times of great change some of the most radical ideas about what the future ought to be like will be located in the books which are written for the new generation.[143]

VI THE CHILD AND HER BOOK

In 1891, when Virginia Woolf would have been nine years old, E. M. Field suggested in one of the earliest histories of children's literature, *The Child and His Book*, that the new interest in child development ought to focus attention on children's books.[144] Zangwill wrote in the *Pall Mall Magazine*: 'How lucky are the children of to-day! – why was I a child too early, born in the crude old days when the fine art of the nursery was not understood?'[145] James Sully recognised that writers such as Stevenson and Frances Hodgson Burnett could teach psychologists as much about children as Rousseau or Pestalozzi.[146]

Sully had no notion of repudiating literary evidence as Lloyd DeMause does, when he complains that 'the literary historians, mistaking books for life, construct a fictional picture of childhood, as though one could know what really happened in the nineteenth-century home by reading *Tom Sawyer*', although DeMause himself asserts that Mary Sherwood's picture of the Fairchild children enjoying an outing to the local gibbet to see 'rotting corpses' describes historical reality.[147] Hardy was deeply impressed by such an incident in his own youth.[148] *The Fairchild Family* (1818), one of the earliest and most widely read Evangelical tales of family life, depicts one kind of 'reality', just as *The Adventures of Tom Sawyer* (1876) shows another in the oscillation in both adult and childhood experience between fact and fantasy. As Heather Glen has argued in relation to Blake's *Songs of Innocence*, the 'charting of real experiences within an actual world' provides the starting-point for an exploration of the ideal which may create a new social reality.[149] Many Victorians lacked a rigid sense of the unreality of the imagined world. Flora Thompson describes in *Lark Rise to Candleford* the practical suggestions of the villagers of Juniper Hill for the improvement of Froggy's constitution in Brenda's melancholy tale of East End children, *Froggy's Little Brother* (1875). A week in Juniper Hill would do him a world of good.[150] If this is an unsophisticated mode of reading, the same could not be said of Sully's own practice. He claimed that psychology employs 'the term "image" for all varieties of representation'.[151] The psychologist projects images of perception in the same way that the creative writer projects the images of his imagination. The development of children's books in the late nineteenth century cannot be separated from the enquiries of a whole society into the nature of children and how they should be treated.

In 1894 Arthur Waugh, whose son Evelyn would be a voice of the thirties, complained in the first issue of the *Yellow Book* that although 'every great productive period of literature has been the result of some internal or external revulsion of feeling, some current of ideas', the present age was barren of upheaval.[152] Not everyone shared that view. Havelock Ellis recalled in 1936 the impact of Bourget's *Essais de psychologie contemporaine* (1885), in which the writer proclaimed that 'the *book* is the great initiator; for it presents the modes of feeling and of action, which the young generation greedily absorbs'.[153] As early as 1839 a contributor to the *London and Westminster Review* wrote of the 'autograph picture' which a society's 'lighter literature' provides of its members – 'the insight we thus acquire into what they desire, or suppose themselves to be, and the shapes which thought takes most readily amongst them. . . . Much of this very value has the literature of children in our eyes; the literature of that innumerable nation of children everywhere spread around and amongst us. . . . Yet has this nation a near and cogent importance to us which no other can equal; for are not children the kings and queens of the future, the heirs of all the promise that surrounds us?'[154]

Critics writing twenty years later believed that the new interest in children fostered by Froebel's teaching would create a new kind of children's book. A contributor to the *London Review* in 1860 remarks on the growth of children's literature: 'It would be pleasant to infer from this obvious fact, that children were better understood than formerly, and that their mental and moral needs had been more accurately gauged. We cannot conceive a higher proof of the wisdom and thoughtfulness of an age than any token which showed it to be specifically capable of sympathizing with childhood. A generation of men distinguished from its predecessors by keener insight into a child's nature, and greater power of adapting itself to his wants, must necessarily be in a very hopeful state.' But the writer criticises a widespread assumption that 'it is an easy thing to write a good juvenile book', lamenting that authors choose that form because they think it will be easy and financially profitable. Part of the problem is that 'paedology, or the science which systematically observes the phaenomena of child-life, and investigates the laws which govern its early development, seems to have fewest professors and least encouragement'. The writer believes that the 'thoughtful study of childhood [is] indispensable for the production of a sound juvenile literature'. The purpose of the children's book 'is not so much to impart instruction, as to promote growth', and to 'give pleasure' to children.[155] Five years later *Alice in Wonderland* demonstrated that Carroll agreed with both principles, although the picture of Alice with a neck like a giraffe's suggests that he took the word growth literally.

Carroll might have remembered the *London and Westminster Review* image of children as kings and queens of the future when he showed Alice progressing into the eighth square of the chess-board in *Through the Looking-Glass*: ' "And what *is* this on my head?" she exclaimed in a tone of dismay, as she put her hands up to something very heavy, that fitted tight all round her head. . . . It was a golden crown.' (*L-G*, 315). The novelty of the destination for its period lies in its secularity – not heaven, but adulthood, as an article on Lewis Carroll in *Child Life* in 1901 pointed out: 'We are all "Alices" more or less, and, if we win the crown, find it heavy at times.'[156]

The *Alice* books bore witness to a secular vision which is nearer to Froebel than to Rousseau, nearer to Edward Lear than to Mary Sherwood, an upheaval of ideas of which Darwin is a part. Carroll made a place in fiction not only for the child in every adult (Virginia Woolf's view of Carroll) but also for the adult in every child, the independent consciousness which judges the world around her and finds it wanting: 'Who cares for *you*?' said Alice (she had grown to her full size by this time). 'You're nothing but a pack of cards!' (*AW*, 161). When Henry James observed in the Preface to *What Maisie Knew* (1897) that Maisie 'treats her friends to the rich little spectacle of objects embalmed in her wonder',[157] he describes the independent vision with which Alice views the creatures of her adventures.[158] William Empson sees in Alice 'the underdog speaking up for itself', although Alice is not 'pert' as he claims.[159] Darton called the *Alice* books 'the spiritual volcano of children's books, as the activities of John Newbery had been their commercial volcano. . . . The directness of such work was a revolution in its sphere. It was the coming to the surface, powerfully and permanently, the first unapologetic, undocumented appearance in print, for readers who sorely needed it, of liberty of thought in children's books.'[160]

When Brian Alderson reissued in 1982 Darton's *Children's Books in England*, he commented on its poor sales in the thirties, suggesting that it was ahead of its time 'in treating so apparently trivial a subject with such attention'.[161] The truth is more likely to be that it came just too late, for in 1932, with the founding of *Scrutiny* – called by a vengeful Virginia Woolf 'that prigs manual. . . . All they can do is to schoolmaster' – the playful spirit in art received a douche of seriousness. Following her meditation on *Scrutiny*'s criticism of her for not thinking, Woolf wrote: 'My brain is jaded with the conflict within of two types of thought, the critical and the creative.'[162] The impact of the child on literature of the late nineteenth century had been to emphasise the creative rather than the critical, the sensual rather than the rational, the sportive rather than the serious. *Scrutiny* required a return to meanings and significances, the moral accountability of the written word. Leavis's criterion of value in *The Great Tradition* (1937) is the concept of maturity, a mood caught in 1966, that other age of youth, by Boas in *The Cult of Childhood*, a work which castigates the adult world for idealising the child and encouraging adults to think, dress and behave like children.[163] When René Wellek accused Leavis of being 'unappreciative of a whole phase of human thought: idealism as it comes down from Plato',[164] one can hear Pater murmuring about coloured walls in a room where a child reads. The distrust of fantasy rife in Rousseau and the Edgeworths becomes, under Leavis's guidance, respectable again. The treacle well has run dry.

In the late nineteenth century many writers read with a sense of shock Tolstoy's essay 'What is Art?' in which he declares that the artist outgrows his art. Perversely, Robert Louis Stevenson, who had done more than any other writer to incorporate the idea of play into writing and to obviate a tradition of preaching in children's books, agreed with him, as Leslie Stephen recalled in an essay on him:

> 'I think *David Balfour* is a nice little book,' he [Stevenson] says, 'and very artistic and just the thing to occupy the leisure of a busy life; but for the top flower of man's life it seems to be inadequate. . . . I could have wished to be otherwise in this world. I ought to have been able to build lighthouses and write *David Balfour* too.'[165]

The parallel had a particular meaning for Stevenson because he came from a family of lighthouse-builders. His grandfather, Robert Stevenson, was a civil engineer who designed and constructed lighthouses.[166] In 1814 he accompanied Sir Walter Scott on an expedition to see his own creation, the Bell Rock lighthouse in the Hebrides, an enterprise which is recorded in Lockhart's *Life*, and which resulted in Scott's novel *The Pirate*.[167] Woolf first read Lockhart in 1897, but she remembered the diary, for in 1902 she wrote to Violet Dickinson that 'in Scott's [Lockhart's] life there is his diary of a voyage to the lighthouses on the Scotch coast'.[168] The original impulse for her own novel, *To the Lighthouse*, probably came from a childhood outing to the Godrevy lighthouse in 1892, from which her brother Adrian, like James in the novel, was excluded.[169] But the lighthouse in the novel is in the outer Hebrides, and Virginia Woolf perhaps knew the Stevenson connection with Scott's lighthouse diary.[170]

In 1883 Robert Louis Stevenson wrote a description of his grandfather's trip with Scott for *Scribner's Magazine*. He describes the old man's determination in 1850 to make one last visit to the light-house, a longing defeated by a sudden revelation of mortal illness:

> I do not suppose he was much dashed at the nearness of a common destiny. But there was something else that would cut him to the quick: the loss of the cruise, the end of all his cruising; the knowledge that he had looked his last on Swinburgh, and the wild crags of Skye, and that Sound of Mull; . . . that he was never again to hear the surf break in Clashcarnock; never again to see lighthouse after lighthouse (all younger than himself and the more part of his own device) open in the hour of the dusk their flowers of fire. . . . To a life of so much activity and danger, a life's work of so much interest and essential beauty, here came the long farewell.
>
> It was in the spring and summer – at first impatiently expecting to revisit the scenes commemorated, and afterwards awaiting death in his own house and following with his mind's eye the course of the yacht now gone without him – that he returned with a memory already dim to the details of the former voyage, and wrote with a hand already failing his reminiscences of Scott.[171]

The powerful elegiac tone, the death which interrupts the voyage to the lighthouse, the return in memory after many years to a rich moment of the past, suggest the imaginative landscape of *To the Lighthouse*, which was already evolving in Woolf's mind as she devoured Lockhart. Two years earlier death had separated her mother, as Mrs Ramsay was to be separated, from that life in which she too had been the builder of lighthouses younger than herself.

More than anyone else except Lewis Carroll, Stevenson created the sensibilities which lie behind Woolf's description of the fictional territory of *To the Lighthouse*: 'This is going to be fairly short; to have father's character done complete in it; and mother's and St Ives; and childhood.'[172] Woolf always resisted the symbolic interpretation of the lighthouse in that book. It may be a beam, but it is also, in Fry's terms, a solid volume in a picture, the cone which Cézanne required in design. Woolf might have replied to Stevenson that for her books and lighthouses were the same thing.

In the *Strand Magazine* for 1892 – a journal which litters Betty Flanders' seaside lodging at the beginning of *Jacob's Room* – the ten-year-old Virginia might have read an account of the opening in 1882 of the Eddystone lighthouse.[173] The author, seated in a boat, describes the light from the new lighthouse flashing across the waves. The account ends with a four-line poem on immutability. A beautiful ink sketch of the building with the boat caught in a beam of light across the water stays in the mind. Whether the picture summons up Alice and the Sheep gliding on the river and plucking at dream rushes, or James and Cam belatedly grasping the dream of childhood, the images it creates allow Carroll and Woolf the same imaginative space in which to challenge both the Victorian establishment and its established narratives.

2
The Voice of the Author

I PIETY, IMPROVEMENT AND PROTEST

In *To the Lighthouse* Virginia Woolf offers the reader no definite standpoint from which to interpret the fictional world and partake in the author's control of it. As Auerbach pointed out in *Mimesis*: 'She does not seem to bear in mind that she is the author and hence ought to know how matters stand with her characters.'[1] She never explains why Mrs Ramsay is sad. There is no voice murmuring, as there is at the end of *Vanity Fair*: 'Ah! *Vanitas Vanitatum*! Which of us is happy in this world? Which of us has his desire? or having it, is satisfied?'[2] When Lily Briscoe mourns Mrs Ramsay what is communicated is not the understanding which emerges from the author's interpretation of her own text, but the reeling dizziness of trying to understand, in which writer and reader are equally caught up:

> Was she crying then for Mrs Ramsay, without being aware of any unhappiness? She addressed old Mr Carmichael again. What was it then? What did it mean? Could things thrust their hands up and grip one; could the blade cut; the fist grasp? Was there no safety? No learning by heart of the ways of the world? No guide, no shelter, but all was miracle, and leaping from the pinnacle of a tower into the air?[3]

The voice of the author, if it can be heard at all, is never the voice of Providence, as it is for Fielding or for George Eliot. Both Woolf and Joyce rebelled against the 'privileged discourse' through which the author commands his own creatures.[4] But that form of insurrection by the author on behalf of the reader had begun much earlier in the children's book:

> 'I don't know what you mean by "glory,"' Alice said.
> Humpty Dumpty smiled contemptuously. 'Of course you don't

41

– till I tell you. I meant "there's a nice knock-down argument for
you!"'

'But "glory" doesn't mean "a nice knock-down
argument,"'Alice objected.

'When *I* use a word,' Humpty Dumpty said, in rather a scornful
tone, 'it means just what I choose it to mean – neither more or
less.'

'The question is,' said Alice, 'whether you *can* make words
mean so many different things.'

'The question is,' said Humpty Dumpty, 'which is to be master
– that's all.'   (*L-G*, 269)

Lewis Carroll, when asked about the meaning of the *Alice* books,
replied serenely that he was content for the meaning to be decided
by the reader.[5] In 1865 such abrogation of authorial mastery in the
children's book was unprecedented. Darton described it as
revolutionary in 1932. The relocation of power in reader rather than
in writer has since then become a central tenet of modern critical
theory. Roland Barthes pointed out that the refusal to assign 'an
ultimate meaning to the text . . . liberates what may be called an
anti-theological activity, an activity that is truly revolutionary since
to refuse to fix meaning is in the end, to refuse God and his
hypostases – reason, science, law'.[6] Virginia Woolf knew perfectly
well what she was repudiating in her withdrawal from her own
created world in *To the Lighthouse*.

A contributor (Elizabeth Rigby) to the *Quarterly Review* in 1844
blamed the pious tale sanctioned by the Religious Tract Society for
encouraging the children's author to intrude on his own fictions:

> The obvious intention of these writers is to do good, but the very
> officiousness of their services renders them unpalatable. The
> truth is, there is no getting rid of them. From the moment you
> open the book the moral treads so close upon your heels as to be
> absolutely in the way. . . . In short, the young idea is not left to
> shoot one moment in peace, but is twitted and snubbed the whole
> way through with a pertinacity of admonition, injunction and
> advice, which, from its studious incorporation into the tale itself,
> is more than usually difficult to elude.[7]

The older style of writing for children, parodied by many later
writers, was to stick the moral on at the end, which Rigby feels was

preferable, because it could then be skipped altogether. Mary Sherwood's *The Fairchild Family* (1818) accumulates hymns and prayers at the end of each chapter, so that the lively incidents to some extent stand on their own, despite encouragements to the adult to end each session of reading aloud with proper devotions. As Lord Frederick Hamilton records, remembering his childhood enjoyment of the book: 'There was plenty about eating and drinking; one could always skip the prayers, and there were three or four very brightly written accounts of funerals in it.'[8] The cautionary tale – Elizabeth Turner's, parodied by Belloc in 1908, appeared in 1807 and 1811 – provided a model of applied morality which many writers imitated.[9] The ubiquitous piety of which the *Quarterly Review* complains was much in evidence in the work of Sarah Trimmer, one of Sherwood's most influential predecessors, and it became increasingly modish as the nineteenth century progressed. A notorious example was Maria Louisa Charlesworth's *Ministering Children*, published in 1854, ten years after Elizabeth Rigby's protest, and eleven years before *Alice in Wonderland*.

The mid-Victorian generation of parents seem to have fallen on *Ministering Children* as though it were indeed an answer to prayer, and complaints about its appearance as Sunday reading, even if not as everyday fare, resound later in the century from those children who suffered from that parental zeal. Stevenson recalled that his youthful fascination with the murder of Archbishop Sharpe by John Burley of Balfour – described in Scott's *Old Mortality* – was augmented by the fact that 'as it was a crime of fine religious flavour, it figured in Sunday books and afforded a grateful relief from *Ministering Children*'.[10] The children of Charlesworth's story are paragons of piety and philanthropy, distributing tracts, prayers and packets of tea with abundant sweetness. Charlotte Yonge, herself the product of a Tractarian home,[11] and author of a wide range of children's books, of which the best known is now *The Daisy Chain* (1856) – although *The Heir of Redclyffe* (1853) made Yonge's name as a novelist – singled out Charlesworth's book when she complained about the simulated piety of the Evangelical tale:

> Without pausing to consider the doctrine they teach, the manner of it is undesirable, because obtrusive. Little children amaze their elders, and sometimes perfect strangers, by sudden inquiries whether they are Christians, or as to their personal love for God. . . . When the Tract Society had pledged itself to introduce the

central doctrine of the Christian Faith in every publication, of whatever size, it undertook what was not possible without frequent irreverence. . . .

The species has of late culminated in 'Ministering Children', a book multiplied by thousands, owing to a certain pleasantness of practical detail in the early pages, running on into the mawkish sweetness and sentiment that is peculiarly acceptable to a certain stage of development in children and nursery maids.[12]

Yonge's objections here are both moral and aesthetic. The story encourages the child to play at religion and to feel self-righteous for doing so, while the language of the obtrusive author expresses through its own inferiority a form of class condescension. Yonge would have agreed with the *London Review* critic who complained in 1860 that people seemed to think that anyone could write a children's story and that it required no literary gifts to do so – a view which has modern parallels.

The real objector to the inferior writing and false religiosity of the Evangelical tale is not the child but the adult, and one suspects that adult uneasiness only partly mirrors childish distaste. Children have only one form of protest against books they do not like, and they use it with devastating effectiveness. They do not listen, or they put the book down. It is as impossible to make a child read a book he does not like as it is to make him vacate his bowels at a time decreed by his parent. Many children probably did hate the preaching in Evangelical books. Kipling's parody of Farrar's *Eric, Or Little by Little* in *Stalky & Co* (1899) and Nesbit's of *Ministering Children* in *The Wouldbegoods* (1901) are as much an adult's revenge on behalf of the child he or she once was as fictions for the new generation, although they are that, too. But children are capable of not noticing aspects of books which would deter adults from reading them. No child objects to Enid Blyton's ethics and language. The readability of the books creates the adult's protest against their pernicious influence, and the same was probably true of the Evangelical book, which, as Yonge observes, was written with a certain power. Field wrote in *The Child and His Book*: 'A child let loose among books is gifted by Nature with the happy faculty of discovering and assimilating that which suits him, and passing by all the rest.'[13] Like Lord Frederick Hamilton, the child reader might ignore the piety. When Huckleberry Finn stays with a Southern family and reads *The Pilgrim's Progress* he remarks that it was 'about a man that left his family and it didn't say why'.[14] No adult could fail to perceive why Christian left his family. C. Day Lewis wrote that 'a book was something I tore through for the story, regardless of the style and impatient of the trimmings'.[15] Stevenson, Nesbit, Kipling and Belloc parodied their originals not because they were dull, but because they presented fake ideals in fake language. The *London Review* critic expostulated: 'No healthy child, who preserves his natural frankness and openness, can or ought to use the language of such books; and every right-minded parent knows that the stilted and artificial phrases which are to be met with in many evangelical stories, cannot possibly correspond to the real experience of a child.'[16] But even before the Evangelical book gained its hold on children's reading, writers of books for children evinced an uneasy awareness of a double readership, the child with the adult peering over his shoulder, purse and principles equally to hand.

In the Preface to *Sandford and Merton* (1783–9) – one of the first books to be written for children on Rousseau's educational model – Thomas Day, supporter of Wilberforce and friend of another educationalist and children's writer, Richard Edgeworth (father of Maria Edgeworth), expressed his wish to avoid theorising and addressing the adult reader over the child's head, although he admits to having done exactly that at one point in the book. However, 'all the rest of the book is intended to form and interest the minds of children; it is to them I have written; it is from their applause alone I shall estimate my success; and if they are uninterested in the work, the praises of a hundred reviewers will not console me for my failure'. Worthy as this sounds, it is none the less somewhat disingenuous, because the work will only reach the child in the first place if it wins adult applause. It is parents, not children, who care about the forming of the child's mind. When Day breaks off his narrative to describe Tommy's new enlightenment about the condition of the negroes, the author's voice surreptitiously castigates not the child reader, but the un-enlightened adult standing behind him: 'He [Tommy] reflected, with shame and contempt, upon the ridiculous prejudices he had once entertained; he learned to consider all men as his brethren and equals; and the foolish distinctions which pride had formerly suggested were gradually obliterated from his mind.' The unlearning of pride and prejudice is the concern of the adult reader, not of the child, who learns them from the adult world with the air he breathes.[17]

Jane Austen, eight years old the year that the first volume of *Sandford and Merton* appeared, may not have noticed that the author required her to consider negroes her equals, but she noticed that the words 'pride and prejudice' had a good sound, as well as some sense.[18] The contrasts which she sets up in her own novel between the sickly well-bred Anne de Bourgh, who would have performed delightfully on the pianoforte had her health permitted her to learn, and Elizabeth Bennet, walking three miles to Netherfield Park to astound Miss Bingley at the breakfast table with a petticoat six inches deep in mud, recalls Day's repudiation of the fashionably delicate Miss Matilda in favour of Miss Sukey: 'His niece was accustomed from her earliest years to plunge into the cold bath at every season of the year, to rise by candlelight in winter, to ride a dozen miles upon a trotting horse, or to walk as many even with the hazard of being splashed or soiling her clothes.' The healthy Miss Sukey is thus disqualified for 'society' in the same way that Harry is, a boy who reacts to fine company much as Elizabeth Bennet reacts to Netherfield: 'What disgusted Harry more than ever was, that his refined companions seemed to consider themselves and a few of their acquaintance as the only beings of any consequence in the world.' When Mrs Merton praises Miss Matilda for her accomplishments, Miss Bingley's effusions over Miss Darcy spring to mind. Mrs Merton declares: 'She plays most divinely upon the harpsichord, talks French even better than she does English, and draws in the style of a master. Indeed, I think that last figure of the naked gladiator the finest thing I ever saw in my life.' Miss Bingley accosts Mr Darcy while he is writing a letter to his sister:

'How can you contrive to write so even?' He was silent.
'Tell your sister I am delighted to hear of her improvement on the harp, and pray let her know that I am quite in raptures with her beautiful little design for a table, and I think it infinitely superior to Miss Grantley's.'
'Will you give me leave to defer your raptures till I write again? At present I have not room to do them justice.'

In Jane Austen's version the naked gladiator becomes a glint in the author's satirical eye. When the ladies in *Sandford and Merton* make music, Day's description anticipates two occasions in the later novel:

Among the rest, Miss Simmons sang a little Scotch song, called Lochaber, in so artless, but sweet and pathetic a manner, that little Harry listened almost with tears in his eyes, though several of the other young ladies by their significant looks and gestures treated it with ineffable contempt. After this Miss Matilda, who was allowed to be a perfect mistress of music, played and sang several celebrated Italian airs.

Harry is suffocated with boredom. When Elizabeth Bennet sings at Sir William Lucas's, her unaffected performance is contrasted with her sister Mary's studied display of her accomplishments:

Mary had neither genius nor taste; and though vanity had given her application, it had given her likewise a pedantic air and conceited manner, which would have injured a higher degree of excellence than she had reached. Elizabeth, easy and unaffected, had been listened to with much more pleasure, though not playing half so well; and Mary, at the end of a long concerto, was glad to purchase praise and gratitude by Scotch and Irish airs.

If Miss Bingley inherits Miss Matilda's finery, Mary is heir to her parade of skills. At the Netherfield ball Elizabeth 'had the mortification of seeing Mary, after very little entreaty, preparing to oblige the company. By many significant looks and silent entreaties did she endeavour to prevent such a proof of complaisance, but in vain. Mary would not understand them.'[19] Jane Austen gave Thomas Day the loudest applause any child could in imitating some of his most piquant moments. Darcy, like Day's protagonist, progresses from pride and prejudice to an awareness of the rights of other people. If Austen did notice Day's intrusive voice, she deflected it onto Mr Collins.

When Day describes Tommy's awakening to a sense of racial equality the author's convictions are passionately sincere, as is evident from his devotion to the abolition movement. But the language in which he expresses them – 'He learned to consider all men as his brethren and his equals' – is pompous and self-righteous. The Biblical 'brethren' might be skated over in silent reading but no adult reading aloud can tolerate the author's tone. Although Day's beliefs were different from those of Evangelical writers, the special vocabulary of philanthropy comes from the pulpit, as E. Nesbit points out when in *The Wouldbegoods* the Bastables pursue a black pig, which they had hoped to make perform in their circus, right into the heart of a missionary tea party. The narrator is the ten-year-old Oswald Bastable: 'Even as he [the pig] crossed the threshold I heard something about "black brothers being already white to the harvest." All the ladies had been sewing flannel things for the poor blacks while the curate read aloud to them. You think they screamed when they saw the Pig and Us? You are right.' Oswald as author withdraws gracefully from the double intrusion, on the tea party and on the reader: 'Nor will I tell you a word of all that was said and done to the intrepid hunters of the Black and Learned. I have told you all the interesting part. Seek not to know the rest. It is better buried in obliquity.'[20] Language also escapes. Oswald might have hoped for oblivion, but obliquity came instead.

When the *London Review* critic complained of the 'stilted and artificial language' of such books as *The Life of a Baby, Little Annie: or, Is Church-Time a Happy-Time?* and *Ministering Children*, he protested that the child 'gets what seems to him an impossible standard of youthful piety before him; he knows that such language and behaviour are very unlike his own'.[21] Such language is the special property of nineteenth-century Evangelical children's books. Charlesworth writes:

> Sweet was the slumber of the ministering boys that night – within the Hall, the farm-house, and the cottage; and sweet the link between them! And pleasant thoughts smoothed the old man's pillow, as, dry and warm through the youthful love of Earth, he turned to rest beneath the shadow of the Eternal, turned to the well-spring, whence those bright and blessed rills of human sympathy had risen and flowed to his aged feet.[22]

Sweet slumbers, well-springs, blessed rills of human sympathy, aged feet. These phrases not only fail to correspond to any child's experience of life, they fail to correspond to anyone's experience of anything except the reading of other books written in the same style, or of a selection of Wordsworth's worst poems. Mary Sherwood's *The Little Woodman and his Dog Caesar* ends in like manner: 'When William grew up he thanked his grandmother for having preserved him from doing wrong. And thus their days were spent happily in diligent labour; while their evenings were closed with reading God's book and praying together; till, at length, the pious old woman died.'[23] What a pity. If one is tempted to recite: 'There was an old woman who swallowed a fly / Silly old woman, she's sure to die', that was surely Edward Lear's feeling when he countered this kind of thing with *A Book of Nonsense* (1846): 'There was an old Derry down Derry, who loved to see little Folks merry.'[24] No doubt he found that the little children of the Earl of Derby, to whom he was tutor, became restive under Sherwood's ministrations. (Or did he just become restive himself?) *Froggy's Little Brother* (1875), by Brenda, captures the same sugar-coated language:

> How many a beautiful lesson can we learn from the poor – for sufferings nobly endured and heavy burdens bravely borne, where can we look better than to them, but what *generosity* they teach us. They show us how to be truly and greatly generous in their willingness to share the last crumb of comfort, whatever that may be, with a neighbour, kindly and ungrudgingly, without hope of return or reward.[25]

However accurate the observation, it will not stand the language which expresses it: beautiful lessons, noble sufferings, heavy burdens, crumbs of comfort.

The comments of E. Nesbit's children define the reader's discomfort, when they agree to found the Society of the Wouldbegoods:

> 'I'm not sure we oughtn't to have put our foot down at the beginning,' Dicky said. 'I don't see much in it, anyhow.'
>
> 'It pleases the girls,' Oswald said, for he is a kind brother.
>
> 'But we're not going to stand jaw, and "words in season", and "loving sisterly warnings". I tell you what it is, Oswald, we'll have to run this thing our way, or it'll be jolly beastly for everybody.'
>
> Oswald saw this plainly.
>
> 'We must do something,' Dicky said; 'it's very hard, though. Still, there must be *some* interesting things that are not wrong.'
>
> 'I suppose so,' Oswald said, 'but being good is so much like being a muff, generally. Anyhow I'm not going to smooth the pillows of the sick, or read to the aged poor, or any rot out of *Ministering Children.*'
>
> 'No more am I,' Dicky said. He was chewing a straw like the head had in its mouth, 'but I suppose we must play the game fair.

Let's begin by looking out for something useful to do – something like mending things or cleaning them, not just showing off.'

'The boys in books chop kindling wood and save their pennies to buy tea and tracts.'

'Little beasts!' said Dick. 'I say, let's talk about something else.' And Oswald was glad to, for he was beginning to feel jolly uncomfortable.[26]

The implication of the boys' discontent with smoothing pillows is that this is the language of the Evangelical lady, but historically that is not so. Dean Frederick Farrar, Master of Trinity (the college of Strachey, Thoby Stephen and Leonard Woolf) could out-sherwood them all, as Kipling realised when he chose to parody *Eric, Or Little by Little* in *Stalky & Co* (1899), in which he coined a new word, 'eric-ing'. Farrar exhorts his hero at a moment of spiritual trial:

Now, Eric, now or never! Life and death, ruin and salvation, corruption and purity , are perhaps in the balance together and the scale of your destiny may hang on a single word of yours. Speak out, boy! Tell these fellows that unseemly words wound your conscience; tell them that they are ruinous, sinful, damnable; speak out and save yourself and the rest. . . .

Good spirits guard that young boy, and give him grace in this his hour of trial. Open his eyes that he may see the fiery chariots of the angels who would defend him, and the dark array of spiritual foes who throng around his bed. Point a pitying finger to the yawning abyss of shame, ruin, and despair that even now perhaps is being cleft under his feet.[27]

Both Kipling and Nesbit attack a language which has no referent beyond itself. Behind the metaphors and euphemisms of pseudo-literary piety, no writer ever says exactly what he or she means. In *Ministering Children* one of the 'good' children asks why another child cannot stay and take care of her ailing mother:

'Could not some one stay with her?' asked Rose.

'No, there is no one to stay, except the children,' replied the daughter-in-law, 'and they are a great deal more trouble than comfort when one's well, and I am sure they would be ten times worse to bear in sickness.'

'Could you not teach them to be kind?' asked Rose.

'Well, as for that, I don't know that they are bad dispositioned, but children will be children – at least, I have always found it so.'[28]

Charlesworth makes it plain, however, that the point of the book is that children must not be children, they must be ministering angels. Elizabeth Rigby, author of the *Quarterly Review* article in 1844, had quoted an Evangelical demur that 'it is too horrid to make religion a matter of *show-off*, which I really think these stories could teach children to be guilty of'. Dicky in *The Wouldbegoods* suggests that the Bastables find something useful to do, not 'just showing-off'. An encouragement to ape religion, according to the *Quarterly Review* critic, is bound to lead, as Charlotte Yonge declared in 1869, to irreverence.

II THE BURDEN OF INSTRUCTION

The possibility that piety might promote irreverence never occurred to Sherwood or to Charlesworth, or to Farrar or to the adherents of the Religious Tract Society, because they followed the fictional model of *The Pilgrim's Progress*, the one book which all the critics of Sherwood and her merry tribe agreed was irreproachable both as religion and literature. Moreover, as Elizabeth Rigby observes: 'What book is more popular with children?'[29]

That question remained rhetorical until 1865, when Alice pushed Christian unceremoniously off the centre of the path of children's reading. In some ways the two stories are not dissimilar. Both are cast in the form of a dream, but in Bunyan the dreamer remains outside the narrative, initiating the action – 'Now I saw in my dream' – and requiring explanations of it from the actors themselves. When Christian is plucked out of the Slough of Despond, the dreamer asks Help why it isn't mended, 'that poor travellers might go thither with more security':

And he said unto me, This *Miry Slough* is such a place as cannot be mended: it is the descent whither the scum and filth that attends conviction for sin doth continually run, and therefore it is called the *Slough of Dispond*: for still as the sinner is awakened about his lost condition, there ariseth in his soul many fears, and doubts, and discouraging apprehensions, which all of them get together, and settle in this place: And this is the reason of the badness of this ground.

The dreamer, Bunyan himself, instructs the reader by demanding from one of his own characters, Help, an explanation ostensibly for himself, the narrator. After Christian has turned out of his way according to the counsels of Mr Worldly-Wiseman he is reprimanded by the Evangelist, who makes him recite the whole episode and then interprets it: '*Give more earnest heed to the things that I shall tell thee of.* I will now show thee who it was who deluded thee, and who 'twas also to whom he sent thee. The man that met thee is one *Worldly-Wiseman*, and rightly is he so called.' In the original this explanation goes on for several pages and a picture, until Christian meets Good Will and journeys to the House of the Interpreter. The next part of the story is a long monologue, broken only by Christian's enquiries: '*Then said* Christian, *What means this?*' (repeated two pages later), followed by '*Then said* Christian *to the* Interpreter, *Expound this matter more fully to me.*' He need not have worried: the Interpreter is anxious to expound things as fully as possible. After another two pages the dreamer returns:

> Then I saw in my Dream, that the *Interpreter* took *Christian* by the hand, and led him into a place, where was a Fire burning against a Wall, and one standing by it always, casting much Water upon it to quench it: Yet did the Fire burn higher and hotter.
>   *Then said* Christian, *What means this*?

The Interpreter responds with a long and detailed explanation.

It is not hard to see that as a fictional model this has disastrous possibilities. Christian, the protagonist, is only once allowed to be a hero. He is, apart from the encounter with Apollyon, always on the receiving end of counsels, admonitions, instruction and endless explanations, and, in that he is the figure with whom the allegory requires the reader to identify, the reader also enjoys these attentions. Or quite enjoys them, depending on what else there is to read. Christian matters, and the reader matters too. Christian's question 'What shall I do to be saved?' is the motive force of the narrative and the answer lies in the reading of the book, as it does for Christian himself in the reading of the Bible:

> Worl.   *How camest thou by thy burden at first?*
> Chr.   By reading this Book in my hand.

If one did not know what one's burden was before reading Bunyan's book, one would certainly know it early on in that work:

Dedic. *This Book will make a Travailer of thee,*
       If by its Counsel thou wilt ruled be;
       It will direct thee to the Holy Land,
       If thou wilt its Directions understand.

A child of eight is capable of perceiving that the burden is not on Christian's back but in his mind, even if, like Huck, that child is not sure why Christian left home in the first place.

The opening of *Alice in Wonderland* bears a genetic relation to the opening of *The Pilgrim's Progress*. Both are prefaced with a poem about the work and its origins. Both begin with a tired person: in Bunyon's book the dreamer, who lies down to sleep and sees a man with a book:

> I looked, and saw him open the Book, and Read therein; and as he Read, he wept, and trembled: and not being able longer to contain, he brake out with a lamentable cry; saying *what shall I do?*[30]

Alice is also ready for sleep:

> Alice was beginning to get very tired of sitting by her sister on the bank, and of having nothing to do: once or twice she had peeped into the book her sister was reading, but it had no pictures or conversations in it, 'and what is the use of a book,' thought Alice, 'without pictures or conversations?'
> So she was considering, in her own mind (as well as she could, for the hot day made her feel very sleepy and stupid), whether the pleasure of making a daisy-chain would be worth the trouble of getting up and picking the daisies, when suddenly a white rabbit with pink eyes ran close by her.
> There was nothing so *very* remarkable in that; nor did Alice think it so *very* much out of the way to hear the Rabbit say to itself, 'Oh dear! Oh dear! I shall be too late.'   (*AW*, 25)

Carroll, whose mind ran to parody like iron filings to a magnet, may have recalled that in Charlotte Yonge's *The Daisy Chain*, published in 1856, the daisy chain is also a dream, interpreted for the boy Martin by his sister Margaret:

> 'And, behold, the tumult and despair were passed. I lay on the grass in the cloisters, and the Daisy Chain hung from the sky, and was drawing me upwards. . . .'
> [Margaret] 'It is what we all feel, is it not? That this little daisy bud is the link between us and heaven.'[31]

We may all feel this, but on the other hand, we may just feel that making a daisy chain is hardly worth the bother of picking the daisies. The tonal link between this passage in Yonge's novel and Bunyan's allegory is as unmistakable as Carroll's implied changing of Christian's cry 'What shall I do [to be saved]?' into that of a bored child: 'What shall I do?'

It has been suggested that Alice's meeting with the Cheshire Cat parodies Christian's encounter with the shepherds of the Delectable Mountains.[32] The local parallel is apt, but in a more general sense the encounter with the Cheshire Cat pinpoints the redirection which Alice gives to the idea of the Christian journey:

'Cheshire Puss,' she began, rather timidly, as she did not at all know whether it would like the name: 'Come, it's pleased so far,' thought Alice, and she went on, 'Would you tell me, please, which way I ought to go from here?'

'That depends a good deal on where you want to get to,' said the Cat.

'I don't much care where –' said Alice.

'Then it doesn't matter which way you go,' said the Cat, '– so long as I get *somewhere*,' Alice added, as an explanation.

'Oh, you're sure to do that,' said the Cat, 'if you only walk long enough.'

Alice felt that this could not be denied, so she tried another question. 'What sort of people live about here?'

'In *that* direction,' the Cat said, waving its right paw round, 'lives a Hatter: and in *that* direction,' waving the other paw, 'lives a March Hare. Visit either you like: they're both mad.'

'But I don't want to go among mad people,' Alice remarked.

'Oh, you can't help that,' said the Cat: 'we're all mad here. I'm mad. You're mad.'

'How do you know I'm mad?' said Alice.

'You must be,' said the Cat, 'or you wouldn't have come here.'

(*AW*, 88–9)

The Cat is the prototype Evangelist, gesturing Alice along an enigmatic path towards various kinds of new acquaintance, all mad according to the tenets of the faith. Both Alice and Christian meet a lot of dictatorial people. The difference is that Christian, an adult, is put into the position of a child by the fact that his experiences are supposed to be improving and instructive. Alice, although much dictated to by her new acquaintances, never loses her independence, her capacity to criticise them as much as they criticise her:

'Everybody says "come on!" here,' thought Alice, as she went slowly after it: 'I never was so ordered about before, in all my life, never!' (*AW*, 25)

The interchanges with Humpty Dumpty read like burlesques of the dialogue between Christian and the Interpreter, as Humpty Dumpty interprets 'Jabberwocky' to a bemused and reluctant Alice:

'When I make a word do a lot of work like that,' said Humpty Dumpty, 'I always pay it extra.' . . . (Alice didn't venture to ask what he paid them with; and so you see I can't tell *you*.)

(*L-G*, 270)

Bunyan would have made certain that Christian did ask, and he would have told the reader the answer at considerable length.

The overblown language of Evangelical writers cannot be laid at poor Bunyan's door, but he can to some extent be held responsible for the voice of the author intruding on the narrative in order to explain its meaning and point its moral. That informative voice dominates children's books certainly into the 1840s, when Edward Lear, Catherine Sinclair, Harriet Martineau and Mary Howitt all pioneered a less loaded relation between writer and reader.

Although the condescension of the Evangelical author gained the greater notoriety in the early nineteenth century, the secular instructive story favoured by the Edgeworths was just as much a form of domination of author over reader, and often much more boring than the pious tale. Anna Barbauld and John Aiken's prose dialogues, *Evenings at Home* (1794), conjure up a supposedly interested child who interrogates the parent–narrator, much as Christian questions the Interpreter. Here is one called 'Dialogue on Things to be Learned', between Mamma and Kitty:

Mamma: Reading and writing are such necessary parts of education, that I need not say much to you about them.

Kitty: O no, for I love reading dearly.

Mamma: I know you do, if you can get entertaining stories to read; but there are many things also to be read for instruction, which perhaps may not be so pleasant at first.

Kitty: But what need is there of so many books of this sort?

Mamma: Some are to teach you your duty to your Maker, and your fellow creatures, of which I hope you are sensible you ought not to be ignorant. Then it is very right to be acquainted with geography; for you remember how poor Miss Blunden laughed at you for saying that if she ever went to France, it should be by land.[33]

The author adopts the parent's voice. The child's response is never free, but always the one author and parents want to hear, which is partly what Darton means when he said that *Alice in Wonderland* inaugurated liberty of thought in children's books. The rebellion of the child who might yawn her way through Anna Barbauld is suddenly part of the story: how bossy and ill-tempered all the creatures are.

Charles Kingsley imitated Barbauld's method in his series 'Madam How and Why', first published in *Good Words for the Young*, edited by George MacDonald. The dialogues form a set of lessons on geography, biology, astronomy and everything imaginable.[34] The tireless adult voice demands: 'What? you have a question more to ask? Oh? I talked about Madam How lifting up Hartford Bridge Flat.

How could she do that? My dear child, that is a long story; and I must tell it you some other time.'[35] Hardly a cliff-hanger, but read on next week. The tone may simulate equality, as in Jean Ingelow's assumption of a sibling role in the same journal:

> Dear little boys and girls who are reading this book, I have a brother and sister who are about as old as you are, and I have told you some of the things that they say and do. I am generally very happy when I am with them, because we talk about sensible things that one can understand, such things as dolls, and lesson books, and fairies, and the Middle Ages, and being good.[36]

How much those little boys and girls must have enjoyed those little conversations and how unerringly they must have chosen one of those lovely little topics which spell childhood to the adult mind. The palpable pretence in the relation between author and child is just as much in evidence as it is in the Evangelical tale, and if the child won't be that sort of child the author won't tell the story. Even pieces which are not couched in dialogue form insist on a reading of information in terms of moral instruction and improvement, as in H. B. Tristram's 'The Spider and its Webs', where the spider's web is not just a marvel in itself, but a lesson on how to live: 'The spider will teach us not only the lesson of perseverance which Robert Bruce learnt when he was nearly giving way to despair – it will teach us how to spin and how to weave, how to hunt and how to snare. It gives lessons in gymnastics, in swimming and in leaping, and it has solved many a problem in mathematics before Euclid was born.'[37] *Charlotte's Web* also teaches, but a lesson which is not fired at the defenceless inferior from the big gun of the condescending author:

> Charlotte stood quietly over the fly, preparing to eat it. Wilbur lay down and closed his eyes. He was tired from his wakeful night and from the excitement of meeting someone for the first time. A breeze brought him the smell of clover – the sweet-smelling world beyond his fence. 'Well,' he thought, 'I've got a new friend, all right. But what a gamble friendship is! Charlotte is fierce, brutal, scheming, bloodthirsty – everything I don't like. How can I learn to like her, even though she is pretty, and, of course, clever?'[38]

An adult may master Euclid and swimming, but will go to her grave reflecting that friendship is a gamble. Author and reader have drawn into collusion over the difficulty of learning to read the world aright.

Alice is the first fictional child to escape from the moral-finder:

> She had quite forgotten the Duchess by this time, and she was a little startled when she heard her voice close to her ear.
>
> 'You're thinking about something, my dear, and that makes you forget to talk. I can't think what the moral of that is, but I shall remember it in a bit.'
>
> 'Perhaps it hasn't one,' Alice ventured to remark.
>
> 'Tut, tut, child!' said the Duchess. 'Everything's got a moral, if only you can find it.' And she squeezed herself up closer to Alice's side as she spoke.
>
> Alice did not much like her keeping so close to her: first, because the Duchess was *very* ugly: and secondly, because she was exactly the right height to rest her chin on Alice's shoulder, and it was an uncomfortably sharp chin. However, she did not like to be rude: so she bore it as well as she could.
>
> 'The game's going on rather better now,' she said, by way of keeping up the conversation a little.
>
> ''Tis so,' said the Duchess: 'and the moral of that is – "Oh, 'tis love, 'tis love, that makes the world go round."'
>
> 'Somebody said,' Alice whispered, 'that it's done by everybody minding their own business!'
>
> 'Ah, well! It means much the same thing,' said the Duchess, digging her sharp little chin into Alice's shoulder as she added, 'and the moral of *that* is – "Take care of the sense, and the sounds will take care of themselves."'
>
> 'How fond she is of finding morals in things!' Alice thought to herself. (*AW*, 120–1)

The physical proximity of the Duchess, the nudging and twitting which Elizabeth Rigby complained of in 1844, allows the child neither physical space – she is edged off her own ground – nor mental space to see the world literally rather than metaphorically. The shift from Bunyan is noticeable. Carroll gives Alice a new place on which to stand firm.

The Pilgrim myth underpins the story of Louisa M. Alcott's *Little Women* published in 1868, three years after *Alice in Wonderland*, but an independent childish voice enters the narrative. The March girls decide to face the difficulties of life while their father is away fighting

in the American Civil War by playing at *The Pilgrim's Progress*. They
hesitate in case they are too old for the game they had liked when
they were little. The moment provides insight into the popularity of
Bunyan's book among children in its capacity for being translated
into play, both as amusement and as dramatic action. Mrs March
replies, in tones not unlike Jean Ingelow's:

> 'We are never too old for this, my dear, because it is a play we are
> playing all the time in one way or another. Our burdens are here,
> our road is before us, and the longing for goodness and happiness
> is the guide that leads us through many troubles and mistakes to
> the peace which is a true Celestial City. Now, my little pilgrims,
> suppose you begin again, not in play, but in earnest and see how
> far on you can get before father comes home.'
>   'Really, Mother? Where are our bundles?' asked Amy, who was
> a very literal young lady.[39]

Amy's literalness is Alice's, and marks a new recognition that things
have the right to be themselves, that they do not have to be
significant, which looks forward not only to Woolf's non-symbolic
lighthouse, but also to the determination of Willa Cather and Laura
Ingalls Wilder to de-signify the road to the American West by
making it a road and not a pilgrimage. Virginia Woolf's first novel,
The Voyage Out, is not a spiritual journey but a literal journey which
has more of *Alice in Wonderland* in its hinterland than it has of *The
Pilgrim's Progress*.

In Carroll's book the passage about moral-pointing is followed by
a discussion between Alice and the Duchess as to whether the
flamingo which Alice is carrying will bite:

> 'Very true,' said the Duchess: 'flamingoes and mustard both
> bite. And the moral of that is – "Birds of a feather flock together."'
>   'Only mustard isn't a bird,' Alice remarked.
>   'Right, as usual,' said the Duchess: 'what a clear way you have
> of putting things!'
>   'It's a mineral, I *think*,' said Alice.
>   'Of course it is,' said the Duchess, who seemed to agree to
> everything that Alice said: 'there's a large mustard-mine near
> here. And the moral of that is – "The more there is of mine, the
> less there is of yours."'   (*AW*, 121–2)

Words are here operating as things in the way that Freud observed in 'Jokes and their Relation to the Unconscious' (1905): 'We notice, too, that children, who, as we know, are in the habit of still treating words as things, tend to expect words that are the same or similar to have the same meaning behind them. . . . We may notice, too, that here jokes are making use of a method of linking things up which is rejected and studiously avoided by serious thought.'[40] The mustard-mine gives the Duchess a mastery over meaning comparable to Humpty Dumpty's even while she pretends to defer to the child.

The morals pointed by the Duchess, about love making the world go round, about taking care of the sense (pence) and letting the sounds (pounds) take care of themselves (a maxim which gives meaning precedence over words in a way which the book itself repudiates), and about the more there is of mine the less there is of yours, create an aura of money-making, morally superior Protestant parenthood, from which Alice rebels with her own moral: ' "Somebody said," Alice whispered, "that it's done by everybody minding their own business." ' Such a thought would never have crossed Christian's mind, but once it had crossed Alice's, a whole generation wondered why it had never occurred to them before, not only that all those people whom Christian encounters might mind their own businesses, but that Bunyan might mind his.

Twenty years before the publication of *Alice*, in 1846, the year of Lear's *A Book of Nonsense*, Edgar Allan Poe attacked allegory in a way which rebounded throughout the rest of the century on the reputation of *The Pilgrim's Progress*. In Johnsonian terms he observes: 'The deepest emotion aroused within us by the happiest allegory, as allegory, is a very imperfectly satisfied sense of the writer's ingenuity in overcoming a difficulty we should have preferred his not having attempted to overcome.' He attacks at its root the argument of Bunyan's dedicatory poem that metaphor has its own solidity and can advance an argument as well as ornament it, and in particular dislikes the necessity of explanation: 'If allegory ever establishes a fact, it is by dint of overturning a fiction.' He calls *The Pilgrim's Progress* 'a ludicrously overrated book',[41] claiming that the allegory forces the author's intrusion on his narrative. The only pleasure it can give the reader is that of ignoring the author's explicit intention in writing the story in the first place.

That generations of children did ignore Bunyan's purpose is certain, however much their parents may have glowed at the thought of the spiritual meanings that they were imbibing. As

Maggie Tulliver in *The Mill on the Floss* grows older the book becomes
an archetype for her own tribulations, but as a child it is the pictures
of the devil which enchant her:

> 'Ah, a beautiful book,' said Mr Riley; 'you can't read a better.'
> 'Well, but there's a great deal about the devil in that,' said
> Maggie, triumphantly, 'and I'll show you the picture of him in his
> true shape, as he fought with Christian.'[42]

When the Bastable children think of playing at *The Pilgrim's Progress*
they none of them want to be Christian: 'We talked about that for
some time, but it did not come to anything, because we all wanted to
be Mr Greatheart, except H. O., who wanted to be the lions, and
you could not have lions in a Society for Goodness.' When they do
go on a pilgrimage it is literal and not spiritual, to the extent that
Denny is soon unable to walk for the peas he has put in his shoes for
extra mortification, and 'in his secret heart Oswald said, "Greedy
young ass." For it *is* greedy to want to have more of anything than
other people, even goodness.'[43] When Froude published his *Life of
Bunyan* in 1880 he claimed that Bunyan's book had 'for two centuries
affected the spiritual opinions of the English race in every part of the
world more powerfully than any book or books except the Bible', but
added that, 'unfortunately, parents do not read Bunyan, he is left to
the children'.

   In an essay written in 1905 which quotes Froude's views, Robert
Bridges attacks *The Pilgrim's Progress*, first, for neglecting 'the
practical side of morals. . . . Though Bunyan's theology supposes
works to be of no account in themselves . . . he should have seen
that works make the true portraiture of faith'; secondly, Bridges
repudiates the 'priggishness and self-complacency' of the writer in
using morality-play names for his characters: 'Mr Worldly-
Wiseman', 'Obstinate', 'Pliable'. He deplores Bunyan's theology,
though recognising 'literary excellence . . . without which he would
have perished long ago'.[44] Bridges' criticisms body forth a double
animus, against Victorian worship of great names – Sir Charles Firth
declared that 'in 1880, with the publication of Froude's life of the
author, Bunyan was formally included in the roll of "English men of
letters"'[45] – and against the author's underlining of a spiritual
message which denies the literal text.

   The demotion of *The Pilgrim's Progress* not only from adult reading
but from its central place in nursery and school-room follows the

secular pattern which the *Alice* books initiate. In *Lark Rise to Candleford*, Flora Thompson's evocation of village life in her own childhood in the 1890s, Laura's uncle calls Bunyan's allegory 'a grand old book', but adds that it 'is a shade dull for some young people'.[46] The child's answer to the dull book is either to put it down or to transform it, as the narrator of Butler's *The Way of All Flesh* does when he adapts *The Pilgrim's Progress* for pantomime, accompanied by jazz Handel, with Vanity Fair as the central scene and Mr Greatheart, Apollyon, Christiana, Mercy and Hopeful, in that order, as leading characters. Christian seems to have dropped out of the cast, perhaps baffled by the Cheshire Cat's directions. The costumes of Mr Greatheart and Hopeful are flamboyant in the Oscar Wilde style, and 'Christiana did not wear much of anything'.[47] The protest against Bunyan is symptomatic of the younger generation's struggle against Evangelicalism in its most extreme form, which Edmund Gosse plangently depicts in *Father and Son* (1907).

III   AUTHOR, PARENT, PREACHER

One of the most interesting of the many transitional figures in the movement from Bunyan to Carroll, and from Carroll to the twentieth century, was Charlotte Yonge, who attacked the obtrusive author for assuming godhead: 'The author, as the Providence of the book, can twist the narrative to point the moral.'[48] The moral purposes of Yonge's own fiction are much less blatant than those of Mary Sherwood. She had no doubt observed the humanising effect of Catherine Sinclair's determination to treat children as children in *Holiday House* (1839), a book which is often treated as a landmark in the history of children's literature, because its author enjoys children's mischievousness and high spirits. Harriet Martineau's *The Crofton Boys* (1841) – volume IV of *The Playfellow* – is one of the first realistic descriptions of life in a boys' school. Martineau presents childhood in terms not coloured by pious persuasions. But family authority goes unquestioned in her work, and Yonge, whatever her disapproval of the pulpit author, could not bring herself to throw a stone at the pulpit parent, a reluctance which makes her Victorian in a way that Kipling, Nesbit, Grahame, Butler and Gosse are not.

Dr May's explication in *The Daisy Chain* of David and Goliath, the one story in the Bible which no child could possibly misunderstand

and which has for every child superb subversive content,
anticipates the honeyed tones of Mrs March explaining about
burdens in Alcott's *Little Women*; Dr May tells his children:

> 'Perhaps little things, now you are little children, may be like the
> lion and the bear – so kill them off – get rid of them – cure yourself
> of whining or dawdling, or whatever it be, and mind your sheep
> well,' said he, smiling sweetly in answer to the children's earnest
> looks as they caught his meaning, 'and if you do, you will not find
> it so hard to deal with your great giant struggle when it comes.'
>   Ah! thought Ethel, it suits me as well as the children. I have a
> great giant on Cocksmoor, and here I am, not allowed to attack
> him, because, perhaps, I am not minding my sheep and letting
> my lion and my bear run loose about the house.

Behind the fatherly admonition stands Charlotte Yonge, pen in
hand, castigating the Ethel May within her own psyche for having
ambitions beyond the pursuit of piety. The book's subtitle is
'Aspirations', and Yonge said in the Preface that her purpose in
writing it was 'that the young should take one hint, to think whether
their hopes and upward-breathings are truly upwards, and founded
in lowliness'. Ethel May's ambition is 'to earn money by writing. . . .
She would compose, publish, earn money – some day call papa,
show him her hoard, beg him to take it, and, never owning whence
it came, raise the building.'[49] If this sounds like the lighthouse
which Stevenson wished to have constructed alongside the plot of
David Balfour, Yonge did achieve practical as well as artistic
fulfilment within her own lifetime. When the *Strand Magazine*
featured her in its 'Portraits of Celebrities' in one of its first issues in
1891, it declared: 'Miss Yonge's books have done good, not only by
their healthy moral teaching, but by the generous use which she had
made of the proceeds of their sale: . . . [donating] the sum of £2,000
which resulted from the sale of "The Daisy Chain", to the erection of
a missionary college at Auckland.'[50] The book allows Yonge both to
question Ethel's purity of heart through the fatherly admonition,
and, in a literal sense, to exonerate her own ambitions from any taint
of worldliness by turning the proceeds from its sale into practical
piety. She wrote to a friend in 1896: 'I think I must tell you that the
Daisy Chain was written just when I was fresh from the influence and
guiding of my father.'[51]
    As an author of children's books Charlotte Yonge embodies

conflicts which many Victorian women writers experienced. Her articles on children's literature in *Macmillan's Magazine* show that in her own line she was as professional as Henry James. She loathed amateurishness and sloppy writing, and thought that her own collection of true stories of heroism, *A Book of Golden Deeds* (1864), contained some grammatical imperfections which made her grieve that it should be used as a reading-book in Bombay.[52] She disliked overt moral-pointing, but she was passionately interested in education and would heartily have endorsed Catherine Sinclair's urging in the Preface to *Holiday House* of authorial responsibility: 'For it is at their early age that the seed can best be sown which shall bear fruit into eternal life.'[53] Yonge hated sentimentality and what she called 'suburban Evangelicalism', but although she was one of the earliest critics to recognise the originality of *Alice in Wonderland*, she could not in her heart justify writing if it was to be done without the ultimate purpose of improving and educating: 'To be overdone with moral is a fatal thing. To force events, even imaginary, to illustrate some maxim is ruinous; yet it seems to us that a book so written has really a better chance of getting a permanent hold on the mind than the whipped syllabub of fiction.'[54] The metaphor of the 'whipped syllabub' owes its genesis to the early Puritans' distrust of fiction as untruth which was reinforced in the eighteenth century by Rousseau's banishing of the fabulous from the child's education.

Rousseau underestimated the difficulties which the systematic suppression of the imagination would cause to both adults and children. The author of an early account of children's literature in the *London and Westminster Review* in 1839, the year of Sinclair's *Holiday House*, complained of the vacuum created in the mind of the child when the 'wonder, amusement, experience and human interest' inherent in the fairy tale was no longer available to him. Would not the consequence be the adaptation of religion for play purposes, causing children to approach the sacred story as though it were a secular fiction? When the child listens to 'Mamma's Bible Stories' he may enquire: 'Does Christ walk on the water like a gnat?' He may notice the cruelty and injustice of much of the Old Testament,[55] as Ellen Key recalls doing in *The Century of the Child* when God's favouritism in preferring Jacob to Esau filled her 'with silent contempt'. The small child has a wondrous faculty for picking up the wrong end of the stick, at least from the adult point of view, as is apparent in the case which Key quotes of the little reader who, 'seeing the pictures of the Christian martyrs in the arena, cried out sympathetically, "Look at that poor tiger; he hasn't got a Christian."'[56] Gwen Raverat seems to have remembered the story in *Period Piece* when she describes a punting picnic in which all the young ladies fell into the river, either accidentally or on purpose, and had to be rescued by the young men: 'There were hardly enough drowning young ladies to go round, and "one poor Tiger didn't get a Christian"; especially as Cordelia managed to climb back into the boat by herself; but for a minute the Ouse was rather like Alice's Pool of Tears, when all the animals were swimming about.'[57] *Alice in Wonderland* not only set children free from having to be serious about what they read; it also questioned the need for the writer to be quite so serious about what she wrote, which looks forward to Virginia Woolf, of whom E. M. Forster said in 1941: 'Though most of us like to write sometimes seriously and sometimes in fun, few of us can so manage the two impulses that they speed each other up, as hers did.'[58]

Yonge shared with Charlotte Brontë and George Eliot an upbringing in which novel-reading would have been considered lax.[59] Ethel May in *The Daisy Chain* reproaches herself for reading a book over her brother's shoulder: 'I forgot, mamma told me not to read those stories in the morning.' Her brother remains unconcerned: 'He was conscious of nothing but his book.'[60] Elizabeth Gaskell wrote of the ceaseless conflict in a woman's life between 'the quiet, regular duties of the daughter, the wife, or the mother', and the creative impulse: 'She must not shrink from the extra responsibility implied by the very fact of her possessing such talents.'[61] Yonge resolved her own difficulty by using her books as a platform for preaching a selflessness and devotion to others which no artist can afford to practise if she is to produce a work of art. Yonge's *A Book of Golden Deeds* emphasises unflaggingly the virtue of what the author calls, with unintentional irony, 'self-devotion', celebrating the heroism inherent in service to others. George Eliot wrote to Macmillan in 1873: 'A little while ago we inquired for Miss Yonge's *Book of Noble Deeds*, and it was out of print. I hope it is to be reproduced.'[62] The slip in the title is significant. 'Noble' is strenuous and adult. 'Golden' is still soothing the sweet slumbers of the ministering child, as Nesbit recognised when she called the minute-book of the Society of Wouldbegoods 'The Book of Golden Deeds'.

The connection between Yonge and George Eliot is not confined to this collection of true stories. The contrast which George Eliot sets up between Dorothea Brooke and Rosamund Vincy in *Middlemarch* develops Yonge's portrait in *The Daisy Chain* of the relation between Ethel – aspiring, large-hearted, near-sighted, rash and self-doubting – and her sister Flora, complacent, worldly, impeccably dressed, self-interested. Rosamund miscarries because she will go out riding in defiance of Lydgate's advice, and Flora's baby dies because she leaves it in the care of a nurse who takes opium.[63] Yonge directs against Flora, as Eliot does against Rosamund, an authorial disapproval neatly identified by E. Nesbit in *The Wouldbegoods*:

> 'Well, then, do you know a book called *The Daisy Chain*?' We didn't.
> 'It's by Miss Charlotte M. Yonge, ' Daisy interrupted, 'and its about a family of poor motherless children who tried so hard to be good, and they were confirmed, and had a bazaar, and went to church at the Minster, and one of them got married and wore black watered silk and silver ornaments. So her baby died, and then she was sorry she had not been a good mother to it. And –'
> Here Dicky got up and said he'd got some snares to attend to, and he'd receive a report of the Council after it was over.[64]

The black watered silk performs the same function as Rosamund Vincy's lace collar. But it is in the portrait of Ethel, bent, like Dorothea, on building cottages for the poor, ambitious for influence and yet afraid of finding herself guilty of self-seeking under the guise of philanthropy, that Yonge draws closest to Eliot, sharing with her the Victorian writer's deep need to justify her own writing by making it purvey truth and good influence. Zangwill wrote that George Eliot's union with Lewes injured her writing not because it hurt her morals, but because it made her so scrupulously moral in her attitude to her readers.[65] Goldsworthy Lowes Dickinson complained to Roger Fry in 1887 that 'George Eliot can never write a single sentence without a page of commentary on it; she ought to have written a philosophy of ethics instead.'[66]

Phyllis Greenacre's research into the guilt which many artists feel about their own creativity, which makes them wonder if it is stolen and whether they themselves are impostors, helps to explain why the preaching voice offers an author so much reassurance about her role as creator of fiction in an age when the fabulous was still under the shadow of Rousseau's disapproval and Evangelical distrust. Both Yonge and Eliot demonstrate a powerful sense of the guilt attached to the artist, as is particularly evident in George Eliot's treatment of Daniel Deronda's opera-singer mother. Greenacre suggests that the artist provides two selves from childhood onwards, one which is conventional and the other which is freakish, abnormal and creative: 'Under many circumstances this struggle continues into adult life, when the more conventional self may be more or less guardian or enemy of the creative self.' The conflicts thus engendered often turn the child in on the family group, creating especially close ties and affinities, a situation evident in George Eliot's case and given by her to Maggie Tulliver, in whom the novelist reproduced her own emotional adhesiveness.[67]

This research throws some light on Virginia Woolf, who was not from a religious home, but who nevertheless had to forge her own reasons for writing, as Yonge had done. Once the woman ceases to see the book as some equivalent to the pulpit, the problem of what it is and what its function is becomes paramount, and carries with it the whole area of the author's relation with the reader. The question of readership dominates all Woolf's work. In refusing to impose herself on the world she created, the novelist carried to its logical extreme protests which many adults had made since the 1840s about the relation of author to child reader. In the two *Alice* books Carroll renegotiated for the children of Nesbit's, Grahame's, and later, Virginia Woolf's generation, the contract between reader and writer. In the experimental art of Woolf and some of her contemporaries the child becomes 'not just a mirror, not only the creature, but also the creator of culture, and in this sense, a dynamic force in his own right'.[68] Alice is her own Interpreter, and the reader, as Woolf pointed out in 'Mr. Bennett and Mrs. Brown' (1924), must share and shoulder the burden, the 'duties and responsibilities' not of the author's message, but of writing the book.[69]

3

Virginia Woolf and the Irreverent Generation

I LEWIS CARROLL

Lewis Carroll had little inkling of the irreverent generation which the *Alice* books would usher in for reasons which reached far beyond them, but in which their overturning of authority was central. He shared the views of some contemporary critics of Evangelical books who feared that the Religious Tract Society's insistence on God in every tale would create hilarity rather than solemnity, fabricated religion as well as fabricated facts. The children's writer Juliana Horatia Ewing recorded the conviction of her mother Margaret Gatty (founder in 1866 of *Aunt Judy's Magazine*) that 'the world would perhaps have less to unlearn and not be so chary of its reverence' if devotional concerns in all writings for both adults and children were subject to 'strict fact and genuine feeling'.[1] Carroll urged parents not to press on children a form of reverence dictated by adult conventions: 'I do not belive God means us to divide life into two halves – to wear a grave face on Sunday, and to think it out-of-place to even so much as mention Him on a week-day. Do you think he cares to see only kneeling figures, and to hear only tones of prayer – and that He does not also love to see the lambs leaping in the sunlight, and to hear the merry voices of the children, as they roll among the hay?'[2] But despite the impeccably decorous tone of this question Carroll set a precedent for an irreverence which went much deeper than an attack on sabbatarianism. Those critics who had feared that the effect of pious pretences would be the destruction of any respect for religion would have been perhaps gratified by their own sagacity if they could have heard Helen Ambrose speaking of religion in Virginia Woolf's first novel, *The Voyage Out*, published in 1915:

'I have had servants,' said Mrs Ambrose, concentrating her

69

gaze. 'At this moment I have a nurse. She's a good woman as they go, but she's determined to make my children pray. So far, owing to great care on my part, they think of God as a kind of walrus; but now that my back's turned – Ridley,' she demanded swinging round upon her husband, 'what shall we do if we find them saying the Lord's Prayer when we get home again?'

Ridley made the sound which is represented by 'Tush'. But Willoughby, whose discomfort as he listened was manifested by a slight rocking movement of his body, said awkwardly, 'Oh surely, Helen, a little religion hurts nobody.'

'I would rather my children told lies,' she replied, and while Willoughby was reflecting that his sister-in-law was even more eccentric than he remembered, pushed her chair back and swept upstairs. In a second they heard her calling back, 'Oh, look! We're out at sea!'[3]

The Stephen children might well have thought that Tenniel's picture of the Walrus would do very well for God, and that his behaviour to the oysters – supported by the Carpenter – in sancti-moniously offering good things which never materialise while exploiting their trust, bore a resemblance to caprices in the Deity which religion tries to conceal. Children who were bored with *Ministering Children* suddenly had something else to talk about:

> 'I like the Walrus best,' said Alice: 'because he was a *little* sorry for the poor oysters.'
>
> 'He ate more than the Carpenter, though,' said Tweedledee. 'You see he held his handkerchief in front, so that the Carpenter couldn't count how many he took: contrariwise.'
>
> 'That was mean!' Alice said indignantly. 'Then I like the Carpenter best – if he didn't eat as many as the Walrus.'
>
> 'But he ate as many as he could get,' said Tweedledum. This was a puzzler. After a pause, Alice began, 'Well! they were *both* very unpleasant characters –' (*L-G*, 236–7)

If the new generation saw God as a walrus, they might have got a good deal further than asking about Christ's similarities to a gnat.

The *Alice* books set a precedent in challenging authority which released the energies of many writers towards a new secular fiction.

Carroll's books were not irreverent in the sense that Humphrey Carpenter argues in *Secret Gardens* (1985), of mocking God and parodying the sacrament ('Eat me; Drink me').[4] These labels speak directly to the experience of children, who are used to bottles marked in red letters 'Not to be taken internally', as is evident from Alice's reaction to the bottle labelled 'DRINK ME':

> It was all very well to say 'Drink me', but the wise little Alice was not going to do *that* in a hurry. 'No, I'll look first,' she said, 'and see whether it's marked "poison" or not': for she had read several nice little stories about children who had got burnt, and eaten up by wild beasts, and other unpleasant things, all because they *would* not remember the simple rules their friends had taught them: such as, that a red-hot poker will burn you if you hold it too long; and that, if you cut your finger *very* deeply with a knife, it usually bleeds; and she had never forgotten that, if you drink much from a bottle marked 'poison', it is almost certain to disagree with you, sooner or later.
>
> However, this bottle was *not* marked 'poison', so Alice ventured to taste it, and, finding it very nice (it had, in fact, a sort of mixed flavour of cherry-tart, custard, pineapple, roast turkey, toffy, and hot buttered toast), she very soon finished it off.
>
> (*AW*, 31)

Alice is not, as Carpenter claims, everyman, but every child, tired of exhortations and books which say 'Don't', just as Carroll, in the poem which he wrote when he was fifteen, is weary of the Fairy whose *Moral* is 'You mustn't.'[5] The child reader escapes from the dull book and the dull exhortation. To see a parody of Isaac Watts's hymns for children as a mockery of God is to accept Watts's own judgement of himself as the Voice of Providence. Carroll does not accept that judgement any more than a modern reader would, or than most people would have done in 1890, although probably many still did in 1865, which is why *Alice* is a significant as well as a funny book. Carroll is not irreverent towards true religion. His scruples about taking full Orders in the Church when he wanted to spend his time on mathematics show not that his faith was shaky but that he took his religion too seriously to accept a sinecure post as many of his contemporaries did.[6] What he did not take seriously was the parade of religion provided for children of his own generation, and of the generation for which *Alice in Wonderland* was written. The Evangelical tale did not, as Carpenter claims, die out in 1830. If it had done so, the protests of critics in 1839, 1844, 1860 and 1869 against the showing-off, self-righteousness and dissembling of piety, which would be bound to create not real religion but real irreverence, would have been superfluous. Writers initially protested against Trimmer and Sherwood, but the later and stronger protests were against *Ministering Children* and *Eric, Or Little by Little*, both written in the 1850s, shortly before *Alice*. The irreverence which Carroll authorised in the *Alice* books was towards the pretensions of the pious author and of the entire adult world in its attitude to children, whom Carroll understood on their own terms as no writer had done before.

Virginia Woolf saw that the Walrus was a perfect Victorian child's image of the man-made God who wanted children to read *Ministering Children* on Sundays and behave like angels in church. The same kind of image-making operated for her contemporary and friend Gwen Raverat, whose world as both child and adult shaped itself in *Alice in Wonderland* terms: 'God had a smooth oval face, with no hair and no beard and no ears. I imagine that He was not descended, as most Gods are, from Father Christmas, but rather from the Sun Insurance Office sign.' It is true that Raverat gave up believing when the Almighty did not answer her prayer that 'the dancing mistress might be dead before we got to the Dancing Class', and when she was nine or ten years old her cousin Frances (later

Frances Cornford) told her, confidentially, while they both
crouched by the Cam under the wooden bridge on the Little Island,
'that it was not at all the thing nowadays to believe in Christianity
any more. It simply wasn't done.'[7] *Alice in Wonderland* is both
symptom and catalyst to a new sceptical generation, not because
Carroll mocks God, but because his book refuses to convey a
religious message, just as Froebel refused to believe that a child must
be kept busy because Satan will seize him if his hands are idle.
Instead Froebel gave the child a ball and taught him to play and
Carroll gave him *Alice in Wonderland* to read.

Carroll laughs at the hierarchies of the adult world in which God
and the author dance a lobster quadrille. He was irreverent not as a
Christian but as an artist, which is why Roger Fry wanted to rescue
the *Alice* books from the deluge in which he would gladly have
submerged most of Victorian culture. In 'Emotion in Art' Fry
reviewed a book by Sir Claude Phillips which sought to estimate 'the
status of the work in question in the hierarchy of art, its ultimal
value, the exact degree of reverence which it might rightly claim
from the devout. Reverence is, indeed, the key to all such religious
attitudes, and reverence is, of course, as inimical to true esthetic
experience as it is to the apprehension of truth.'[8] The impetus to
Helen Ambrose's loathing of religion in *The Voyage Out* comes from
the same source as her hatred of hierarchies, whether social,
academic, political or aesthetic. In *The Voyage Out* Woolf writes from
a sensibility in which a contempt for reverence in art, which she
shares with Roger Fry, originates in Alice's polite but determined
refusal to see her world in terms dictated by the Duchess, Humpty
Dumpty, the Mad Hatter, the Walrus or even the Carpenter.

Carroll wrote for children because he liked them and wanted
them to enjoy themselves. He carried the concept of art for art's
sake, in full flood in the adult world in the 1860s, into the nursery,
sharing with Catherine Sinclair and Pre-Raphaelites such as William
Morris the fear that the child would prove to be the casualty of
mechanisation, as Dickens had protested in *Hard Times* (1854).
Carroll wrote to one of his child friends, May Forshall: 'Did you ever
play at games? Or is your idea of life "breakfast, lessons, dinner,
lessons", and so on? It is a very neat plan of life and almost as
interesting as being a sewing machine or a coffee grinder.'[9]
Catherine Sinclair's Harry in *Holiday House* exclaims against the
monotonous march of meals and instruction. Sinclair observed that
'in this age of wonderful mechanical inventions, the very mind of

youth seems in danger of becoming a machine'. In consequence 'the minds of young people are now manufactured like webs of linen, all alike, and nothing left to nature'. Carroll was unusual for his century, class and sex in spending time playing with children in a way that has only become common in men's experience in the last twenty years of the present century. But he wrote the *Alice* books as much for himself as for the Liddell children, or indeed for any children. As he lectured in mathematics to polite young men from impeccably prosperous and well-bred schools and homes, he must sometimes have wondered whether the adult world was inhabited by an extinct species of which he himself was a member – the Dodo got its name from his stutter and George Eliot gave its name to another example of an extinct species, Dorothea Brooke in *Middlemarch* – or whether the whole race of children, irrepressible, irreverent, spontaneous and joyful, had been rendered extinct by Victorian conventionality. Sinclair wrote of *Holiday House*: 'In these pages the author has endeavoured to paint that species of noisy, frolicsome, mischievous children, now almost extinct, wishing to preserve a sort of fabulous remembrance of days long past, when young people were like wild horses on the prairies, rather than like well-broken hacks on the road; and when amidst many faults and eccentricities, there was still some individuality of character and feeling allowed to remain.'[10] The attack on Victorian stuffiness, humbug, self-importance, moral earnestness, utilitarianism and middle-class complacency was nurtured in a generation of children who needed the alternative world of *Alice in Wonderland* and *Through the Looking-Glass*. The children's writers who followed Carroll – Stevenson, Nesbit, Kipling, Kenneth Grahame, Mary Molesworth, Mark Twain, Louisa M. Alcott, Joel Chandler Harris, Susan Coolidge, Frances Hodgson Burnett – pioneered in the children's book a new relation between adult and child, religion and living, the world and the book. Their dissent from mid-century habits of writing varied, but they anticipated in different ways the radical experiments not only of Woolf's later novels but also of *The Voyage Out*, *Night and Day* and *Jacob's Room*.

II ACCOMPLICES: WRITER AND READER

The changes in the relation between writer and reader at the turn of the century are by no means simply a result of a changed ethos in attitudes to children. The production of books has always been a business enterprise[11] as well as an artistic venture, and some of the new aims of writers for children reflect the demands of a market which publishers, and in particular, Macmillan, Carroll's publisher, were eager to exploit.[12] Macmillan began its specialist children's list, publishing *Tom Brown's Schooldays*, *The Water-Babies* and Crane's *Grimm*, as well as acquiring the Kipling copyright.[13] In 1896 for the first time the *Bookman*'s Christmas supplement contained a children's book section.[14] Not only did the cheap reissue of established writers create economic pressure for new writers, but the growing fashion for single-volume works in the nineties provided an opening for the children's book, where the three-volume novel could not have been filled from that smaller reservoir of experience.[15] The observation that other kinds of writing for children than the Evangelical tale or instructive dialogue would sell better no doubt spurred new writers such as E. Nesbit and Frances Hodgson Burnett, who were always desperately in need of money,[16] to write for the eager readership created by *Alice in Wonderland* rather than for the reluctant readers of *Ministering Children*.

Writers from Charlotte Yonge onwards were much more reader-conscious than they had been earlier. Hilaire Belloc's epitaph 'On his Books' captured a new mood:

> When I am dead, I hope it may be said:
> His sins were scarlet, but his books were read.[17]

Juliana Horatia Ewing remarked that 'all real fairy-tales . . . should be written down as if they were oral traditions, taken down from the lips of a "story-teller". This is where modern ones fail.'[18] When E. Nesbit published *The Story of the Treasure Seekers* in 1899 she gave Oswald Bastable, her ten-year-old narrator, guardianship over the rights of both author and reader: 'I have often thought that if the people who wrote books for children knew a little more it would be better. I shall not tell you anything about us except what I should like to know about if I was reading the story and you were writing it. Albert's uncle says I ought to have put this in the preface, but I never read prefaces, and it is not much good writing things just for people to skip. I wonder other authors have never thought of this.'[19] Thirty-one years earlier, another writer had thought hard about what children might actually like to read: 'I plod away, though I don't enjoy this sort of thing. Never liked girls or knew many, except my sisters; but our queer plays and experiences may prove interesting, though I doubt it.' Her publisher was not hopeful, either, and she wrote that he 'thought it dull; so do I. But work away and mean to try the experiment, for lively, simple books are very much needed for girls, and perhaps I can supply the need.'[20] The book based on the author's experiences with her sisters is *Little Women* (1868), and the grumbling tomboyish tone is authentically that of Jo March, a heroine who found the part of ministering child hard to play.

Mark Twain wrote in the Foreword to *The Adventures of Tom Sawyer* (1876): 'Although my book is intended mainly for the entertainment of boys and girls, I hope it will not be shunned by men and women on that account, for part of my plan has been to try pleasantly to remind adults of what they once were themselves, of how they felt and thought and talked, and what queer enterprises they sometimes engaged in.' The realisation that 'parents and children are of the same flesh' is there in some of Ewing's work,[21] notably *Mrs Overtheway's Remembrances* (1869), which Carpenter describes as a pioneering book in its recognition not only that childhood has special perceptions and impressions but also that adults can relive those experiences.[22] Mary Howitt anticipated Ewing in *The Children's Year* (1847) when she wrote: 'I have often wished that in books for children the writer would endeavour to enter more fully into the feelings and reasonings of the child; that he would look at things from the child's point of view.'[23] Mark Twain set in *The Adventures of Tom Sawyer* a fashion for writing about children not only for the amusement of the child reader, but in order too that the adult might recapture the child that he had been.[24]

Samuel Rutherford Crockett's stories, which were popular in the 1890s and admired by Nesbit's Bastables, drew, as many other books of the period did, on *Tom Sawyer*, which with *The Adventures of Huckleberry Finn* (1884) provided an antidote to *Little Women*.[25] In Crockett's *The Surprising Adventures of Sir Toady Lion* (1897) the boy hero accosts his father:

an I says to him, ' 'Cause, father *you* never clumb up no trees on Sundays when you was little boy!' An' then he didn't speak no more down here that trimbly way, but laughed, and pulled me down, and roded me home in front of him, and gived me big hunk of pie – yes, indeedy![26]

The 'Yes, indeedy' echoes Jim in *Huckleberry Finn*. The title page of *Sir Toady Lion* reads:

The Surprising Adventures of
Sir Toady Lion
with those of General Napoleon Smith
and improving history
for
old boys, young boys, good boys, bad boys,
big boys, little boys, cow boys and Tom-boys.

Opposite the title page is a drawing of a placard with an urchin with a catapult sitting astride it:

TOO GOOD BOYS
NOT ALLOWED
TO READ THIS BOOK
by order
HEAD MARSHALL NAPOLEON SMITH

This is of course joyously cribbed from the title page of *The Adventures of Huckleberry Finn*, which reads as follows:

NOTICE

Persons attempting to find a motive in this narrative will be prosecuted; persons attempting to find a moral in it will be banished; persons attempting to find a plot in it will be shot.

BY ORDER OF THE AUTHOR
per G. G., CHIEF ORDNANCE

The repudiation of moral purpose and the repudiation of plot form a revealing partnership which looks forward to Virginia Woolf's hatred of both.[27] Crockett's story, *Sir Toady Lion*, continues after Napoleon Smith's order with the same acute awareness of audience which the title page demonstrates:

Prissy and Napoleon Smith were by no means model children, though Prissy was afterwards marvellously improved. Even their best friends admitted as much, and as for their enemies – well, their old gardener's remarks when they chased each other over his newly planted beds would be out of place even in a military periodical, and might be the means of preventing a book with Mr Gordon Browne's nice pictures from being included in some well-conducted Sunday-school libraries.

The same jovial flouting style, the same jolly but calculating eye for a new secular market governs the whole story, in which at one point the hero engineers getting a good-conduct prize and threatens to fight any boy who won't vote for him: 'Hugh John had mentioned that he would be on the look-out for any fellow that was a sneak and didn't cheer like blazes. MORAL. – There is no moral to this chapter.'[28] The writing is more self-conscious than Mark Twain's, but the sending-up of Sunday schools and the pious rewards of the adult system looks back to Tom Sawyer's fielding of yellow tickets through the barter of dead cats and the like, and being rewarded with the prize Bible as a boy who has two thousand verses of scripture stored in his head.[29] The satire on moral-pointing comes from Lewis Carroll, whose poem 'Brother and Sister' starts in true Victorian style –

> 'Sister, sister, go to bed!
> Go and rest your weary head.'
> Thus the prudent brother said

– but continues in a much brisker vein with the sister answering back shrewishly, and the brother then demanding from the cook the loan of her frying-pan:

> 'And wherefore should I lend it you?'
> 'The reason, Cook, is plain to view.
> I wish to make an Irish stew.'
>
> 'What meat is in that stew to go?'
> 'My sister'll be the contents!'
>   'Oh!'
> 'You'll lend the pan to me, Cook?'
>   'No!'

> *Moral*: Never stew your sister.[30]

The presentation of Crockett's book courts the lending library's multiple readership through an assumption of equality between adults and children. Both are united in repudiating a 'Moral'.

In claiming a new equality the author claims also a new familiarity. Nesbit declared that she wrote from her own childhood memories, because 'I was a child as other children.' When Albert's uncle in *The Story of the Treasure Seekers* advises Oswald on how to write rather than on how to live, Oswald reflects: 'He always talks like a book, and yet you can always understand what he means. I think he is more like us, inside of his mind than most grown-up people are.'[31] When George Eliot re-created her own childhood in Tom and Maggie Tulliver in *The Mill on the Floss* (1860) she asked: 'Is there anyone who can recover the experience of his childhood, not merely with a memory of what he did and what happened to him, of what he liked and disliked when he was in frock and trousers, but with an intimate penetration, a revived consciousness of what he felt then – when it was so long from one Midsummer to another? . . . Surely, if we could recall that early bitterness, and the dim guesses, the strangely perspectiveless conception of life that gave the bitterness its intensity, we should not pooh-pooh the griefs of our children.'[32] True as this observation is, its tone of one superior addressing another over the head of the suffering minor comes from a world which still patronises children. Much water is to flow over the wheel of Dorlcote Mill before Walter de la Mare can say in 1935 that the motive of his book on childhood, *Early One Morning*, is not to explain or condescend to children – 'a house might as well condescend to its foundations'.[33] Heather Glen suggests that the 'coercive admonitions of the children's books' which Blake parodied in his *Songs of Innocence* 'are the products not of assurance' but of fear.[34] Research into education, psychology and human origins closed the gap between adults and children and in so doing made adults less afraid of children's differences from them, because those differences seemed less.

Virginia Woolf wrote in 'How Should One Read a Book?': 'Do not dictate to your author; try to become him. Be his fellow-worker and accomplice.'[35] C. S. Lewis identifies the collusion between writer and reader, adult and child within the children's book in an essay entitled 'On Three Ways of Writing for Children':

Once in a hotel dining-room I said, rather too loudly, 'I loathe prunes.' 'So do I', came the unexpected six-year-old voice from another table. Neither of us thought it funny. We both knew that

prunes are far too nasty to be funny. That is the proper meeting
between man and child as independent personalities. Of the
higher and more difficult relations between a child and parent or
child and teacher, I say nothing. An author, a mere author, is
outside all that. He is not even an uncle. He is a freeman and an
equal, like the postman, the butcher, and the dog next door.[36]

It is, like Thomas Day's Preface to *Sandford and Merton*, still slightly
disingenuous. Prunes can be funny, as Virginia Woolf proved in *A
Room of One's Own* when she contrasted the Newnham prunes with
the King's confection. Children, who are always made to eat
prunes for a purpose, wreak their revenge by refusing to dissociate
them from that purpose, a tendency which caught Freud, like
Lewis, at his most solemn. The theory of equality, like some of
Charlotte Yonge's theories, is hardly borne out in the *Narnia* books,
for Lewis is too much the product of a world of exclusively male,
middle-class, Anglo-Saxon privilege to notice how exclusively those
values are underwritten in his good fair children and wicked dark
ones, or how much the inhabitants of his new Jerusalem look like
the best sort of Oxbridge freshmen – Peter is the shining example.
They are all Percivals and God is not a walrus but a really lovely
Margaret Mahy lion. Lewis is more at home in an authoritarian
world however much he may acknowledge the equality of author
and reader. The perception which burst on the Lewis Carroll
generation was that the whole system needed reclassifying. Alice
voiced criticisms of the adult world which spoke not only to the child
in every adult but to an integrated consciousness in which the
Victorian authority figure, whether parent, author, teacher,
preacher or even Deity, suddenly seemed ridiculous.

III   EGOTISTIC AUTHOR

The Adventures of Tom Sawyer, published in 1876, still allows Mark
Twain to reflect from a position of superiority on the limitations of
boyish vision. Tom has just hoodwinked his friends into
whitewashing a wall for him:

> He had discovered a great law of human action, without knowing
> it, namely, that, in order to make a man or a boy covet a thing, it is
> only necessary to make the thing difficult to attain. If he had been

a great and wise philosopher, like the writer of this book, he would now have comprehended that work consists of whatever a body is obliged to do, and that play consists of whatever a body is not obliged to do.

The intrusion is, however, unlike that of Mary Sherwood, or even of Brenda in *Froggy's Little Brother* (published one year earlier), secular and self-mocking.[37] Mark Twain's admission that he is the writer of the book, and therefore the fabricator of its philosophy, already places him beyond the assumption of an authority which is somehow more than human and individual. Zangwill addressed the same issue when he commented on his own use in his *Pall Mall Magazine* column of the first-person pronoun:

> I am sometimes accused of egotism myself because of the capital I that figures in this *causerie*. . . . By a singular fallacy which ought scarcely to deceive children, it is forgotten that everything that has ever been written since the world began has been written by some one person. . . . Every new thought must pass through the brain, every moral ideal through the conscience of an individual.[38]

In *Huckleberry Finn*, published eight years after *Tom Sawyer*, Twain retreated further from his own creation. The first-person voice never claims to be more knowing than that of an individual within the narrative relating and reflecting upon personal experience:

> As they went by, I see they had the king and the duke astraddle of a rail – that is, I knowed it *was* the king and the duke, though they was all over tar and feathers, and didn't look like nothing in the world that was human – just looked like a couple of monstrous big soldier-plumes. Well, it made me sick to see it; and I was sorry for them poor pitiful rascals, it seemed like I couldn't ever feel any hardness against them any more in the world. It was a dreadful thing to see. Human beings *can* be awful cruel to one another.[39]

The judgement carries no adult authority, for it proceeds from Huck's own observation of the world.

Between the appearance of *Tom Sawyer* in 1876 and *Huckleberry Finn* in 1884, Stevenson produced *Treasure Island* (1883), a book in which the story is told largely by the boy Jim Hawkins, but in part by the Doctor. The modern reader is so used to children's books which do not stop to harangue her about godliness and sobriety that it is hard to recapture the astonished delight which greeted *Treasure Island*,[40] a story told by two voices, neither of which appear to belong to the author. Leslie Stephen wrote that 'it would require some courage to infer from *Treasure Island* that the author held any philosophy', and quoted Henry James's remark that 'the love of youth is the beginning and end of Stevenson's message'.[41] If Stevenson's pirates derive in part from Tom, Huck and Joe in *Tom Sawyer*, Twain's decision in *Huckleberry Finn* to dump the philosopher author follows Stevenson's lead in *Treasure Island*. Mark Twain wrote to Stevenson in June 1893 in reply to a letter which no longer exists, but which must have described the enthusiasm of Fanny Stevenson's son for *Tom Sawyer*: 'I have a warm place in me for that student of Tom Sawyer. He deserves to arrive at a high place in this world's regard. . . . We are square now. My wife keeps re-reading Kidnapped & neglecting my works.' One month later Twain's publishing-firm wrote to Stevenson in reply to a request from the author that they consider the possibility of publishing his own work.[42] This appears to have come to nothing, but it does show that Stevenson had a keen interest in Mark Twain, and a sense that they were both doing the same thing. This belief was shared by some of their contemporaries. Andrew Lang wrote to W. E. Henley, 'Luckily, or Huckily (already that infernal paper is telling on me) Huckleberry Finn came in, and I had a Fortune by me. . . . Yes, Huck may be read, but I don't set him by Treasure Island.'[43] Stevenson's romance seemed to free both writer and reader from moral responsibility for the world of the book, to liberate them from the dust and heat of personality. Stevenson only allows Jim temporary control of his own narrative and only partial insight into its outcome. In Virginia Woolf's novels many of the voices which claim centrality provoke their author to consign them mockingly to a territory she shares with them on the margins of the narrative.

When Zangwill denied the egotism of the first-person narrative, he explained that 'egoism should be distinguished from egotism. The egoist thinks for himself, the egotist about himself. Mr Meredith's Sir Willoughby should not have been styled the *Egoist*.'[44] The writer, in Zangwill's view, must speak out as an independent voice. The demand to be heard comes from the self-realisation of the egoist not from the self-regard of the egotist. Virginia Woolf's rejection of the egotistical author is inseparable from her criticism of the self-absorbtion and self-satisfaction of men in positions of authority. In *The Voyage Out* Rachel's father, like Meredith's hero, is named Willoughby, and Helen's husband Ridley – perhaps after the Protestant martyr whose name adorns the theological college which sits cheek by jowl with Newnham, where Virginia Woolf ate up her prunes and custard. The discoveries of neither Copernicus nor Darwin have had the slightest effect in altering the conviction of both men that the world is oyster to their Walrus and Carpenter. Ridley behaves like a prima donna on board ship until his wife has fixed his working-space:

> 'I daresay he isn't very strong,' said Mrs Chailey, looking at Mrs Ambrose compassionately, as she helped to shift and carry.
> 'It's books,' sighed Helen, lifting an armful of sad volumes from the floor to the shelf. 'Greek from morning to night. If ever Miss Rachel marries, Chailey, pray that she may marry a man who doesn't know his ABC.'

Willoughby is anxious to bring his daughter Rachel up as her dead mother would have wished – apparently – but is even more anxious to bring her up to take her mother's place in furthering his political career. As Mr Pepper remarks of Jenkinson of Cats [a Cambridge college, not a Cheshire puss], whose wife is dead: 'There's an unmarried daughter who keeps house for him, I believe, but it's never the same, not at his age.' Helen 'could not help laughing at the notion of it – Rachel a Tory hostess! – and marvelling as she left him at the astonishing ignorance of a father.' The egotism of the male world in Virginia Woolf's view exerts a stranglehold equally on life and on books, both in the way men behave to women and children and in the books they provide for them to read. Burke and Gibbon are both recommended as reading for Rachel – writers who would never dream of considering that they only wrote with a little 'I'.

St John Hirst (modelled on Lytton Strachey), Ridley, Richard Dalloway and Mr Pepper in *The Voyage Out* are all men thinking *about* themselves, not *for* themselves. Richard Dalloway's sonorous platitudes carry the weight of Parliamentary oration behind them. Every speech he makes refers to his own position in Parliament as a politician, as when he recalls the pleasures of scholarship:

> 'It's the arguing that counts. It's the things like that that stand out in life. Nothing's been quite so vivid since. It's the

philosophers, it's the scholars,' he continued, 'they're the people who pass the torch, who keep the light burning by which we live. Being a politician doesn't blind one to that, Mrs Ambrose.'

'No. Why should it?' said Helen. 'But can you remember if your wife takes sugar?'

St John Hirst is equally devoted to his own prospects:

> He sat staring intently at the head of a dead match, while Helen considered – so it seemed from the expression of her eyes – something not closely connected with the present moment.
>
> At last St John exclaimed, 'Damn! Damn everything! Damn everybody!' he added. 'At Cambridge there are people to talk to.'
>
> 'At Cambridge there are people to talk to,' Helen echoed him rhythmically and absent-mindedly. Then she woke up.
>
> 'By the way, have you settled what you're going to do – is it to be Cambridge or the Bar?'
>
> He pursed his lips, but made no immediate answer, for Helen was still slightly inattentive.

The only man who is an egoist rather than an egotist in the novel is Hewet, who himself attacks Hirst's world:

> 'Look at Hirst now. I assure you,' he said, 'not a day's passed since we came here without a discussion as to whether he's to stay on at Cambridge or go to the Bar. It's his career – his sacred career. And if I've heard it twenty times, I'm sure his mother and sister have heard it five hundred times. . . . But St John's sister –' Hewet puffed in silence. 'No one takes her seriously, poor dear. She feeds the rabbits.'
>
> 'Yes,' said Rachel. 'I've fed rabbits for twenty-four years; it seems odd now.'

The traditional form of the novel, as Hewet sees it, mirrors the self-absorption of the male world and readers seem content for it to do so. He wants 'to write a novel about Silence . . . the things people don't say'.[45]

Although Virginia Woolf when under fire from the critics often vowed, as her own character Orlando does, to write to please herself, she did not really believe that writing could exist without a public, because it is 'a method of communication; and the crocus is an imperfect crocus until it has been shared'. In the same essay, 'The Patron and the Crocus', she outlines the risks involved in writing for a 'submissive public. . . . For in that case the writer remains conscious of the public, yet is superior to it – an uncomfortable and unfortunate combination, as the works of Samuel Butler, George Meredith, and Henry James may be taken to prove. Each despised the public; each desired a public; each failed to attain a public; and each wreaked his failure upon the public by a succession, gradually increasing in intensity, of angularities, obscurities, and affectations which no writer whose patron was his equal and friend would have thought it necessary to inflict.'[46] She was always afraid of writing *about* herself rather than *for* herself. 'Do I write essays about myself?' Dadie Rylands' observation that she had no logical power and wrote in an opium dream worried her; she reflected: 'The dream is too often about myself.' She criticised Maurice Baring's writing as though it were Richard Dalloway's: 'He can only do one thing; himself to wit; charming, clean, modest, sensitive Englishman.' The problem was a double one: the author's voice must speak to the reader, otherwise 'the convention of writing is destroyed: therefore one does not write at all'.[47] But if the author must also efface herself, how was she to speak at all? She would have agreed with Zangwill who remarked that both Gissing and George Moore ruined their work by intruding on the world they had created: 'The business of the faithful novelist is to represent life as it does not appear to him.'[48] Woolf complained of Lawrence's insistent voice: 'Why does Aldous say he was an "artist"? Art is being rid of all preaching.'

When Woolf visited Shakespeare's grave at Stratford she noted the 'queer impression of sunny impersonality. . . . He is serenely absent–present. . . . What I had not reckoned for was the worn simple slab, turned the wrong way, Kind friend for Jesus' sake forbear – again he seemed to be all air and sun smiling serenely; and yet down there one foot from me lay the little bones that had spread over the world this vast illumination.' In her own writing she sought that same freedom: 'I think writing, my writing, is a species of mediumship. I become the person.'[49] William James called for 'the re-instatement of the vague to its proper place in our mental life'.[50] Did Virginia Woolf remember that plea when she called her greatest novel of shared consciousness *The Waves*, of which the French translation would be *Les vagues*? The reader in Woolf's novels remains as vague as the author, part of a shared consciousness created by the book.[51]

Gautier had urged as early as 1835 that 'it is the character who speaks and not the author': 'It is as absurd to say that a man is a drunkard because he describes an orgy, or a rake because he recounts a debauch, as to pretend that a man is virtuous because he has written a moral book; one sees the opposite every day.'[52] In *What Katy Did* (1872), Susan Coolidge mocks authorial piety in Katy who – before her accident – reads to her brothers and sisters on Sunday afternoons from her own serial magazine *The Sunday Visitor* a story of her own creation called 'Little Maria and Her Sisters': 'A dreadful tale in which Katy drew so much moral, and made such personal allusions to the faults of the rest, that it was almost more than they could bear.'[53] In a fit of revolt the other children stuff the manuscript into the boiler. Katy is on weekdays the naughtiest of them all. Mark Twain, describing in *Tom Sawyer* the female pupils' compositions which were recited at the school prize-day, declares: 'The sermon of the most frivolous and least religious girl in the school is always the longest and the most relentlessly pious.'[54] There is little to be gained from speculating about the religious faith and virtues of Dean Frederick Farrar, Master of Trinity College, Cambridge, author of *Eric, Or Little by Little*, compared with those of his colleague, the mathematics don at Christ Church, Oxford, Charles Lutwidge Dodgson, author of *Alice in Wonderland*. The heart may be reverent, but irreverence begins, as Moses kept explaining to the idolatrous Jews, with representation.

William James pointed out in *The Will to Believe* (1897): 'We of the nineteenth century, with our evolutionary theories and our mechanical philosophies, already know nature too impartially and too well to worship unreservedly any God of whose character she can be an adequate expression. Truly, all we know of good and duty proceeds from nature; but none the less so all we know of evil. Visible nature is all plasticity and indifference, – a moral multiverse, as one might call it, and not a moral universe.'[55] Woolf wrote of George Eliot's heroines that 'each has the deep feminine passion for goodness, which makes the place where she stands in aspiration and agony the heart of the book – still and cloistered like a place of worship, but that she no longer knows to whom to pray'.[56] When Virginia was fifteen she read avidly Hakluyt's account of Elizabethan travels to exotic lands and practised 'their style in my copybook. I was then writing a long picturesque essay upon the

Christian religion, I think; called Religio Laici, I believe, proving that man has need of a God; but the God was described in a process of change.' Her nature craved not the authoritarian God of the Evangelical author, but spiritual refuge. She wrote in 1928: 'This has been a very animated summer; a summer lived almost too much in public. Often down here I have entered into a sanctuary; a nunnery; had a religious retreat; of great agony once; and always some terror; so afraid one is of loneliness; of seeing to the bottom of the vessel. That is one of the experiences I have had here in some Augusts; and got then to a consciousness of what I call 'reality': a thing I see before me: something abstract; but residing in the downs or sky; beside which nothing matters; in which I shall rest and continue to exist.'[57] Art allows the artist to admit moral multiplicity without losing her identity, which must be separated from that of preacher or moralist because the voices of both are contaminated by egotism.

IV   REBELS

When Edmund Gosse depicts family prayers in the mid-Victorian household of his childhood, he says of his father who conducted them: 'I cannot help thinking that he liked to hear himself speak to God in the presence of an admiring listener. . . . My father took at all times a singular pleasure in repeating that "our God is a jealous God".'[58] Behind closed eyes and folded hands the praying child meditated on his father's satisfaction in representing the Almighty. In *The Way of All Flesh* Butler describes Theobald and Christiana's extracting information from Ernest about his friends' misdemeanours, to send to the headmaster: 'They [his parents] were not idle, but Satan can find as much mischief for busy hands as for idle ones, so he sent a little job in the direction of Battersby which Theobald and Christiana undertook immediately.' The child Ernest in Butler's novel does not rebel with any vigour because he never questions his parents' assumption that he is the one who is wrong. The author insists on telling the reader what Ernest might have thought but didn't, as when he has to learn Mrs Hemans' poem 'Casabianca': 'It never occurred to him that the moral of the poem was that young people cannot begin too soon to exercise discretion in the obedience they pay to their Papa and Mamma.'[59] The adult, Butler, reflects instead of the child, but in Gosse's account the child censures the adult world while pretending to pray. When *Father and Son* was published, the novelist received many letters from men and women brought up under the shadow of Evangelicalism, among them Kipling, who wrote that he had tried to protect himself by ' "a natural magic" (in my own case by a charm. I used to make 'em out of old bones stuffed with wool and camphor-scented)'. He added: 'The devil of it is that that life still persists. . . . As the reviews *won't* say – the book "ought to be in the hands of all parents and teachers".'[60] The world had moved quietly but perceptibly on since 1875, when Brenda proclaimed in *Froggy's Little Brother*: 'There is no sin more grievous in Christ's eyes than that of rebelliousness towards parents. Whatever may be our parents' failings, and short-comings, we are bound to love, honour, and succour them.'[61]

When Virginia Woolf named 1910 as the beginning of the modern movement in the arts she admitted that 'the change was not sudden and definite like that. . . . The first signs of it are recorded in the books of Samuel Butler, in *The Way of All Flesh* in particular.' Despite her scorn of Gosse as both man and critic – 'I know a mean skunk when I see one, or rather smell one, for its his writing I abominate' – *Father and Son* captured her imagination against her will. She wrote to Vita Sackville West that Gosse's description of 'all the coast of England . . . fringed with little sea anemones and lovely tassels of seaweed and sprays of emerald moss' which was then ravaged by 'hordes of clergy and spinsters in mushroom hats and goggles' was a parable of 'what we have done to deposits of family happiness'. Strachey accused her of narrow-mindedness towards Gosse, perhaps recognising that Butler and the younger writer were more akin than Woolf would admit.[62]

Charlotte Yonge moderated her admiration of *Alice* with a demur about the growth of burlesque in children's books: 'Extravagance becomes destructive of reverence.'[63] After the Caucus Race 'Alice thought the whole thing absurd, but they all looked so grave that she did not dare to laugh; and, as she could not think of anything to say, she simply bowed, and took the thimble, looking as solemn as she could' (*AW*, 50). Harry Levin remarks that 'so it is that children learn to suppress their native instinct for laughter in the company of adults'.[64] Socially that may be true, but in the book laughter is not suppressed, because the child reader laughs on Alice's behalf at the folly and false dignity of the creatures, just as the Fool in a Shakespearean comedy stands aside from the action and directs the audience's laughter at the scene in which he is both participant and observer.

Roger Fry observed that the new generation of children 'are entirely lacking in reverence'.[65] Woolf herself noticed it in Cambridge, half regretting, from the vantage point of middle age, the new world which she and her peers had helped to create.[66] When other children with whom Vanessa and Virginia Stephen associated discoursed on the meaning of Good Friday, 'Virginia had to be hurriedly banished, shrieking with laughter.'[67] She resented Victorian saintliness as evidenced in the Fisher cousins, declaring: 'The Fishers would have made Eden uninhabitable.'[68] But as a child her irreverence was not confined to religion. Vanessa Bell recalls her sister's asking her which she liked best, her mother or her father: 'This seemed to begin an age of much freer speech between us. If one could criticise one's parents, what or whom could one not criticise? Dimly some freedom of thought and speech seemed born, created by her question.'[69]

Carroll's picture in *Alice in Wonderland* of a child set free from parental authority provided a fictional model in which the author might also escape from sounding like a parent. In Mary Molesworth's *The Cuckoo Clock* (1877) Griselda's mother and father are abroad and she is left with two elderly aunts – as Rachel is in *The Voyage Out* – but Molesworth quietly criticises Miss Tabitha and Miss Grizzel for being out of touch with children's needs. Katy's Mamma in *What Katy Did* (1872) is dead, and the children enjoy liberty in their hayloft. Huck Finn is an orphan, a state envied by all his friends. Stevenson quickly killed off Jim Hawkins' father in *Treasure Island* (1883) and dispatched him on a voyage while his mother remained safely at home. In the 1890s, with a shout of glee from author, fictional child and reader, the parent is finally ditched. Mowgli in *The Jungle Books* (1894 and 1895) is brought up by wolves, not moral wolves, but real ones. Zangwill was one of the first critics to realise that the change was a revolution in children's reading:

> Beast stories are as old as the Vedas, but the beasts in them have almost always existed for moral ends, and for the edification of the ethical mind. . . . In Mr. Kipling's stories the animals exist for their own ends. . . . People speak of the theory of Evolution as if it degraded man. But even if the theory were true I should prefer to look upon it as elevating the beasts, into the skins of which Mr. Kipling so skilfully helps us to get. Children, who I am credibly

informed will not read fairy tales, will perhaps find this quasi-realistic treatment of the beast-world more to their sophisticated taste.[70]

Kipling's vision of a new relationship between children and animals may have been prompted in part by Anna Sewell's *Black Beauty* (1877), in which everything is told from the horses' point of view. The adult world is judged and found wanting. Roger Fry, aged twelve, wrote home from school to his mother in 1878: 'I am reading Black Beauty and I like it very much.'[71] Modern research into children's reading-habits has seen in *Black Beauty*'s sustained criticism of 'the folly, blindness, insensitivity, selfishness or cruelty of the adult human beings'[72] the main reason for its enduring popularity.

The child unhampered by parents has become a commonplace of twentieth-century children's books since Arthur Ransome. But Ransome's children in *Swallows and Amazons* (1930) owe their freedom to *Tom Sawyer* – a homesick pirate – to Richard Jefferies' *Bevis* (1882), and above all to *Treasure Island*, which Ransome used as parent text in the same way that Alcott used *The Pilgrim's Progress* in *Little Women*. John Rowe Townsend's regret that the Walker children and the Blacketts are not shown in living relation to their parents[73] ignores their relation to a tradition of dispensing with parents which began with Carroll and reached its apotheosis in Kenneth Grahame's *The Golden Age* (1895), in which the Olympians identified by Stevenson in his essay 'Child's Play' are seen through the alienated eyes of a new race, their children: 'We were supposed to be denied the faculty for putting two and two together, and like the monkeys, who very sensibly refrain from speech lest they should be set to earn their livings, we were careful to conceal our capabilities for a simple syllogism. Thus we were rarely taken by surprise, and so were considered by our disappointed elders to be apathetic and to lack the divine capacity for wonder.'[74] Freud wrote ten years later that 'children often represent themselves as naïve, so as to enjoy a liberty that they would not otherwise be granted'.[75] Grahame's clear glance not, as in Butler's novel, at adult cruelty and stupidity, but at the real child's mockery of an adult dream, looks forward to Nesbit and Virginia Woolf.

Grahame's children see in adults the creators of false fictions as well as the stolid worshippers of the literal: 'As a rule . . . grown-up people are fairly correct on matters of fact; it is in the higher gift of imagination that they are so sadly to seek.' They have no sense of humour. Uncle Thomas is condemned because 'his rooted conviction seemed to be that the reason of a child's existence was to serve as a butt for senseless adult jokes – or what, from the accompanying guffaws of laughter, appeared to be intended for jokes.' Above all, adults possess no just estimate of the significant and the trivial: 'It was perennial matter for amazement how these Olympians would talk over our heads – during meals, for instance – of this or the other social or political inanity, under the delusion that these pale phantasms of reality were among the importances of life. We *illuminati*, eating silently, our heads full of plans and conspiracies, could have told them what real life was.'[76] If the tone of the last sentence seems to locate the author uneasily in both camps, the same could not be said of the depictor of the silent observers of another Mad Hatter's tea party, held on board the *Euphrosyne* in *The Voyage Out*.

The prime concerns of the talkers in this scene are judged by the speaking silence of the listeners:

Both gentlemen nodded sagely as they carved their apples.

'There was a book, wasn't there?' Ridley inquired.

'There *was* a book, but there never *will* be a book,' said Mr Pepper with such fierceness that both ladies looked up at him.

'There never will be a book, because someone else has written it for him.' said Mr Pepper with considerable acidity.

'That's what comes of putting things off, and collecting fossils, and sticking Norman arches on one's pigsties.'

'I confess I sympathise,' said Ridley with a melancholy sigh. 'I have a weakness for people who can't begin.'

'... The accumulations of a lifetime wasted,' continued Mr Pepper. 'He had accumulations enough to fill a barn.'

'It's a vice that some of us escape,' said Ridley. 'Our friend Miles has another work out today.'

Mr Pepper gave an acid laugh. 'According to my calculations,' he said, 'he has produced two volumes and a half annually, which, allowing for time spent in the cradle and so forth, shows a commendable industry.'

'Yes, the old Master's saying of him has been pretty well realized,' said Ridley.

'A way they had,' said Mr Pepper. 'You know the Bruce collection? – not for publication, of course.'

'I should suppose not,' said Ridley significantly. 'For a Divine
he was – remarkably free.'

'The Pump in Neville's Row, for example?' inquired Mr Pepper.
'Precisely,' said Ambrose.

Each of the ladies, being after the fashion of their sex, highly
trained in promoting men's talk without listening to it, could
think – about the education of children, about the use of fog sirens
in an opera – without betraying herself. Only it struck Helen that
Rachel was perhaps too still for a hostess, and that she might have
done something with her hands.

'Perhaps, – ?' she said at length, upon which they rose and left,
vaguely to the surprise of the gentlemen, who had either thought
them attentive or had forgotten their presence.

Even the reluctance to think about beginning, places the dialogue in
Lewis Carroll country:

'But what happens when you come to the beginning again?'
Alice ventured to ask.

'Suppose we change the subject', the March Hare interrupted,
yawning.   (*AW*, 99–100)

There is both Pig and Pepper in Woolf's scene. In a later social
gathering Mr Dalloway's story about the Skye terrier proceeds with
the inconsequentiality of some of the Dormouse's remarks, the
author observing: 'The story seemed to have no climax.' It turns out
that the dog died, which leads Mr Dalloway to another anecdote:
'The first sorrow I can remember was for the death of a dormouse.'[77]
In both this conversation, and in the earlier one between Ridley and
Willoughby, the main discourse is framed in the powerful but silent
subtext of the listener's dissent, which Woolf would have found in
Alice, but even more explicitly in *The Golden Age*.

Carroll, Grahame and Woolf provide an alternative tradition to
that of family cohesiveness as upheld by Ethel May in Yonge's *The
Daisy Chain*: 'I never could bear the way the Mackenzies used to
have of thinking their parents must be like enemies, and keeping
secrets from them.'[78] Yonge, who feared irreverence, might have
heard a note she distrusted in Edward Lear's story of the seven
parents: 'Sending out to various shops, they purchased great
quantities of Cayenne Pepper, and Brandy, and Vinegar, and blue
sealing-wax, besides seven immense glass Bottles of air-tight

stoppers. And having done this, they ate a light supper of brown bread and Jerusalem Artichokes, and took an affecting and formal leave of the whole of their acquaintance, which was very numerous and distinguished, and select, and responsible, and ridiculous.'[79] Roger Fry blamed the family for Victorian patriarchalism: 'I have so little family feeling, so little feeling that it's by the family that one goes into the future.'[80] For him, as for Virginia Woolf, family life authorised the conventionality which Ruskin had declared in *Modern Painters* to be the enemy of art, which men and women can only see with new eyes if they become as little children.[81]

Woolf wrote in 'The Mark on the Wall' of how the horrors of Victorian conventional family life are in her mind inseparable from the military sound of the word 'generalization', that propensity of the authoritarian author:

> Generalizations bring back somehow Sunday in London, Sunday afternoon walks, Sunday luncheons, and also ways of speaking of the dead, clothes, and habits – like the habit of sitting all together in one room until a certain hour, although nobody liked it. There was a rule for everything. . . . What now takes the place of those things I wonder, those real standard things? Men perhaps, should you be a woman; the masculine point of view which governs our lives, which sets the standard, which established Whitaker's Table of Precedency, which has become, I suppose, since the war, half a phantom to many men and women, which soon, one may hope, will be laughed into the dustbin where the phantoms go, the mahogany sideboards and the Landseer prints, Gods and Devils, Hell and so forth, leaving us all with an intoxicating sense of illegitimate freedom – if freedom exists.[82]

E. Nesbit recalled in the *Girl's Own Paper* a comparable mid-Victorian child's day, remembering her own boredom – 'children are bored much more often and much more deeply than their elders suppose':

> The dining-room was mahogany and leather with two books in it, the Bible and Family Prayers. They stood on the side-board, flanked on one side by a terra-cotta water-bottle oozing sad tears all day into a terra-cotta saucer, and on the other by a tea-caddy. Upstairs in the drawing-room, which was only used on Sundays, were a few illustrated gift-books, albums and types of beauty

book arranged on a polished, oval, walnut centre table. The piano was kept locked. There were a few old bound volumes of *Good Words*, which I had read again and again.[83]

The first real rebels against Victorian stuffiness were children, and the first rebels in print wrote books for them.

V EMINENT VICTORIANS

The voice which rambles through 'The Mark on the Wall' is one the reader has heard before: inconsequential, easily distracted, light, conversational, intimate. It is Alice talking to the kitten at the beginning of *Through the Looking-Glass*:

> Now, if you'll only attend, Kitty, and not talk so much, I'll tell you all my ideas about Looking-Glass House. First, there's the room you can see through the glass – that's just the same as our drawing-room, only the things go the other way. I can see all of it when I get upon a chair – all but the bit just behind the fireplace. Oh! I do wish I could see *that* bit! I want so much to know whether they've a fire in the winter: you never *can* tell, you know, unless our fire smokes, and then smoke comes up in that room too – but that may be only pretence, just to make it look as if they had a fire. Well then, the books are something like our books, only the words go the wrong way: I know *that*, because I've held up one of our books to the glass, and they they hold up one in the other room.
>
> (*L-G*, 180–1)

Here is Woolf's version of that other room:

> Supposing the looking-glass smashes, the image disappears, and the romantic figure with the green of forest depths all about it is there no longer, but only that shell of a person which is seen by other people – what an airless, shallow, bald, prominent world it becomes! A world not to be lived in. As we face each other in omnibuses and underground railways we are looking into the mirror; that accounts for the vagueness, the gleam of glassiness, in our eyes. And the novelists in future will realize more and more the importance of these reflections for of course there is not one reflection but an almost infinite number; those are the depths they

6 Looking-Glass House (from *Through the Looking-Glass*)

will explore, those the phantoms they will pursue, leaving the description of reality more and more out of their stories.[84]

Both passages muse on the fascination of the phantom, but Woolf's essay is a mirror image of Carroll's monologue not so much in the subject matter, with its Platonic and Freudian resonances, as in tone and syntax, which beguile the reader into thinking that she hears her own voice and not that of the author.

Virginia Woolf believed that reading both demands and creates liberty: 'To admit authorities, however heavily furred and gowned, into our libraries and let them tell us how to read, what to read, what value to place upon what we read, is to destroy the spirit of freedom which is the breath of those sanctuaries.'[85] The adversary of that freedom is the great man, sanctioned by the various forms of the establishment. When Neville attends school chapel in *The Waves* he feels confined by the headmaster's utterances: ' "The brute menaces my liberty," said Neville, "when he prays. . . . The words of authority are corrupted by those who speak them." ' At the farewell ceremony he muses: 'I cannot endure the Doctor's pompous mummery and faked emotions.'[86] Lytton Strachey, on whom Neville was modelled, was to become, with the appearance of *Eminent Victorians* in 1918 (when Woolf was composing her own verison of the same theme in *Night and Day*, published the following year), a byword for the new generation's irreverence towards the great men and women of Victorian culture, toppling Florence Nightingale unceremoniously off the plinth on which she stands in the frontispiece to Charlotte Yonge's *A Book of Golden Deeds*. The great woman and her great work fell together. The enshrining of Bunyan as a great man of letters was enough to make *The Pilgrim's Progress* unreadable in the next generation. Carroll's parody of Alfred Bunn's 'Bohemian Song' conjures up the farewell ceremony which oppresses Neville:

> I dreamt I dwelt in marble halls,
> And each damp thing that creeps and crawls
> Went wobble-wobble on the walls.
>
> Faint odours of departed cheese,
> Blown on the dank, unwholesome breeze,
> Awoke the never-ending sneeze.

Strange pictures decked the arras drear
Strange characters of woe and fear,
The humbugs of the social sphere.

. . .

Oh yet my spirit inly crawls
What time it shudderingly recalls
That horrid dream of marble halls![87]

Woolf repudiated the voice of the great man in criticism, the 'London Library atmosphere . . . the second hand, frozen fingered, university specialist, don trying to be creative, don all stuffed with books, writer.'[88] And if one were to protest that she was pretty stuffed with books herself, she probably would have retorted with Margaret in Shakespeare's *Much Ado About Nothing*: 'A *maid*, and stuffed?' The male world was stuffed with such men as Macaulay, of whose essay on Addison she remarked: 'Even now, at a distance of seventy-six years, the words seem to issue from the mouth of the chosen representative of the people. There is an authority about them, a sonority, a sense of responsibility, which puts us in mind of a Prime Minister making a proclamation on behalf of a great empire rather than of a magazine. . . . Florid, and at the same time extremely solid, the phrases seem to build up a monument.' But she adds: 'It has never occurred to us, strangely enough, to believe that it is true.'[89] Of Herbert (H. A. L.) Fisher and his colleagues in Parliament she murmured (in a letter to Roger Fry) as she might have done of Richard Dalloway: 'What humbugs they all are!'[90]

Rachel Vinrace in *The Voyage Out* perceives an adult world riddled with dignified falsehood: 'It appeared that nobody ever said a thing they meant, or ever talked of a feeling they felt, but that was what music was for.'[91] Great men and women authorise this deception. Woolf conjures up a moment in one of George Eliot's famous Sunday afternoons at the Priory:

A scrap of her talk is preserved. 'We ought to respect our influence,' she said. 'We know by our experience how very much others affect our lives, and we must remember that we in turn must have the same effect upon others.' Jealously treasured, committed to memory, one can imagine recalling the scene, repeating the words, thirty years later and suddenly, for the first time, bursting with laughter.[92]

She found the whole notion of character, whether in the novel, or in actual life, false; when Arnold Bennett complained that *Jacob's Room* contained no characters who would survive she retorted: 'My answer is – but I leave that to the Nation: it's only the old argument that character is dissipated into shreds now.'[93] She might equally well have said, I leave that to Leslie Stephen and the *Dictionary of National Biography*, for the burst of laughter at the Victorian enshrining of its great *is*, as much as is Alice's suppressed laughter at the Caucus Race, that of a child overturning her parent's household gods.

All of Virginia Woolf's writings – both fiction and non-fiction – eschew the making of monuments to either the living or the dead. *Orlando*, subtitled a biography – which she feared would reduce its sales and prove an expensive joke – parodies the notion of academic biography, with its acknowledgements to the dead great, to the living friends and relatives, the British Museum, the Record Office, Mr Sydney Turner's erudition, Mr Arthur Waley's knowledge of Chinese (how much Chinese is there in *Orlando*?), the mysterious gratitude to 'my niece Miss Angelica Bell, for a service which none but she could have rendered', the patient husband working away in the background. In *Orlando* the multiple selves of Orlando are set against traditional methods of writing biography: 'The true length of a person's life, whatever the *Dictionary of National Biography* may say, is always a matter of dispute.' Sir Leslie had been dead too long to be offended. Woolf burlesques the straightforward mode of biographical writing:

> It was now November. After November, comes December. Then January, February, March, and April. After April comes May. June, July, August follow. Next is September. Then October, and so, behold, here we are back at November again, with a whole year accomplished.

Or, as the children's rhyme adapted by Flanders and Swann might put it, bloody January again. Woolf continues: 'This method of writing biography, though it has its merits, is a little bare.' The problem is that nothing at all has happened in Orlando's external world. The writer laments that according to 'everyone whose opinion is worth consulting', life, as it presents itself to the biographer, 'has nothing whatever to do with sitting still in a chair and thinking. . . . Therefore – since sitting in a chair and thinking is precisely what Orlando is doing now – there is nothing for it but to recite the calendar, tell one's beads, blow one's nose, stir the fire, look out of the window, until she has done. Orlando sat so still that you could have heard a pin drop. Would, indeed, that a pin had dropped! That would have been life of a kind.'[94] The external uneventfulness of most people's, and especially most women's lives, drew Woolf to the idea of writing the 'Lives of the Obscure' essays in *The Common Reader*, of which the first series was published in 1925, three years before *Orlando*.

The Stephen children grew up under the shadow of a great family, just as Katharine Hilbery – ostensibly a portrait of Vanessa but containing much of her author's own experience – does in *Night and Day* (1919): 'Denham had accused Katharine Hilbery of belonging to one of the most distinguished families in England, and if any one will take the trouble to consult Mr Galton's "Hereditary Genius", he will find that this assertion is not far from the truth.'[95] Quentin Bell has written of Leslie Stephen's great-grandfather, James Stephen, that 'he was (so far as I know) the first of the Stephens to write a book and from that time on there was scarcely a one who did not publish and never, certainly, a generation which did not add something to the literary achievements of the family'. His son, another James, devoted his life to the anti-slavery cause and was a member of the Clapham sect.[96] James's second son, Leslie Stephen, who began work as editor of the *Dictionary of National Biography* in 1882, published in 1895 a life of his elder brother, Sir James Fitzjames Stephen. In *Night and Day* Katharine and her mother are both engaged on a biography of Mrs Hilbery's father, Richard Alardyce: 'the rarest flower that any family can boast, a great writer, a poet eminent among the poets of England'.

Virginia Woolf uses a particular metaphor for the distinction of the Alardyce family: 'When they were not lighthouses firmly based on a rock for the guidance of their generation, they were steady serviceable candles, illuminating the ordinary chambers of life.'[97] The image, with its echo of Stephen's essay on the author of *Treasure Island*, recurs in *Orlando*, after Orlando's encounter with Alexander Pope, in a passage which quietly parodies Leslie Stephen's mode of writing, just as the whole book pokes fun at the *Dictionary of National Biography*:

From the foregoing passage, however, it must not be supposed that genius (but the disease is now stamped out in the British

Isles, the late Lord Tennyson, it is said, being the last person to suffer from it) is constantly alight, for then we should see everything plain and perhaps should be scorched to death in the process. Rather it resembles the lighthouse in its working, which sends one ray and then no more for a time. . . . To steer by its beams is therefore impossible, and when the dark spell is on them men of genius are, it is said, much like other people.[98]

The paragraph is set up in such a way that the last sentence has an almost blasphemous ring, which is exactly how Virginia Woolf felt about the worship of family idols, that activity which great Victorian men and women bequeathed to their early-twentieth-century offspring. It must have been meat and drink to Woolf to hear Roger Fry's challenge to the fixity of that metaphorical lighthouse:

Baudelaire compared the great names in art to lighthouses posted along the track of historic time. The simile, as he used it, seizes the imagination and represents a great truth, but it allows of an interpretation which the limits of a sonnet form forbade him to develop. He takes the lights of his beacons as much for granted as the sailor does the lights of real lighthouses. But the lighthouses of art do not burn with so fixed and unvarying a lustre. The light they give is always changing insensibly with each generation, now brighter, now dimmer, and often enough growing bright once more.[99]

This fitfulness Woolf herself noted in 'Lives of the Obscure': 'Memories of great men are no infallible specific. They fall upon the race of life like beams from a lighthouse. They flash, they shock, they reveal, they vanish.'[100]

In *Night and Day* Katharine lives in an extended family consisting not only of 'uncles and aunts and cousins "from India", to be reverenced for their relationship alone', but also of 'an august circle of beings to whom she gave the names of Shakespeare, Milton, Wordsworth, Shelley, and so on, who were, for some reason, much more nearly akin to the Hilberys than to other people'. Such relatives seemed to be larger than life in the same way that in Henry James's story 'The Real Thing' (1893) the real-life models, Major and Mrs Monarch, when used by the professional illustrator, seem out of scale with the other represented figures. The problem of living is, in *Night and Day* as in James's story, inseparable from the artistic problem of representing life. Mrs Hilbery as biographer is unable to 'decide how far the public was to be told the truth about the poet's separation from his wife'. The point of the biography for both Mrs Hilbery and Katharine is to establish 'indisputably that her grandfather was a very great man'.[101]

Virginia Woolf's aunt Julia Cameron, who made her name as a photographer both of Victorian great men and of children, once left Tennyson under a dust-sheet for several hours, somewhat as Aunt Etty leaves Uncle Richard in *Period Piece*: 'He sat there as patient as a statue, till he could be unveiled',[102] and Tennyson seems to have done the same. Irreverence was not Mrs Cameron's intention, however; she was merely, like Mrs Hilbery, absent-minded. The Preface to an album of her photographs observes: 'Her portraits of famous men . . . enshrine a monumental view of human personality. Mrs Cameron believed that great thoughts shone, like haloes, from the heads of her thinkers, so her pictures are acts of homage towards her heroes.'[103] Her portraits were literary and her sitters conscious of their own dignity. Roger Fry wrote in an introduction to the same collection: 'In that protected garden of culture women grew to strange beauty, and the men – how lush and rank are their growths! How they abound in the sense of their own personalities.'[104] But, although Mrs Cameron's photographic portraits 'attempt to transmit the aura of the great figures of the time', she was perfectly well aware that photography was a new art and a new technique 'which was turning painting upside down',[105] and some of her most striking effects – the notable portrait of Carlyle which seems to surround him in a halo of light – were the consequence of technical imprecisions in the use of wet plates.[106] But Mrs Cameron was not the woman to be put down either by machine or conventional critic. She wrote to Sir John Herschel, in tones worthy of Virginia Woolf: 'What is focus – and who has a right to say what focus is the legitimate focus?'[107] Her soft-focus photography challenged traditional painterly modes of representation. By 1916 photography had become part of the modernist experiment, as the photographer Alvin Langdon Coburn declared when he wrote:

There are the 'moderns' in Painting, in Music, and in Literature. What would our grandfathers have said of the work of Matisse, Stravinsky and Gertrude Stein? What *do* our grandfathers say? . . .

Yes, if we are alive to the spirit of our time it is these moderns who interest us. They are . . . building afresh, in colour and sound and grammatical construction, the scintillating vision of their minds. . . . Why should not the camera also throw off the shackles of conventional representation and attempt something fresh and untried? . . . Think of the joy of doing something which it would be impossible to classify.[108]

The determination to resist established classifications connects Julia Cameron's ideas about representation to those of Virginia Woolf, Willa Cather and Proust, who described himself as a child gazing at a photograph of St Mark's in Rome, and reflecting how 'I might myself be the minute personage whom, in an enlarged photograph of St Mark's that had been lent to me, the illustrator had portrayed, in a bowler hat, in front of the portico.'[109] The snapshot dwarfs the human figure, where Mrs Cameron had enlarged it, but both Proust and Mrs Cameron recognise that the camera 'signals the decline of portrait painting as a straightforward representation'.[110]

The advent of the family camera and the snapshot destroyed the monumental vision of human personality created by the portrait. As one critic has written of the selection of self implied in Cézanne's self-portraits: 'A good photograph is an accurate record of the individual's visual appearance at one particular instant; but the portrait can never do more than select a personality.'[111] The camera arrests a moment to be relished for what it is – as Walter Pater urges in the conclusion to *The Renaissance* – but not to be interpreted. Alain Robbe-Grillet argues in *Snapshots and Towards a New Novel* that the writer should reproduce objectively as the photographer does, allowing multiple interpretations.[112] Orlando's fame is celebrated not by a portrait, as Richard Alardyce's is in *Night and Day*, but by the ephemeral photograph in the evening paper. Even the recognition that the great had not always been great, but had once been little children like everybody else, was much more apparent and tangible when the *Strand Magazine* published its monthly photographic records of the childhood of great men and women. Stuart Collingwood, Carroll's biographer, wrote after Carroll's death in 1898:

A peculiar interest belongs to the childhood of a man who has afterwards become famous . . . for the boy in his tastes and tendencies is prophetic of the man. . . . They were all children once – these famous writers and lawyers and statesmen; but it is more than probable that hardly any of those who knew them in their early days were able to dissociate them from the other children with whom they worked and played. Their mothers, no doubt, felt convinced that they were the cleverest and most attractive of all conceivable boys; but then, so do all mothers, and we can, therefore, give them no credit for acumen.[113]

These sentiments are oddly poised between *Little Lord Fauntleroy* (1885), which enshrines a mother's adoration of her child, and *The Waves*, where the children have no parents and move together in a pattern as group rather than individual until Bernard muses in middle age: 'I am not so gifted as at one time seemed likely.'[114] The *Strand* article captures a transitional moment between the revering of the great man and the awareness that he was a child like other children, not a different and special species called 'man of genius', but a being who might be dwarfed by the dome of St Mark's.

In *To the Lighthouse* William Bankes, surveying Lily Briscoe's painting, sees something irreverent in her challenge to traditional modes of representing the human figure in art:

> What did she wish to indicate by the triangular purple shape, 'just there?' he asked.
>
> It was Mrs Ramsay reading to James, she said. She knew his objection – that no one could tell it for a human shape. But she made no attempt at likeness, she said. For what reason had she introduced them then? he asked. Why indeed? – except that if there, in that corner, it was bright, here, in this, she felt the need for darkness. Simple, obvious, commonplace, as it was, Mr Bankes was interested. Mother and child then – objects of universal veneration, and in this case the mother was famous for her beauty – might be reduced, he pondered, to a purple shadow without irreverence.

Lily explains that 'her tribute took that form, if, as she vaguely supposed, a picture must be a tribute. A mother and child might be reduced to a shadow without irreverence. A light here required a shadow there.' The human figure is not the motive for painting, nor is the painting an act of homage to the individual, because personality is subjugated to form, placed in a landscape of light and shade as Scott placed his figures in *Old Mortality*. Lily shares with

William Bankes her vision of a soft focus not dictated by the
conventions of other people's art, and they walk off arm-in-arm in a
new intimacy: 'She nicked the catch of her paint-box to, more firmly
than was necessary, and the nick seemed to surround in a circle for
ever the paint-box, the lawn, Mr Bankes, and that wild villain, Cam,
dashing past.'[115] The click which closes the paint box is
unmistakably the sound of a camera shutter as the moment is
arrested in a snapshot.

The camera's eye, unmediated by notions of tribute, is more
ruthless than the painter's. The spirit which reduces human
pretension looks beyond the draperies in which Mrs Cameron clad
her sitters and asks the question, not, how are they so great and
different, but in what ways are they all the same? Orlando gazes at a
line of eminent Victorians:

> The ladies held card-cases between their fingers; the gentlemen
> balanced gold-pointed canes between their knees. She stood
> there gazing, admiring, awe-struck. One thought only disturbed
> her, a thought familiar to all who behold great elephants, or
> whales of an incredible magnitude, and that is how do these
> leviathans to whom obviously stress, change and activity are
> repugnant, propagate their kind? Perhaps, thought Orlando,
> looking at the stately, still faces, their time of propagation is over;
> this is the fruit; this is the consummation. What she now beheld
> was the triumph of an age. Portly and splendid there they sat.[116]

Kenneth Grahame would not have recorded anything so improper.
But the subversive mood is there in *The Golden Age* (1895), the
undermining of the static, monolithic, venerated Olympian world,
just as the undermining of the monolithic text is there in his writing:

> You must please remember that a theme, a thesis, a subject, is in
> most cases little more than a sort of clothes-line, on which one
> pegs a string of ideas, quotations, allusions and so on, one's
> mental undergarments, of all shapes and sizes, some possibly
> fairly new, but most rather old and patched; and they dance and
> sway in the breeze, and flap and flutter, or hang limp and lifeless;
> and some are ordinary enough, and some are of a rather private
> and intimate shape, and rather give their owner away and show
> up his or her peculiarities. And owing to the invisible clothes-line
> they seem to have some connexion and continuity.[117]

If Grahame's clothes-line sounds a little like Mrs Hilbery's book – 'a wild dance of will-o'-the-wisps, without form or continuity'[118] – it nevertheless describes the biographical methods of Woolf rather than of Leslie Stephen.

Stevenson wrote in an essay ostensibly about Victor Hugo of the way in which in Scott's novels 'the individual characters begin to occupy a comparatively small proportion of that canvas on which armies manoeuvre, and great wills pile themselves upon each others shoulders. . . . Already in Scott we begin to have a sense of the subtle influences that moderate and qualify a man's personality.'[119] Woolf thought Scott preached, but wrote in her diary that *Old Mortality* had her 'by the hair once more', and described the placing of figures in terms which Fry might have used to analyse a Gainsborough: 'Everything is so much in keeping – even his odd monochromatic landscape painting, done in smooth washes of sepia and burnt senna. Edith and Henry too might be typical figures by an old master, put in exactly in the right place.'[120] Stevenson speaks of the 'revolutionary tradition' of Scott in subordinating personality to landscape and even weather, and praises Scott because 'he does not believe in novels having any moral influence at all'.[121]

A new irreverence towards the great men and women of late Victorian society thus becomes part of a movement in the writing of fiction, away from the monumental author with rights over his characters and over his readers' reaction to them. Orlando may reflect on the motives of politicians, but her creator breaks off: 'These moralities belong, and should be left to the historian, since they are as dull as ditch water.' The dissenting consciousness fostered in books for children, whether in *The Golden Age*, *The Adventures of Huckleberry Finn*, or even in Griselda's impatience in Molesworth's *The Cuckoo Clock* not only with her aunts but also with the Cuckoo's momentary lapses into instruction and improvement, has become the distinctive territory not of the reader resisting the preaching voice, but of the author herself. Even as Orlando, Elizabethan nobleman, observes his own munificence – a penance for fornication: 'Twelve poor old women of the parish to-day drink tea and to-night bless his Lordship for a roof above their heads; so that illicit love is a treasure ship' – a voice interrupts, as though it had heard Alice whisper: 'How fond she is of finding morals in things', announcing firmly: 'But we omit the moral.'[122]

VI   SACRED TEXTS

Virginia Woolf might have found in Zangwill's column in the *Pall Mall Magazine* in the 1890s an anticipation not only of her own mode of writing novels,[123] but also of Katharine's Hilbery's sense that Shakespeare and Milton were part of the illustrious Victorian family from which she was trying to escape. He wrote of the inevitable literary reading of life which a well-read person was obliged to make: 'There is a drop of ink in the blood of the most natural of us; we are all hybrids, crossed with literature, and Shakespeare is as much the author of our being as either of our parents.'[124] In Kipling's *Stalky & Co*, published in 1899, Stalky and his friends, having hidden a dead cat in the rafters of School House so that the whole place stinks, are flogged by Mr King:

> King enjoyed himself most thoroughly for by virtue of their seniority the boys were exempt from his hand, save under special order. Luckily, he was no expert in the gentle art.
> ' "Strange, how desire doth outrun performance," ' said Beetle irreverently, quoting from some Shakespeare play that they were cramming that term. They regained their study and settled down to the imposition.
> 'You're quite right, Beetle,' Stalky spoke in silky and propitiating tones. 'Now if the Head had sent us up to a prefect, we'd have got something to remember!'[125]

Kipling's readers in 1899 would not have needed Bowdler to inform them that Shakespeare had in mind a different kind of performance when he gave this speech to Poins observing Falstaff's courtship of Doll Tearsheet in *II Henry IV*. The choice of quotation is all the more ribald in view of Farrar's veiled warnings in *Eric, Or Little by Little* against the sexual corruption which awaits the unwary in an all-boys school. For Farrar, Shakespeare is as much sacred text as the Bible, as is evident in the authorial exhortation to Eric to resist the carnal in word, and of course, deed: 'Lose your purity of heart, Eric, and you have lost a jewel which the whole world, if it were "one entire and perfect chrysolite", cannot replace.' Othello's lament for the loss of Desdemona is then resolved into an appeal to the Almighty: 'Good spirits guard that young boy, and give him grace in this his hour of trial. . . . Point a pitying finger to the yawning abyss of shame, ruin, and despair that even now perhaps is being cleft under his feet.'[126] The pointing finger is Farrar's, God's and Shakespeare's.

Virginia Woolf wrote to Emma Vaughan in 1900: 'I do hope Vere [Isham] is reading Thackeray. There is no picture in my mind that gives me more pleasure than that of him reading and rereading Thackeray and playing a tune on the Cello between whiles. It takes me back to the days of my childhood.'[127] The childhood reading Woolf refers to may have included not only *The Rose and the Ring* but another children's Christmas book, *The Kickleburys on the Rhine* (1850), in which 'Lady Kicklebury remarks that Shakespeare was very right in stating how much sharper than a thankless tooth it is to have a serpent child.'[128] Nesbit adapted this line in *The Railway Children* (1906) in which Phyllis remarks: 'It's quite right what it says in the poetry book about sharper than a serpent it is to have a toothless child, – but it means ungrateful when it says toothless.'[129] Thackeray, who murmured that he thought great writers a bore,[130] would have loved to hear in *The Voyage Out* not only Clarissa's calling Rachel a monster for not liking Jane Austen, and then bringing *Persuasion* on deck to read 'because I thought it was a little less threadbare than the others', but also her quoting of Shelley's 'Adonais':

'At your age I only liked Shelley. I can remember sobbing over him in the garden.

> He has outsoared the shadow of our night,
> Envy and calumny and hate and pain –

you remember?

> Can touch him not and torture not again
> From the contagion of the world's slow stain.

How divine! – and yet what nonsense!' She looked lightly round the room. 'I always think it's *living*, not dying, that counts. . . .'
She pressed Rachel's shoulder.
'Um-m-m –' she went on quoting –

> Unrest which men miscall delight.[131]

Clarissa is plainly the Duchess in *Alice in Wonderland*, quoting, pointing morals, edging nearer all the time with her chin on Rachel's shoulder.

Lewis Carroll's parodies of Tennyson, Longfellow, Swinburne and many other poets provided an escape from revered texts. In 'The Hunting of the Snark' the Captain begins: ' "Friends, Romans and countrymen, lend me your ears!" / (They were all of them fond of quotations:)'; the Bellman continues:

> For England expects – I forbear to proceed:
> 'Tis a maximum tremendous, but trite.[132]

In *The Waves* the Doctor 'has bid us "quit ourselves like men". (On his lips quotations from the Bible, from *The Times*, seem equally magnificent.)'[133] The concept of authority vested in the sacred text, whether Bible or great author, receives a wigging at the hands of the new generation.

In Nesbit's *The Story of the Treasure Seekers* Dora demurs at divining as a way of looking for treasure:

> 'I hope the divining rod isn't wrong. I believe it's wrong in the Bible.'
> 'So is eating pork and ducks,' said Dicky, 'You can't go by that.'[134]

The children in *The Wouldbegoods* want to make a fashionable watering-place when they are playing in the stream. Oswald refuses: 'We do not like fashionableness':

> '*You* ought to, at any rate,' Denny said. 'A Mr Collins wrote an Ode to the Fashions, and he was a great poet.'
> 'The poet Milton wrote a long book about Satan,' Noel said, 'but I'm not bound to like *Him*.'[135]

If *Ministering Children* can be a model for behaviour then the Bastables think that the *Arabian Nights* ought also to qualify:

> 'There are ways of being robbers that are not wrong,' said Noel; 'if you can rob a robber it is a right act.'
> 'But you can't,' said Dora; 'he is too clever, and besides, it's wrong anyway.'
> 'Yes you can, and it isn't; and murdering him with boiling oil is

a right act too, so there!' said Noel. 'What about Ali Baba? Now then!'[136]

The impulse which has always led children to deface their books by drawing in the margin dictates Cam's rebellion in *To the Lighthouse* against Mr Ramsay's quoting of Cowper: ' "But I beneath a rougher sea / Was whelmed in deeper gulfs than he." '[137] Woolf's sinuous prose in *Orlando* conceals a burlesque of Longfellow worthy of Lewis Carroll, but also shoots a mocking glance at T. S. Eliot, whom she accused of letting the '-ing' termination become a habit,[138] and whose poem 'The Love Song of J. Alfred Prufrock' begins 'Let us go then, you and I'. Woolf's prose can be written out as verse, thus:

> Let us go, then, exploring,
> this summer morning,
> when all are adoring
> the plum blossom and the bee.
> And humming and hawing,
> let us ask of the starling
> (who is a more social bird than the lark)
> what he may think
> on the brink
> of the dust-bin,
> whence he picks
> among the sticks
> combings of scullion's hair.[139]

Woolf might have found in E. Nesbit's books for children that same challenge to the extended family of great authors which she gave to Katharine Hilbery. When the butter tubs have been drowned in the moat in *The Wouldbegoods*, Denny observes, as Thackeray might have done, that 'after the mud in that moat not all the perfumes of somewhere or other could make them fit to use for butter again'.[140]

The oscillation between adult and child consciousness which critics found so disconcerting in Kenneth Grahame and which Beerbohm complained of in *Peter Pan* – as many have done since – represented a transitional movement between the writer as authority figure and the repudiation of that authority which is so marked in Virginia Woolf's novels. In 1881 Kenneth Grahame was devouring Joel Chandler Harris's *Uncle Remus*, in which the adventures of Brer Rabbit are told by Uncle Remus to the plantation-owner's child.[141] The narrative novelty of these stories lies in the interchange between narrator and child, as the child is not always satisfied with Uncle Remus's endings – which seem unjust by the standards of the white child's story book – nor with his resuscitation of characters who have been killed off:

> 'And was that the last of the Rabbit, too, Uncle Remus?' the little boy asked, with something like a sigh.
>
> 'Don't push me too close, honey' responded the old man; 'don't shove me up in no cornder. I don't wander tel you no stories. . . . Some tells one tale en some tells nudder. . . . Let dem tell you w'at knows. Dat w'at I years you gits it straight like I yeard it.'[142]

When Grahame wrote to his son Alistair on his birthday in 1907 he told him the first adventure of Toad, and added that he was sending him Brer Rabbit to read.[143] Virginia Woolf wrote in 'How It Strikes a Contemporary' that the new generation of writers 'cannot tell stories because they do not believe the stories are true'.[144]

The exposing of the Great Wizard of Oz in Frank Baum's book, first published in 1902, is the exposing of a 'humbug' made possible by other people's reverence: ' "No; you are all wrong," said the little man meekly. "I have been making believe." '[145] The worship of humbug creates false gods, whether sacred or secular, and when Virginia Woolf told H. G. Wells that children were more at ease with their parents than they had been, she might have added that it was because her generation of both children and writers had turned on the Duchess and said: 'Don't push me too close, honey . . . don't shove me up in no cornder.'

4
Death

1 DEATH-BED SCENES

Virginia Woolf was thirteen when her mother died. Recalling that time from a distance of forty-four years, only two years before her own death, Woolf wrote: 'The tragedy of her death was not that it made one, now and then and very intensely, unhappy. It was that it made her unreal; and us solemn, and self-conscious. We were made to act parts that we did not feel; to fumble for words that we did not know. It obscured, it dulled. It made one hypocritical and immeshed in the conventions of sorrow.'[1] Earlier she had described how 'her death, on the 5th of May, 1895, began a period of Oriental gloom, for surely there was something in the darkened room, the groans, the passionate lamentations that passed the normal limits of sorrow, and hung about the genuine tragedy with folds of Eastern drapery'.[2] When bidding her mother farewell, she was afflicted by an impulse to laugh: 'I remember very clearly how even as I was taken to the bedside I noted that one nurse was sobbing, and a desire to laugh came over me, and I said to myself as I have often done at moments of crisis since, "I feel nothing whatever." ' The next day Stella took her to her mother's room to kiss her for the last time:

> Her face looked immeasurably distant, hollow and stern. When I kissed her, it was like kissing cold iron. Whenever I touch cold iron the feeling comes back to me – the feeling of my mother's face, iron cold, and granulated. I started back. Then Stella stroked her cheek, and undid a button on her nightgown. 'She always liked to have it like that,' she said. When she came up to the nursery later she said to me, 'Forgive me. I saw you were afraid.' She had noticed that I had started.[3]

It is a curious fact that the critic is uncertain when recording this sequence whether to use the historical past: 'Stella took', or the

111

fictional present: 'Stella takes.' The scene in being written down becomes a fiction, gathered to all those other fictional Victorian death-beds, and is thus part of the unreality which Virginia Woolf describes. The effect of unreality is enhanced by its distance from modern customs, but it is also part of the sense which Woolf tries to convey of the family's being forced to live up to the death-bed, to some literary or stage representation of death which then dominates its realities and obscures their true nature.

Virginia Woolf was as much at home in the Elizabethan period as T. S. Eliot was. Her own creation, Orlando, is at his most vigorous, zestful and uninhibited in that early period. The Elizabethans combined a capacity for extreme staginess about death – Donne rigged himself up in his shroud, having preached his own death sermon, 'Death's Duell'[4] – with distrust of such theatricality. Bacon wrote in his essay 'Of Death' that 'groanes and Convulsions, and a discoloured Face, and Friends Weeping, and Blackes, and Obsequies, and the like shew *Death* Terrible'. The recounting of death is for Bacon an exacerbation of terror: 'Men feare Death, as Children feare to goe in the darke: And as that Natural Feare in Children, is increased with Tales, so is the other.'[5] Woolf admired Montaigne's essays, and spoke of his 'great bug-bears, convention and ceremony'.[6] When Jacques Raverat died, she recorded:

> Jacques died, I say. . . . I do not any longer feel inclined to doff the cap to death. I like to go out of the room talking, with an unfinished casual sentence on my lips. That is the effect it had on me – no leavetaking, no submission, but someone stepping out into the darkness. For her though the nightmare was terrific. All I can do now is to keep natural with her, which is I believe a matter of considerable importance. More and more do I repeat my own version of Montaigne – it's life that matters.[7]

The words refer to Montaigne's essay 'That to Philosophize, is to Learne How to Die', in which the writer argues that 'to know how to die, doth free us from all subjection and constraint'. He continues: 'Were I a composer of books, I would keepe a register, commented of the divers deaths, which in teaching men to die, should after teach them to live.'[8] In her biography of Roger Fry Woolf records Fry's quoting of Spinoza: 'The free man thinks less of death than of anything else and all his wisdom is the contemplation of life.'[9]

The Stephen children found themselves forced into all the

externals of Victorian mourning, as if they had to play out a drama in which their parts were already written for them. Woolf remarks: 'There was a struggle, for soon we revived, and there was a conflict between what we ought to be and what we were. Thoby put this into words. One day before he went back to school, he said: "It's silly going on like this ...", sobbing, sitting shrouded, he meant. I was shocked at his heartlessness yet he was right, I know; and yet how could we escape?'[10] The proper manner of behaving at death seemed to have been prescribed in the cheapest sort of novelette. In fact, the way the Stephen family conducted itself is emotionally in tune with the way in which Eric and his friends carried on after the death of Russell in *Eric, Or Little by Little*, the same lugubrious dwelling on the sacred moments, the same living by the pattern of the dead, the same impelling obligations to the dead. Gosse describes the same phenomenon in *Father and Son* when his mother dies – he is seven years old:

> Almost in the last hour of her life, urged to confess her 'joy' in the Lord, my Mother, rigidly honest, meticulous in self-analysis, as ever, replied: 'I have peace, but not *joy*. It would not do to go into eternity with a lie in my mouth.'
>
> When the very end approached, and her mind was growing clouded, she gathered her strength together to say to my Father, 'I shall walk with Him in white. Won't you take your lamb and walk with me?' Confused with sorrow and alarm, my Father failed to understand her meaning. She became agitated, and she repeated two or three times: 'Take our lamb, and walk with me!' Then my father comprehended, and pressed me forward; her hand fell softly upon mine and she seemed content. Thus was my dedication, that had begun in my cradle, sealed with the most solemn, the most poignant and irresistible insistence, at the death-bed of the holiest and purest of women. But what a weight, intolerable as the burden of Atlas, to lay on the shoulders of a little fragile child![11]

The weight which was laid on the Stephen children was dedication not to God, but to the altar of their father's suffering, or so it seemed to them: 'We were his only hope, his only comfort, he would say. And there kneeling on the floor one would try – perhaps only to cry.'[12] More than forty years later, in *The Years*, Virginia Woolf described with some savagery a death scene which bore a

"Mudder! Mudder, dear! are you going to a new land?" he cried with excitement.

7   Death of Froggy's Mother (from Brenda, *Froggy's Little Brother*, 1875)

resemblance to her mother's, but was more stagey in that it followed a long illness. A death scene was always about to be played but ended in a false alarm. The actual death scene is presented through the consciousness of Delia, one of the daughters:

There were so many of them in the room that she could get no farther than the doorway. She could see two nurses standing with their backs to the wall opposite. One of them was crying – the one, she observed, who had only come that afternoon. She could not see the bed from where she stood. But she could see that Morris had fallen on his knees. Ought I to kneel too? she wondered. Not in the passage, she decided. She looked away; she saw the little window at the end of the passage. Rain was falling; there was a light somewhere that made the raindrops shine. One drop after another slid down the pane; they slid and they paused; one drop joined another drop and then they slid down again. There was complete silence in the bedroom.

'Is this death?' Delia asked herself. For a moment there seemed to be something there. A wall of water seemed to gape apart; the two walls held themselves apart. She listened. There was complete silence. Then there was a stir, a shuffle of feet in the bedroom and out came her father, stumbling.

'Rose!' he cried. 'Rose! Rose!' He held his arms with the fists clenched out in front of him.

You did that very well, Delia told him as he passed her. It was like a scene in a play. She observed quite dispassionately that the raindrops were still falling. One sliding met another and together in one drop they rolled to the bottom of the window-pane.[13]

The raindrops do not become a rain of tears. The only person weeping is the hired nurse. When Roger Fry died, Virginia Woolf remembered Maupassant's description of the writer's detachment from every feeling, which he must observe for the sake of his art: 'Ne jamais souffrir, penser, aimer, sentir comme tout le monde, bonnement, franchement, simplement, sans s'analyser soi-meme après chaque joie et après chaque sanglot.' She added: 'I remember turning aside at mother's bed, when she had died, and Stella took us in, to laugh, secretly, at the nurse crying. She's pretending, I said: aged 13. & was afraid I was not feeling enough. So now.'[14] But, although she recalls that childish urge to laugh, at once irreverent, nervous, anguished and embarrassed, brooding as a woman on another failure to feel as strongly as the occasion seems to require, she had access to a literary representation of her own predicament in Tolstoy's semi-autobiographical description of the simulated emotion which surrounded his own mother's death.

In *Childhood* Tolstoy records how the children and their father are summoned to the mother's death-bed and ushered into the sick-room: 'I was in great distress at that moment, yet I automatically noticed every little detail. It was almost dark in the room, and very hot; there was a mingled smell of mint, eau-de-cologne, camomile and Hoffmann's drops. The smell struck me so forcibly that, not only when I happen to smell it but when I even recall it, my imagination instantly carries me back to that stifling room and reproduces every minute detail of that terrible moment.'[15] That spur to memory anticipates not only Proust, but *The Voyage Out*. Rachel is reading:

> Next she picked up *Cowper's Letters*, the classic prescribed by her father which had bored her, so that one sentence chancing to say something about the smell of broom in his garden, she had thereupon seen the little hall at Richmond, laden with flowers on the day of her mother's funeral, smelling so strong that now any flower-scent brought back the sickly horrible sensation; and so from one scene she passed, half-hearing, half-seeing, to another. She saw her Aunt Lucy arranging flowers in the drawing-room.
> 'Aunt Lucy,' she volunteered, 'I don't like the smell of broom; it reminds me of funerals.'
> 'Nonsense, Rachel,' Aunt Lucy replied; 'don't say such foolish things, dear. I always think it is a particularly cheerful plant.'

Whereas earlier drafts of the novel emphasise Rachel's rage and her dead mother's dominion over her survivors, in the final version Woolf has toned these down, partly by expunging an authorial comment: 'Nothing is stronger than the position of the dead among the living', an utterance which reminds the reader of Rachel's fascination with Ibsen.[16]

The unreality which Woolf felt that death bestowed on her mother strikes Tolstoy's Nikolai as he slips into the music room where his mother's body lies in state. The open coffin, flanked with candles, is in the middle of the room; a professional chanter intones continuously from the Psalter. The child hardly recognises the impassive face: 'I kept forgetting that the dead body which lay before me and which I gazed at so absently, as on some object that had nothing to do with my memories, was *she*.' When another chanter enters to relieve the wake, the boy feels that his curiosity may not make a good impression, so he begins to cry. But when he looks back on the scene, the novelist declares that the only genuine emotion preceded the tears, when the child registered the loss of the real mother. Every later manifestation seemed tainted with self-regard, with awareness of the impression which was being created in the minds of other witnesses: 'I despised myself for not experiencing sorrow to the exclusion of everything else, and I tried to conceal all other feelings: this made my grief insincere and unnatural. Moreover, I felt a kind of enjoyment in knowing that I was unhappy and I tried to stimulate my sense of unhappiness, and this interest in myself did more than anything else to stifle real sorrow in me.' The artificial pumping-up of grief is equally evident in the adults, and Tolstoy, who retained as writer and artist his child's honesty about feelings, allows Nikolai to recognise in them the condition of his own heart and behaviour. Mimi weeps, but she also covers her face with her handkerchief: 'I fancied she did so in order to hide her face from the spectators and rest a moment from forced sobbing.' As French governess her livelihood is endangered by her mistress's death. Tolstoy remarks: 'Perhaps her grief was genuine but not entirely pure and disinterested.' The friends who mourn jar on the child: 'All the outsiders who were present at the service I found intolerable. The expressions of sympathy they addressed to my father – that she would be better off there, that she was not for this world – aroused a kind of anger in me.' The only grief which seems real is that of the old nurse: 'With clasped hands and eyes raised to heaven she was not weeping but was praying. . . . "There is one who loved her truly", I thought, and I felt ashamed of myself.' After the service is finished all those present go to kiss the corpse's face, including a young peasant woman carrying a five-year-old girl, 'whom she had brought with her, heaven knows why':

At that moment I dropped my wet handkerchief by mistake and was just stooping to pick it up when I was startled by an awful piercing cry of such horror that I shall never forget it if I live to be a hundred: whenever I think of it a cold shudder runs down my body. I raised my head – the peasant woman was standing on a stool by the coffin and struggling to hold the little girl in her arms.

The child was pushing with her little fists, throwing back her frightened little face and staring with dilated eyes at the dead woman as she uttered a succession of dreadful frenzied shrieks. I too uttered a cry that, I think, must have been even more terrible than the one which had startled me, and ran from the room.[17]

The little child's terror communicates to Nikolai the reality of physical decay. What stands out from the whole is the total inability of either child to meet the enormous demands of the adult world in her or his reaction to death, either in the specific, of the little peasant girl's kissing the dead face of a complete stranger, or in the general, of Nikolai's actual feelings. For him, as for Virginia Woolf, the dead woman is nothing to do with the live one. But that child's perception is not allowed any place in the world of adult feeling, which requires him to operate only within its own modes of representation.

In *Boyhood* Tolstoy describes, much more briefly, the death of his grandmother. She has been ill a long time: 'There is the same oppressive odour in her room that I had smelt five years before in mamma's room.' Then one day they are sent out for a drive in the morning, and see that the street is covered with straw: 'The reason never dawns on me why we are being sent out at such an unusual hour. During the whole drive Lyuba and I, we don't know why, are in that particular state of high spirits when the least trifle, the least word or movement, starts one laughing.' Everything sets them off:

Mimi looks displeased and remarks that it is only *silly people* who laugh for no reason, and Lyuba, crimson in the face with suppressed mirth, casts a sidelong glance at me. Our eyes meet and we break into such Homeric laughter that the tears fill our eyes, and we cannot restrain our paroxysms although they nearly choke us. We have no sooner quieted down to some extent than I look at Lyuba and utter a private catchword which has been in favour among us for some time, and we are off again.

As we drive up to the house on the way back I open my mouth to make a fine face at Lyuba when my eyes are startled by a black coffin-lid leaning against one panel of our front door, and my mouth remains fixed in its distorted grimace.

'*Votre grand'mere est morte!*' says St Jerome with a pale face, coming out to meet us.

All the time grandmamma's body is in the house I have an oppressive feeling of fear of death – that is, the dead body reminds me vividly and unpleasantly that I too must die some day. It is a feeling that is often somehow taken for grief. I do not regret grandmamma, indeed I doubt whether any one sincerely regrets her. Though the house is full of mourning callers nobody regrets her death except one person, whose vehement grief surprises me beyond expression. And that person is her maid, Gasha. . . .

I repeat once more that inconsistency in matters of feeling is the surest sign of their genuineness.[18]

The children's laughter marks rebellion: a release of nervous energy from the powerless, directed against a power structure which allows them no breathing-space. Where the younger child in the first incident is unable to dissemble, and his mixed emotions escape in terror, the older boy protests through irreverence, as did the thirteen-year-old Virginia, wanting to laugh. For Tolstoy adult hypocrisy has its roots in a vain effort at consistency where the child is true to genuine feeling in being the prey of contradictory emotions.

Separated as they are by religion and culture, Woolf and Tolstoy record scenes of mummery capable of provoking Montaigne's scorn. Montaigne saw in the trappings of death an affirmation of social hierarchies: 'The very children are afraid of their friends, when they see them masked; and so are we: The maske must as well be taken from things, as from men, which being removed, we shall finde nothing hid under it, but the very same death, that a seely varlet, or a simple maid-servant, did lately suffer without amazement or feare. Happie is that death, which takes all leasure from the preparations of such an equipage.'[19] In both *The Years* and in Tolstoy's novel the death scenes are stage-managed by religion to worldly ends: a show of wealth – nurses, professional chanters – and family power in which children are necessary as emblems of hierarchical structure. Those who are high in that structure act out a tragic scene for the benefit of those who are low in it, as Laertes and Hamlet do when they wrestle in Ophelia's grave, watched by the men who have dug it. Death offers men and women a final statement not just of their individual importance, but of their social standing, and, in a wider sense, of the 'hierarchy of values' which José Ortega y Gasset sees as the central construct of life itself.[20] Montaigne declared in another essay, 'Of Judging of Others Death', that 'most men set a sterne countenance on the matter, looke big, and speake stoutly, thereby to acquire reputation, which if they chance to live, they hope to enjoy'.[21] The big death scene and its trappings become ceremonials to self-importance, as in the rituals surrounding Mr Featherstone's demise in *Middlemarch*.

The pressing of reluctant and terrified children into the service of such adult rituals is translated from the old world into the new in Willa Cather's *My Ántonia* (1918), which describes an open-air burial service after the suicide of Ántonia's father, Mr Shimerda, who has shot himself from homesickness for his native Bohemia. While the adults debate the form of service available to a man who has taken his own life, and Mrs Shimerda decides from superstition to bury him at the crossroads, Jim is left in charge of his grandmother's house:

> I felt a considerable extension of power and authority, and was anxious to acquit myself creditably. I carried in cobs and wood from the long cellar, and filled both the stoves. I remembered that in the hurry and excitement of the morning nobody had thought of the chickens, and the eggs had not been gathered. Going out through the tunnel, I gave the hens their corn, emptied the ice from their drinking-pan, and filled it with water. After the cat had had his milk, I could think of nothing else to do, and I sat down to get warm. . . . Presently, as I looked with satisfaction about our comfortable sitting-room, it flashed upon me that if Mr. Shimerda's soul were lingering about in this world at all, it would be here in our house, which had been more to his liking than any other in the neighbourhood. . . .
>
> I knew it was homesickness that had killed Mr. Shimerda, and I wondered whether his released spirit would not eventually find its way back to his own country. . . . Surely, his exhausted spirit, so tired of cold and crowding and the struggle with the ever-falling snow, was resting now in this quiet house.
>
> I was not frightened, but I made no noise. I did not wish to disturb him. I went softly down to the kitchen which, tucked away so snugly underground, always seemed to me the heart and centre of the house. There, on the bench behind the stove, I thought and thought about Mr. Shimerda.

Instead of religion, there is here a domestic intimacy which emphasises not only the child's function and responsibility – he becomes himself a part of his world's 'authority' – but also his equality with the dead man. Obviously, his real relation with Mr

Shimerda is less close than Tolstoy's with his mother. But in some ways it is closer. The pioneers live in a state of interdependence in which everyone is necessary. The children in Tolstoy's novel have been for a long time in a different town from their mother and are only summoned back for her death-bed. In *The Years* they are distanced from the mother by her illness, but also by the father's demands on them for a special kind of behaviour. By contrast, Jim has real power. The chickens, the hens, the cat are all dependent on him. Even Mr Shimerda's spirit is allowed a freedom to be itself, to rest with Jim in the warm kitchen, and not to compete with a scene which creates unreality – the corpse and the chanters.

The same easy atmosphere carries over into the funeral itself, which is conducted in the open air without a priest. There has been some discussion between the Catholic Bohemians who believe that Mr Shimerda will be years and years in Purgatory, and Jim's grandparents, who believe no such thing. The young Bohemian Anton Jelinek tells how he and a priest were preserved from cholera carrying the sacrament to soldiers in the war, and that he feels bad that Mr Shimerda should die without it:

> We listened attentively. It was impossible not to admire his frank, manly faith.
>
> 'I am always glad to meet a young man who thinks seriously about these things,' said grandfather, 'and I would never be the one to say you were not in God's care when you were among the soldiers.'

Respect for other people's beliefs is part of a larger respect for human liberty, evident when the family all come to bid farewell to the dead man, a scene which compares interestingly with Tolstoy's:

> Mrs. Shimerda came out and placed an open prayer-book against the body, making the sign of the cross on the bandaged head with her fingers. Ambrosch knelt down and made the same gesture, and after him Ántonia and Marek. Yulka hung back. Her mother pushed her forward, and kept saying something to her over and over. Yulka knelt down, shut her eyes, and put out her hand a little way, but she drew it back and began to cry wildly. She was afraid to touch the bandage. Mrs. Shimerda caught her by the shoulders and pushed her toward the coffin, but grandmother interfered.

Alice to the Lighthouse

'No, Mrs. Shimerda,' she said firmly, 'I won't stand by and see that child frightened into spasms. She is too little to understand what you want of her. Let her alone.'

At a look from grandfather, Fuchs and Jelinek placed the lid on the box, and began to nail it down over Mr. Shimerda. I was afraid to look at Ántonia. She put her arms round Yulka and held the little girl close to her.

The old world tries to assert itself over the child. But the new world allows no such domination. The child is free to be a child, to be unable to partake of the adult ritual, not to understand its significance and requirements. Adult prestige does not in Cather's account depend on the child's audience or its organised participation. Jim suffers no feeling that the adults are pretending when his grandfather offers a prayer 'in English, for the neighbours to understand':

Grandmother looked anxiously at grandfather. He took off his hat, and the other men did likewise. I thought his prayer remarkable. I still remember it. He began, 'Oh, great and just God, no man among us knows what the sleeper knows, nor is it for us to judge what lies between him and Thee.' He prayed that if any man there had been remiss toward the stranger come to a far country, God would forgive him and soften his heart.

They sing a hymn. The open air atmosphere is symbolic of the casting-off of oppression imposed through religion, through human theatricality and through the hierarchical ordering of family and society. In the new air the child is still part of a family structure, but is allowed to breathe. 'Ántonia was washing dishes. When she saw me, she ran out of her dark corner and threw her arms around me. "Oh, Jimmy," she sobbed, "what you tink for my lovely papa!" It seemed to me that I could feel her heart breaking as she clung to me.'[22] Cather gives the child not only social space, but space in the book to pioneer new ways of expressing feeling.

Willa Cather abdicates her own right as author to impose on her characters an affecting death scene. If anyone has written the death scene in *My Ántonia*, it is Jim Burden, whereas in Tolstoy the reactions of Nikolai are, like those of Delia in *The Years*, a subversive subtext, in which the author traces out an alternative scene by a process of undermining her fictional establishment. The dominant voice in Cather's account is not that of the grandmother refusing to let a child be terrified, but that of another child who observes that the adult world sanctions and enjoys that terror. Even Stella made her young sister kiss her mother's iron-cold and granulated skin and felt obliged to apologise when she witnessed the start of fear which Virginia could not suppress. There was no voice available to say: 'Don't make her do it.' Woolf, like Tolstoy, feeds revolution against the whole system into the mind of a child, who refuses to legitimate adult practices. In *To the Lighthouse* that refusal creates the famous brackets: '[Mr Ramsay stumbling along a passage stretched his arms out one dark morning, but, Mrs Ramsay having died rather suddenly the night before, he stretched his arms out. They remained empty.]'[23] The death itself has become subtext, as it had earlier in Dorothy Richardson's *Pilgrimage*, where the suicide of Miriam Henderson's mother is not named, but inferred from the heroine's emotions. The growth of reticence and the refusal to represent death began in the late nineteenth century in children's books, in which the dying child had been ruthlessly exploited.

II CHILDREN AND DEATH

Wordsworth pointed out in the notorious 'We are Seven' that children cannot conceive of death, but his just observation was largely ignored by most writers for and about children. A poem called 'Child's Play', published in *Good Words* five years before Stevenson wrote his very different essay of the same name for the *Cornhill*, painted a sombre picture of small children playing in a churchyard (accurate in so far as churchyards do make wonderful playgrounds). After an introductory verse of melancholy wisdom the poet exclaims:

> Angel, cry aloud!
> Tell them of life's long winter – of the shroud.
> No! Let them play – for Age, alas! and Care,
> Too soon will frown, to teach them what they are.
> . . .
> When they look up, and high in air admire
> The lessening shaft of that aerial spire;
> So be their thoughts uplifted from the sod,
> Where Time's brief flowers they gather to their God![24]

When Kenneth Grahame published *The Cambridge Book of Poetry for Children* in 1916 he commented on the necrophilia of children's writers:

> In the output of those writers who have deliberately written for children, it is surprising how largely the subject of *death* is found to bulk. Dead fathers and mothers, dead brothers and sisters, dead uncles and aunts, dead puppies and kittens, dead birds, dead flowers, dead dolls – a compiler of Obituary Verse for the delight of children could make a fine fat volume with little difficulty. I have turned off this mournful tap of tears as far as possible, preferring that children should read of the joy of life, rather than revel in sentimental thrills of imagined bereavement.[25]

Walter de la Mare noted the same tendency in *Early One Morning*: 'Few novelists nowadays are as prone to the pathos of describing the death of a child as were those of the last century – *Eric*, *Misunderstood*, *Uncle Tom's Cabin*, *Bleak House*, immediately come to mind.' De la Mare discusses a little-known work of Maria Charlesworth's:

> In a tiny volume entitled Letters to a Child, written by the author of *Ministering Children*, Letter iv begins, not very winningly: 'Dear Child, Do you know what an Allegory is?' and Letter ix: 'My dear Child, You know that men, and women, and children may be called at any age to leave this world. . . . I will tell you in this Letter of four children who were all called away from one village . . . .' The gentle authoress believed that it is imperative to persuade a young child, who might be as eager with life as a dewdrop is with the colours of a rainbow, to brood on its brevity. Almost every sentence of her minute volume is in a hushed, candied, yet faintly menacing strain.[26]

De la Mare sees the insistence on death as a form of harrassment practised by the 'gentle authoress' on the gentle reader.

The situation cannot be completely explained away as Evangelical lugubriousness. Children – and indeed very small children – are fascinated by death and only gradually learn the inhibitions and euphemisms with which adults surround it – and used to surround it even in the nineteenth century when it was described at length in fiction. When Virginia Woolf's Orlando becomes a Victorian she finds that 'love, birth, and death were all swaddled in a variety of fine phrases. The sexes drew further and further apart. No open conversation was tolerated. Evasions and concealments were sedulously practised on both sides.' Although no doubt Woolf is here thinking more of sex than of death, she includes the great physical experiences of life, of which death is one, in the swaddling-process which is connected in her mind with that refusal to acknowledge the body which she and her friends – and particularly Roger Fry – considered to be one of the main factors in keeping a false 'reverence' alive. When Orlando tries to write she finds that 'the pen ma[d]e one large lachrymose blot after another, or it ambled off, more alarmingly still, into mellifluous fluencies about early death and corruption'.[27] But children breathe an altogether different air, as Freud was to argue in *The Unconscious*: 'When it comes to someone else's death, the civilized man will carefully avoid speaking of such a possibility in the hearing of the person under sentence. Children alone disregard this restriction; they unashamedly threaten one another with the possibility of dying, and even go so far as to do the same thing to someone whom they love, as, for instance: "Dear Mummy, when you're dead I'll do this or that." '[28] Not only that, but they love playing at funerals, as Ann Thwaite observes of Frances Hodgson Burnett, who buried her doll in ceremony and strewed the grave with flowers.[29] Children find death intriguing rather than melancholy, and the more intriguing because of the secretive atmosphere in which adults envelop it. They can be immensely sentimental about their toys,[30] as well as about animals, and are not offended by either sentiment or lugubriousness. Their taste is not at all the same as an adult's. Margaret Gatty captures the difference when in *Aunt Sally's Life* (1865) she gives a child the chance to write a funeral oration:

> This is a doll. It was once a tree, and lived in a wood, and birds sat on the top of it and sang. Then came carpenters and cut it down, and made it into a doll, and (perhaps) a coffin as well. So when the doll's mistress is grown old enough to die, there will be the coffin ready for both, and then all the tree will come together again, and birds will sit outside the grave and sing.[31]

The matter-of-fact tone and joy in the birdsong as well as in the union of child and doll is as authentic as the practical concern which

makes a funeral a good play possibility. The child is not near enough
to death to find the prospect of popping into the coffin with a
favourite doll daunting in the way that an adult would.
Nevertheless Gatty wrings a good deal of pathos out of the tale
because the doll's owner does die in childhood. The doll, however,
survives three burials in lusty sort, providing her different
protectors with splendid funereal entertainment. When Rumer
Godden published *The Dolls' House* in 1947 she drew on Gatty's story
in her description of Tottie, the doll who was one hundred years old:

> How strange that a little farthing doll should last so long. Tottie
> was made of wood and it was good wood. She liked to think
> sometimes of the tree of whose wood she was made, of its
> strength and of the sap that ran through it and made it bud and
> put out leaves every spring and summer, that kept it standing
> through the winter storms and wind. 'A little, a very little of that
> tree is in me,' said Tottie, 'I am a little of that tree.' She liked to
> think of it.[32]

The hundred years which have elapsed since Gatty's tale cause the
wooden doll's permanence to appear in a less graveyard package,
but that is dedicated by an adult's sensibility, not a child's.

The disjunction between a child's taste and an adult's is
beautifully captured in Penelope Lively's *A Stitch in Time* (1976), in
which the child Maria visits a church and pauses in front of a
Victorian memorial plaque:

> A lady, much draped in white marble, reclined upon a marble
> sofa. Across her lap stretched a boy of about ten, with a nightdress
> on, his eyes closed. He had a lock of marble hair across his
> forehead and a most angelic expression. The lady, though, on
> closer inspection, could be seen to be weeping white marble tears.
> On the other side of her were clustered very fat cherubs, also
> weeping.
> ' "Erected by his Grieving Mother," ' read Mrs Lucas, ' "In
> Ever-Loving Memory ..." What a ghastly piece of work.' She
> moved away to look at the font.
> 'I think it's beautiful,' said Maria, very quietly, too quietly for
> anyone to hear. Her eyes pricked with not unenjoyable tears – the
> kind of tears prompted by a sad book. She had sometimes thought
> herself of dying young. In moments of extreme resentment

MRS. BLACKAMOOR'S GRAVE.

8 Mrs Blackamoor's Grave (from Margaret Gatty, *Aunt Sally's Life*, 1865)

against her parents she had relished the thought of them weeping over a pathetic (but extremely grand) little tomb in some enormous cemetery, feeling sorry that they had been so cruel to her.[33]

The story is not only about Maria, but also about Harriet, the little girl of a hundred years ago who still seems to be playing on the swing in that Victorian house in Lyme Regis, and around whom Maria builds up a Victorian children's book fantasy of early death which turns out to be only fantasy: Harriet's little dog died but not Harriet. The child's enjoyment of cultivated lugubriousness is measured against adult repudiation of it.

The mood evoked, however fleetingly, by Mrs Gatty parallels the change of spirit which had prompted the protests of Bacon and Montaigne against funereal flummery. When the Cuckoo in Molesworth's *The Cuckoo Clock* (1877) shows Griselda pictures of her grandmother Sybilla's life and early death, no religious or moral lessons are pointed. The child finds the scene sad but natural:

> One more picture.
> Griselda looked again. She saw before her a country road in full summer time; the sun was shining, the birds were singing, the trees covered with their bright green leaves – everything appeared happy and joyful. But at last in the distance she saw, slowly approaching, a group of a few people, all walking together, carrying in their centre something long and narrow, which, though the black cloth covering it was almost hidden by the white flowers with which it was thickly strewn, Griselda knew to be a coffin.
> It was a funeral procession, and in the place of chief mourner, with pale, set face, walked the same young man whom Griselda had last seen dancing with the girl Sybilla in the great saloon.
> The sad group passed slowly out of sight; but as it disappeared there fell upon the ear the sounds of sweet music, lovelier far than she had heard before – lovelier than the magic cuckoo's most lovely songs – and somehow, in the music, it seemed to the child's fancy there were mingled the soft strains of a woman's voice.
> 'It is Sybilla singing,' thought Griselda dreamily, and with that she fell asleep again.[34]

The dead person becomes a part of Griselda's consciousness in the same way that the birds and the trees are vivid to the child in *Aunt Sally's Life*, making death easily assimilable to a known reality.

When Tom Sawyer appears with his disreputable friends in the middle of his own funeral service, the tender sentiments which have been worked up for the occasion are rendered ridiculous:

> As the service proceeded, the clergyman drew such pictures of the graces, the winning ways, and the rare promise of the lost lads, that every soul there, thinking he recognized these pictures, felt a pang in remembering that he had persistently blinded himself to them always before, and had as persistently seen only faults and flaws in the poor boys. The minister related many a touching incident in the lives of the departed, too, which illustrated their sweet, generous natures, and the people could easily see, now, how noble and beautiful those episodes were, and remembered with grief that at the time they occurred they had seemed rank rascalities, well deserving the cowhide.[35]

The scene plays out the childish fantasy, indulged to the full by Tom and his friends, that the adult world will be sorry for its mean behaviour when they are dead. For the adult reader the comedy is somewhat marred by an awareness of Aunt Polly's real grief, but no such qualms afflict a child, for whom the entry of Tom into the church carries the Dionysiac exhilaration of Toad's triumphant escape from prison, disguised as a washerwoman, in *The Wind in the Willows*, or of the children's flying in *Peter Pan*. In *Huckleberry Finn* Peter Wilks's funeral is taken over by the drama of a dog chasing a rat in the cellar below, which culminates in the undertaker's killing the dog. This incident provides relief for Huck who observes that 'the funeral sermon was very good, but pison long and tiresome; and then the king he shoved in and got off some of his usual rubbage, and at last the job was through, and the undertaker begun to sneak up on the coffin with his screw-driver'. As Huck has hidden the deceased's money in the coffin along with the corpse he 'was in a sweat then'.[36] By a happy accident of the pen which anticipates Oswald Bastable, funeral obsequies become in Huck's account 'funeral orgies'. In both books the drama of death descends into pantomime.

When Mary Lennox in Frances Hodgson Burnett's *The Secret Garden* (1911) finds Colin lying ill in the great house with a hundred rooms, most of which are locked up, she is taken aback by his certainty that he is going to die:

> 'How do you know?' said Mary unsympathetically. She didn't like the way he had of talking about dying. She did not feel very sympathetic. She felt rather as if he almost boasted about it.[37]

One can almost hear the echo of Montaigne: 'We deeme our death to be some great matter, and which passeth not so easily, nor without a solemn consultation of the Starres.'[38] The notion that he will die young gives Colin a spurious sense of power which Mary is quick to relocate in the adults who allow him such self-indulgence:

> 'Oh, I've heard it ever since I remember,' he answered crossly. 'They are always whispering about it and thinking I don't notice. They wish I would, too.'
> Mistress Mary felt quite contrary. She pinched her lips together.
> 'If they wished I would,' she said, 'I wouldn't. Who wishes you would?'
> 'The servants – and of course Dr Craven, because he would get Misselthwaite and be rich instead of poor. He daren't say so, but he always looks cheerful when I am worse. When I had typhoid fever his face got quite fat. I think my father wishes it, too.'
> 'I don't believe he does,' said Mary quite obstinately.
> That made Colin turn and look at her again.
> 'Don't you?' he said.
> And then he lay back on his cushion and was still, as if he were thinking. And there was quite a long silence. Perhaps they were both of them thinking strange things children do not usually think of.

Both children are shadowed by death. The book opens with cholera striking the Lennox family in India, and Mary, the plain daughter of a beautiful woman, forgotten in a bungalow where only a little snake remains alive. Colin explains his own situation to Mary: 'My mother died when I was born and it makes him wretched to look at me. He thinks I don't know, but I've heard people talking. He almost hates me.'[39] The air the children breathe is heavy with adult inability to come to terms with death.

In an earlier book, *In the Closed Room* (1904), Burnett allowed herself a prolonged meditation on the dead child, in the manner of the traditional Victorian children's book. A working-class couple and their little daughter take care of a great house in which, unknown to them, another little girl has died, her parents having gone away to recover from their grief. The working-class child is able to go through the door of the closed room and play with the little ghost, with her toys, and with her roof garden, in which the touch of the mysterious ghost child's hand can make 'the leaves . . . stir and uncurl and become fresh and tender again . . . roses were nodding, blooming on the stems'.[40] The fascination which Burnett evinces with the secret place in which the dead survive, and withered flowers come to life again, prefigures *The Secret Garden*, published seven years later, in which the lugubrious Victorian death story has been transformed into a child's celebration of living. The author rejected in the story of Mary Lennox and Colin Craven that adult fascination with death which she had allowed herself to indulge in, in the earlier story, as a means of consolation after the death of her own son Lionel. Burnett found in herself the creative spirit to turn away from the conventional solace of the bereaved woman writer in order to produce *The Secret Garden*, which proclaims, as Montaigne had done, and as Thoby Stephen had urged his sisters, that it is life that matters. Mary Lennox accosts Colin:

'See here,' she said. 'Don't let us talk about dying; I don't like it. Let us talk about living. Let us talk and talk about Dickon. And then we will look at your pictures.'

It was the best thing she could have said. To talk about Dickon meant to talk about the moor and about the cottage and the fourteen people who lived in it on sixteen shillings a week – and the children who got fat on the moor grass like the wild ponies. And about Dickon's mother – and the skipping-rope – and the moor with the sun on it – and about pale green points sticking up out of the black sod. And it was all so alive that Mary talked more than she had ever talked before – and Colin both talked and listened as he had never done either before. And they both began to laugh over nothings as children will when they are happy together. And they laughed so that in the end they were making as much noise as if they had been two ordinary healthy natural ten-year-old creatures – instead of a hard, little, unloving girl and a sickly boy who believed that he was going to die.

The laughter is not just laughter at the theatricality of adult grief, but the easy laughter of children left on their own.

Mary Lennox and Colin Craven are both spoilt children in the traditional Rousseauesque sense of indulged, but they are also spoiled in a different sense. They are the victims of adult self-centredness which keeps gardens locked, and children cooped up in grand rooms with foolish servants to satisfy their whims without satisfying their needs. The clergyman's wife with whom Mary boards before going to England remarks: 'Her mother was such a pretty creature. She had a very pretty manner, too, and Mary has the most unattractive ways I ever saw in a child.' Her husband retorts: 'Perhaps if her mother had carried her pretty face and her pretty manners oftener into the nursery Mary might have learned some pretty ways too.'[41] The moral admonition directed not at children but at their parents recalls Day's *Sandford and Merton* (Burnett's Dickon is to some extent modelled on Harry Sandford), but Burnett is more forthright in her redirection of criticism away from the child and onto the adult.

The Secret Garden owes its imaginative intensity and mellowness to Burnett's reworking of rich literary sources in the light of deeply meditated personal experience. She seems in this book to have had a sense, as George Eliot did when reading Charlotte Yonge, of the incomplete narrative which cries out for further exploration. The two books which lie in the subsoil of *The Secret Garden* are Elizabeth Gaskell's *North and South* (1855) and Mary Molesworth's *An Enchanted Garden* (1892), although Burnett also owed some of the atmosphere of her story to Oscar Wilde.

North and South opens with the wedding of Margaret Hale's beautiful but feather-brained society cousin, Edith, to the handsome Captain Lennox, with whom she departs to Corfu. Burnett transports her own similar pair in *The Secret Garden* to British India and gives Edith an unwanted plain child to cramp her style, asking what such a woman might make of the demands of motherhood. The answer is Mary Lennox, a little yellow shrimp, sullen and sallow, spoilt silly by a succession of Ayahs. Molesworth's *An Enchanted Garden* tells the story of an old garden to which a robin shows two children a way through the wall, although the tale ends sadly and abruptly with their being whisked away to a new place and never seeing the garden again, a moment which remains mercifully free from allegory, but which spurs Burnett to create a counter-myth in which children can re-enter a garden adults have forsaken. The magic and elusive old caretaker of the now vanished house to which the enchanted garden belonged tells the children of two sisters who may each have a wish, but whose wishes will not come true until they both wish the same third thing – the other's success. In *The Secret Garden* Burnett refocuses Molesworth's lesson about unselfishness, with the consequence that adult selfishness rather than childhood peevishness bears the brunt of the argument as it does also in Wilde's story 'The Selfish Giant'. The giant refuses to let the poor children play in his garden and is punished by perpetual winter. Burnett, a Christian Scientist, gave her children a garden more full of natural magic than either Molesworth's or Wilde's, a place Gertude Jekyll would have recognised and tended as eagerly as the garden she created for Roger Fry at Durbins.[42] Burnett criticises a whole realm of fiction in which adults battened like parasites on the dying child.

Lawrence's *Sons and Lovers*, a book which at various points in the narrative enters Burnett's emotional climate, depicts the death of Mrs Morel's first son, William, from brain fever, that disease which has a particularly Victorian ring. The coffin is brought back home and laid in state:

> The family was alone in the parlour with the great polished box. William, when laid out, was six feet four inches long. Like a monument lay the bright brown, ponderous coffin. Paul thought it would never be got out of the room again. His mother was stroking the polished wood.
> They buried him on the Monday in the little cemetery on the hillside that looks over the fields at the big church and the houses. It was sunny, and the white chrysanthemums frilled themselves in the warmth.
> Mrs Morel could not be persuaded, after this, to talk and take her old bright interest in life. She remained shut off. All the way home in the train she said to herself: 'If only it would have been me!'

The withdrawal from life and absorption in the dead recalls Archibald Craven, wasting with grief after his wife's death in *The Secret Garden*. The same morbid inability to cast off the death scene lay in the background of *Peter Pan*, with Barrie's mother always mourning a dead boy, always trying to remake the living one in his image. In *Sons and Lovers* Mrs Morel is jolted back into life by Paul's illness – it was so nearly another death-bed: 'Paul was in bed for seven weeks. He got up white and fragile. His father had bought him a pot of scarlet and gold tulips. They used to flame in the window in the March sunshine as he sat on the sofa chattering to his mother. The two knitted together in perfect intimacy. Mrs Morel's life now rooted itself in Paul's.'[43] The recovery of Paul and Mrs Morel might be Lawrence's retort to *Peter Pan*, as *The Secret Garden* is perhaps Burnett's. The moment when Colin takes his father, Archibald Craven, into the garden at the end of the book anticipates Lawrence in celebrating natural life:

> The place was a wilderness of autumn gold and purple and violet blue and flaming scarlet, and on every side were sheaves of late lilies standing together – lilies which were white or white and ruby. . . . He looked round and round.
> 'I thought it would be dead,' he said.
> 'Mary thought so at first,' said Colin. 'But it came alive.'[44]

Burnett's insistence that Colin's mother remains with him in the garden grows from her own belief, which she tried to convey even in *In the Closed Room*, that the dead stay with the living: 'I am not thinking of your dearests as conventional angels with flapping wings or as spiritualistic creatures lifting tables and cushions about – I am thinking of them as real – real – as themselves.'[45]

When Alice takes to instructing the Duchess on the movement of the earth the response from that dignitary is one many children might have liked to make to Anna Barbauld: [Alice] ' "You see the earth takes twenty-four hours to turn upon its axis –" "Talking of axes," said the Duchess, "chop off her head!" ' (*AW*, 84). Or at the Mad Hatter's tea party:

> 'Well, I'd hardly finished the first verse,' said the Hatter, 'when the Queen bawled out "He's murdering the time! Off with his head!" '
> 'How dreadfully savage!' exclaimed Alice. (*AW*, 99)

It did not take long for Lewis Carroll's irreverence about death to penetrate children's books. If the death of Beth in *Good Wives* is one of the most touching in the old tradition, already in *What Katy Did* three years later Katy Carr is not managing to be a lovely little mamma to all her brothers and sisters, despite the death-bed charge

9   'It Made Her Look Spidery' (from *The Adventures of Huckleberry Finn*)

and the pious model of Margaret in Charlotte Yonge's *The Daisy Chain* (1856). Katy's Aunt Izzie may be the first of an illustrious line of people who died quietly in the night, even if she is not put in brackets. Mentally, as far as the book is concerned, the death is in a bracket, because its purpose is to show Katy rising to the challenge of doing the housekeeping efficiently despite her disability.

In the Southern family with whom Huckleberry Finn stays Miss Emmeline Grangerford died at fifteen, leaving a lot of crayon pictures of mourning figures, all ladies, clad in black, lamenting lost lovers and dead birds, with captions such as 'Shall I Never See Thee More Alas?' and 'I Shall Never Hear Thy Sweet Chirrup More Alas!' and 'And Art Thou Gone Yes Thou Art Gone Alas!' One drawing remained unfinished at her death, in which the young lady has six arms, because the artist was going to scratch out the less successful pairs but 'she died before she got her mind made up'. Huck finds that the pictures give him 'the fan-tods', and although everyone regrets Emmeline's passing: 'I reckoned, what with her disposition, she was having a better time in the graveyard.' Emmeline's enjoyment of death had indeed been spoilt by her one failure to get her 'tribute' to the corpse's relatives 'before he was cold'.[46] On that occasion the undertaker had beaten her to it because she had been unable to find a word to rhyme with the deceased's name, which was Whistler. The idea of murdering a rhyme had done for poor Emmeline just as murdering the time had almost finished off the Mad Hatter.

With irreverence towards death in children's books comes a new reticence. Whereas Charlotte Yonge in *The Daisy Chain* presents death as educative, E. Nesbit believes only that it is a fact of life. Edwardian versions of Sherwood's *The Fairchild Family* and of Catherine Sinclair's *Holiday House* omit the improving death scenes.[47] In Nesbit's books there are things that the reader has no right to pry into and that the author will not tell. Oswald in *The Story of the Treasure Seekers* informs the reader smartly: 'Our Mother is dead, and if you think we don't care because I don't tell you much about her you only show that you do not understand people at all.' Just occasionally Oswald mentions his mother – she would have liked the garden in *The Wouldbegoods*. She had planted seeds with him and Dora: the others were too little to remember it. Once in *The Treasure Seekers* he and Alice are made to feel loss. They try to sell their money-making commission sherry 'Castilian Amoroso' to a lady collecting for dead sailors. Having taken a swig of their much sweetened sherry she is outraged, and, accusing them of trying to poison her, threatens to write to their mother. Alice, almost crying, begs her not to, as it will make their father unhappy:

> 'What do you mean, you silly child?' said the lady, looking quite bright and interested. 'Why doesn't your Father like your Mother to have letters – eh?'
> And Alice said, "*Oh*, you .....!" and began to cry, and bolted out of the room.
> Then I said, 'Our Mother is dead, and will you please go away now?'
> The lady looked at me a minute, and then she looked quite different, and she said, 'I'm very sorry. I didn't know. Never mind about the wine. I daresay your little sister meant it kindly.' And she looked round the room just like the butcher had done. Then she said again, 'I didn't know – I'm very sorry ...'
> So I said, 'Don't mention it,' and shook hands with her, and let her out. Of course we couldn't have asked her to buy the wine after what she'd said. But I think she was not a bad sort of person. I do like a person to say they're sorry when they ought to be – especially a grown-up. They do it so seldom. I suppose that's why we think so much of it.
> But Alice and I didn't feel jolly for ever so long afterwards. And when I went back into the dining-room I saw how different it was from when Mother was here, and we are different, and Father is different, and nothing is like it was. I am glad I am not made to think about it every day.
> I went and found Alice, and told her what the lady had said, and when she had finished crying we put away the bottle and said we would not try to sell any more to people who came. And we did not tell the others – we only said the lady did not buy any – but we went up on the Heath, and some soldiers went by and there was a Punch-and-Judy show, and when we came back we were better.[48]

The consolation offered is secular. It never occurs to the children to take refuge in any kind of religious faith; but rather in the consolations of childhood, which Nesbit remembered more vividly and authentically than almost any other writer except Frances Hodgson Burnett: the soldiers and the Punch-and-Judy show. The passage is genuine in its lack of analysis of feeling. Children feel acutely, but they have no interest in analysing their feelings and do not know how to do it, as De Quincey points out when he recalls the dire effects on his childhood of his elder sister's death: 'The reader must not forget, in reading this and other passages, that, though a child's feelings are spoken of, it is not the child who speaks. I decipher what the child only felt in ciphers.'[49]

Irreverence about death is for the new generation of writers after Lewis Carroll an act of defiance of authority,[50] whether of great men, parents, or writers of books. This spirit erupts in Woolf's writings, as in her recollection of a visit to Scott's grave: the novelist reposed 'in a caddy made of chocolate blancmange' with his wife beside him 'covered with the same chocolate slab'. After Hardy's funeral she noted: 'I doubt the capacity of the human animal for being dignified in ceremony. . . . Over all this broods for me some uneasy sense of change and mortality and how partings are deaths.'[51] Woolf wrote to Violet Dickinson on Christmas Day 1906, just one month after her brother Thoby's death: 'I am reading now a book by Renan called his Memories of Childhood [*Cahiers de Jeunesse*, 1906]: O my word it is beautiful – like the chime of silver bells.'[52] In that work Renan declared that when his mother died 'it was the memory of their shared deprivations which were most poignant to him: "I had been happy with her, I had been *poor* with her." '[53] Virginia Woolf, like Burnett, Barrie, Lawrence, Renan, and innumerable others saw in the child's vision a way of evading the unreality in which the living shroud the dead.

III   MRS RAMSAY'S BRACKETS

In *The Voyage Out, Jacob's Room* and *To the Lighthouse* Woolf explores the question of how to kill off the book's central consciousness[54] without simultaneously killing off both writer and reader. Freud wrote in *The Unconscious* (1914–16), in a section entitled 'Our Attitude to Death': 'We . . . seek in the world of fiction, in literature and in the theatre compensation for what has been lost in life. There we still find people who know how to die – who indeed, even manage to kill someone else. There alone too the condition can be fulfilled which makes it possible for us to reconcile ourselves with death: namely, that behind all the vicissitudes of life we should still be able to preserve a life intact. . . . In the realm of fiction we find the plurality of lives which we need. We die with the hero with whom we have identified ourselves; yet we survive him, and are ready to die again just as safely with another hero'.[55] Woolf as artist returned constantly to the problem of how both writer and reader may survive the fictional dead.

The author as surrogate god has even greater power over life and death than that assigned by Freud to the reader. Flora Thompson in *Lark Rise to Candleford* recalls her mother's gifts as a story-teller. On one occasion she grew impatient with the children's demands for a further episode in a serial, 'and startled them by saying, "and then he came to the sea and fell in and was eaten by a shark, and that was the end of poor Jimmy", and the end of their story too, for what further developments were possible?'[56] The author's dispatching of characters impresses the reader with a display of authorial power, but offers her no right of protest, which is why Joel Chandler Harris's *Uncle Remus* (1881) seemed such an innovation. The child listener points out to Uncle Remus that he has arbitrarily resuscitated Wolf who is dead, at which the story-teller fetches a whip to beat the listener into submission and is only melted by the child's tears.[57] When Zangwill reviewed *Jude the Obscure* in the *Pall Mall Magazine* in 1896 he complained that when Father Time 'murders the two other children and then himself, I find myself more on the brink of laughter than of horror'.[58] If the author's disposing of his creatures' lives is too palpably contrived the story becomes the cautionary tale of which Hilaire Belloc wrote in 1908:

> And is it True? It is not True.
> And if it were it wouldn't do,
> . . .
> Because if things were really so,
> You would have perished long ago,
> And I would not have lived to write
> The noble lines that meet your sight.[59]

The author must be careful how he doles out death or he will find, like Marvell's Mower, that he has mown himself down as well as the grass.

In the survival which the work of fiction offers to the reader, the author and her characters are implicated in more complex ways than Freud's simple analysis suggests. Virginia Woolf recognised that interrelation in 'The Patron and the Crocus' when she claimed that 'to know whom to write for is to know how to write. . . . They are twins indeed, one dying if the other dies, one flourishing if the other flourishes.'[60] She provides carefully for the reader's conciousness in each of her books, but it was not until *To the Lighthouse* that she found a completely convincing way of dealing out death to her central characters while allowing herself and her readers to survive.[61]

At the beginning of *The Voyage Out* the reader experiences the world of the novel through Helen Ambrose, but by the time Rachel Vinrace has decided to stay with Helen rather than complete the voyage with her father, the reader's consciousness has become identified with hers rather than with the older woman's. Up till this point Helen – modelled on Vanessa Stephen[62] – has been set up as a substitute parent through whom Willoughby, the real parent, is tried and found wanting. Helen Ambrose, forty and wise, takes Rachel out of a Victorian story-book childhood with two maiden aunts, in which she trails round Richmond Park like Mary Lennox at Misselthwaite Manor, into a room of her own peopled by Meredith's *Diana of the Crossways* and Ibsen's Nora in *A Dolls' House*. When Rachel recalls for Hewet her aunts' decorous home her memory explodes in violent protest: 'All her rages had been against them; it was their world with its four meals, its punctuality, and servants on the stairs at half-past ten, that she examined so closely and wanted so vehemently to smash to atoms.' However, once Rachel has entered into Hewet's orbit, Helen, who had helped to rescue her from that claustrophobic setting, becomes summarily redundant. Her sympathy is replaced by his, her experience of the world surpassed by Miss Allan's, and her nonconformity, compared with Evelyn's, becomes conventionality. As she recedes from Rachel's consciousness, so she ceases to represent the reader's interests in the novel.

Rachel has some of the qualities of Lewis Carroll's Alice: literal where others are literary, solid in a world of strangely wispy and grotesque human beings, tasting ginger because she has never had it before, and tempted to take a little swig of crème de menthe out of a green bottle Miss Allan has had for twenty-six years. It almost might make her shrink – or perhaps grow? There is even a moment when she and Hewet seem exposed by the looking-glass world: 'It chilled them to see themselves in the glass, for instead of being vast and indivisible they were really very small and separate, the size of the glass leaving a large space for the reflection of other things.' When Rachel falls ill it is a real Victorian child's malady with delirium and crises and googly old night nurses. Helen dwindles to nothing: she is no longer anything but a voice to comment on Rachel's illness. Rachel's fever is a strange phantasmagoria, a treacle well and a pool of tears, and the bottom of the sea where they teach reeling and writhing: 'She fell into a deep pool of sticky water, which eventually closed over her head. . . . While all her tormentors thought that she was dead, she was not dead, but curled up at the bottom of the sea. There she lay, sometimes seeing darkness, sometimes light, while every now and then someone turned her over at the bottom of the sea.' The description prefigures Woolf's own death by drowning, while also suggesting the madness which engulfed her during the writing of the book. Finally Rachel dies: 'This was death. It was nothing; it was to cease to breathe. It was happiness, it was perfect happiness. They had now what they had always wanted to have, the union which had been impossible while they lived.' Hewet, with a gesture which anticipates Mr Ramsay's, rushes from the room with outstretched arms.

In the remaining pages of the book Rachel's death is recounted to various acquaintances who react, as Mrs Paley does, with Ibsenesque inconsequence:

'Dead?' she said vaguely. 'Miss Vinrace dead? Dear me ... that's very sad. But I don't at the moment remember which she was.'

Mrs Elliot and Mrs Thornbury are too busy with their knitting to think of anything else, and Helen never appears again. The closing words of the book suggest a fading into unconsciousness, as at the end of *Through the Looking-Glass*, a resolving of narrator, narrative and reader into a ball of wool, a kitten and sleep: 'All these voices sounded gratefully in St John's ears as he lay half-asleep, and yet vividly conscious of everything around him. Across his eyes passed a procession of objects, black and indistinct, the figures of people picking up their books, their cards, their balls of wool, their work-baskets, and passing him one after another on their way to bed.'[63] It is almost as if the reader had dreamt the book.

In dispensing with Helen Virginia Woolf obliterates the parental role which she represents, which although not domineering, is relentlessly patronising. The reader is glad to be shot of her complacent knowledge of the world. Both Rachel and the reader have more real freedom without her, meeting the author within the shared consciousness of equals. But when Rachel dies Virginia

Woolf audaciously deprives herself, as author, of control, by refusing to accommodate Rachel to the conventions of the novel. In the fictional models to which Woolf relates the book – the children's story, Jane Austen, *Alice* – endings complete expectations. *Alice* contains nothing more violent than an awakening from sleep. But *The Voyage Out* disrupts its own pattern, as if James in *The Portrait of a Lady* had polished off Isabel instead of Ralph Touchett. If the central

consciousness is gone, how can there be a novel? What has happened to the reader? Woolf has made Rachel a reader of the book's inmates and events. When she dies, the author's medium – Woolf's word – is annihilated, but the reader expires too, because the life which the author gave her in reading the novel was inseparable from that of Rachel, who also read its world. The author's determination to prize open the closed shell of the novel and let something else in results in a curious void. We do not, as

Freud lightly observed, identify with Rachel Vinrace and survive her through the plurality of selves. The ground on which we stand, the territory of the novel, ceases to be solid when she ceases to be.

There are two real deaths in *Jacob's Room* (1919), despite the fact that only Jacob physically dies, for here also Woolf kills off the reader's representative, Betty Flanders, who at the beginning of the book provides the consciousness through which the reader enters the action. Betty Flanders is weeping not, like Helen Ambrose, for a parting from her children, but for death itself, her husband's: 'The entire bay quivered; the lighthouse wobbled. . . . Tears made all the dahlias in her garden undulate in red waves.' The landscape refracted through tears looks like a Van Gogh painting.[64] The child Jacob is compelling because presented through the medium of his mother's melancholy and passionate solicitude for him. But once Woolf moves him out of the circle of that intense gaze he becomes a dull young man at Cambridge, despite her attempts to make him fascinating – attempts courageously abandoned in *The Waves*, where Percival is allowed to be conventional, a hero whose heroism exists solely in other people's adoration of him. Jacob cannot stand on his own without Betty Flanders, any more than Percival can exist apart from his friends' consciousness of him. Betty herself remains for the reader the most compelling person in the book, waiting, like Christina Light in James's *Roderick Hudson*,[65] for another book in which her unused energy can be expended. Betty's spirit is subsumed in Mrs Ramsay.

In *To the Lighthouse* the death of the central character, Mrs Ramsay, does not destroy the fiction. Woolf, while investing her own vision as author in Mrs Ramsay's consciousness, creates alternatives to it[66] not only in other adults, but in the generation which will outlive Mrs Ramsay.

In the first part of the book the Ramsays control their world. It will rain and stop the outing to the lighthouse, states Mr Ramsay, provoking unawares the suppressed violence registered by Rachel in the earlier novel:

Had there been an axe handy, a poker, or any weapon that would have gashed a hole in his father's breast and killed him, there and then, James would have seized it. Such were the extremes of emotion that Mr Ramsay excited in his children's breasts by his mere presence; standing, as now, lean as a knife, narrow as the blade of one, grinning sarcastically, not only with the pleasure of disillusioning his son and casting ridicule upon his wife, who was ten thousand times better in every way than he was (James thought), but also with some secret conceit at his own accuracy of judgement.

By contrast Mrs Ramsay is fluid: 'It may rain.' But she too loves power and exercises it with the same ruthlessness as the Fisherman's Wife in the Grimm's fairy tale which she reads aloud to James. She matchmakes, pairing off successfully Paul and Minta, and planning to marry Lily to William Bankes. She soothes her husband; she creates myths so that the skull and the green shawl will not frighten Cam but will remain there to satisfy James. At the dinner party she is not simply a hostess, but the author of a scene, making all the parts knit together like the stocking that she is knitting for the lighthouse-keeper's child. The reader enters into her consciousness but also, like Lily Briscoe, watches her manipulations: 'There was something frightening about her. She was irresistible. Always she got her own way in the end, Lily thought. Now she had brought this off – Paul and Minta, one might suppose, were engaged. Mr Bankes was dining here. She put a spell on them all, by wishing so simply, so directly; . . . Mrs Ramsay, Lily felt, . . . having brought it all about, somehow laughed, led her victims, Lily felt, to the altar.'

Mrs Ramsay's dreams for her family are inordinate: 'She would have liked always to have had a baby. She was happiest carrying one in her arms. Then people might say she was tyrannical, domineering, masterful, if they chose; she did not mind.' She does not want their childhood, and her own mastery of it, to end: 'Why must they grow up and lose it all?' Her power must be prolonged and extended like that of the Fisherman's Wife in Grimm's story to whom the Flounder gave all her wishes, except when she wished to be God, and then she found herself back where she started:

> She turned the page; there were only a few lines more, so that she would finish the story, though it was past bed-time. It was getting late. . . .
> But she did not let her voice change in the least as she finished the story, and added, shutting the book, and speaking the last words as if she had made them up herself, looking into James's eyes: 'And there they are living still at this very time.'
> 'And that's the end,' she said, and she saw in his eyes, as the

interest of the story died away in them, something else take its
place; something wondering, pale, like the reflection of a light,
which at once made him gaze and marvel. Turning, she looked
across the bay, and there, sure enough, coming regularly across
the waves first two quick strokes and then one long steady stroke,
was the light of the Lighthouse. It had been lit.

The beam of the lighthouse reminds Mrs Ramsay of the limits of her
own power to create the reality James wants: 'She was certain that
he was thinking, we are not going to the Lighthouse tomorrow; and
she thought, he will remember that all his life.'[67] The power of the
woman in the fairy tale came to an end even before Mrs Ramsay
closed the book on her. In the draft of *To the Lighthouse* Mrs Ramsay
reads James the story of the Three Dwarfs and Woolf has added a
pencilled note in brackets '(the strain of having told lies)' and relates
this to Mrs Ramsay's 'not being quite sure of the entire truth of what
she said'. Woolf obviously searched for a fairy story which would
underline Mrs Ramsay's role as an inventor of plots for other
peoples' lives: the original choice centres on fictions and lying. The
later decision to use 'The Fisherman's Wife' still underwrites Mrs
Ramsay's lust for power, but relates it more precisely to the author's
role because the woman in the story wants to be God.[68] In the final
version the reading-aloud takes much longer and is given more
importance, but the changing of the story is significant of a major
change in the presentation of Mrs Ramsay. In the first draft she is set
at a disadvantage – in a position of weakness, almost as suppliant –
in relation to her husband and the other characters, but in the final
version has become the powerful and magical figure conjured up by
Grimm's fairy tale.

Mrs Ramsay's dinner party marks both the height and the end of
her power because she cannot avert her own death or arrest the time
which will carry the children into adult life, any more than she can
control the elements: 'It was necessary now to carry everything a
step further. With her foot on the threshold she waited a moment
longer in a scene which was vanishing even as she looked, and then,
as she moved and took Minta's arm and left the room, it changed, it
shaped itself differently; it had become, she knew, giving one last
look at it over her shoulder, already the past.' She moves into the
drawing-room and she and her husband read, he in Scott's novel
The Antiquary, and she in Shakespeare's sonnets, while she reviews
the day: 'The children being awake; Charles Tansley waking them

with his book's falling – oh no, that she had invented.' Even in memory she fabricates. And the stocking is too short: ' "No," she said, flattening the stocking out upon her knee, "I shan't finish it." '[69]

The end of the story is beyond her; it lies not only in Lily's consciousness but in the next generation. Woolf wrote on 15 January 1926 at the beginning of her revision of *To the Lighthouse*: 'The idea has grown in the interval since I wrote the beginning. ~~It~~ The presence of the 8 children, undifferentiated, should be important, to bring out the sense of life in opposition to fate – i.e. Waves, Lighthouse.' On the plan of the ten chapters she had written: 'We are handed on by our children.'[70] But the handing-on is not to the respectful descendants represented by Mrs Hilbery and Katharine in *Night and Day*. Even at the height of Mrs Ramsay's triumph at the dinner table the children, like those children in *The Golden Age*, have escaped and pass judgement on the Olympians:

> How odd to see them sitting there, in a row, her children, Jasper, Rose, Prue, Andrew, almost silent, but with some joke of their own going on, she guessed, from the twitching at their lips. It was something quite apart from everything else, something they were hoarding up to laugh over in their own room. It was not about their father, she hoped. No, she thought not. What was it, she wondered, sadly rather, for it seemed to her that they would laugh when she was not there. There was all that hoarded behind those rather set, still, mask-like faces, for they did not join in easily; they were like watchers, surveyors, a little raised or set apart from the grown-up people.[71]

In the draft the description of the children is longer and more explicit, reminding one of that original question asked by the child Virginia which Vanessa Bell had seen as the beginning of freedom: which parent did she like best? One of the children at the party experiences 'a spasm of merriment, of criticism (for why were old people so absurd?)'.[72] Mrs Ramsay cannot control the laughter, nor the subversive consciousness: it evades her, but in doing so it also survives her extinction.

It is only by being a child in her own book that Woolf as author can claim the triumph over time and death which Mrs Ramsay sees in her children, and her husband hopes for in his writing. For their daughter the life of the book is dependent on the child's capacity both to create it and to survive it. She wrote of *To the Lighthouse* that she described her parents from a child's point of view: 'How serene and gay even, their life reads to me: no mud: no whirlpools. And so human – with the children and the little hum and song of the nursery. But if I read as a contemporary I shall lose my child's vision and must stop.'[73] Although Mrs Ramsay seems to stand in for her author and control the world around her as the author controls the fiction, the author's power lies elsewhere. The eye which witnesses Mrs Ramsay's mastery is that of the child at the dinner table, a watcher ready to burst out laughing, whose consciousness will remain when she is gone. Woolf wrote: 'Until I was in the forties – I could settle the date by seeing when I wrote *To the Lighthouse*, but am too casual here to bother to do it – the presence of my mother obsessed me. I could hear her voice, see her, imagine what she would do or say as I went about my day's doings.' She explains: 'I wrote the book very quickly; and when it was written, I ceased to be obsessed by my mother. I no longer hear her voice; I do not see her.' She continues:

> I suppose that I did for myself what psycho-analysts do for their patients. I expressed some very long felt and deeply felt emotion. And in expressing it I explained it and then laid it to rest. But what is the meaning of 'explained' it? Why, because I described her and my feeling for her in that book, should my vision of her and my feelings for her become so much dimmer and weaker? Perhaps one of these days I shall hit on the reason; and if so, I will give it, but at the moment I will go on, describing what I can remember, for it may be true that what I remember of her now will weaken still further.[74]

This was not the first time that either she or Vanessa spoke of the book as having laid a ghost: 'Nessa enthusiastic – a sublime, almost upsetting spectacle. She says it is an amazing portrait of mother; a supreme portrait painter; has lived in it; found the rising of the dead almost painful.' But when Woolf began the book she had thought of it more in terms of being about her father. The germ of it was a mental image of his sitting in the boat, like Scott on his way to the Bell Rock, reciting 'We perished'. Remembering his birthday in her diary, his daughter seemed to think of the book as an exorcism of his spirit as much as of her mother's:

Father's birthday. He would have been 96, 96, yes, today; and could have been 96, like other people one has known: but mercifully was not. His life would have entirely ended mine. What would have happened? No writing, no books; – inconceivable.

I used to think of him and mother daily: but writing *To the Lighthouse* laid them in my mind.[75]

The act of writing has given Woolf the power over her parents which Mrs Ramsay's capacity to fabricate allowed her to exert over her children. Woolf evades both parents by becoming their author and exploring the limits of their control of the world of which she herself was a part. She gazes at it with wonder and suppressed laughter. If James wants to chop off his father's head, Cam thinks only, like Alice at the Caucus Race, that the scene is ridiculously solemn.

E. Nesbit wrote a story about dragons in a book which are let out by a little boy's opening the pages, but at the end are carefully replaced within those restraining covers, with the author's conclusion that that is the best place for a dragon.[76] Virginia Woolf closes the first part of *To the Lighthouse*, 'The Window', on her parents, leaving them, like the figures on the Grecian Urn, arrested in a moment of ritual triumph, at their own dinner table. But that is the end of their reign: the stocking is too short and the outing to the Lighthouse is deferred. In the next section, 'Time Passes', Woolf, by a dramatic speeding-up of sequence, destroys her own perfect fiction, just as Shakespeare destroys his own courtly comedy in the last act of *Love's Labour's Lost* when the Princess hears of her father's death. The end of the play, with its direction either to players or audience: 'You that way: we this way', which Woolf echoed at the end of her story 'The String Quartet' – ' "Good night, good night. You go this way?" / "Alas. I go that" '[77] – provides a model for the author's dismissal of Mrs Ramsay in death and of Mr Ramsay to a bygone generation: 'An old man, very sad, reading his book.' The letters which Woolf wrote after her father's death – letters which were followed by a severe breakdown (as also afflicted her after her mother's death) – show how deeply she needed to rid herself of a tie so close[78] that it dominated her until she found her own way of ending the story. In containing that power within the book, letting the book live, grow and finish independently of the Ramsays, Woolf found a way of dealing death to her characters while creating survival for both herself as author, and for the reader. The writing of

10   Mr and Mrs Leslie Stephen and Virginia

To the Lighthouse restores to the dead a place where they can be themselves, untouched, like Keats's figures, by time and change. Mrs Ramsay knew that the children would laugh when she was gone, but in that laughter she returns from the unreality of death to a fictional space in which she can live, encounter the living, and be laid to rest when the book is closed.

5

The Medium of Art

I LANGUAGE

The Waves carries to its logical extreme Twain's determination to have no plot and no moral,[1] as well as Stevenson's insistence that the writer's true calling is to words as medium not as meaning. That belief had dominated the experience of Lewis Carroll's Alice, for whom words are a form of play: 'Alice had not the slightest idea what Latitude was, or Longitude either, but she thought they were nice grand words to say' (*AW*, 27). Even the disposition of individual letters can be arbitrary: 'Do cats eat bats?' or 'Do bats eat cats?' (*AW*, 28). Woolf repudiates in *The Waves* the author's right to construct out of language a shaped vision of the future such as she allowed to Mrs Ramsay in *To the Lighthouse*. Instead she explores other ways of using words[2] and of defining their relation to the passage of time as it conditions the development of the self from childhood to old age. Some writers for children realised that the rejection of the moral and improving tale implied a rejection of cause and consequence, of destinies worked out in time. Sully and many others recognised that the idea of sequence was foreign to the young child, who had to learn that concept through the body and through the acquisition of language.[3]

In 'A Sketch of the Past' Woolf re-created her passion for St Ives: 'I am hardly aware of myself, but only of the sensation. I am only the container of the feeling of ecstasy, of the feeling of rapture. Perhaps this is characteristic of all childhood memories; perhaps it accounts for their strength.' Her impressions are of colour and sound, 'highly sensual': 'It is of hearing the waves breaking, one, two, one, two, and sending a splash of water over the beach; and then breaking, one, two, one, two, behind a yellow blind.' The vividness of the senses seems to demand a different medium of expression:

If I were a painter I should paint these first impressions in pale yellow, silver, and green. There was the pale yellow blind; the

green sea; and the silver of the passion flowers. I should make a
picture that was globular; semi-transparent. . . . Sound and sight
seem to make equal parts of these first impressions. . . . The
rooks cawing is part of the waves breaking – one, two, one, two –
and the splash as the wave drew back and then it gathered again,
and I lay there half awake, half asleep, drawing in such ecstasy as I
cannot describe.[4]

In *To the Lighthouse* Woolf had transposed her vision into that of a
painter: Lily Briscoe explaining that the purple triangle is Mrs
Ramsay and James. In *The Waves* she tries to recapture that
childhood ecstasy through a penetration of the properties of
language.

The book opens with the sea at dawn, imaged as a woman raising
a lamp in a room of sleepers. The swell of the sea, like the wrinkles
on a grey coverlet, is the swell of 'a sleeper whose breath comes and
goes unconsciously'. As the lamp rises higher 'the fibres of the
burning bonfire were fused into one haze, one incandescence which
lifted the weight of the woollen grey sky on top of it. . . . The sea
blazed gold.' The light reaches the garden, 'one bird chirped high
up; there was a pause; another chirped lower down'. The sun rests
on the blind of the bedroom window: 'The blind stirred slightly, but
all within was dim and unsubstantial. The birds sang their blank
melody outside.'[5] Within the room the sleepers stir and wake. It is
an opening from film, or from music, an *aubade* reminiscent of
Debussy's *La mer*. The dawn is both literal and metaphorical – the
dawn of consciousness in the children – just as the waves are real but
also a metaphor for language itself, the breaking of silence. The
children wake and speak in single statements of sensation, as Woolf
noted on the plan of her draft, 'Sensations':[6]

> 'I hear a sound,' said Rhoda, 'cheep, chirp; cheep, chirp; going
> up and down.'
> 'I see a globe,' said Neville, 'hanging down in a drop against the
> enormous flanks of some hill.'
> 'I see a crimson tassel,' said Jinny, 'twisted with gold threads.'
> 'I hear something stamping,' said Louis, 'A great beast's foot is
> chained. It stamps, and stamps, and stamps.'

The simple present without auxiliary, and the present participle,
capture a moment unflanked by past or future, brief and blank as the

bird's singing in the dawn air. The first perceived sequence comes with the use of the word 'now'. It is still present, but contains an awareness that some things are not now, they are past. What is past is the brief span of consciousness, the birdsong, the rising sun. The reader is thus introduced to the processes of memory, but develops memory only as the child develops it:

> 'Stones are cold to my feet,' said Neville. 'I feel each one, round or pointed, separately.'
> 'The back of my hand burns,' said Jinny, 'but the palm is clammy and damp with dew.'
> 'Now the cock crows like a spurt of hard, red water in the white tide,' said Bernard.[7]

Sully asserted in *Outlines of Psychology* that in the very young child 'images do not appear till sense-knowledge has reached a certain stage of development. Retentiveness in the early period exists only as the power of recognizing objects when they are present.'[8] Woolf shows the children unaware of self, as she herself had been, because they have not acquired the concept of sequence which creates memory.

In the same year as *The Waves*, 1932, Laura Ingalls Wilder published the first of her books about her own childhood memories of pioneer life, *Little House in the Big Woods*. Although from the beginning Wilder describes the passage of time, the child registers it through externals: 'The first snow came, and the bitter cold'; 'the little log house was almost buried in snow'; 'then one day Pa said that spring was coming'; 'it was a warm night. The fire had gone to coals on the hearth, and Pa did not build it up.' Wilder, unlike Woolf, makes no attempt to challenge the consecutiveness of language itself, although in this book, when the children are youngest, she limits herself to the simplest grammatical structures: partly to allow a child of the same age to read the book, but partly to reflect the perceptions of the children in the story: 'Now the winter seemed long.'[9] The pattern of the narrative follows that of the seasons much more rigidly than in any of Wilder's later books when the children are progressively older and capable of a more complex relationship with their world, because they have already developed a sense of self against the passage of time. Woolf wrote of the children's speeches in *The Waves*: 'The thing is to keep them running homogeneously in and out in the rhythm of the waves.' That the rhythm of the waves is also the rhythm of language is apparent from a note which she made when she came to revise the book: 'I begin to see what I had in mind; and want to begin cutting out masses of irrelevance and clearing, sharpening and making the good phrases shine. One wave after another. No room.'[10] What there is no room for is the author herself interrupting and interpreting the flow of words.

The relation of language to time was central to the writing of Bergson, William James and Edmund Husserl. James wrote: 'As we take, in fact, a general view of the wonderful stream of our consciousness, what strikes us first is this different pace of its parts. Like a bird's life, it seems to be made of an alternation of flights and perchings. The rhythm of language expresses this, where every thought is expressed in a sentence, and every sentence enclosed by a period.'[11] The children's single statements at the beginning of *The Waves* perch and chirp like the birdsong they describe. But once Bernard has introduced the word 'now' then the first time-clause appears in the writing, and marks the first constructing of a timed relation between discrete events. It is immediately followed by the first use of the past tense and of adverbs of sequence: 'first', 'then'. The concept of consequence enters, and the children's observations, although not answering each other, become much nearer to dialogue than before. With the toll of the church bell the official measurement of time joins the new awareness that sensations have a specific duration, and then suddenly the whole scene is over – all the children except Louis have gone to breakfast:

'*When* the smoke *rises*, sleep curls off the roof *like a mist*,' said Louis.

'The birds *sang* in chorus *first*,' said Rhoda. '*Now* the scullery door is unbarred. Off they fly. Off they fly *like a fling of seed*. But *one* sings by the bedroom window *alone*.'

'Bubbles form on the floor of the saucepan,' said Jinny. '*Then* they *rise*, quicker and quicker, in a silver chain to the top.'

'*Now* Biddy scrapes the fish-scales with a jagged knife on to a wooden board,' said Neville.

'The dining-room window is dark blue *now*,' said Bernard, 'and the air ripples above the chimneys.'

'A swallow *is perched* on the lightning-conductor,' said Susan. 'And Biddy *has smacked* down the bucket on the kitchen flags.'

'That is the *first stroke of the church bell*,' said Louis. '*Then the others follow*; one, two; one, two; one, two.'

'Look at the table-cloth, flying along the table,' said Rhoda. '*Now* there are rounds of white china, and silver streaks beside each plate.'

'*Suddenly* a bee booms in *my* ear,' said Neville. 'It is *here*; it is *past.*'

'*I* burn, *I* shiver,' said Jinny, '*out of this sun, into this shadow.*'

'Now *they* have *all gone*,' said Louis, '*I* am *alone*.' [my italics][12]

The first-person pronoun which began the children's utterances has moved from being virtually impersonal and incantatory, to being defined distinctly as a separate entity. The birds sang together first, then one sang alone, as Rhoda perceives just before Louis is left singing alone when the others fly off. The voices of both children and birds, though forced apart by language, register simultaneous impressions. The church bells, tolling in sequence, imitate the waves, and the waves resemble phrases which describe consciousness, rather than reproducing the sensations of consciousness itself. The apprehension of sequence gives a new meaning to the pronoun 'I' because it is no longer a collective statement but a separate 'I' defined by absence and change: they were here, but now they are gone and I am alone.[13]

William James declared that 'the literally present moment is a purely verbal supposition, not a position'. He argued that 'to remember a thing as past it is necessary that the notion of "past" should be one of our ideas'.[14] The capacity of Louis and Rhoda to construct a metaphor – 'like a mist', 'like a fling of seed' – demonstrates that they can call up past experience in order to illuminate the present. Although when the children first start to speak they seem to exist in a world of sensation without either past or future, the elaborate temporal distinctions of language force them to order their sense impressions. '"Each tense," said Neville, "means differently. There is an order in this world; there are distinctions, there are differences in the world upon whose verge I step. For this is only a beginning."'[15]

Both Bergson and William James argued that language falsified experience by creating separation where there should be a continuous process of flow. Bergson wrote that 'we instinctively tend to solidify our impressions in order to express them in language. . . . Not only does language make us believe in the unchangeableness of our sensations, but it will sometimes deceive us as to the nature of the sensation felt.' Language is the code through which society assumes uniformity between the experience of individuals, which allows them to generalise – a word Woolf hated. The real art of the novelist in Bergson's view depends on stripping experience of the cloak in which language hides it: 'We estimate the talent of a novelist by the power with which he lifts out of the common domain, to which language had thus brought them down, feelings and ideas to which he strives to restore, by adding detail to detail, their original and living individuality.' But even the novelist is obliged to spread out 'the indefinite plurality of conscious states in this homogeneous medium which some call duration, but which is in reality space'. Bergson argues that the human being fails to translate completely what the soul experiences: 'There is no common measure between mind and language.' His own writing demonstrates that, 'by the very language which I was compelled to use, I betrayed the deeply ingrained habit of setting out time in space'. The children's speeches at the beginning of *The Waves* are measured out in language on the space of the page, whereas in fact the author only records simultaneous thoughts and impressions.

Both James and Bergson feel that language is inadequate to express states of consciousness. Bergson wrote: 'By giving first the person and then the feelings by which he is moved a fixed form by means of sharply defined words, it deprives them in advance of every kind of living activity.'[16] James argued that words could only ever approximate to the feelings which they tried to represent: 'Take a train of words passing through the mind and leading to a certain conclusion on the one hand, and on the other hand an almost wordless set of tactile, visual and other fancies leading to the same conclusion. Can the halo, fringe, or scheme in which we feel the words to live be the same as that in which we feel the images to lie? Does not the discrepancy of terms involve a discrepancy of felt relations among them?'[17] Nevertheless James must have been aware, as Woolf certainly was when she used his images to describe her own ideas about consciousness, that he himself uses language brilliantly to convey states of being which he claims are beyond its reach, as in his description of time: 'Our feeling of time, that it is different from space, that it somehow involves past, present, and future, and that it somehow pervades the whole of our experience – all these facts and relations are dimly apprehended as its fringes, without being clearly distinguished and spelled out.'[18] He concludes: 'These feelings of relation, these psychic overtones, halos, suffusions, or fringes about the terms, may be the same in very different systems of imagery.'[19] Woolf's own famous description in 'Modern Fiction' of the mind receiving a myriad impressions – 'trivial, fantastic, evanescent, or engraved with the sharpness of steel' – and her belief that 'life is a luminous halo, a semi-transparent envelope surrounding us from beginning of consciousness to the end' echo James's own images and his conclusion that 'the great continua of time, space and the self envelop everything betwixt them, and flow together without interfering.'[20] But the novelist differs from both philosophers, and particularly from Bergson, in her estimate of the accuracy of language in conveying the vagueness and liquid character of sense impressions.

This difference derives largely from Woolf's conviction that words are a medium of expression for the writer in the same way that paint is for the artist. She described revising *The Waves* as 'sweeping over an entire canvas with a wet brush'.[21] She castigated Forster for ignoring the importance of language in *Aspects of the Novel* (1927):

> Thus, though it is impossible to imagine a book on painting in which not a word should be said about the medium in which a painter works, a wise and brilliant book, like Mr Forster's, can be written about fiction without saying more than a sentence or two about the medium in which a novelist works. Almost nothing is said about words. . . .
>
> Strange though this unaesthetic attitude would be in the critic of any other art, it does not surprise us in the critic of fiction. For one thing, the problem is extremely difficult. A book fades like a mist, like a dream. How are we to take a stick and point to that tone, that relation, in the vanishing pages, as Mr Roger Fry points with his wand at a line or a colour in the picture displayed before him?[22]

When 'The Mark on the Wall' appeared in 1918 – quietly mocked in Forster's book – Roger Fry wrote to Virginia Woolf that, although there were many good living writers, 'you're the only one now Henry James is gone who uses language as a medium of art, who makes the very texture of the words have a meaning and quality really almost apart from what you are talking about'.[23]

The insistence on words as medium, and on writing as pattern, was as important to Henry James's friend Robert Louis Stevenson as it was later to be to Fry and Woolf. In an essay, 'On Style in Literature', published in 1885, Stevenson drew parallels between literature, and music and painting, pointing out that 'the sister arts enjoy the use of a plastic and ductile material, like the modeller's clay; literature alone is condemned to work in mosaic with finite and quite rigid words'. He observed that 'music and literature, the two temporal arts, contrive their pattern of sounds in time: or, in other words, of sounds and pauses', and claimed that phrases must be constructed 'to gratify the sensual ear'. He concluded: 'The motive end of any art whatever is to make a pattern; a pattern, it may be, of colours, of sounds, of changing attitudes, geometric figures, or imitative lines; but still a pattern.'[24] He would have agreed entirely with Woolf's criticism of Forster's book, and all three critics – Woolf, Fry and Stevenson – would have entered joyously into Alice's skirmish with Humpty Dumpty about meaning:

> 'Don't stand chattering to yourself like that,' Humpty Dumpty said, looking at her for the first time, 'but tell me your name and your business.'
> 'My *name* is Alice, but –'
> 'It's a stupid name enough!' Humpty Dumpty interrupted impatiently. 'What does it mean?'
> '*Must* a name mean something?' Alice asked doubtfully.
> 'Of course it must,' Humpty Dumpty said with a short laugh: '*my* name means the shape I am – and a good handsome shape it is, too. With a name like yours, you might be any shape, almost.'
>
> (*L-G*, 263)

Alice assumes that to talk about meaning is to imply significance. But Humpty Dumpty sees words as a poet might, as capable of realising volume in space, or, as in one of the Duchess's morals, sounds not sense. In *Freshwater*, the burlesque on her aunt Julia Cameron's establishment which Virginia Woolf wrote in 1923 but which was not performed until 1935 (in a revised version), the earlier version contains an interchange between Watts and Tennyson, in which the painter proposes a symbolic rendering of 'Mammon trampling upon Maternity. The sound is certainly excellent; but what about the sense?' Tennyson retorts: 'Take care of the sound and the sense will take care of itself.'[25] In the 1935 version the quotation from Carroll is omitted, perhaps because it has acquired the status of cliché. But in 1923 Carroll's word games still caught Woolf's verbal imagination. She wrote the previous year to David Garnett about Eliot's 'The Waste Land': 'I expect you're rather hard on Tom Eliot's poem. I have only the sound of it in my ears, when he read it aloud; and have not yet tackled the sense. But I liked the sound.'[26]

Walter Pater observed that the true artist must be 'a lover of words for their own sake, to whom nothing about them is unimportant, a minute and constant observer of their physiognomy'.[27] Virginia Woolf sometimes asked herself, as Bernard does in *The Waves*, whether she was only a phrase-maker: 'One must write from deep feeling, said Dostoievsky. And do I? Or do I fabricate with words, loving them as I do?'[28] Her father wrote of Stevenson: 'A singular delicacy of organisation gave him a love of words for their own sake; the mere sound of "Jehovah Tsidkenu" gave him a thrill (it does not thrill me!); he was sensitive from childhood to assonance and alliteration. . . . Language, in short, had to him a music independently of its meaning.'[29] Woolf wrote scathingly to Janet Case in 1925 that 'Stevenson is a poor writer, because his thought is poor, and therefore, fidget though he may, his style is obnoxious. And I don't see how you can enjoy technique apart from the matter.'[30] But her irritation was sparked off by Case's criticism of *Mrs Dalloway* and throws something of a smokescreen around her own debt to Stevenson.

In the draft of the essay on *Robinson Crusoe*, which appears in the same notebook as *To the Lighthouse*, Woolf compared Defoe with Stevenson, although in the finished version the comparison has been excised. She wrote of Defoe's novel:

> &
> [It rouses] in us a sense of ~~excitement~~ of Romance ~~of Stevenson~~ with all his art ~~craft never~~ wrote. None of Stevenson's romances have the same power; ~~to stir us~~ because, ~~though every device of art has been employed~~ they lack ~~this the power~~ to ~~convince.~~[31]

Her contempt comes from a long and easy familiarity which may also explain the tepid comments she made in 1939 on Lewis Carroll, against whom almost every new writer in the early twentieth century formed her or his artistic identity. Woolf despised Stevenson from self-defence. He belonged to her father's world, although also to her own childhood. Leslie Stephen wrote to him in 1884:

> I have been thinking of you lately . . . for I confiscated (*temporarily*) a work called Treasure Island wh. had been given to one of my boys, and having sat down to it after dinner did not rise till I had finished it. I think it firstrate in its kind; and I fancy from what I have heard that my opinion is the common one. John Morley spoke of it to me in the same sense. I dont know when I have read anything more excellent in the way of story telling. I shall read it again, when I rescue it from the family.[32]

The gift was probably to one of the Duckworth boys, but Stephen read the book aloud to the smaller children.[33]

Woolf recorded in one of her early diaries under 13 March 1905 that she had dispatched an order to Hatchard's for Stevenson and Pater because she wanted to study both authors, not for the purpose of copying, but in order to see how the writing worked. She added that there was an element of trickery in Stevenson's art, and that Pater was infinitely superior to him.[34] That diary ends in May 1905, but a new one, the 'Cornwall' diary, begins three months later on 11 August and continues till 14 September 1905. It describes the return of the Stephen children to St Ives and their peering through the escalonia hedge at the strangers who now inhabit Talland House. The account is unique among Woolf's writings in being written in a consciously literary and mellifluous manner which conjures up both Stevenson and Kenneth Grahame. The sentences are decorated with conventional archaisms of the sort which both Grahame and Stevenson use. The train journey to Cornwall is transposed, in a manner which Grahame would have approved of, into a fairy tale of wizardry by which the young Stephen adults are conveyed not only to a far-away place, but to the far-away time of their own childhood at St Ives.[35] The well-worn imagery of enchantment and the frequent crossings-out suggest that the writer was 'composing' rather than scratching out an impromptu record. Woolf discarded that style completely when she wrote *To the Lighthouse*, but remained anxious that the book was 'sentimental', which the earlier account is, as she no doubt later realised, observing of the novel: 'I am making more use of symbolism, I observe; and I go in dread of "sentimentality."'[36] When, in the 'Cornwall' diary, she practised Stevenson's style she ruined her own, which is naturally more acerbic. But she was too sensitive a critic not to perceive, as the more dispassionate Henry James did, that Stevenson was not cast in the high Victorian mould and that his concentration on the medium of writing made him, however reluctant she was to acknowledge it, the natural ally of herself and Roger Fry.

Stevenson argued that the writer deals with words rather than thoughts: 'None but he appreciates the influence of jingling words; so that he looks upon life, with something of a covert smile, seeing people led by what they fancy to be thoughts and what are really the accustomed artifices of his own trade, or roused by what they take to be principles and are really picturesque effects.' In an essay called 'Random Memories' Stevenson recalls a question put to a schoolboy at a meeting of the school philosophical society:

> 'What would be the result of putting a pound of potassium in a pot of porter?' 'I should think there would be a number of interesting bi-products,' said a smatterer at my elbow; but for me the tale itself has a bi-product, and stands as a type of much that is most human. For this inquirer who conceived himself to burn with a zeal entirely chemical, was really immersed in a design of a quite different nature; unconsciously to his own recently breached intelligence, he was engaged in literature. Putting, pound, potassium, pot, porter; initial p, mediant t – that was his idea, poor little boy.[37]

Orlando's medium is words, just as the schoolboy's was:

> For to him, said the Archduke Harry, she was and would ever be the Pink, the Pearl, the Perfection of her sex. The three p's would have been more persuasive if they had not been interspersed with tee-hees and haw-haws of the strangest kind. 'If this is love,' said Orlando to herself, looking at the Archduke on the other side of the fender, and now from a woman's point of view, 'there is something highly ridiculous in it.'

Woolf declares in the novel that 'for all her travels and adventures and profound thinkings and turnings this way and that, she [Orlando] was only in process of fabrication. . . . "Of what odds and ends are we compounded," she said. . . . "What a phantasmagoria the mind is and the meeting-place of dissemblables!"' When Orlando reflects, with Mary Queen of Scots' prayer book in her hand, on the power of the Word, she decides that

The letter S . . . is the serpent in the poet's Eden. Do what she would there were still too many of these sinful reptiles in the first stanzas of 'The Oak Tree'. But 'S' was nothing, in her opinion, compared with the termination 'ing'. . . . We must shape our words till they are the thinnest integument for our thoughts. Thoughts are divine, etc.[38]

The serpent is no longer the devil or little girl, but instead a typographical statement of signifier and signified, the signs on the page.[39] Orlando's meditations conjure up Alice's world:

'You promised to tell me your history, you know,' said Alice, 'and why it is you hate – C and D,' she added in a whisper, half afraid that it would be offended again.

'Mine is a long and sad tale!' said the Mouse, turning to Alice and sighing.

'It *is* a long tail, certainly,' said Alice, looking down with wonder at the Mouse's tail; 'buy why do you call it sad?'

(*AW*, 50)

> "Fury said to
> a mouse, That
> he met
> in the
> house,
> ' Let us
> both go
> to law :
> *I* will
> prosecute
> *you.* —
> Come, I 'll
> take no
> denial ;
> We must
> have a
> trial :
> For
> really
> this
> morning
> I 've
> nothing
> to do.'
> Said the
> mouse to
> the cur,
> 'Such a
> trial,
> dear sir,
> With no
> jury or
> judge,
> would be
> wasting
> our breath.'
> ' I 'll be
> judge,
> I 'll be
> jury,'
> Said
> cunning
> old Fury ;
> ' I 'll try
> the whole
> cause,
> and
> condemn
> you
> to
> death.

The tale is then printed to mirror Alice's arrangement of it in her mind as a long tail, a typographical sequence as well as a time sequence. In *The Waves* Bernard also sees words as creatures: 'I must open the little trap-door and let out these linked phrases.'[40]

Stevenson wrote in an essay called 'Child's Play', first published in 1878 in the *Cornhill Magazine*, edited by Leslie Stephen, a sentence which Woolf herself might have composed: 'We make to ourselves day by day, out of history, gossip, and economical speculations, and God knows what, a medium in which we walk and through which we look abroad.'[41] The children in *The Waves* use words as a protective medium to cover the rawness of pure sensation, as when they have to go to school. Bernard muses: 'I must make phrases and phrases and so interpose something hard between myself and the stare of housemaids, the stare of clocks, staring faces, indifferent faces, or I shall cry.' Words create connections between people by flowing round separate bodies, like James's flow of consciousness: ' "But when we sit together, close," said Bernard, "we melt into each other with phrases. We are edged with mist. We make an insubstantial territory." ' When Susan weeps, Bernard tells her that words will break up the 'knot of hardness' which is her grief.

All the children in *The Waves* discover a sense of self when they find in language their own medium for experience. Each has a special relationship with words. Neville will be 'a clinger to the outsides of words all my life', Woolf's private view of Strachey's writing. Neville is the one who talks like Oswald Bastable: 'I will use this hour of solitude, this reprieve from conversation, to coast round the purlieus of the house. . . . I will continue to make my survey of the purlieus of the house in the late afternoon, in the sunset, when the sun makes oleaginous spots on the linoleum.'[42] The language is faintly self-parodying, recalling both Lewis Carroll, and the pseudo-grandiose diction of an estate agent's brochure aped by Oswald Bastable in his description in *The Wouldbegoods* of the Indian uncle's splendid dwelling: 'When we were taken to the beautiful big Blackheath house we thought now all would be well, because it was a house with vineries and pineries, and gas and water, and shrubberies and stabling, and replete with every modern convenience, like it says in Dyer & Hilton's list of Eligible House Property. I read all about it, and I have copied the words quite right.'[43] Neville uses words to shield himself from his headmaster, whose 'words fall cold on my head like paving-stones, while the gilt cross heaves on his waistcoat'. For Susan they describe things which are distinct and separate: ' "I see the beetle," said Susan. "It is black, I see; it is green, I see; I am tied down with single words. But you wander off; you slip away; you rise up higher, with words and words in phrases." ' Jinny's words are coloured – a phenomenon which Sully researched: ' "Those are yellow words, those are fiery words," said Jinny. "I should like a fiery dress, a yellow dress, a

fulvous dress to wear in the evening."'' The children recognise
Bernard's greater power with words, his capacity to form patterns,
create sequences and thus establish directions. Neville remarks: 'We
are all phrases in Bernard's story, things he writes down in his
note-book under A or under B. He tells our story with extraordinary
understanding except of what we most feel. For he does not need
us. He is never at our mercy.' Woolf gives Bernard her own love of
words. He reflects: 'I am a natural coiner of words, a blower of
bubbles through one thing and another.'[44] She herself wrote of the
book that she had never made prose move so fluently before 'from
the chuckle, the babble to the rhapsody'.[45] But it is true of the
novelist's emotion in *The Waves*, as it is of Bernard's, that it is
subjugated to the act of representation. Woolf does not need her
characters any more than Bernard needs the other children. She
never acquires George Eliot's almost painful closeness to her own
heroines. Instead, she shows the children learning the world
through language, and charts their discoveries, which are also her
own.

The book questions the power of language. Neville expresses
Bergson's scepticism: 'Nothing should be named lest by so doing we
change it.' Language may be a 'balloon that sails over tree-tops', but
it is also a way of defining and thus limiting the experience which it
seems to set free. Bernard comes, as all the children implicitly do, to
an understanding that they are imprisoned in a world of time:

> 'Had I been born,' said Bernard, 'not knowing that one word
> follows another I might have been, who knows, perhaps
> anything. As it is, finding sequences everywhere, I cannot bear
> the pressure of solitude. When I cannot see words curling like
> rings of smoke round me I am in darkness – I am nothing.'

Bernard believes that the naming of things is a means of controlling
them: 'I wish to add to my collection of valuable observations upon
the true nature of human life. My book will certainly run to many
volumes, embracing every known variety of man and woman.' To
grow up is to have the ability to name everything:

> When I am grown up I shall carry a notebook – a fat book with
> heavy pages, methodically lettered. I shall enter my phrases.
> Under B shall come 'Butterfly powder'. If, in my novel, I describe

the sun on the window-sill, I shall look under B and find butterfly powder. That will be useful.

But the problem which the children gradually perceive is that words may control *them*, just as they controlled Stevenson's enquirer after potassium and porter. Louis observes: 'The time approaches when these soliloquies shall be shared. We shall not always give out a sound like a beaten gong as one sensation strikes and then another. Children, our lives have been gongs striking.'[46] But he himself gravitates to the passive mood, to the chained beast who stamps on the shore, just as his racial memories are of the captivity of the Jews.[47] Although Bernard is 'eternally engaged . . . [in] finding some perfect phrase that fits this very moment exactly', he begins to wonder whether his access to phrases constitutes any real authority in a world of things: 'I am not an authority on law, or medicine, or finance. I am wrapped round with phrases, like damp straw; I glow, phosphorescent.' But if it is straw, author and reader may both murmur, I'll huff and I'll puff and I'll blow your house down. The question which runs in harness with Bernard's sense of mastering the medium, is whether in truth the medium has mastered Bernard.

The children learn in the first section of *The Waves* that the body is subject to compulsions defined by words. This is evident in the use of the word 'must':

'The heat is going,' said Bernard, 'from the Jungle. The leaves flap black wings over us. Miss Curry has blown her whistle on the terrace. We *must* creep out from the awnings of the currant leaves and stand upright. There are twigs in your hair, Jinny. There is a green caterpillar on your neck. We *must* form, two by two.' [my italics]

The formation is a physical necessity which is dictated by an uncomprehended moral necessity: ' "We must form into pairs," said Susan, "and walk in order, not shuffling our feet, not lagging, with Louis going first to lead us, because Louis is alert and not a wool-gatherer." ' The word 'must' is for the children like the chain which for Louis binds the great beast and creates his stamping. But it is also the condition of adult bondage, from which very young children are fleetingly exempt. The adult Bernard reflects: 'We must go; must catch our train; must walk back to the station – must, must,

must.'[48] Lewis Carroll's poem 'My Fairy', written when he was fifteen, battles with that word:

> I have a fairy by my side
>   Which says I must not sleep,
> When once in pain I loudly cried
>   It said 'You must not weep.'
>
> If, full of mirth, I smile and grin,
>   It says 'You must not laugh':
> When once I wished to drink some gin
>   It said 'You must not quaff.'
>
> When once a meal I wished to taste
>   It said 'You must not bite';
> When to the wars I went in haste
>   It said 'You must not fight.'
>
> 'What may I do?' at length I cried,
>   Tired of the painful task,
> The fairy quietly replied,
>   And said 'You must not ask.'
>
> *Moral*: 'You mustn't.'[49]

The introduction of the new form 'may' in the final verse of the poem lets in a world of alternatives comparable to those suggested in Mrs Ramsay's 'It may be fine.'

Carroll was the first of his generation to identify the linguistic centre of a child's subjection to the adult world but other writers were quick to follow him. In *The Cuckoo Clock* Griselda, cooped up in her solitary schoolroom, rebels against the confinement of life with her two aunts:

> 'I hate winter,' said Griselda, pressing her cold little face against the colder window-pane, 'I hate winter, and I hate lessons. I would give up being a *person* in a minute if I might be a – a – what would I best like to be? Oh yes, I know – a butterfly. Butterflies never see winter, and they *certainly* never have any lessons or any kind of work to do. I hate *must*-ing to do anything.'[50]

Flush, in Woolf's effervescent biography of Elizabeth Barrett Browning's spaniel, enters Regent's Park in a new spirit of anarchy once he perceives that he has been ousted in his mistress's heart by the poet Robert Browning: ' "Dogs must be led on chains" – there was the usual placard; there were the park-keepers with their top-hats and their truncheons to enforce it. But "must" no longer had any meaning for him. The chain of love was broken. He would run where he liked.' When he is eventually reconciled to the marriage he finds, as the Brownings also do, new liberty in Italy: 'Now in Florence the last threads of his old fetters fell from him. . . . Where was "must" now? Where were chains now? . . . He had no need of a chain in this new world.'[51] What child, trailing round the park at an adult's heels, has not, like Flush, balked at bondage, and what adult has not scented freedom as the white cliffs of Dover fade into mist? When Orlando in an earlier biography stood remembering the visit of Queen Elizabeth to her home, she recalled the royal protest against 'must': ' "Little man, little man," – Orlando could hear her say – "is 'must' a word to be addressed to princes?" '[52]

Virginia Woolf found the concept of 'must' extremely inhibiting for the novelist. She wrote of the paleness and dullness which comes from writing from a sense of duty, and was sometimes distracted by the conflicting obligations which had loomed so large for Elizabeth Gaskell, but which the earlier novelist had mastered:

All books now seem to me surrounded by a circle of invisible censors. . . . I read 'Ruth' after breakfast. Its stillness, its unconsciousness, its lack of distraction, its concentration and the resulting 'beauty' struck me. As if the mind must be allowed to settle undisturbed over the object in order to secrete the pearl. . . . Ought I to go to the village sports? 'Ought' thus breaks into my contemplation.[53]

Many of Woolf's essays deal with the particular conditions of 'must' under which women write: 'They adopt a view in deference to authority.' She points to the difficulty of even deciding what to write about: 'Often nothing tangible remains of a woman's day. The food that has been cooked is eaten; the children that have been nursed have gone out into the world. Where does the accent fall? What is the silent point for the novelist to seize upon? It is difficult to say. Her life has an anonymous character which is baffling and puzzling

Alice to the Lighthouse

in the extreme. For the first time, this dark country is beginning to be explored in fiction.'[54] For both women and children the word 'must' has special force.

When Virginia Woolf made the Queen in *Orlando* protest against the compulsions of language she might have remembered the brilliant and capricious lady created by Kipling in *Rewards and Fairies* (1910), who anticipates her own Queen Elizabeth in *Between the Acts* – stagey, vital, amoral. Kipling's children find the Queen with Puck's help in the wood from which they have excluded grown-ups: their kingdom. She enacts for them a scene in her conflict with Philip of Spain, reading from a letter: 'Therefore he requires (which is a word Gloriana loves not), *requires* that she shall hang 'em when they return to England, and afterwards shall account to him for all the goods and gold they have plundered.'[55] The lady, whom they do not recognise as Elizabeth I, and who does not enlighten them, is, like the women Orlando remembers, a creature of fitful but electric power in a world governed by male authority.

Whether or not the novelist echoed Kipling's 'Gloriana' in *Orlando*, she evidently remembered 'Cold Iron', the first story in *Rewards and Fairies*, in which a slave child is captured by Puck and brought up amongst the fairies, but he must not touch Cold Iron, or he will become human. The first thing he touches will dictate his fortune. Thor makes a ring of iron, and one day the changeling child, lighting upon it, clasps it round his neck, to be forever a slave. When Bernard has his hair cut in *The Waves*, the scissors are both Time's scythe, the scissors of Delilah, and Kipling's Cold Iron: 'I leant my head back and was swathed in a sheet. Looking-glasses confronted me in which I could see my pinioned body and people passing; stopping, looking and going on indifferent. The hairdresser began to move his scissors to and fro. I felt myself powerless to stop the oscillations of the cold steel.' Earlier in the book the ring which reminds the reader of Kipling's slave is language: 'This I see for a second, and shall try to-night to fix in words, to forge in a ring of steel.'[56] The fixing of experience in words involves both permanence and bondage.

Woolf wrote: 'If a writer were a freeman and not a slave, if he could write what he chose, not what he must, if he could base his work upon his own feeling and not upon convention, there would be no plot, no comedy, no tragedy, no love interest or catastrophe in the accepted style, and perhaps not a single button sewn on as the Bond Street tailors would have it.' In the same essay she complained: 'The writer seems constrained, not by his own free will but by some powerful and unscrupulous tyrant who has him in thrall, to provide a plot. . . . Must novels be like this?'[57] The 'must' is a condition of sequence, as it is for the children in *The Waves*: 'We must form into pairs . . . and walk in order.' Even the rhythm of Woolf's sentence, 'If a writer were a freeman and not a slave', echoes Kipling's poem 'If' in *Rewards and Fairies*. The poem has come to signify everything in leadership which Woolf disliked: 'If you can keep your head when all about you / Are losing theirs and blaming it on you / . . . you'll be a Man, my son!' But it also contains an impassioned and rhythmic plea for defiance:

> If you can make one heap of all your winnings
>   And risk it on one turn of pitch-and-toss,
> And lose, and start again at the beginnings
>   And never breathe a word about your loss.[58]

Queen Elizabeth in Kipling's story gambles everything and takes the loss with the gain. Woolf wrote of her own image of the Queen in 'Reading':

> If we could see also what we can smell – if, at this moment crushing the southernwood, I could go back through the long corridor of sunny mornings, boring my way through hundreds of Augusts, I should come in the end, passing a host of less-important figures, to no less a figure than Queen Elizabeth herself. Whether some tinted waxwork is the foundation of my view, I do not know; but she always appears very distinctly in the same guise. She flaunts across the terrace superbly and a little stiffly like the peacock spreading its tail . . . her imagination still young in its wrinkled and fantastic casket.[59]

When Una suggests to Kipling's Gloriana that in her machinations she did not know what she in truth wanted to achieve, the Queen replies: ' "May it please your Majesty" – the lady bowed her head low – "this Gloriana whom I have represented for your pleasure was both a woman and a Queen. Remember her when you come to your Kingdom." '[60] The tones of Miss La Trobe in *Between the Acts*, author and presenter of a stage play in which she is both ruler and subject, can be heard as clearly as the echo both of the thief on Calvary, and of Virginia Woolf's own voice demanding whether 'must' is a word to be used to those who rule in the kingdom of language.[61]

Stevenson's picture of the writer secretly mocking people who think they are rejoicing in principles when in fact they are the slaves of picturesque effects becomes in 'Random Memories' a mockery of himself. He recalls his determination to be a writer, in a piece which anticipates Woolf's diary descriptions of the inception of *The Waves*, which she had originally planned to call 'The Moths' until she remembered that moths only fly by night. Stevenson recounts his first struggles with composition, in '*Voces Fidelium*, a series of dramatic monologues in verse', in which he was spurred on by 'intimations of early death and immortality' – not purely poetic in Stevenson's case, as his health was extremely precarious from a small child. He sat late at night at the window, 'toiling to leave a memory behind me', framed in the scorn of the grown man he has become, 'so ridiculous a picture (to my elderly wisdom) does the fool present'. In the end a particular circumstance stopped his effusions:

The weather was then so warm that I must keep the windows open; the night without was populous with moths. As the late darkness deepened, my literary papers beaconed forth more brightly; thicker and thicker came the dusty night-fliers, to gyrate for one brilliant instant round the flame and fall in agonies upon my paper. Flesh and blood could not endure the spectacle; to capture immortality was doubtless a noble enterprise, but not to capture it at such cost of suffering; and out would go the candles, and off would I go to bed in the darkness, raging to think that the blow might fall tomorrow, and there was *Voces Fidelium* still incomplete. Well, the moths are all gone, and *Voces Fidelium* along with them; only the fool is still on hand and practises new follies.[62]

Virginia Woolf would not have had to think about Stevenson in order to dream up the flight of the moth: the Stephen children's passion for moth-hunting colours the essay 'Reading'. Nevertheless, in her mind, just as the subject of reading made her think of the beautiful moth, and Roger Fry's love of pictures seemed to her like a hawkmoth hovering over a red flower, so the original conception of 'The Moths' embodied a scene not unlike the one

Stevenson describes, in which someone is writing at a window with the moths flying towards a lamp:

> Every morning I write a little sketch, to amuse myself. I am not saying, I might say, that these sketches have any relevance. I am not trying to tell a story. Yet perhaps it might be done in that way. A mind thinking. They might be islands of light – islands in the stream that I am trying to convey; life itself going on. The current of the moths flying strongly this way. A lamp and a flower pot in the centre. The flower can always be changing. But there must be more unity between each scene than I can find at present. Autobiography it might be called. How am I to make one lap, or act, between the coming of the moths, more intense than another; if there are only scenes? One must get the sense that this is the beginning; this the middle; that the climax – when she opens the window and the moth comes in.[63]

What remains of this early sketch is the lamp (the image of the sun rising and the flowerpot): Louis as plant, and a lady writing whom the children see and who is somehow mysteriously there throughout the whole scene. Who is the lady? It is never said. Yet she is, unmistakably, Virginia Woolf herself, and the children in the book recognise both their separateness from her, and a mysterious tie between them. She is, in different form, the fool who still writes after the moths have ceased to suffer. The voices of the faithful are echoed in the children's voices, and eventually they too will cease, but not while 'the lady sits between the two long windows, writing'.[64] Woolf described herself 'writing perhaps a few phrases here at my window in the morning'.[65]

But at the end of the book Bernard, who is the one who makes phrases, finds that with the cold steel of the hairdresser's scissors Puck has deserted him. He is only human after all. The lady writing seems a dream:

> The woods had vanished; the earth was a waste of shadow. No sound broke the silence of the wintry landscape. No cock crowed; no smoke rose; no train moved. A man without a self, I said. A heavy body leaning on a gate. A dead man. With dispassionate despair, with entire disillusionment, I surveyed the dust dance; my life, my friends' lives, and those fabulous presences, men with brooms, women writing, the willow tree by the river – clouds and

phantoms made of dust too, of dust that changed, as clouds lose and gain and take gold or red and lose their summits and billow this way and that, mutable, vain. I, carrying a note-book, making phrases, had recorded mere changes; a shadow, I had been sedulous to take note of shadows. How can I proceed now, I said, without a self, weightless and visionless, through a world weightless, without illusion?[66]

When the slave child clasped the steel round his neck in Kipling's story he bade farewell to Sir Huon and his knights, the fairy king who in *A Midsummer Night's Dream* lies behind Oberon, king of shadows. At the beginning of *Puck of Pook's Hill* the children rehearse a scene from Shakespeare's play. The mood of Bernard's speech echoes Theseus' words to Hippolyta: 'The best in this kind are but shadows.' The lady writing has become in Bernard's reverie vague and impersonal: women writing. Have the children imagined her? Has she imagined the children? Is it the writer or is it the writer's creation which is unreal? Is illusion weightless, or is the world weightless without it? The young Stevenson, writing at the window while the moths flew at the lamp, fighting his own extinction with candles flaring in the theatre of the mind, tried feverishly to capture the phantom of immortality as he recorded, in a series of dramatic monologues in verse, not meanings, but voices. In *The Waves* Virginia Woolf explores through those same voices, more searchingly than she had done in *To the Lighthouse*, the power of the medium, words, and the capacity of the design they make to defy the flux they describe.

II   FORM

In *Puck of Pook's Hill* (1906) and *Rewards and Fairies* (1910) Kipling suggests a new formal possibility in the construction of narrative for children, although he did not consider the two books to be written for children. The children's adventures in travelling in time have no causal framework, no utopian direction, such as Ortega y Gasset claimed to have 'dominated the European mind during the whole of the modern epoch in science, in morals, in religion and in art'.[67] Through Puck's device of the Oak and Ash leaves – or Kipling's device as narrator of framing the children's adventures with Puck's magic and his own poems – the children never remember what has happened to them and so are not improved or educated by their experiences. The enriching of consciousness is the reader's not the fictional character's. The children grow out of one pair of boots and into another, but their minds show no such expansion. Kierkegaard declared that only through the development of the ethical self could the human personality acquire independence or significance. Moral development is dependent on time, and when the aesthetes insisted on seizing the moment, in Kierkegaard's view they cut themselves off from the possibility of maturity.[68] Woolf sought, while still giving form to the novel, to divest it of the moral and spiritual direction which Fry complained about in British painting. In *Mrs Dalloway* she achieved her effects through a circular structure. Writing to her about *To the Lighthouse* Roger Fry – to whom the novel would have been dedicated except that its author thought it was not good enough – observed: 'You're no longer bothered by the simultaneity of things and go backwards and forwards in time with extraordinary enrichment of each moment of consciousness.'[69] In *The Waves* she endorsed Kipling's determination to use narrative in defiance of spiritual or moral ends, but she reached that point after much meditation and experimenting with the relation between form and meaning.

William James argued that through the selecting processes of consciousness[70] children create meanings for themselves in the same way that they extract meaning from books even when half of the words are unknown to them: 'Their thinking is in form just what ours is when it is rapid. Both of us make flying leaps over large portions of the sentences uttered and we give attention only to substantive starting points, turning points, and conclusions here and there. . . . The children probably feel no gap when through a lot of unintelligible words they are swiftly carried to a familiar and intelligible terminus.'[71] Woolf wrote that 'a great part of every day is not lived consciously. One walks, eats, sees things, deals with what has to be done; the broken vacuum cleaner. . . . As a child then, my days, just as they do now, contained a large proportion of this cotton wool, this non-being.'[72] In *The Waves* the children depend on Bernard to select for them the moments of their own significance: 'Bernard says there is always a story.'

But as Bernard gets older he begins to wonder whether the tale in the mind is after all only a tail on the page: 'I can see a dozen pictures. But what are stories? Toys I twist, bubbles I blow, one ring passing through another. And sometimes I begin to doubt if there are stories. What is my story? What is Rhoda's? What is Neville's? There are facts.' The story implies meaning and control. As Bernard sees thin places in the stories, he falls back on the sequences of the external world, the biographical continuum which imposes itself so falsely and yet irrevocably on the shape of a life: 'The mind grows rings; . . . How fast the stream flows from January to December. We are swept on by the torrent of things grown so familiar that they cast no shadow.'[73] The rings are both the rings added to a tree each year, which spell age, but also the ring of the slave child in Kipling's story, opening and shutting, forever presenting a possibility of freedom and yet denying it, forcing on the individual the bondage of mortals, which consists both of inheritance – the savage lurking in the gut of every being, the women at the Nile gathering water – and of the race against time:

> The Queen propped her up against a tree, and said kindly, 'You may rest a little, now.'
> Alice looked round her in great surprise. 'Why, I do believe we've been under this tree the whole time! Everything's just as it was!'
> 'Of course it is,' said the Queen. 'What would you have it?'
> 'Well, in *our* country,' said Alice, still panting a little, 'You'd generally get to somewhere else – if you ran very fast for a long time as we've been doing.'
> 'A slow sort of country!' said the Queen. 'Now, here, you see, it takes all the running *you* can do, to keep in the same place. If you want to get somewhere else, you must run at least twice as fast as that.'   (*L-G*, 210)

Bernard's perception in *The Waves* is that you have to keep running but it doesn't get you anywhere. It is sequence without goal or direction, without the significance of story. In the final scene in the restaurant Bernard muses: 'Should this be the end of the story? a kind of sigh? a last ripple of the wave? A trickle of water in some gutter where, burbling, it dies away? Let me touch the table – so – and thus recover my sense of the moment. A side-board covered with cruets; a basket full of rolls; a plate of bananas – these are comfortable sights. But if there are no stories, what end can there be, or what beginning? Life is not susceptible perhaps to the treatment we give it when we try to tell it.'[74] We are back with the Caucus Race, start where you like and end where you like.

The ponderous woman looked through the pattern of falling words at the flowers standing cool, firm and upright in the earth, with a curious expression. She saw them as a sleeper waking from a heavy sleep sees a brass candlestick reflecting the light in an unfamiliar way, and closes his eyes and opens them, and seeing the brass candlestick again, finally starts wide awake and stares at the candlestick with all his powers. So the heavy woman came to a standstill opposite the oval shaped flower bed, and ceased even to pretend to listen to what the other woman was saying. She stood there letting the words fall over her, swaying the top part of her body slowly backwards and forwards, looking at the flowers. Then she suggested that they should find a seat and have their tea.

11 *Kew Gardens* (decorated by Vanessa Bell, 1927)

Virginia Woolf thus confronts the central aesthetic dilemma which the artist must encounter if there is no God and no ethical direction to either life or art. Narrative demands to be set out in time and space as human life is set out. If there is no pilgrimage, what is to take the place of the pilgrim's arrival at the Delectable Mountains? Where and what is the little wicket gate which he must go through in order to start his meaningful existence? If it is birth only into physical but not into moral existence, the words which describe it patter like rain on the growing flower as they do in *Kew Gardens*[75] and stop when the shower is over. Without a moral, as Mark Twain saw perfectly well as he pushed the raft bearing Huck and Jim out into the main stream of the Mississippi, there can be no plot. If the work of art ceases to mirror the designs of God because life has ceased to mirror them, how is the artist to give a design in art to his vision of life, and without design, how can it be a vision? It can only be continuous flux, but although that may represent the medium of life for human beings, as words represent the medium of the novel, it can never represent form, without which neither art nor life can have meaning. The sea is a fact; it is not a story.

The problem was solved in *To the Lighthouse* by making the novelist's art into painting. The representative medium of the novel is thus one of volumes, colours and shapes, relations in spatial design. Lily's mode of painting defines its own direction through aesthetic rather than moral choices.

Virginia Woolf drew her descriptions of Lily's painting directly from Roger Fry's essay 'The Artist's Vision' in *Vision and Design* (1920), a book he gave her in return for addressing envelopes at the Omega. She wrote to him in December: 'I'm in the middle of your book and fascinated. 200 envelopes have been despatched.'[76] Fry claims that 'the artist's main business in life . . . is carried on by means of yet a fourth kind of vision, which I will call the creative vision. . . . It demands the most complete detachment from any of the meanings and implications of appearances. . . . As he contemplates the particular field of vision, the (aesthetically) chaotic and accidental conjunction of forms and colours begins to crystallise into a harmony; and as this harmony becomes clear to the artist, his actual vision becomes distorted by the emphasis of the rhythm which has been set up within him.'[77] This view of design lies behind Lily's explanations to William Bankes that Mrs Ramsay and James are subordinate to a design of lights and shadows, of solid masses seen in relation to each other.

Like the stocking, and like the first section of Woolf's own book, the picture remains unfinished, and Lily, returning to it ten years later, must see it afresh and recompose those masses, as Woolf herself must reconstruct her own picture of the Ramsays in the final section of the book after 'Time Passes'. Fry analyses 'the process by which such a picture is arrived at . . . – the actual objects presented to the artist's vision are first deprived of all those specific characters by which we ordinarily apprehend their concrete existence – they are reduced to pure elements of space and volume.' The artist's 'sensual intelligence' creates from these abstract masses a design which is then 'brought back into the concrete world of real things not by giving them back their specific peculiarities, but by expressing them in an incessantly varying and shifting texture'. The second section of *To the Lighthouse* creates the shifting texture, the third restores the reality of concrete things. Fry declares that the process is an unconscious one, but that 'no doubt all great art arrives at some such solution of the apparently insoluble problem of artistic creation'.[78] Lily as artist moves from the chaotic to the ordered, but also from the actual vision to the artistically rhythmic one:

> Quickly, as if she were recalled by something over there, she turned to her canvas. There it was – her picture. Yes, with all its greens and blues, its lines running up and across, its attempt at something. It would be hung in the attics, she thought; it would be destroyed. But what did that matter? she asked herself, taking up her brush again. She looked at the steps; they were empty; she looked at the canvas; it was blurred. With a sudden intensity, as if she saw it clear for a second, she drew a line there, in the centre. It was done; it was finished. Yes, she thought, laying down her brush in extreme fatigue. I have had my vision.

The final statement is one of having realised something in a medium which seemed to resist it. Earlier, while she was painting, Lily had meditated on how Mr Carmichael, a poet, would have answered the question: 'What does it mean?' 'She looked at her picture. That would have been his answer, presumably – how "you" and "I" and "she" pass and vanish; nothing stays; all changes; but not words, not paint.'[79] The work of art defines itself within a tradition of art as permanence.

To the Lighthouse is defined not only in relation to a tradition, but also in relation to specific parent texts, in which the *bildungsroman*,[80]

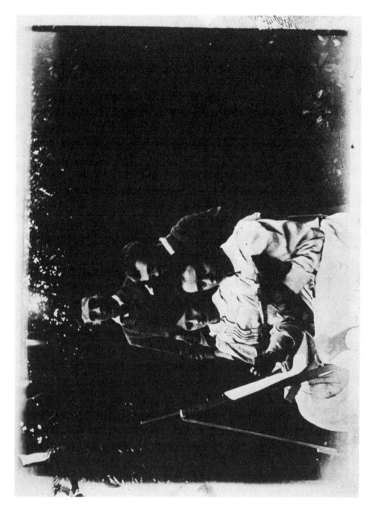

12 At the easel: Virginia, Vanessa, Thoby and Adrian Stephen

which traces the journey of the hero through life, is undercut by a speeding-up and fracturing of narrative sequences comparable to Carroll's in *Through the Looking-Glass*. Woolf's whole novel might be viewed as a railway journey – a metaphor that she often used for writing – in which the first section, 'The Window', shows a view neatly contained within a frame, as Mrs Ramsay and James will

ultimately be contained within the frame of Lily's picture.[81] In the second section the train moves on, gathering speed and momentum, with the landscape flashing by as it does in Stevenson's poem 'From a Railway Carriage' in *A Child's Garden of Verses*. In the last part of the novel the train arrives at the destination which had been proclaimed from the beginning: the Lighthouse.

Carroll created moments capable of sparking off the reader's imagination, so that both the *Alice* books, read at an age when the mind is at its freshest and most retentive, fed back to adult writers in the early twentieth century a fund of remembered images. If Woolf had in the back of her mind Alice and the Sheep in their boat with the dream rushes, she might have remembered that Tenniel's picture places it in front of a large empty window which is all that remains of the Sheep's shop. The Sheep, like Mrs Ramsay, is still knitting, despite the dissolution of her world. Eliot said that the opening of *Burnt Norton*, the first of *Four Quartets*, came from the beginning of *Alice in Wonderland*, where 'Alice hears the footsteps of the White Rabbit in the passage and cannot get through the door into the rose-garden':[82]

> Footfalls echo in the memory
> Down the passage which we did not take
> Towards the door we never opened
> Into the rose-garden. My words echo
> Thus, in your mind.[83]

Carroll's words echoed in the minds of Woolf's and Eliot's generation. The Guard looks at Alice 'through a telescope, then

through a microscope, and then through an opera-glass', and tells her she is travelling the wrong way, at which another passenger, dressed in white paper, rebukes her for not knowing her name. Like Bernard in *The Waves* she has not got a ticket.

'Don't make excuses,' said the Guard: 'you should have bought one from the engine-driver.' And once more the chorus of voices went on with 'The man that drives the engine. Why, the smoke alone is worth a thousand pounds a puff.'
   Alice thought to herself 'Then there's no use in speaking.' The voices didn't join in, *this* time, as she hadn't spoken, but to her great surprise, they all *thought* in chorus (I hope you understand what *thinking in chorus* means – for I must confess that *I* don't), 'Better say nothing at all. Language is worth a thousand pounds a year.' (*L-G*, 217)

If the testiness of the other passengers suggests Charles Tansley's dismissiveness towards Lily, both the insistence on the value of the language, and the thinking in chorus, anticipate the children's voices at the opening of *The Waves*.
   Although Woolf may have culled hints for *The Waves* from *Through the Looking-Glass*, the later novel, when compared with *To the Lighthouse*, does not establish its identity primarily through its relation to recognised traditions of writing. If, like Kenneth Grahame in *The Golden Age*, Woolf dispensed in *The Waves* with parents so that the children might possess their own consciousness in peace, she also claimed for herself as writer freedom from parent texts. While she was writing the novel she insisted: 'I am not trying to tell a story.' *Orlando* had taught her 'continuity and narrative and how to keep the realities at bay'. But she repudiates in *The Waves* traditional narrative structures: 'Suppose I could run all the scenes together more? – by rhythms chiefly. . . . I want to avoid chapters.'[84] The word 'rhythm' returns her to Fry's analysis of Cézanne's later work: 'Whatever the technique, we find in this last phase a tendency to break up the volumes, to arrive almost at a refusal to accept the unity of each object, to allow the planes to move freely in space. We get, in fact, a kind of abstract system of plastic rhythms, from which we can no doubt build up the separate volumes for ourselves, but in which these are not clearly enforced on us.'[85]
   At the conclusion of the chapter 'Vision and Design' in her biography of Roger Fry, Virginia Woolf recalled Fry's belief that

aesthetic choices must be continually remade: 'No crust must be allowed to form, even if the purely external conditions of life must have a certain solid texture.'[86] She herself never stopped experimenting with form: 'I have to some extent forced myself to break every mould and find a fresh form of being, that is of expression, for everything I feel or think. So that when it is working I get the sense of being fully energised – nothing stunted.'[87] This was written after *The Waves*, but it was true of all her books. Rebellion against conventions and authority included rebellion against her own conventions of writing. Bernard declared in *The Waves*: 'I begin to seek some design. . . . Great clouds always changing, and movement. . . . Of story, of design, I do not see a trace then.' This perception of rhythm, and of a meaning not related to the fabrications of narrative, follows Bernard's fullest statement of the inadequacies of stories and of phrase-making: 'How tired I am of stories, how tired I am of phrases that come down beautifully with all their feet on the ground! Also, how I distrust neat designs of life that are drawn upon half-sheets of note-paper. I begin to long for some little language such as lovers use, broken words, inarticulate words, like the shuffling of feet on the pavement.'[88] Fry had written – and Woolf quoted him in the biography – that 'art and life are two rhythms',[89] and that although they might interact, in the main they stayed separate. Virginia Woolf, for all her experimenting, clung to the belief that 'writing must be formal' and that only in form could the egotism of the artist be written out of the text; but she did not think that art and life were distinct. They were in fact inextricably bound together, like lovers, each giving meaning to the other. After the publication of *The Waves* she mused: 'I thought, driving through Richmond last night, something very profound about the synthesis of my being: how only writing composes it: how nothing makes a whole unless I am writing.'[90]

The children in *The Waves* apprehend death long before Percival dies, when the man is found by the apple-tree with his throat cut, a moment poised between fact and fantasy.[91] Percival dies in the noontide of their day: 'The sun had risen to its full height' – and their sense of time is measured against his passing: 'We are doomed, all of us. Women shuffle past with shopping-bags. People keep on passing.' Bernard's son is born as Percival dies. Rhoda declares that Bernard will enter in his book 'under D . . . "Phrases to be used on the deaths of friends" '.[92] In the next section the light has already left the meridian. On one level Percival's death is trivialised by his unreality. On another, it constructs reality for the reader. He becomes a self through the children's accommodation of his death. Kierkegaard argued that death teaches subjectivity, forcing men to define themselves against its reality.[93] Bernard muses: 'I saw the first leaf fall on his grave. I saw us push beyond this moment, and leave it behind us for ever.'[94] Ortega wrote in *The Modern Theme* that 'the essential note in the new sensibility is actually the determination never in any way to forget that spiritual and cultural functions are equally and simultaneously biological functions'.[95] The rhythm of art in *The Waves* traces the great sequences of the physical world, both in the individual and in the cycles of nature.

Woolf wrote in her diary: 'All writers are unhappy. . . . The wordless are the happy.'[96] Bernard declares that 'for pain words are lacking. There should be cries, cracks, fissures, whiteness passing over chintz covers, interference with the sense of time, of space.'[97] But although pain may evade description, to describe how it defies language is still to locate it in language, as William James knew. Grahame had written in *Dream Days*:

> Of certain supreme moments it is not easy to write. The varying shades and currents of emotion may indeed be put into words by those specially skilled that way; they often are, at considerable length. But the sheer, crude article itself – the strong, live thing that leaps up inside you and swells and strangles you, the dizziness of revulsion that takes the breath like cold water – who shall depict this and live?[98]

In an article in the *Yellow Book* in 1895 called 'The Inner Ear' Grahame identified an inner silence, in which if heeded 'the very rush of sap, the thrust and foison of germination, will join in the din, and go far to deafen us'.[99] For Louis 'grass and trees . . . hint at some other order, and better, which makes a reason everlastingly'.[100]

The order of nature may give meaning to life, but what sort of meaning does it give to art? Can art really only trace the rhythms of physical existence without shaping them into some utopian vision, some pattern of cause and effect? Virginia Woolf had insisted in *Orlando* on the multiplicity of selves, on the falsehood involved in creating a unified character. But when she finished the draft of *The Waves* she wrote: 'It occurred to me last night while listening to a Beethoven quartet that I would merge all the interjected passages into Bernard's final speech and end with the words O solitude: thus making him absorb all those scenes and having no further break. This is also to show that the theme effort, effort, dominates; not the waves: and personality: and defiance: but I am not sure of the effect artistically, because the proportions may need the intervention of the waves finally so as to make a conclusion.'[101] Although Bernard's final soliloquy is not to solitude but to death, this diary entry contains a revealing statement of direction, for in the novel the children move from group to discrete entity through learning the language of defiant self, which arrests flux. In the end Bernard is partially reconciled to renunciation: 'Now no one sees me and I change no more. Heaven be praised for solitude that has removed the pressure of the eye, the solicitation of the body, and all need of lies and phrases.' The state of aloneness is the precondition of strength. But he still asks: 'By what name are we to call death? I do not know. I need a little language such as lovers use, . . . I need a howl; a cry.'[102] The echo of *King Lear* is insistent. On 19 July 1897 Virginia Woolf recorded in her diary that at three in the morning George and Vanessa had broken the news to her that Stella Duckworth had died. The lines sprawl unevenly across the small and otherwise blank page on which she notes that that event has absorbed all their thoughts and that she cannot write about it. Two days later the diary notes that Stella had been buried next to her mother in the churchyard at Highgate and that none of the Stephen children had attended the funeral.[103] In *The Waves* Virginia Woolf forces the impossible, the writing about death, onto the page.

The children's separation from each other as, in the novel, they grow older, is described in an extraordinarily plastic image: 'We were all different. The wax – the virginal wax that coats the spine melted in different patches for each of us. . . . We suffered terribly as we became separate bodies.' In becoming separate they become mortal and fallible, subject to the physical world. But the power which separates them, language, also controls that world.

Bernard has practised ways of naming death, and the book ends with an amazing apostrophe to both death and life, which recaptures the original moment of the children's awakening to birdsong and light:

A redness gathers on the roses, even on the pale rose that hangs by the bedroom window. A bird chirps. Cottagers light their early candles. Yes, this is the eternal renewal, the incessant rise and fall and fall and rise again.

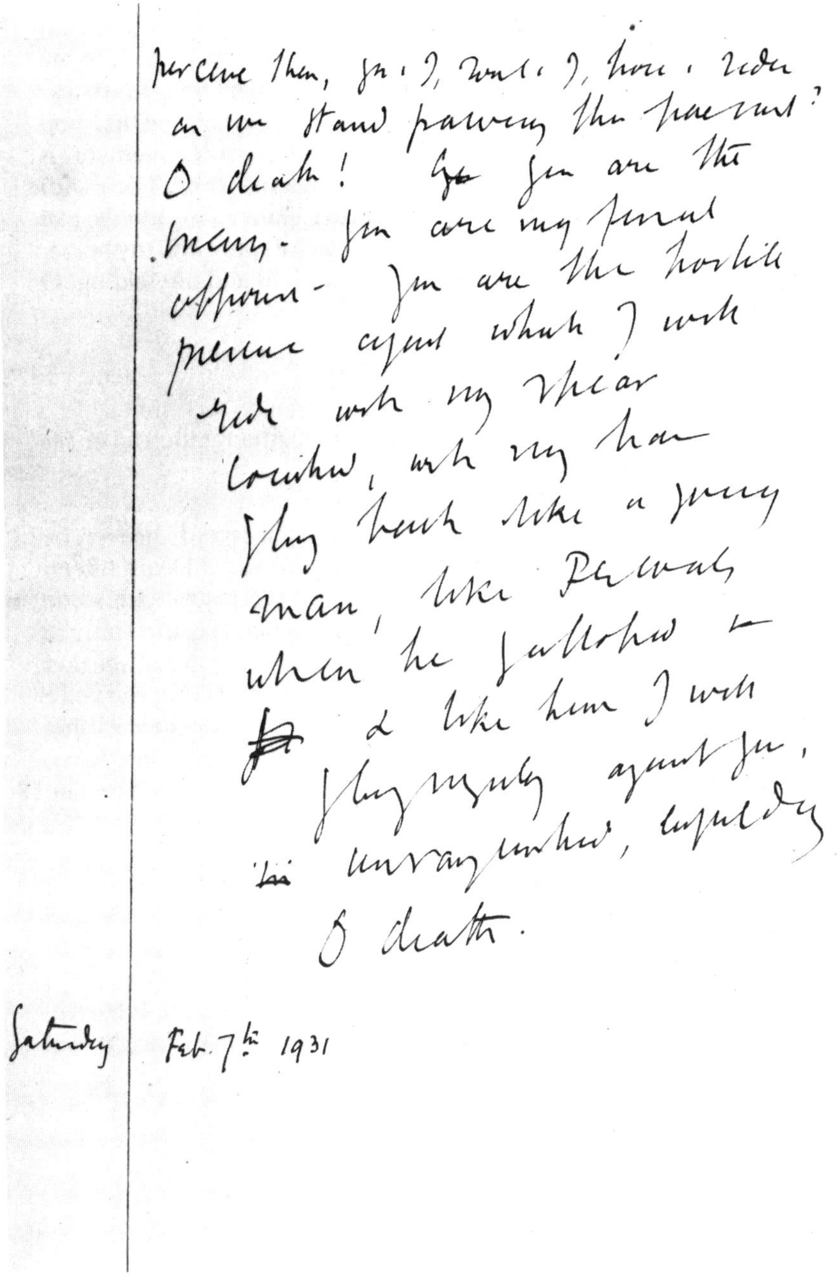
perceive them, go I, would I, horse. Ride
on we stand pawing this pavement?
O death! ~~Yo~~ You are the
enemy. You are my final
opponent. You are the hostile
presence against which I will
ride with my spear
couched, with my hair
flying back like a young
man, like Percival's
when he galloped in
~~In~~ & like him I will
fling myself against you,
~~in~~ unvanquished, unyielding
O death.

Saturday Feb. 7th 1931

13 Virginia Woolf, holograph draft of the end of *The Waves*

And in me too the wave rises. It swells; it arches its back. I am aware once more of a new desire, something rising beneath me like a proud horse whose rider first spurs and then pulls him back. What enemy do we now perceive advancing against us, you whom I ride now, as we stand pawing this stretch of pavement? It is death. Death is the enemy. It is death against whom I ride with my spear couched and my hair flying back like a young man's, like Percival's, when he galloped in India. I strike spurs into my horse. Against you I will fling myself, unvanquished and unyielding, O Death!'[104]

The waves broke on the shore.

What is the nature of the defiance which is breathed at the end of *The Waves*? Woolf wrote:

Here in the few minutes that remain, I must record, heaven be praised, the end of *The Waves*. I wrote the words O Death fifteen minutes ago, having reeled across the last ten pages with some moments of such intensity and intoxication that I seemed only to stumble after my own voice, or almost, after some sort of speaker (as when I was mad) I was almost afraid, remembering the voice that used to fly ahead. Anyhow it is done; and I have been sitting these 15 minutes in a state of glory, and calm, and some tears, thinking of Thoby and if I could write Julian Thoby Stephen 1881–1906 on the first page. I suppose not.[105]

In *The Waves* death is fully represented as a form of life, as a solid volume subject to the same rhythms as physical existence and capable of description in words. In naming death, in forcing it to become part of the medium of art, words, Woolf makes it also part of the process of creation, as her brother's death becomes the subject of her own defiance of time in words which create life, if not permanence.

6

Making Space for a Child

When Alice sits down at the Mad Hatter's tea table the occupants assure her that there is no room: ' "There's *plenty* of room!" said Alice indignantly, and she sat down in a large arm-chair at one end of the table" ' (*AW*, 93). Not being allowed to sit down becomes comparable to not having a place in language. The Dormouse remarks:

> 'Did you ever see such a thing as a drawing of a muchness!'
> 'Really, now you ask me,' said Alice, very much confused, 'I don't think –'
> 'Then you shouldn't talk,' said the Hatter.
> This piece of rudeness was more than Alice could bear: she got up in great disgust and walked off.   (*AW*, 103)

The Mad Hatter is determined not to allow Alice any space, and her retort is to find her own, first by taking some of his, and then by moving elsewhere.

In *The Voyage Out* Rachel's silent judgement on the breakfast table occupied by Willoughby, Ridley and Mr Pepper makes a space which is both her own, the author's and the reader's.

Woolf declared that 'the test of a book (to a writer) is if it makes a space in which, quite naturally, you can say what you want to say. . . . This proves that the book itself is alive'.[1] Her complaint against the realism of Arnold Bennett and H. G. Wells was that 'they have laid an enormous stress upon the fabric of things', but that Bennett 'is trying to hypnotize us into the belief that, because he has made a house, there must be a person living there'. The book, like the house, opens on a void, whereas Woolf wants it to open on a new freedom: 'I ask myself, what is reality? And who are the judges of reality? A character may be real to Mr Bennett and quite unreal to me.'[2] The protest is Alice's: whose table is it and why do they think there is no room for her?

Woolf was anticipated in this protest by Robert Louis Stevenson. In 'A Note on Realism' published in the *Magazine of Art* in November 1883 he argued: 'The immediate danger of the realist is to sacrifice the beauty and significance of the whole to local dexterity, or in the insane pursuit of completion, to immolate his readers under facts . . . to discard all design, abjure all choice, and . . . to communicate matter which is not worth learning.' He declared that 'in literature . . . the great change of the past century has been effected by the admission of detail [Scott, Balzac]. . . . But it has recently . . . fallen into a more technical and decorative stage. . . . With a movement of alarm, the wiser or more timid begin to aspire after a more naked narrative articulation . . . after a general lightening of this baggage of detail.'[3] Ten years later he expostulated to Henry James: 'How to get over, how to escape from the besotted particularity of fiction. "Roland approached the house; it had green doors and window blinds; and there was a scraper on the upper step." To hell with Roland and the scraper.'[4] Virginia Woolf confided to her diary in 1909 that her own descriptions suffered from being too precise and concrete.[5] Stevenson was one of the first writers to attack the notion that definiteness – which Woolf accuses herself of in this early diary – constitutes realism. He argued that 'representative art, which can be said to live, is both realistic and ideal; and the realism about which we quarrel is a matter purely of externals'.[6] Woolf declared of Orlando's passion for books: 'It was the fatal nature of this disease to substitute a phantom for reality.'[7] But she had already argued in 'The Mark on the Wall' that the phantom was inseparable from the

14   Illustration from Robert Louis Stevenson's *A Child's Garden of Verses*

reality. In demanding that the author make a place in the book for both, and recognise their interdependence, Woolf entered the imaginative territory of the child.

Stevenson argued in 'Child's Play' (1878) that a child's apprehension of reality differs radically from an adult's: 'They walk in a vain show, and among mists and rainbows; they are passionate after dreams and unconcerned about realities.' He pointed out that 'children are ever content to forego what we call the realities, and prefer the shadow to the substance'. The example he gives is of the games they play with their food: 'We need pickles nowadays to make Wednesday's cold mutton please our Friday's appetite; and I can remember the time when to call it red venison, and tell myself a hunter's story, would have made it more palatable than the best of sauces. To the grown person, cold mutton is cold mutton all the world over.'[8] For children the imaginary world clothes and adorns the unpalatable real, as it did for Virginia Woolf, who wrote that 'the only exciting life is the imaginary one'.[9] When Nesbit shows the Bastable children in *The Story of the Treasure Seekers* transforming their drab everyday existence into a fable, she enters as artist a country bounded by Stevenson on one side and Oscar Wilde on the other. If the Bastables have to eat cold mutton, 'Oswald said it was a savoury stew made of red deer that Edward shot. So then we were the Children of the New Forest, and the mutton tasted much better.'[10] Stevenson attacked the notion that children should be expected to tell the truth, and poured scorn on parental demands for 'peddling exactitude about matters of fact'.[11] Only a dozen years later Oscar Wilde pleaded in *The Decay of Lying* for a return to fiction and lies, bewailing the predominance of 'the solid stolid British intellect' and groaning that 'we are all bored to death with the commonplace character of modern fiction'. Wilde longs for the day when

> Facts will be regarded as discreditable, truth will be found mourning over her fetters, and Romance, with her temper of wonder, will return to the land. The very aspect of the world will change to our startled eyes. Out of the sea will rise Behemoth and Leviathan, and sail round the high-pooped galleys, as they do on the delightful maps of those ages when books on geography were actually readable. Dragons will wander about the waste places, and the phoenix will soar from her nest of fire into the air. We shall

lay our hands upon the basilisk, and see the jewel in the toad's head.[12]

The pioneers of the return of the phoenix, the toad and the high-pooped galley to British fiction were the writers of children's books: E. Nesbit (*The Phoenix and the Carpet*), Kenneth Grahame (*The Wind in the Willows*) and Stevenson himself (*Treasure Island*). Behind all of them lay *Through the Looking-Glass*, as Nesbit knew when she allowed Anthea in *The Story of the Amulet* to compare the orchards of ancient Babylon intersected with brooks to the squares and lines on the chessboard landscape of Alice's adventures.[13]

Carroll's looking-glass, superimposed on older mirror images, helped to shape the mental landscape of these writers. Kipling shows Gloriana parading before it in *Rewards and Fairies*:

Backwards and forwards and sideways did she pass,
Making up her mind to face the cruel looking-glass.
The cruel looking-glass which will never show a lass
As comely or as kindly or as young as she once was.[14]

In *The Waves* 'the looking-glass whitened its pool upon the wall. The real flower on the window-sill was attended by a phantom flower. Yet the phantom was part of the flower, for when a bud broke free the paler flower in the glass opened a bud too.'[15] Nesbit wrote at the beginning of *Five Children and It*, in which the children find a sand-fairy, that she was not going to put anything in the book which would enable the adult reading out loud to pencil into the margin '"How true!" or "How like life!"'[16] Author, reader, and child within the book share a space which allows them to sport with the adult obsession with facts.

As the modern Orlando enters the lift in Marshall and Snelgrove's she muses: 'The very fabric of life now . . . is magic. In the eighteenth century, we knew how everything was done; but here I rise through the air; I listen to voices in America; I see men flying – but how it's done, I can't even begin to wonder. So my belief in magic returns.'[17] Woolf was only a child when in the 1890s men and women began to realise that the new century would make unprecedented demands on their capacity for belief. An article on submarines in the *Strand Magazine* in 1898 observed that in the days of Jules Verne's *Twenty Thousand Leagues under the Seas* 'the submarine boat was but the invention of a fertile imagination. . . . To-day [it] is

an actual fact.'[18] The popular literature of the late nineteenth
century records an astonishment amounting to disbelief as each
technological invention emerges: the train, the camera, the
telephone, the submarine, the flying-machine, even, in an early
children's story in *Good Words for the Young* in 1872, the idea of the
gramophone. Flora Thompson captures that mood of wonder when
in *Lark Rise to Candleford* she describes a walk the children take in the
1890s from Juniper Hill:

> Their father pointed out some earthworks which he said were
> thrown up by the Romans and described those old warriors in
> their brass helmets so well that the children seemed to see them;
> but neither he, nor they, dreamed that another field within sight
> would one day be surrounded by buildings called 'hangars', or
> that one day, within their own lifetimes, other warriors would
> soar from it into the sky, armed with more deadly weapons than
> the Romans ever knew. No, that field lay dreaming in the
> sunshine, flat and green, waiting for a future of which they knew
> nothing.[19]

Lewis Carroll had anticipated in *Through the Looking-Glass* that
moment of bemused astonishment at the evidence presented by the
world of the real.

When the Unicorn espies Alice he 'stood for some time looking at
her with an air of deepest disgust':

> 'What – is – this?' he said at last.
> 'This is a child!' Haigha replied eagerly, coming in front of Alice
> to introduce her, and spreading out both his hands towards her in
> an Anglo-Saxon attitude. 'We only found it to-day. It's as large as
> life, and twice as natural!'
> 'I always thought they were fabulous monsters!' said the
> Unicorn. 'Is it alive?'
> 'It can talk,' said Haigha solemnly.
> The Unicorn looked dreamily at Alice, and said 'Talk, child.'
> Alice could not help her lips curling up into a smile as she
> began: 'Do you know, I always thought Unicorns were fabulous
> monsters, too? I never saw one alive before!'
> 'Well, now that we *have* seen each other,' said the Unicorn, 'if
> you'll believe in me, I'll believe in you. Is that a bargain?'
> 'Yes, if you like,' said Alice. (*L-G*, 287)

For a moment the reader sides with the Unicorn: can one really believe in a child? Where has it come from? Where is it going? What are the laws of its existence? Many adults would admit that such questions cross their minds, just as, when the baby turns into a pig, Alice feels this to be its true identity: it makes a rather handsome

pig, whereas it was a hideous baby. Most mothers would recognise this emotion too, although society does not sanction its public expression. Virginia Woolf exclaimed about her baby nephew Julian Bell: 'A child is the very devil – calling out, as I believe, all the worst and least explicable passions of the parents – and of the Aunts.' A fortnight later she wrote: 'I had a fortnight at St Ives; Adrian and Nessa and Clive came for the last week. I doubt that I shall ever have a baby. Its voice is too terrible, a senseless scream, like an ill omened cat. Nobody could wish to comfort it, or pretend that it was a human

being.'[20] Well, as the Unicorn said, I'll believe in you if you'll believe in me. The child's capacity for belief, as Stevenson averred, is infinitely greater than the adult's because every aspect of his experience tests it. He has no ground of acquired knowledge from which to divide the phenomena of the world into the real and the unreal.

The child's search for truth is thus different in kind from the adult's. Stevenson observed the child's eager preservation of the text of his stories, but claimed that for him the question 'Is it true?' had nothing to do with the accurate purveying of information. It means: 'Is he, or is he not, to look out for magicians, kindly or potent? May he, or may he not, reasonably hope to be cast away upon a desert island, or turned to such diminutive proportions that he can live on equal terms with his lead soldiery, and go on a cruise in his own toy schooner?'[21] J. R. R. Tolkien in *Tree and Leaf* (1964) stated that the child's question about truth meant: ' "Am I safe in

bed?'' The answer: ''There is certainly no dragon in England today'',
is all that they want to hear.'[22] However, the evidence of children's
stories written at the turn of the century suggests that, although
children wanted to be safe in their beds, they were happy to hear
that a new dragon was skulking on the horizon within walking-
distance. It was the adults who didn't like it.

When the child in Kenneth Grahame's 'The Reluctant Dragon'
(1899) breaks the news to his parents that a dragon has taken up
residence on the hill above their farm they are far from pleased:

> 'Only a dragon?' cried his father. 'What do you mean, sitting
> there, you and your dragons? *Only* a dragon indeed! And what do
> *you* know about it?'
> ''Cos it *is*, and 'cos I *do* know,' replied the Boy, quietly. 'Look
> here, father, you know we've each of us got our line. *You* know
> about sheep, and weather, and things; *I* know about dragons.'[23]

James Ramsay should have made a comparable speech to his father
at the beginning of *To the Lighthouse*. Leslie Stephen's daughter
made it to him every time she wrote a novel. The answer which Mr
Ramsay might have given his son appeared in a feature in *Good
Words for the Young* in 1870, called 'Dragons and Dragon-Slayers', in
which the writer informs the child reader that dragons are not *real*,
they are metaphors for evil, and that the dragon-slayers of the world
were 'real conquerors over sin and tyranny, flood and pain, over
paganism and heresy, and godless evil, in all its forms and
shapes'.[24] Life, as Mr Ramsay points out, narrowing his little blue
eyes upon the horizon, is a struggle 'that needs, above all, courage,
truth, and the power to endure'.[25] It takes St George in Grahame's
story a long time to understand that his dragon is not a
representative of evil and that therefore he can stop playing his
saintly part and take notice of the world around him, where the
populace are gambling on the dragon's success in the combat: ' ''Six
to four on the dragon!'' murmured St George sadly, resting his
cheek on his hand. ''This is an evil world, and sometimes I begin to
think that all the wickedness in it is not entirely bottled up inside
dragons.'' ' When the dragon makes a snap at his horse's tail, 'the
language of the Saint, who had lost a stirrup, was fortunately
inaudible to the general assemblage'.[26] The dragon, who likes best
to bask in the sun making up poetry, ambles back to his cave,
singing. He is still a dragon, but not the sort that adults are used to

finding in the books they select for the improvement of their children.

Grahame suggested in an introduction to Aesop's *Fables* that 'a dragon . . . is a more enduring animal than a pterodactyl'.[27] The new dragons at the turn of the century are just as fiery, noisy, cumbersome and terrifying as the old, but it is adults rather than children who feel that they would prefer to see horses on the hillside rather than the more exotic slumbering beast. Many people felt Orlando's disorientation at ' "that stupendous invention, which had (the historians say) completely changed the face of Europe in the past twenty years" (as, indeed, happens much more frequently than historians suppose). She noticed only that it was extremely smutty; rattled horribly; and the windows stuck.'[28] The nineteenth century rings with laments about the way in which the railway has destroyed man's relation to his environment so that the experience of travelling is no longer measured by a discernible relation between time, speed, distance and animal effort. Emerson wrote that 'it was dream-like travelling on the railroad'.[29] The landscape itself seemed like a mirage, a moving picture, as in Stevenson's poem: 'And ever again, in the wink of an eye, / Painted stations whistle by'.[30] When Victor Hugo describes a view from a train window, it becomes a Van Gogh painting, all colour and sinuous lines: 'The flowers by the side of the road are no longer flowers but flecks, or rather streaks, of red or white; there are no longer any points, everything becomes a streak; the grainfields are great shocks of yellow hair.'[31] *Struwwelpeter* or stooks of corn, the landscape speeding past the window seemed, like Fry's Post-Impressionist exhibition, to catapult adults into the world of children's tales and rudimentary surrealist drawings.

But children felt differently. They had a fiction ready to hand by which to interpret and imagine the new reality: 'In the distance, they could see its eyes of fire growing bigger and brighter every instant. "It *is* a dragon – I always knew it was – it takes its own shape in here, in the dark," shouted Phyllis. But nobody heard her. You see the train was shouting, too, and its voice was bigger than hers.' Nesbit's railway children name the trains the 'Green Dragon', the 'Worm of Wantley' and the 'Fearsome Fly-by-Night'.[32] In *The Waves* the train acquires the same identity: 'the very powerful, bottle-green engine without a neck, all back and thighs, breathing steam', which 'stamps heavily, breathes stertorously, as it climbs up and up', is a creature capable of representing life itself – 'This is part of the emerging monster to which we are attached.'[33] But whereas the adult, as in Jean Ingelow's story of travelling into the future on a train, feels 'a sense of desolation and isolation',[34] the child is exhilarated by his own capacity to see in the reality of his actual world the creature of a world often more real to him: that of the book.

II TIME-TRAVEL AND TERRITORY

The writing of fiction is stimulated, as Arthur Waugh observed in the *Yellow Book* in the 1890s, by times of upheaval, because they highlight its vital function of feeding the imagination with images through which change may be understood and interpreted. Shakespeare's plays bodied forth the Renaissance for his own times as well as for the future, just as Milton and Bunyan created for the Puritans of the seventeenth century images through which they might recognise and define themselves in relation to their faith. The time theory which emerges in Bergson, William James and other writers in the late nineteenth and early twentieth centuries is an attempt to understand a human consciousness disoriented by different kinds of relativity. Both scientific discovery and technological invention unite in a new popular form in H. G. Wells's futurist fantasy *The Time Machine* (1895). Wells's traveller voyages through the fourth dimension into the future in a creaking but marvellous machine, and discovers a world in which survival of the fittest has created a bizarre dichotomy between, on the one hand, the beautiful, the good and the weak, and, on the other, the ugly, the evil and the strong. Reviewing the story in the *Pall Mall Magazine* Zangwill criticised Wells for naïveté, claiming that all men must now consider themselves to be time travellers, because 'the whole Past of the earth is still playing itself out – to an eye conceived as stationed to-day in space, and moving now forwards to catch the Middle Ages, now backwards to watch Nero fiddling over the burning of Rome. . . . Terrible, solemn thought that the Past can never die.'[35] The new function of the author is to mirror not God's moral judgements nor his prompting of the human conscience, but his simultaneity, which sees the Roman camp and the 1914 hangar coexisting on the same landscape. Many writers perceived that memory offers everyone a paradigm of travelling in time because it provides access to childhood, which is both past and not-past.

The brand of time travel which Wells's story depicts is in fact less in evidence at the turn of the century than a rather different impulse set in motion by *The Golden Age*, which appeared in the same year. In an incident called 'The Secret Drawer' the boy narrator slips away from his companions into an old blue-brocaded room to explore an antique Sheraton bureau, hoping to find that it has a secret drawer stocked with treasure trove. He alights instead on a jumble of odds and ends: birds' eggs, a ferret's muzzle, a portrait of a monarch. The point of the story is twofold. The room has the secrecy of a place of refuge: 'A power of making the intruder feel that he *was* intruding – perhaps even a faculty of hinting that some one might have been sitting on those chairs, writing at the bureau, or fingering the china, just a second before one entered.' Secondly, the contents of the secret drawer, given up 'with a sort of small sigh, almost a sob – as it were – of relief', appeal to the finder as 'a real boy's hoard. . . . He too had found out the secret drawer. . . . Across the void stretch of years I seemed to touch hands a moment with my little comrade of seasons – how many seasons? – long since dead.' Poised at the door of the quiet chamber the boy narrator hovers in spirit between past and present: 'In another minute I would be in the thick of it, in all the warmth and light and laughter. And yet – what a long way off it all seemed, both in space and time, to me yet lingering on the threshold of that old-world chamber.'[36] The whole experience encapsulates the writer's absorption in the book he creates. Woolf mused in her diary: 'What leagues I travel in time.'[37] Long before the impassioned outburst of *A Room of One's Own*, she had herself given the refuge of Grahame's boy narrator to Rachel Vinrace in *The Voyage Out*. Helen Ambrose finds for Rachel in her own house 'a room cut off from the rest of the house, large, private – a room in which she could play, read, think, defy the world, a fortress as well as a sanctuary. Rooms, she knew, became more like worlds than rooms at the age of twenty-four.'[38] The old room in which Grahame's narrator finds a private space and an ally from another time provides an image for many late-nineteenth-century children's books, and one which Virginia Woolf drew on in her own writing. The author uses the book to make for the child a space which has not been there before, and in so doing makes a new space for what she herself wants to say.

In 'A Sketch of the Past' Virginia Woolf remembers herself as a small child in the garden at St Ives: 'I was looking at a plant with a spread of leaves; and it seemed suddenly plain that the flower itself was a part of the earth; that a ring enclosed what was the flower; and that was the real flower; part earth; part flower. It was a thought I put away as being likely to be very useful to me later.'[39] She used it many years later in *The Waves*, where the child Louis muses: 'I hold a stalk in my hand. I am the stalk. My roots go down to the depths of the world, through earth dry with brick, and damp earth, through veins of lead and silver. I am all fibre.'[40] The image of the child rooted in the earth and needing its own ground may derive initially from the teaching of both Rousseau and Froebel, but it becomes in many late-nineteenth- and early-twentieth-century children's books an emblem of protest against adult refusal to allow children their own territory.

When Archibald Craven in *The Secret Garden* remembers his niece Mary he sends for her to enquire: 'Do you want toys, books, dolls?' Her tremulous question 'Might I have a bit of earth?' seems to leap out of the page:

> 'Earth!' he repeated. 'What do you mean?'
> 'To plant seeds in – to make things grow – to see them come alive.' Mary faltered.[41]

Froebel had urged that children should be given gardens, not Arcadias to dream in or Never-Never lands to ensure perpetual childhood, but territories for the exercise of real power: 'To be a child who has never called a piece of ground its own, has never tilled it in the sweat of its brow, has never expended its fostering love on plants and animals, there will always be a gap in the development of the soul, and it will be difficult for that child to attain the capacity for human nurture in a comprehensive sense.'[42] In Stevenson's *A Child's Garden of Verses* the child is lord of the outdoors in a way that he never can be in the house, which belongs to adults. Outside 'All about was mine, I said /. . . . This was the world and I was king.'[43] The boy narrator in *Dream Days* invites a little girl into the garden where they discover the common ground of childhood: 'From worms we passed, naturally enough, to frogs, and thence to pigs, aunts, gardeners, rocking-horses, and other fellow-citizens of our common kingdom.'[44] The frogs are real, not Arcadian, more likely to produce a healthy batch of tadpoles than to turn into fairy princes. When Dan and Una in *Rewards and Fairies* encounter the grotesque and extravagant figure of the Queen, she is trespassing on their kingdom, into which 'grown-ups are not allowed . . . unless brought'.[45] Behind that notice pinned on the edge of the wood lies

15 Newly Saved Seeds (from Gertrude Jekyll, *Children and Gardens*, 1908)

no symbol of an unattainable childish world, but only hundreds of notices in parks and gardens, on green lawns, around ponds and rockeries, that children must stay out unless kept on a lead. These writers give children not a dream place to be inhabited by tired adults, but a piece of ground which is their own, from which they can exclude adults, tired or energetic as the case may be.

In *The Secret Garden* the two children whom nobody wants find not only earth to cultivate, but their own earth, in which they too can grow and come alive. Dickon buys seeds for Mary to plant and asks her where her garden is:

> 'I've stolen a garden,' she said very fast.
>
> 'It isn't mine. It isn't anybody's. Nobody wants it, nobody cares for it, nobody ever goes into it. Perhaps everything is dead in it already; I don't know.'
>
> She began to feel hot and as contrary as she had ever felt in her life.
>
> 'I don't care, I don't care! Nobody has any right to take it from me when I care about it and they don't. They're letting it die, all shut in by itself,' she ended passionately, and she threw her arms over her face and burst out crying – poor little Mistress Mary.
>
> Dickon's curious blue eyes grew rounder and rounder.
>
> 'Eh-h-h!' he said, drawing his exclamation out slowly, and the way he did it meant both wonder and sympathy.
>
> 'I've nothing to do,' said Mary. 'Nothing belongs to me. I found it myself and I got into it myself. I was only like the robin, and they wouldn't take it from a robin.'[46]

The request for a bit of earth voices a need for emotional space as much as for physical territory, as it also does in a contemporary children's book, *Tom's Midnight Garden* by Philippa Pearce. The lonely twentieth-century apartment child, Tom Long, escapes at night into an old Victorian garden where he plays with Hatty, a little Victorian girl: 'She had made this garden a kind of kingdom.'[47] Only at the end of the book does the reader learn that the loneliness is an adult's, for the owner of the house which has been divided into flats is old Mrs Bartholomew, Hatty herself, still an outsider in her own home, and dreaming of childhood in the garden. *The Secret Garden* gives Mary and Colin a physical kingdom but also the kingdom of the mind in their freedom from adults. In claiming that the two are

16   The Proper Place for Shoes and Stockings (from Gertrude Jekyll, *Children and Gardens*, 1908)

inseparable Burnett spoke for the Stephen children, who found in Bloomsbury their own bit of earth.

The place of refuge is not complete without the ally whom Grahame's narrator recognised in the hidden presence of the owner of that boy's hoard. Mary Molesworth, writing as early as 1877, gives Griselda a secret place within the Cuckoo Clock itself, a special travelling-compartment of her own: 'Inside there was the most charming little snuggery imaginable. It was something like a saloon railway carriage – it seemed to be lined and carpeted and everything, with rich mossy red velvet.' But in the end the Cuckoo finds Griselda another child to be 'better friends than the mandarins, or the butterflies, or even than your own faithful old cuckoo'.[48] *The Cuckoo Clock* does not reinforce comfortable Victorian values. Molesworth is as critical of the stifling environment of Miss Grizzel and Miss Tabitha as Mrs Sowerby in *The Secret Garden* is of Misselthwaite Manor: 'My word! . . . It was a good thing that little lass came to th' manor. It's been th' makin' o' her an' th' savin' o' him.'[49] But even in 1872 Susan Coolidge had let Katy in *What Katy Did* escape to a hayloft and the fantastic fictions of her own brain, more than twenty years before the exuberant flight from adult environments chronicled in *The Golden Age*.

When Virginia Woolf, amid disapproving stares from her Duckworth and Fisher relatives, went to live in the sleazy area of Fitzroy Square, she set foot in the shoddy lodging-house neighbourhood which Nesbit's children escape from through the amulet in *The Story of the Amulet*. They find in their time travel a dates and cream repast in ancient Babylon which 'was the kind of dinner you hardly ever get in Fitzroy Street', discover that the Ancient Britons thought 'a child was something to make a fuss about, not a bit of rubbish to be hustled about the streets and hidden away in the workhouse', and that the brave new world of the future provides children with an ideal room of their own full of soft furniture they can't hurt themselves on, because 'they are more than half of the people'.[50] But despite the pleasure of these fantastic excursions into more enlightened times, the children know intimately the society to which they must return. Nesbit conveys better than any other children's writer of this period the plight of a child caught in a world of social transition in which keeping up appearances becomes the god which it is in Samuel Butler's *Erewhon*. The adults in Nesbit's books cannot afford private education, nursemaids for their children, servants, decent or even nourishing food, or the maintenance of an Edwardian middle-class home. The silver is pawned, the clothes need mending, the carpet has a hole in it, the wallpaper is coming off the wall. But the adults still pretend that they are the affluent organisers of a great Victorian household. The children know that they are part not of a real family community, but of a pretence of community which is no longer economically viable. Orwell in *The Road to Wigan Pier* describes this kind of family as 'shabby-genteel': 'There is far more *consciousness* of poverty than in any working-class family above the level of the dole. . . . Most clergymen and schoolmasters, for instance, nearly all Anglo-Indian officials, a sprinkling of soldiers and sailors, and a fair number of professional men and artists, fall into this category . . . struggling to live genteel lives on what are virtually working-class incomes.'[51] Nesbit grew up in such a family, married into one, and wrote about that predicament continuously in her children's books.[52]

Nesbit's children travel in time as joyously as Stevenson's child who voyages to ancient Egypt, where he will 'in a corner find the toys / Of the old Egyptian boys'.[53] In Ancient Babylon Jane in *The Story of the Amulet* escapes from the official adventure to play ball with the little Queen from Egypt: 'She told me about the larks they have in Egypt.' The children's visit to Ancient Babylon is returned with interest, and both Nesbit and the Queen of Babylon have a good deal to say about the free world:

> 'But how badly you keep your slaves. How wretched and poor and neglected they seem,' she said, as the cab rattled along the Mile End Road.
> 'They aren't slaves; they're working-people,' said Jane.

The Queen retorts that of course they are working people: that's what slaves are, but why aren't they better fed and clothed?

> No one answered. The wage-system of modern England is a little difficult to explain in three words even if you understand it – which the children didn't.
> 'You'll have a revolt of your slaves if you're not careful,' said the Queen.
> 'Oh, no,' said Cyril; 'you see they have votes – that makes them safe not to revolt. It makes all the difference. Father told me so.'
> 'What is this vote?' asked the Queen. 'Is it a charm? What do they do with it?'

'I don't know,' said the harassed Cyril; 'it's just a vote, that's all! They don't do anything particular with it.'

'I see,' said the Queen; 'a sort of plaything.'

Later in the book the children's nurse, with whom they are lodging, stages her own revolt against their ignoring of her work: 'Slave, slave, slave for you day and night, and never a word of thanks.'[54] The equally down-trodden Cook in *The Phoenix and the Carpet* decides to stay and be a queen in the South Sea Islands instead of returning to the sweat and drudgery of the children's mother's kitchen. Nesbit was often not prosperous enough to have a cook and had the experience unusual for an educated woman of her time of doing her own domestic work, which gives her an unexpected insight into the feelings of those whom children themselves are capable of exploiting. Nevertheless in her books the only hope for a new society lies in the irreverence, truthfulness and imagination of the new generation, as it did for that other Fitzroy Square inhabitant, Virginia Stephen.

Only two of Nesbit's books deal with a working-class child hero, *The House of Arden* (1908) and *Harding's Luck* (1909). In the later book Dickie Harding is the only descendant, like John Durbeyfield in *Tess of the d'Urbervilles*, of the Elizabethan Ardens: 'The house where he lived was one of a row of horrid little houses built on the slope where once green fields ran down the hill to the river, and the old houses of the Deptford merchants stood stately in their pleasant gardens and fruitful orchards.' Nesbit adds bitterly: 'All those good fields and happy gardens are built over now', and creates an image worthy of William Morris in *News from Nowhere* (1873), or of Woolf sweeping over the canvas of *The Waves* with a wet brush: 'It is as though some wicked giant had taken a big brush full of ochre paint, and another full of mud-colour, and had painted out the green in streaks of dull yellow and filthy brown; and the brown is the roads and the yellow is the houses.' In this mud-coloured environment the healthy child has become disabled, but Nesbit allows him to travel back to the time which gave him the great Deptford garden to play in. There he meets the shabby-genteel children who are all that remain of the once aristocratic family, and launches a passionate protest against the twentieth century:

'I hate your times. They're ugly, they're cruel,' said Richard.

'They don't cut your head off for nothing anyhow in our times,' said Edred, 'and shut you up in the Tower.'

'They do worse things,' Richard said. '*I* know. They make people work fourteen hours a day for nine shillings a week, so that they never have enough to eat or wear, and no time to sleep or to be happy in. They won't give people food or clothes, or let them work to get them; and then they put the people in prison if they take enough to keep them alive. They let people get horrid diseases, till their jaws drop off, so as to have a particular kind of china. Women have to go out to work instead of looking after their babies, and the little girl that's left in charge drops the baby and it's crippled for life. Oh, I know! I won't go back with you. You might keep me there for ever.' He shuddered.

'I wouldn't. And I can't help about people working, and not enough money and that,' said Edred.[55]

Edred's response saves Nesbit from priggishness, striking the note which Helen Ambrose sounds in *The Voyage Out* when Clarissa Dalloway inveighs against the irrelevance of art in a world where children are hungry:

'It's dreadful,' said Mrs Dalloway, who, while her husband spoke, had been thinking. 'When I'm with artists I feel so intensely the delights of shutting oneself up in a little world of one's own, with pictures and music and everything beautiful, and then I go out into the streets and the first child I meet with its poor, hungry, dirty little face makes me turn round and say, "No, I *can't* shut myself up – I won't live in a world of my own. I should like to stop all the painting and writing and music until this kind of thing exists no longer." Don't you feel,' she wound up, addressing Helen, 'that life's a perpetual conflict?'

Helen considered for a moment. 'No,' she said, 'I don't think I do.'

There was a pause, which was decidedly uncomfortable. Mrs Dalloway then gave a little shiver, and asked whether she might have her fur cloak brought to her.[56]

Louise DeSalvo notes the enormous number of social and political issues aired in the early drafts of *The Voyage Out*, remarking that it is 'covertly and . . . fiercely seditious' in a way which makes it 'impossible to think of Virginia Woolf as an effete dreamer spinning out her private fantasies in the solitude of her study between bouts of madness'.[57] *The Voyage Out* makes the political implications of

Clarissa's philanthropy in a fur coat subversive rather than aggressive.[58] Woolf's seditious comedy is in *The Voyage Out* as reminiscent of Nesbit as the suggestion in *Harding's Luck*, 'Is this a dream? Or was the other the dream?',[59] is evocative of Woolf's phantom flower in *The Waves*, although Nesbit might not have been capable of the retort which Woolf gives to Tennyson in *Freshwater* after Mr Cameron has announced that life is a dream: 'Rather a wet one, Charles.'[60]

III PSYCHOANALYSIS AND CONSCIENCE

New theories about time throw doubt on the concept of human destiny and the part played in it by conscience. If there is, as William James argued, no real present,[61] there can be no identifiable moment of choice when the human being exercises free will. Freud's research into the origins of human consciousness seemed to deprive grown men and women of the ability to break free from past experience. They must remain entrapped in a consciousness determined by a past beyond their control. When Alice encounters Humpty Dumpty he perches blithely on the wall, convinced that he won't fall off, while she waits with arms outstretched to catch him, knowing that his future, which he thinks free, is already decided because 'it's in a book' (*L-G*, 264). The completion of the nursery rhyme is the completion of his destiny, as James Joyce realised when he made him the symbol of a new Fall in *Finnegans Wake*. Carroll does not offer, as Martin Gardner suggests, a moral that 'pride goeth before a fall',[62] but observes that to move from the present to the past whose history is already written down is to inhibit the present freedom of those dwellers in the past. The question, intensified by psychoanalysis, is not, who is virtuous, but can anyone be other than he is, and has been since childhood? Is Alice truly the only being who is free, because she is still a child? Or is her history determined by the book, just as the book, and thus the writer, is determined by her – a question which leads into the country of Pirandello's *Six Characters in Search of an Author*, in which the characters of an unfinished play beg their author to complete their story.

In 1920 Woolf wrote a review in the *Times Literary Supplement* of J. D. Beresford's novel *An Imperfect Mother*. In this piece, entitled 'Freudian Fiction', she complained that Beresford's characters belonged to 'the very numerous progeny of Dr Freud', and that 'in becoming cases they have ceased to be individuals'. She continues: 'If it is true that our conduct in crucial moments is immensely influenced, if not decided, by some forgotten incident in childhood, then surely it is cowardice on the part of the novelist to persist in ascribing our behaviour to untrue causes.' But although she allows that the novelist 'must use any key that seems to fit the human mind', she protests that in the novel in question 'the new key is a patent key which opens every door. It simplifies rather than complicates, detracts rather than enriches. The door swings open briskly enough, but the apartment to which we are admitted is a bare little room with no outlook whatever',[63] not even the narrowed horizon which in 1908 she had found at the end of Forster's *A Room with a View*. The space created by the book has become not the blue-brocaded refuge of Grahame's *The Golden Age*, which nurtures the imagination of author and character alike, but a void, or even, for child, reader and writer, all equally trapped within their own psychic histories, a prison cell.

The bareness of that little room is much in evidence in Freud's analysis of William Jensen's *Gradiva* (1895), a story which the psychologist turns into a case study of sexual repression. The hero, an archaeologist who falls in love with the sculptured image of a woman on a bas-relief in Rome, traces his beloved's origins to ancient Pompeii, sees in a dream the fall of the city, and eventually discovers the same woman in his own present in the guise of Zoë, the German girl across the street in his home town. The girl Zoë humours her lover's fantasies, and through her 'cure' of his repressed sexuality he is able to release feelings buried within him since childhood, just as Gradiva was buried in the ancient city of Pompeii. Freud's analysis of the story serves his own purpose extremely well, allowing him the credit of discovering in Jensen's characters the sexual drives which their creator gave them. But as psychology it is rigged, in that the characters are a figment of the novelist's much more intriguing psyche, and as literary criticism it is misleading because it ignores the real focus of the fiction.

Jensen believed, as Michel Foucault argues in *The Order of Things*, that human consciousness is an archaeology, recording experience in layers, as the earth itself does. His obsessions in *Gradiva* are not with sexual repression, but with racial origins. He was himself from Sylt,[64] one of the North Frisian islands which now lie within German territory, but which until 1864 retained a personal connection with the Danish monarch. The name Jensen is a common Scandinavian one. Two of Jensen's other stories besides *Gradiva* deal with sexual attraction between people of mixed racial origin. In *Fair Isle*, translated into English in 1881, the hero deserts the fair-haired Nordic girl who has been his comrade since childhood and escapes with the Spanish–Jewish maiden who has landed on the island with other Spaniards. In *Runic Rocks* (English translation 1895) the blond young man is torn between two loves: the dark and the fair. The romance is complicated by the French invasion of Holland, with the demand that the islanders lose their racial identity. In these two stories the author explores both the difficulties of translating the love between children into adult passion, and the conflict within the hero's psyche between his passion for dark women who are not of his race and fair ones who are. It sounds, in a period influenced by Nietzsche's idea of the superman, and by the conviction of supporters of the eugenics movement that racial purity produced the finest offspring, alarmingly like incipient Aryan racism, especially in view of the Jewish origins of the foreign love in *Fair Isle*. Both stories throw light on *Gradiva*, suggesting a richer and more complex fiction than Freud's analysis allows.

The archaeologist hero of *Gradiva* falls in love with the heroine because of the high arch of her foot in stepping out, which spells to him not Roman but Greek origin, as does the name Zoë ('life') in the German girl he eventually marries. Jensen has given Gradiva the mark not only of beauty but of racial superiority. Ellen Key in *The Century of the Child* quotes Westermarck's argument that the purest racial selection contributes to the highest development of physical beauty, creating survival of the fittest. Key, quoting another, unnamed writer (possibly Herbert Spencer, who had described marriage between different races as 'the house divided against itself'), observes:

> The small high-arched foot with the fine ankle is always, he says, regarded as the most beautiful. But such a foot is only combined with a fine, strong, and elastic bony structure. Such a foot besides has, by its great elasticity, a considerably higher power of bearing weight than the flat foot. The high vaulted foot, in walking and jumping, increases the activity of the lungs and heart. This again makes the walk elastic, strong and easy, agile and stately. These traits, for the same reason as the beauty of the foot itself, are

looked upon as a racial sign. This physical power and ease influence the mind and produce self-confidence, so increase the feeling of superiority and the joy of living, marks of distinction in human beings.[65]

Gradiva provides the author with a space in which to explore racial origins, buried in the ashes of Pompeii, and to assimilate them back into German culture: Zoë is both German and Greek. In *Runic Rocks* Cora Lindstrom's name derives from the Greek for maiden, but also suggests the *chora*, the word used by Julia Kristeva to describe the 'pre-socialised space'[66] which allows the child to find its identity in the world. Jensen uses the space which his own fiction makes in all these stories to return to the origins of consciousness and of race, so that the adult may restore his wholeness by re-entering his childhood, buried in the ashes of the psychical city. Freud used the same metaphor in *Civilization and Its Discontents* (1930) but declared himself dissatisfied with the irrationality of imagining the ancient to coexist with the modern.[67]

All Woolf's characters possess a layered consciousness such as Jensen gives to the hero in *Gradiva*. Not even Septimus Smith in *Mrs Dalloway* has a psychical history in Freudian terms. Clarissa's memories in *Mrs Dalloway* illumine and humanise not a past Clarissa, but the living reality of the present.[68] When the children in *The Waves* move into the full midday sun they carry with them the birdsong and the lady writing, but they are still free agents, undetermined by their own past.

If the children in *The Waves* have no bondage to their own psychological development, they also lack conscience. Stevenson had urged that children have no moral sense and do not understand the adult distinction between romancing and lying, fiction and falsehood. When Wilfrid Trotter argued in *Instincts of the Herd* (1916) that children learn conscience from the herd, he stood on the same ground as Mark Twain in *Huckleberry Finn*.

Analysing the systems of morality on which her family and the society she knew operated, Gwen Raverat concluded in *Period Piece*:

Guiltiness was a permanent condition, like rheumatism; and one just had to learn to disregard it, and to carry on under it, as best one could. Huckleberry Finn has the last word on conscience – and I was as consci[ence]ous-ridden as poor Huck himself.

'It don't make no difference whether you do right or wrong, a person's

conscience ain't got no sense, and just goes for him anyway. If I had a yaller dog that didn't know more than a person's conscience, I would pison him. It takes up more room than all the rest of a person's insides, and yet ain't no good, nohow.'

This is most terribly TRUE.[69]

The first time that conscience afflicts Huck is when he and Jim believe, mistakenly, that they are almost at Cairo and that Jim will shortly be free. As the runaway slave's excitement mounts, Huck grows uneasy:

I begun to get it through my head that he *was* most free – and who was to blame for it? Why, *me.* I couldn't get that out of my conscience, no how nor no way. . . . Conscience says to me, 'What had poor Miss Watson done to you, that you could see her nigger go off right under your eyes and never say one single word?'

Jim's ecstatic ruminations about buying his wife and children out of slavery once he is free horrify Huck: 'It most froze me to hear such talk. He wouldn't ever dared to talk such talk in his life before. Just see what a difference it made in him the minute he judged he was about free. It was according to the old saying, "Give a nigger an inch and he'll take an ell". . . . I was sorry to hear Jim say that, it was such a lowering of him. My conscience got to stirring me up hotter than ever, until at last I says to it, "Let up on me – it ain't too late, yet – I'll paddle ashore at the first light, and tell." ' As he makes off in the canoe, hot with resolution, Jim calls after him that he won't forget him when he's free because Huck is the best friend Jim ever had: 'When he says this, it seemed to kind of take the tuck all out of me.' He encounters a boat with two men looking for runaway slaves who challenge him: is the man on the raft black or white? The reader holds her breath, uncertain of Huck's response:

I didn't answer up prompt. I tried to, but the words wouldn't come. I tried, for a second or two, to brace up and out with it, but I warn't man enough – hadn't the spunk of a rabbit. I see I was weakening; so I just give up trying, and up and says: 'He's white.'

In Twain's *Table of Contents* this moment is described as 'A White Lie'. Huck prevents a search with an Iago-like technique of telling the searchers that the man on the raft has smallpox, at which they give him forty dollars conscience money for not carrying their own job any further, and Huck swears to lay his hands on any runaway slaves he comes across. His conscience then gives him trouble:

> They went off and I got aboard the raft, feeling bad and low, because I knowed very well I had done wrong, and I see it warn't no use for me to try to learn to do right; a body that don't get *started* right when he's little, ain't got no show – when the pinch comes there ain't nothin to back him up and keep him to his work, and so he gets beat. Then I thought a minute, and says to myself, hold on, – s'pose you'd a done right and give Jim up; would you felt better than what you do now? No, says I, I'd feel bad – I'd feel just the same way I do now. Well, then, says I, what's the use you learning to do right, when it's troublesome to do right and ain't no trouble to do wrong, and the wages is just the same? I was stuck. I couldn't answer that. So I reckoned I wouldn't bother no more about it, but after this always do whichever come handiest at the time.[70]

Trotter observed in 1916 that 'the judgments of conscience vary in different circles, and are dependent on local environments. . . . Conscience is an indirect result of the gregarious instinct, and is in no sense derived from a special instinct forcing men to consider the good of the race rather than individual desires.'[71] Huck, who has only ever been superficially integrated into the herd of so-called civilised beings, can recite its morality, but has not acquired its instincts. In this incident Twain does not, however, provide Huck with a childish innocence of adult corruption. He shows instead that the boy has learnt to evade the herd, and that under pressure he is true to his own sense that the civilisation of the adult world means that neither he nor Jim has room to breathe.

Conscience afflicts Huck again when he considers writing to Miss Watson, Jim's owner, to tell her that Jim is caught, so that at least Jim will not be sold to strange owners. But he is inhibited by his awareness that his own position is not an impregnable one, as he had aided Jim's escape in the first place. The way events have turned out is Providence's revenge on him for 'stealing a poor old woman's nigger that hadn't ever done me no harm'. The grammar (the real antecedent is 'nigger' not 'woman') suggests that it is not Miss Watson but Jim who has done Huck no harm. Huck tries to listen to his conscience: 'Something inside of me kept saying, "There was the Sunday-school, you could a gone to it; and if you'd a done it they'd a learnt you, there, that people that acts as I'd been acting about that nigger goes to everlasting fire."' Writing the letter to Miss Watson brings instant relief, but he drifts into a memory of life on the raft: 'We a floating along, talking, and singing, and laughing.' He remembers Jim taking a double turn at the watch so that Huck could sleep, calling him honey and doing 'everything he could think of for me', and of Jim's gratitude over the smallpox trick: 'Then I happened to look around, and see that paper.' He tears it up, resolving: 'All right, then I'll *go* to hell':

> It was awful thoughts, and awful words, but they was said. And I let them stay said; and never thought no more about reforming. I shoved the whole thing out of my head; and said I would take up wickedness again, which was in my line, being brung up to it, and the other warn't. And for a starter, I would go to work and steal Jim out of slavery again.[72]

Huck's decision is not based on an abstract notion of right and wrong. If it were, he would have taken the opposite decision, as the only teaching he had had, condemned his harbouring of Jim. He violates those taught precepts because Jim offers him a space which the herd denied him: to be a child, loved, nurtured, protected. Jim gives Huck the territory of childhood, and Huck rewards him with the territory of the free man.

In Henry James's novel *What Maisie Knew* (1897), Maisie is not true to Mrs Wix because she has learnt the moral sense her governess tries to teach her. She is loyal because Mrs Wix is loyal to her in fighting for a place for her which is her own, not the sparring-ground of either Beale, her father, or Ida, her mother. When Maisie's stepfather first suggests to her that she desert Mrs Wix, the proposition is so muffled in fine phrases and propriety that Maisie hardly understands what is said. Nevertheless she perceives with the uncanny instinct of childhood an undertow of meaning: 'There was a word that hummed all through it.' The word is 'sacrifice'. But Maisie will not sacrifice the person who has given her a bit of earth, any more than Dickie in *Harding's Luck* will desert Beale, the tramp who looks after him in the present, for the luxury of the past. Just as Colin Craven in *The Secret Garden* recognises in Dickon's mother a functional role which will guarantee him fresh air, so Maisie draws from Mrs Wix 'a sense of a support, like a breast-high banister in place of "drops", that would never give way'.[73] In Russell Hoban's *The Mouse and His Child* (1967), the Child reflects: 'He had no idea what a mamma might be but he knew at once that he needed one badly.'[74] Payne had argued in *The Child in Human Progress*, published the same year as Trotter's book, that the maternal instinct was the only civilising instinct in human nature because it created emotional space for another human being.[75] In Anne Holm's *I am David* (1963), the boy's quest is not for a celestial city but for the mother who will allow him to be David.

The fiction which Huck invents for himself and Jim about smallpox returns both of them to the freedom of the raft. In *The Waves* the children are not Freud's progeny. They belong to the lady writing who has given them both a room of their own and a view.

IV NARRATIVE AND POWER

The transforming of experience into narrative gives children a place in which they are powerful, as the writer is powerful. Kenneth Grahame observed in 'Saturnalia' that 'whenever a child is set down in a situation that is distasteful, out of harmony, jarring – and he is very easily jarred – that very moment he begins, without conscious effort, to throw out and to build up an environment really suitable to his soul, and to transport himself thereto'.[76] When Sara Crewe in Frances Hodgson Burnett's *A Little Princess* (1905) loses her fortune and is banished by her schoolmistresses, who had fawned upon her when rich, to a rat-ridden attic, she pretends it is the Bastille, and contacts the other prisoner – a servant girl – by knocking on the wall:

Ermingarde quite beamed with delight.
   'Oh, Sara,' she whispered joyfully, 'it is like a story!'
   'It is a story,' said Sara. '*Everything's* a story. You are a story – I am a story. Miss Minchin is a story.'[77]

Neville in *The Waves* needs Bernard to compose reality into narrative: 'Let him describe what we have all seen so that it becomes a sequence. Bernard says there is always a story. I am a story. Louis is a story.'[78] When the prosperous schoolchild in Burnett's tale castigates Sara for telling the other children stories in front of the servants, pouting that *her* mamma would not like her to demean herself in that way, Sara retorts that *her* mother 'knows that stories belong to everybody'.[79] As Virginia Woolf wanders through Trinity College in *A Room of One's Own*, trying to find space to stand – not on the turf, only for Fellows and Scholars; not in the Library, only if you have a letter of introduction and are accompanied by a Fellow – she finds that 'old stories of old deans and old dons came back to mind'.[80] Roger Fry declared that 'the day-dreams of a child are filled with extravagant romances in which he is always the invincible hero',[81] but Nietzsche would have retorted that the Dionysiac impulse is not confined to children. When Toad in *The Wind in the Willows* prepares a concert programme he is the soloist in every item, as all children would be if not suppressed by the adult rebukes of Mole and Rat – 'Don't show off' – and as most adults would be too if they had the chance. Narrative, as Shakespeare knew when he gave Falstaff a dramatist's ability to re-create his adventures with himself as hero, spells control.

Ted Hughes has described the Gospel story as 'an acquisition, a kind of wealth', without which life is empty because it lacks enriching fictions: 'We solve the problem by never looking inward. . . . We sit, closely cramped in the cockpit behind the eyes, steering through the brilliantly crowded landscape beyond the lenses, focused on details and distinctions.' That was written before the poet had a chance to see a new generation of children hunched behind computers, pressing buttons and talking Basic. Those children may in time rebel against the new education without fable and without the capacity to shape experience which the book offers to the child. Hughes wrote that 'stories think for themselves. . . . New revelations of meaning open out of their images and patterns continually, stirred into reach by our own growth and changing circumstances.'[82] The computer programmes the child in a more devastating way than religion did, because a machine can only give out what the human brain in its limited capacities has fed into it. But that has never been the case with the book. Words are free once they have been written and can feed the reader in ways the writer might never have imagined.

The perception of the new century and its new writing was that no artist can fully know or control either the world she creates or the readers for whom she creates it. She can only say, with the Unicorn, that 'I'll believe in you if you'll believe in me.' Flora Thompson's mother once told her a story of a child who crept under a bush, almost like the children in *The Waves*, and 'found a concealed opening which led to an underground palace in which all the furniture and hangings were pale blue and silver. . . . The heroine had marvellous adventures, but they left no impression on Laura's mind, while the blue and silver, deep down under the earth, shone with a kind of moonlight radiance in her imagination.' Her mother was never able to recapture that moment. When she 'tried to tell the story again the magic was gone'.[83] The writers who seized on the children's book in the latter half of the nineteenth century found that it offered them a space in which both child and artist could share common ground. Henry James declared: 'It appears to me that no one can ever have made a seriously artistic attempt without becoming conscious of an immense increase – a kind of revelation – of freedom. . . . The province of art is all life, all feeling, all observation, all vision. . . . That is a sufficient answer to those who maintain that it must not touch the painful, who stick into its divine unconscious bosom little prohibitory inscriptions on the end of sticks, such as we see in public gardens – "It is forbidden to walk on the grass; it is forbidden to touch the flowers; it is not allowed to introduce dogs, or to remain after dark; it is requested to keep to the right."' [84] If this sounds like Flush bounding round Florence and Virginia Woolf rebelling against Cambridge exclusiveness, it also conjures up Carroll's Alice and Burnett's Mary Lennox, insisting in their separate ways that there is plenty of room for each of them.

Freud wrote that 'every child at play behaves like a creative writer, in that he creates a world of his own, or, rather, rearranges the things of his world in a new way which pleases him'.[85] Stevenson claimed that children loved *Robinson Crusoe* because it prompted play. Oswald Bastable in Nesbit's *The Wouldbegoods* laments that Daisy 'had not been taught how to play':

> I talked to Albert's uncle about it one day, when the others had gone to church, and I did not go because of ear-ache, and he said it came from reading the wrong sort of books partly – she has read *Ministering Children*, and *Anna Ross or The Orphan of Waterloo*, and *Ready Work for Willing Hands* and *Elsie or Like a Little Candle*, and even a horrid little blue book about the something or other of Little Sins. After this conversation Oswald took care she had plenty of the right sort of books to read, and he was surprised and pleased when she got up early one morning to finish *Monte Cristo*. Oswald felt that he was really being useful to a suffering fellow-creature when he gave Daisy books that were not all about being good.[86]

Sully noticed children's capacity to create play from the books they read, as Dickens shows David Copperfield doing, but the philosopher thought that 'Paul Dombey and Little Nell do not satisfy this generation's keener sense of the realities of child-life.' They are too passive, too much society's victims, the victims of the fictional world, and indeed their author's victims.[87]

For Nesbit's children a keen sense of their own reality involves a rewriting of the books they have read. When the Phoenix sets the theatre on fire at the end of *The Phoenix and the Carpet*, the children do not suffer heroic deaths:

> 'Oh, how *could* you!' cried Jane. 'Let's get out.'
> 'Father said stay here,' said Anthea, very pale, and trying to speak in her ordinary voice.
> 'He didn't mean stay and be roasted,' said Robert. 'No boys on burning decks for me, thank you.'
> 'Not much,' said Cyril, and he opened the door of the box.[88]

The child uses the text to create for herself alternative action, just as the children in *Swallows and Amazons* use *Treasure Island* to colour the narrative of their own exploring.

This revision of the children's book is the most interesting in the case of the creative writer. When George Eliot depicts Maggie Tulliver shearing off her long black hair in the attic in *The Mill on the Floss* and facing the mockery of her mother's guests, she may have drawn on a real memory, or on a memory of reading. In Sinclair's *Holiday House* Laura persuades Harry to cut off her hair and revels in the snipping scissors and the showering of shorn locks, until brought to confront the 'shame and distress' of public exposure round the dinner table (Sinclair), rebuked by 'severe eyes and severe words' (George Eliot). But where Sinclair's incident leads to a local homily on Laura's virtue in not telling a lie about her hair George Eliot uses the occasion to underline both the irrevocability of Maggie's action and Mr Tulliver's fidelity, which his daughter rewards as faithfully as Huck rewards Jim.[89]

The recollection of childhood is always a process of re-creation, because memory itself is a form of narrative. At the end of *A Child's Garden of Verses* Stevenson conjures up a vision of the child in the garden:

> As from the house your mother sees
> You playing round the garden trees,
> So may you see, if you will look
> Through the windows of this book,
> Another child, far, far away,
> And in another garden, play.[90]

The child in the lines is both reader, child in the book and Stevenson himself, sharing the kingdom he has given to the child he both remembers and creates. Gaston Bachelard observes in *The Poetics of Reverie* (1969) that in accounts of childhood 'the writer's reveries become reveries experienced for the reader. By reading "childhoods", my childhood is enriched.'[91] Gosse describes in *Father and Son* his isolation after his mother's death: 'In memory, my childhood was long, long with interminable hours, hours with the pale cheek pressed against the windowpane.'[92] But the actual event[93] may have fused in his mind with Rodenbach's image of the melancholy child in *The Mirror of the Native Sky* (1898):

> Gentleness of recovering one's thinner face
> As a pensive child, forehead against the windowpane.[94]

The image in the book allows the writer to construct an image of the self he remembers.

Alison Uttley's *A Traveller in Time* (1939) draws on childhood memories of both real places and events, and on the author's dreams. These dreams become in the book the landscape of Penelope's return to the life of the Elizabethan Babingtons, which flows alongside her own twentieth-century existence in the old house, Thackers, in Derbyshire, drawn from Uttley's own home. The imagined story fused with the remembered dreams shapes, out of Penelope's experience of travelling into the past, an image of the writer's ability to enter her own created world, and her fear of losing it: 'My hands glided over smooth stone, and I could find no opening.' Penelope, caught up in the past, is also, as the artist must be, terrified of being overwhelmed by the phantom world, as Septimus Smith is in *Mrs Dalloway*; Penelope fears that 'I should be left behind in that life of the past.'[95] Grahame had used the same image of finding a hidden entry to a secret room not only in *Dream Days*, but also in one of his short stories in which the narrator dreams of escaping to a private chamber in another world: 'Could my fingers but pass over the smooth surface of those oak balustrades so familiar to me, in a trice I would stand at the enchanted door.'[96] The story gives the character a room, but the room is, for the creator of that character, the story itself, his own capacity to enter another place and another time. *A Traveller in Time* ends with a passionate lament not only for the passing of lived time, but also for the created world to which the author, like Penelope, must bid farewell: 'The peacefulness of Thackers which had held the seasons for five hundred years flowed through me, giving me strength and courage as it had done to those others, uniting me to them. I knew I had seen them for the last time on this earth, but some day I shall return to be with that brave company of shadows.'[97] In its echo of Shakespeare's adieu to his own king of shadows at the end of *A Midsummer Night's Dream*, and of Emily Brontë's lingering, as Lockwood himself lingers at the graves of Cathy and Heathcliff at the end of *Wuthering Heights*, Uttley's elegy speaks for all writers, forced to re-enter the sorry present.

Nevertheless, memory allows each adult the capacity to re-live as well as to remember his own past. When the curate in *Lark Rise to Candleford* describes stealing a horse as a boy, '[He] leaned forward with such a flush on his cheek and such a light in his eye that, for one moment, Laura could almost see in the ageing man the boy he had once been.'[98] The story permits the past to re-enter the present, to become what Thomas Mann described as the 'Eucharistic' now.[99] Laura Ingalls Wilder's *Little House in the Big Woods* begins like a fairy tale: 'Once upon a time, sixty years ago, a little girl lived in the Big Woods of Wisconsin, in a little grey house made of logs.' But it ends in a present shared between the child Laura, the reader and the old woman narrating:

> Laura lay awake a little while, listening to Pa's fiddle softly playing and to the lonely sound of the wind in the Big Woods. She looked at Pa sitting on the bench by the hearth, the fire-light gleaming on his brown hair and beard and glistening on the honey-brown fiddle. She looked at Ma, gently rocking and knitting.
>
> She thought to herself, 'This is now.'
>
> She was glad that the cosy house, and Pa and Ma and the firelight and the music, were now. They could not be forgotten, she thought, because now is now. It can never be a long time ago.[100]

Whatever the origins of experience – dream, memory, fable – the story, whether written or remembered, makes it contemporaneous.

Rome, in Grahame's story 'The Roman Road', provides a territory for both artist and child, each weary of a world where 'I never do anything right.'[101] In Nesbit's *The Story of the Treasure Seekers*, the approach of adulthood is identified as a dwindling of imaginative power. Oswald muses: 'I'd rather have the pot of gold we used to dig for when we were little', and notices the decline in his own power to transform the factual world into something other than it is. He feels 'grown-upness creeping inordiously upon him'.[102] Bernard in *The Waves* defines middle age as a turning-away from Stevenson's country: 'I shall never now take ship for the South Sea Islands. A journey to Rome is the limit of my travelling.'[103] The present becomes dead when it loses the capacity to be the dream of the past, the future of its living images.[104] In Bernard's image Rome spells renunciation, not release.

Stevenson tells the tale in 'The Lantern-Bearers' of a monk who wanders into the monastery woods and hears a nightingale, only to find on his return that fifty years have passed. Stevenson launches into a passionate attack on 'the mud and old iron, cheap desires and cheap fears' of the realist writer: 'Of the note of that time-devouring nightingale we hear no more.' He urges: 'It is not only in the woods that this enchanter carols, though perhaps he is native there. . . . All life that is not merely mechanical is spun out of two strands: seeking for the bird and hearing him.'[105] Orlando, musing on the honours showered on the twentieth-century writer, asks: 'Was not writing a secret transaction, a voice answering a voice? . . . What could have been more secret, she thought, more slow, and like the intercourse of lovers, than the stammering answer she had made all these years to the old crooning song of the woods?'[106] When the writer allows the child space in her book, she herself becomes the child in the garden who hears the bird sing.

7

The Literary and the Literal

I PLACES

Carroll allowed an ancient sage to give an aspiring young poet instructions, in 'Poeta Fit, non Nascitur', on how to acquire a 'literary' style:

> Then, fourthly, there are epithets
>   That suit with any word –
> As well as Harvey's Reading Sauce
>   With fish, or flesh, or bird –
> Of these, 'wild', 'lonely', 'weary', 'strange',
>   Are much to be preferred.[1]

The special literary language which Tennyson, Longfellow and Swinburne inherit from the Romantics is presented as a trick, performed by the great writer with the suavity with which a conjurer pulls a string of coloured scarves out of an empty box. But the children remain more impressed by the fact that there was nothing in the box than they are by the display of showy silks. All grin and no Cat can become tiresome. Such language conjures up only other literary works, the other books in which it has been used. But it never breaks out of that magic circle to find something which has never been colonised into language within a book. 'Literary' language is conservative, in that the world it creates remains, with minor variations, the world it has always created. Its pleasures are those of recognition and its function is to authorise categories and reinforce established dichotomies – the beautiful and the ugly, good and evil, the serious and the frivolous – and through doing so to identify for the reader a scale of values:

> 'You are sad,' the Knight said in an anxious tone: 'let me sing you a song to comfort you.'
> 'Is it very long?' Alice asked, for she had heard a good deal of poetry that day.

'It's long,' said the Knight, 'but it's very, *very* beautiful.
Everybody that hears me sing it – either it brings the *tears* into their
eyes, or else –'

'Or else what?' said Alice, for the Knight had made a sudden
pause.

'Or else it doesn't, you know. The name of the song is
"*Haddocks' Eyes*".'

'Oh, that's the name of the song, is it?' Alice said, trying to feel
interested.   (*L-G*, 305–6)

The song is a revised version of Carroll's parody, first published in
1856, of Wordsworth's *Resolution and Independence*. It begins:

> I met an aged, aged man,
> Upon the lonely moor:
> I knew I was a gentleman,
> And he was but a boor.[2]

Wordsworth, who had fought to replace eighteenth-century literary
language with 'a selection of the language really spoken by men',
became for the Victorians a dignified effigy in the marble halls
of great literature. Gwen Raverat wrote of her Aunt Etty that
'Wordsworth was her religion', though she was often dissatisfied
with his lines, which she did not always understand and liked to
emend: 'I remember that Wordsworth's

> *The wind comes to me from the fields of sleep*

did not please her. What does it mean anyhow? Sleep does not grow
in fields. I said, why not try *fields of sheep*. This was not well
received.'[3] Woolf records in her biography of Roger Fry: 'The
cottages of the Lake poets left him cold, but at least he was
vouchsafed a vision of William Wordsworth. "I have very little
doubt that I have seen William Wordsworth. I found him in the form
of a very old sheep lying under a tree. I sat down close to him and
did a drawing. He never moved but looked over my shoulder and
coughed occasionally." '[4] One reason why Gwen Raverat's version
of Wordsworth's line won't do is that it substitutes the actual for the
metaphorical, animals in a field with the breeze blowing over them,
for a man in his bed metaphorically refreshed by the soothing
exhalations of slumber. The literary has been ousted by the literal.

The substitution of the literal for the literary challenges the authenticity of the poet's vision and often – as in this case – returns the reader to the original metaphor with an enhanced awareness of its suggestiveness, the double landscape it evokes. The metaphor proclaims the poet's control of the reflections in the mirror, the flower and its phantom. But the suggestiveness of the metaphor itself imposes limits on perception. The literal world is freer. You don't have to be someone with special gifts in order to see it. It proclaims its right to be considered for what it is rather than for what it might be. A woman does not want always to be someone's muse or someone else's temptress, any more than a child wants to be part of an iconography: slip of Satan or cherub, baby Jesus or changeling boy, man's only inspiration or someone who always tells lies. The image is a form of bondage. It is not true that a rose by any other name would smell as sweet – or, as Bergson argues, that it smells different to every individual sniffer[5] – because literature has given the rose a special place in perception. Nor is that perception the privilege of the well-educated, because the symbolic rose has become so popularised that it usurps the literal flower. Only a small child can smell a rose without romance.

Many of Lewis Carroll's word games in the two *Alice* books consist of taking metaphorically what was meant literally, or the other way round.[6] When the Mouse proposes to dry all those creatures who got soaked in the salt pool of Alice's tears he does it by telling them 'the driest thing I know', intoning a quotation from one of Alice Liddell's lesson books – 'William the Conquerer, whose cause was favoured by the pope':

> 'How are you getting on now, my dear?' it continued turning to Alice as it spoke.
> 'As wet as ever,' said Alice in a melancholy tone: 'it doesn't seem to dry me at all.'   (*AW*, 46–7)

When Alice hears the Dormouse tell of the three little sisters who lived on treacle in a treacle well, she retorts firmly: 'They couldn't have done that, you know, . . . They'd have been ill' (*AW*, 100). When she is rowing, the Sheep keeps instructing her to 'feather' or she will catch a crab. ' "A dear little crab!" thought Alice. "I should like that" ' (*L-G*, 254). Carroll knew that children perceive analogy very early in life. It is one of the ways in which they learn to codify their environment: Humpty Dumpty is *like* an egg (*LG*, 262). But metaphor comes much later. If you asked a church-going child the meaning of 'Rock of Ages, cleft for me / Let me hide myself in thee', she would probably answer that it was something to do with looking for winkles. (What *does* it mean, come to think of it?[7]) Adults move easily and comfortably in a metaphorical medium to which a child has no access, and where her errors of interpretation are often ridiculed. In *Alice in Wonderland* and *Through the Looking-Glass* it is the adult metaphors which create a mad world, not Alice's failure to understand them. Grahame's children in *The Golden Age* observe that the Olympians are literal: cold mutton is never red game. But these adults are literal because they are literary. They divide their experience into actual happenings and revered texts, and then they imagine only what is available to them from the received 'literature' of the past. When James Ramsay meditates that he would like to kill his father, it is partly for Mr Ramsay's refusal to imagine that the weather might be fine in defiance of facts, and it is partly because the journey to the lighthouse is translated in Mr Ramsay's philosophy into literary journey, not just an outing in a boat but 'the passage to that fabled land where our brightest hopes are extinguished, our frail barks founder in darkness'.[8] The revolt of Virginia Woolf's generation against Victorian morality was as much as anything a revolt against its metaphors, against the conviction shared by both writers and readers that what one read in a book might control what one read in the book of life – not a real sheep in sight. Carroll's answer was to insist on exposing metaphors, and thus revivifying language and opening a window on experiences which could not be prepackaged and labelled as literary, and therefore respectable.

Virginia Woolf in *To the Lighthouse* observes Leslie Stephen through a lens which magnifies the egotism and morbidity which enveloped the philosopher after his wife's death and found expression in the *Mausoleum Book* which he wrote for his children.[9] No one could guess, from scrutinising Mr Ramsay, Leslie Stephen's quickness, sense of humour, his astute judgement of people and of writers, and his ear for affectation and cant. Nevertheless the portrait of Mr Ramsay cruelly reproduces a tendency in Stephen's essays towards a consciously 'literary' style, which he did not in fact encourage in contributors to the *Cornhill*, among whom was Robert Louis Stevenson. When Stevenson wrote an essay on walking, Stephen wrote to him that he himself did not share the young man's admiration for Hazlitt's essay on the same theme, as he found it shallow and egotistical.[10] But the editor's ear for his own prose was less finely tuned than it was for other people's. His piece, 'In Praise of Walking', conjures up Mr Ramsay's inability to divest a journey of spiritual significance. Every walk is a pilgrimage. Stephen's favourite passage in *The Pilgrim's Progress* depicts Christian and Hopeful leaving the highroad and crossing the stile into Bypath Meadow which took them to the Castle of Giant Despair: 'The incident really added that spice of adventure which is delightful to the genuine pilgrim. We defied giant Despair; and if our walks were not quite so edifying as those of Christian and his friends, they add a pleasant strand to the thread of memory which joins the past years.' (Or, literally, they liked taking short cuts). He enjoyed getting out of London and walking in the mountains; but what he said is: 'I feel convinced that, if I am not a thorough scoundrel, I owe that relative excellence to the harmless monomania which so often took me, to appropriate Bunyan's phrase, from the amusements of *Vanity Fair* to the *Delectable Mountains* of pedestrianism.' As he opens 'the intellectual album which memory is always compiling' he looks back on 'a long series of little vignettes . . . each representing a definite state of my earthly pilgrimage summed up and embodied in a walk'. A walk is a literary walk: 'You are in the world of Lavengro. . . . Borrow, of course, took the life more seriously than the literary gentleman who is only escaping and ticket-of-leave from the prison-house of respectability.'[11] One can understand why his daughter, reading such stuff, might have wanted to chop off his head, or to sit him in a real boat to go to a real lighthouse, even if he continued quoting all the way and conducting imaginary symphony orchestras. Lily Briscoe deals with Mr Ramsay in the same spirit:

> 'What beautiful boots!' she exclaimed. She was ashamed of herself. To praise his boots when he asked her to solace his soul; when he had shown her his bleeding hands, his lacerated heart.

Lily Briscoe expects an outburst of wrath at her inability to enter Mr Ramsay's metaphorical universe, but he smiles: 'His pall, his draperies, his infirmities fell from him. Ah yes, he said, holding his foot for her to look at, they were first-rate boots. There was only one man in England who could make boots like that.'[12] Mr Ramsay is a prisoner of his own inability to call a boat a boat rather than a bark, and when Stephen looked across the St Ives bay at the lighthouse he may have wondered not how it was built, but whether he himself was a man of genius, or someone who could only get as far as Q in the race for immortality.

Rosemary Freeman suggests that the *The Pilgrim's Progress* 'is the last coherent formulation' of the allegorical mode of thought in the sixteenth and seventeenth centuries. Arnold Kettle argues that the secular version of the story is *Robinson Crusoe*, where spiritual gain is translated into worldly prosperity.[13] Freeman declares that 'it became possible, and then customary, to observe the river independently of its significance, and individual experience broke free of the haunting presence of a perpetual *memento mori*'.[14] Nineteenth-century children's books hardly bear out her assertion. The March girls in *Little Women* are firmly enacting an earthly pilgrimage even if Amy is a literal young lady who thinks a knapsack on her back would give her a better notion of the burden within. The point about Huck Finn's not being able to figure out why Christian left home is that he is the only person in the Western world who has that problem. It is also quite plain to the reader why a family with a good collection of deathy pictures, made by a daughter who was the local epitaph-writer, would have a copy of Bunyan in the house. The chapter in which Beth dies in *Good Wives*, is called 'The Valley of the Shadow of Death'. But other children's writers began to feel that they would like to describe real places and real journeys – that is, happenings which, though imagined, did not stand for something other than what they literally were. Margery Fisher claims in *Intent Upon Reading* that the impulse which makes a writer write for children is, 'almost literally, a journey, for it will be more often associated with places than with people'.[15] Kenneth Grahame accosted his wife: 'You *like* people. They interest you. But I am interested in *places!*'[16]

Virginia Woolf demanded rather irritably why the novelist had to spend so much time on people when places were more interesting. She wrote that 'when they took Talland House, my father and mother gave me, at any rate, something I think invaluable. Suppose I had only Surrey or Sussex or the Isle of Wight to think about when I think about my childhood.'[17] In the diary which she kept of her visit to Greece in 1906 she wrote of her longing – no doubt increased by the illness of both Vanessa and Thoby, which in her brother's case culminated in his death in November of the same year – for England, not for friends but for the place, which seemed to send electric charges across the water summoning her home.[18]

In 1926 Woolf turned down an opportunity to write an article on

Willa Cather,[19] who gave to Jim Burden at the beginning of *My Ántonia* the reflection that 'no one who had not grown up in a little prairie town could know anything about it. It was a kind of freemasonry, we said.'[20]

Willa Cather despised children's writers and thought they were usually failed writers for adults. She singled out for particular scorn *Little Women* and *Little Lord Fauntleroy*, stating that a boy who could read would do better to cut his teeth on Bunyan and Defoe, Virgil, and Foxe's *Book of Martyrs*, though she admired Stevenson intensely.[21] (Never mind about girls' teeth, is strongly implied by Cather, who hated to be labelled a woman writer, because she thought women wrote of nothing but sex. One might hear Virginia Woolf's voice in *Orlando* in a comparable if less strident protest: 'Let other pens treat of sex and sexuality.') But despite Cather's championing of *The Pilgrim's Progress* she spent her life as a novelist trying to slough off the allegorical journey and the spiritual landscape, and to replace them with literal journey and literal landscape. Laura Ingalls Wilder achieved these ends more successfully than Cather did, largely because she wrote books for children.

Cather never attempted Woolf's experiments with form, but she constantly fretted herself about the rigidity of the novel, preferring the looser structures of romance and always moving towards myth and epic.[22] She found the idea of having to make up a plot just as irksome as Mark Twain or Woolf did. She was more interested in legend than in drama, and preferred mood to situation. She wrote of *Shadows on the Rock*: 'I took the incomplete air, and tried to give it what would correspond to a sympathetic musical setting; tried to develop it into a prose composition not too conclusive, not too definite: a series of pictures remembered rather than experienced.' She thought that the power of *The Pilgrim's Progress* came from 'scenes of the most satisfying kind; where little is said but much felt and communicated'.[23]

Daiches remarks that Cather needed more radical experimentation in technique to achieve the 'delicate texture' of *To the Lighthouse*.[24] But delicate texture was the last thing in the world that she wanted to achieve. The pioneers were heavy, earthy, hardy slow folk and 'to attempt to convey this hardihood of spirit one must use language a little stiff, a little formal, one must not be afraid of the old trite phraseology of the frontier. . . . It was like going back and playing the early composers after a surfeit of modern music.'[25] Her first novel, *Alexander's Bridge*, had been in the Jamesian mode, but her second, *O Pioneers!*, marked a deliberate turning-away from the literary world and its traditions: 'From the first chapter I decided not to "write" at all.'[26]

This eschewing of the literary is more complex than that apparently simple ambition would suggest. Laura Ingalls Wilder's daughter Rose urged on her mother the same unselfconsciousness: 'Just think you are writing a diary that no one anywhere will ever see, and put down all the things you think, regardless.' When Virginia Kirkus at Harper's read the Wilder manuscripts she 'felt that the writing had a distinctive folk flavor; was honestly conceived on the basis of her own childhood experiences'.[27] Cather described the genesis of *O Pioneers!*:

> When I got back to Pittsburgh I began to write a book entirely for myself; a story about some Scandinavians and Bohemians who had been neighbours of ours when I lived on a ranch in Nebraska, when I was eight or nine years old. I found it a much more absorbing occupation than writing *Alexander's Bridge*; a different process altogether. Here there was no arranging or 'inventing'; everything was spontaneous and took its own place, right or wrong. This was like taking a ride through a familiar country on a horse that knew the way – on a fine morning when you felt like riding.

When she came to write *My Ántonia*, she described the same natural process. When the book 'came along, quite of itself, and with no direction from me, it took the road of *O Pioneers!*'[28] For many readers the best writing seems transparent, reality itself rather than the representation of reality. Isabelle Jan has called Laura Ingalls Wilder the 'Grandma Moses of fiction. . . . Literary reminiscences play no part in her natural ability to observe each gesture with a little girl's inquisitive eyes.'[29] Some disappointment has accompanied Rosa Ann Moore's uncovering in Laura Ingalls Wilder's notebooks of just that process of editing and arranging of both experience and writing which Cather declared to be no longer necessary when she wrote of her own pioneering childhood. Yet Wilder was not without literary culture. She recalled in *The First Four Years* – her one unedited and rather unhappy description not of childhood, but of the struggles of herself and her husband as young adults – that escaping into Scott's novels was the only thing which made her own life tolerable.[30] She knew what the literary could make out of the literal environment, but she chose not to do it in her own books. Defoe, who wrote of another pioneer struggling to master an alien physical environment, provided for both Wilder and Cather a literary model of writing which did not seem to be 'writing'. The repudiation of the literary is itself a 'literary' statement with a respectable literary history.

Edgar Allan Poe wrote of *Robinson Crusoe*: 'Men do not look upon it in the light of a literary performance. Defoe has none of their thoughts – Robinson all. . . . We close the book, and are quite satisfied that we could have written as well ourselves.'[31] The book communicates power over two kinds of medium. The reader could survive on a desert island (most of the interviewees on Desert Island Discs think they would manage perfectly all right) but he could also write the narrative of his survival just as well as Defoe does. The book, in Poe's view, saps up the self, so that the reader is absorbed in Robinson's identity. This process also happened to the author. He refused to separate himself from his character and wrote testily in the Preface to volume III:

> I have heard, that the envious and ill-disposed Part of the World have rais'd some Objections against the two first Volumes, on the Pretence, *for want of a better Reason*; That (*as they say*) the Story is feign'd, that the Names are borrow'd, and it is all a Romance; that there never were any such Man or Place, or Circumstances in any Mans Life; that it is all form'd and embellish'd by Invention to impose upon the World.
>
> I *Robinson Crusoe* being at this Time in perfect and sound Mind and Memory, Thanks be to God therefore; do hereby declare, their Objection is an Invention scandalous in Design, and false in Fact; and do affirm, that the Story, though Allegorical, is also Historical.[32]

He had, as Cather pointed out in her Preface to *The Fortunate Mistress* – which she did not admire at all and thought suffered from not being based on true experience – received from Alexander Selkirk the account of his own expedition which formed the factual basis for Crusoe's adventures.[33] Defoe also makes it plain that being marooned was a condition of life that he knew well and that, like Frances Hodgson Burnett's Sara Crewe, he had used the story to transform a different kind of desert island: 'All these Reflections are just History of a State of forc'd Confinement, which in my real History is represented by a confin'd Retreat in an Island.'[34] Bunyan's pilgrimage is one way out of the prison house and Defoe's is the more literal description of it, but they are neither of them the literal transcription which Crusoe insisted that he was making. Lamb observed that 'the narrator chains us down to an implicit belief in every thing he says. There is all the minute detail of a log-book in it. Dates are painfully pressed upon the memory. Facts are repeated over and over in varying phrases, till you cannot chuse but believe them. It is like reading evidence in a court of Justice.'[35] Rousseau thought children ought to be allowed to read *Robinson Crusoe* because it dispensed with the fabulous and encouraged the acquisition of practical skills, a view which demonstrates that Rousseau himself was deceived by the author's fiction of veracity.

For children books represent literal reality, as Charlotte Brontë shows in her description of Jane Eyre reading *Gulliver's Travels* to console herself for Mrs Reed's cruelty: 'This book I had again and again perused with delight; I considered it a narrative of facts, and discovered in it a vein of interest deeper than what I found in fairy tales.' Jane had come to the melancholy conclusion that there were no more fairies in England – the advent of the factory drives them out at the end of *Shirley* – but 'Lilliput and Brobdignag being, in my creed, solid parts of the earth's surface, I doubted not that I might one day, by taking a long voyage, see with my own eyes the little fields, houses, and trees, the diminutive people. . . .'[36] For many Victorian children it was not necessary to step through the looking-glass to enter Alice's world. Gwen Raverat writes of her terror at sharing a bedroom with an American great-aunt who 'began her toilet by taking off her skirt, and then came up to my cot dressed in her bonnet and bodice and feather-boa, but tailing off sadly lower down into a skimpy under-petticoat'. This apparition, reproduced in a drawing worth of Tenniel, stimulated such a squalling that the small Gwen had to be transferred to another room: 'I still think the costume was both sinister and indecent, but I admit that my memory of the poor lady has become hopelessly mixed up with the pictures of the Duchess in *Alice Through the Looking-Glass*.'[37] Virginia Woolf described the way in which *Robinson Crusoe* becomes part of a child's consciousness: 'The book resembles one of the anonymous productions of the race rather than the effort of a single mind. . . . Something of this we may attribute to the fact that we have all had *Robinson Crusoe* read aloud to us as children, and were thus much in the same state of mind towards Defoe and the story that the Greeks were in towards Homer. . . . The impressions of childhood are those that last longest and cut deepest. It still seems that the name of Daniel Defoe has no right to appear upon the title-page of *Robinson Crusoe*.'[38]

Woolf's reference to Homer throws light on the aims of both Willa Cather and Laura Ingalls Wilder. Both wanted to record a past which was not just the childhood memories of the individual but the group memory of the pioneer generation. Writing it down becomes the making of a history – the written rather than the oral tradition – in the work of art. Giving to the future the real experiences of the pioneer past is also a giving to the literary future a tradition of writing: Homer, the name subsequent ages give to a work of more than one hand and more than one oral tradition, becomes a source, a point of reference for all future poets. If there is no story of the pioneer past it possesses no imaginative future, no possibility of re-creation in the mind of the present, and thus the present becomes that inconceivably impoverished being, a man without childhood memories, with no access to the origins of consciousness. The aesthetic problem for both Cather and Wilder centred on how to embody the pioneer spirit in words without rooting it, not in the pioneer present, but in the anterior consciousness of the old world. The problem did not exist for Homer, but it did exist for Virgil, who wanted to found a new literature in a new land, Roman not Greek. How could a writer, to use Harold Bloom's phrase, cast off the anxiety of influence?

The difficulty lay in ways of seeing places. Vivian in Wilde's essay *The Decay of Lying* claims that 'the highest art rejects the burden of the human spirit, and gains more from a new medium of fresh material than she does from any enthusiasm for art. . . . She is not symbolic of any age. It is the age that are her symbols.'[39] Cather and Wilder do not want the prairie to symbolise human consciousness. It was hard for anyone whose cultural heritage included Bunyan – which was the vast majority of Protestants in England and America – to look at a road and see it literally as a road, without seeing it as a metaphor for the journey of life.

Pater wrote of Wordsworth that he conveys 'the whole complex sentiment of a particular place, the abstract expression of desolation in the long white road, or peacefulness in a particular folding of the hills'. Pater admits that 'human life, indeed, is for him [Wordsworth], at first, only an additional accidental grace on an expressive landscape'. Nevertheless it was a landscape humanised by 'the habitual association of his thoughts and feelings with a particular spot of earth. . . . For Wordsworth these influences tended to the dignity of human nature, because they tended to tranquillise it' (Fields of sheep do in the end induce fields of sleep.) Pater drew from Wordsworth the perception that 'religious sentiment, consecrating the affections and natural regrets of the human heart . . . has always had much to do with localities, with the thoughts which attach themselves to actual scenes and places.'[40] In 'The Spirit of the Place' (1898) the essayist and poet Alice Meynell revels in exactly that view of physical landscape which the Victorians associated with Wordsworth, and which Cather and Wilder reject. The place itself is subsumed in abstraction, has become all spirit and no place:

> Spirit of place! It is for this we travel, to surprise its subtlety. . . . Long white roads outside have mere suggestions of it and prophecies. . . . And if by good fortune it is a child who is the pilgrim, the spirit of the place gives him a peculiar welcome, for antiquity and the conceiver of antiquity, (who is only a child) know one another; nor is there a more delicate perceiver of locality than a child. He is well used to words and voices that he does not understand, and this is a condition of his simplicity; and when these unknown words are bells, loud in the night, they are to him as lovely and as old as lullabies.[41]

Subtleties, suggestions, pilgrimages, prophecies, singularities, simplicities, antiquities, localities: it begins to sound like a Gilbert and Sullivan pattersong: they'd none of them be missed. By the end the child is not the only one who hears words and voices he does not understand. The reader is left enquiring, in Aunt Etty-ish tones, whether bells at night don't wake one up rather than making a lovely lullaby. One thing is clear: the white road is still there, and, whether barefooted or best-booted, a child plods along it on his earthly pilgrimage, bearing on his back whatever he may, but in his heart the burden of its significance.

The literary associations of that white road do not derive solely from Bunyan, but from the Old Testament and from landscape itself. The Roman road in Grahame's story is both landscape history and spiritual way, whether it leads to the city of Marcus Aurelius or to that of St Peter.[42] The white road at the beginning of Hardy's *The*

Return of the Native, which bisects 'that vast dark surface like the parting-line on a head of black hair',[43] stands for man's futile but enduring attempts to tame a wild landscape, mirrored in Clym's vain efforts to tame Eustacia Vye. The same white road may symbolise hope: the track of the future, as when Jane Eyre gazes out from the window at Lowood and dreams of freedom: 'I traced the white road winding round the base of one mountain and vanishing in a gorge between two: how I longed to follow it further!'[44] Its physical history – an ancient track which bears witness to the passage of diverse civilisations across the face of the earth – enriches its literary representation in which the Biblical, pastoral and allegorical allow many writers to absorb and become part of an ancient literary landscape.

But for Cather and Wilder the new world of the American prairie offered no ancient tracks either on the earth or on the written page. Jim Burden's first journey into Nebraska in *My Ántonia* baffles him: 'If there was a road, I could not make it out in the faint starlight. There was nothing but land: not a country at all, but the material out of which countries are made. . . . I had the feeling that the world was left behind, that we had got over the edge of it, and were outside man's jurisdiction. . . . Between that earth and that sky I felt erased, blotted out. I did not say my prayers that night: here, I felt, what would be would be.' Being outside man's jurisdiction, it is also outside God's: a place empty of spirits: 'I did not believe that my dead father and mother were watching me from up there: they would still be looking for me at the sheep-fold down by the creek, or along the white road that led to the mountain pastures. I had left even their spirits behind me.'[45] Without those marks of locality – sheep-fold, white road, pasture – the land has no road into the imagination. Woolf wrote in an essay entitled 'American Fiction' that 'the English tradition is already unable to cope with this vast land, these prairies, these cornfields, these lonely little groups of men and women scattered at immense distances from each other'.[46] Wilder describes the same empty landscape at the beginning of *Little House in the Big Woods* when the Ingalls family are still in Wisconsin: 'There were no houses. There were no roads. There were no people.'[47] Jim Burden recalls: 'As I looked about me I felt that the grass was the country, as the water is the sea',[48] featureless, fluid, vast, uninhabited. This is no landscape for the enhancing of human dignity. Wilder wrote in the second of her books, *Little House on the Prairie*: 'No road, not even the faintest trace of wheels or of a rider's passing, could be seen anywhere. That prairie looked as if no human eye had ever seen it before.'[49] At the opening of *O Pioneers!* the settlers are talking of giving up and going home, beaten 'by the last struggle of a wild soil against the encroaching plowshare. . . . The great fact was the land itself, which seemed to overwhelm the little beginnings of human society that struggled in its sombre wastes.' Cather wrote that 'of all the bewildering things about a new country, the absence of human landmarks is one of the most depressing and disheartening'.[50] Here was indeed abundance of fresh material to be translated into the medium of art. But how was a writer to describe in a language saturated with literary associations a land without ghosts?

As territory for art Nebraska remained recalcitrant. Cather wrote defiantly: 'A New York critic voiced a very general opinion when he said: "I simply don't care a damn what happens in Nebraska, no matter who writes about it." ' In a lesser form Hardy had felt the same lack of modishness in writing about Dorset. Literary skill, Cather insisted, had little to do with the fact that 'London is supposed to be more engaging than, let us say, Gopher Prairie; even if the writer knows Gopher Prairie very well and London very casually.'[51] Enlisting the imagination for the improvement of homely subject matter would only result in 'a brilliant sham, which, like a badly built and pretentious house, looks poor and shabby after a few years'.[52] *My Ántonia* begins with Jim Burden's offering to his former fellow traveller a bald record of his life in Nebraska:

> 'Here is the thing about Ántonia. . . . I didn't take time to arrange it; I simply wrote down pretty much all that her name recalls to me. I suppose it hasn't any form. It hasn't any title either.' He went into the next room, sat down at my desk and wrote across the face of the portfolio the word 'Ántonia'. He frowned at this a moment, then prefixed another word, making 'My Ántonia'. That seemed to satisfy him.

He explains that Ántonia Shimerda 'more than any other person we remembered . . . seemed to mean to us the country, the conditions, the whole adventure of our childhood'.[53] The addition of the possessive 'my' reminds the reader of Mr Shimerda – it was his way of speaking of his daughter – and that the experiences recorded in the book can only be partly shared with the reader who looks over Jim's shoulder at that unliterary record. Ántonia is not the heroine of a novel in the way that Jane Eyre or Anna Karenina is. The reader can never become her, as she becomes Robinson Crusoe. The journey into the pioneering past is narrative not spiritual journey. Cather, like Woolf, shied away from the word 'novel' and declared that if her books were difficult to classify, as one critic observed, she would simply call them narratives.[54]

The author does not invite the reader to discover truths about the journey of life, but only to be present at the heroic moment before civilisation, when there was, literally, no writing on the land. That moment is tangible for Jim one evening when he and Ántonia are out playing in the open air:

> Presently we saw a curious thing: There were no clouds, the sun was going down in a limpid, gold-washed sky. Just as the lower edge of the red disk rested on the high fields against the horizon, a great black figure suddenly appeared on the face of the sun. We sprang to our feet, straining our eyes toward it. In a moment we realized what it was. On some upland farm, a plough had been left standing in the field. The sun was sinking just behind it. Magnified across the distance by the horizontal light, it stood out against the sun, was exactly contained within the circle of the disk; the handles, the tongue, the share – black against the molten red. There it was, heroic in size, a picture writing on the sun.
>
> Even while we whispered about it, our vision disappeared; the ball dropped and dropped until the red tip went beneath the earth. The fields below us were dark, the sky was growing pale, and that forgotten plough had sunk back to its own littleness somewhere on the prairie.

When Jim Burden studies classical literature with Gaston Cleric at Lincoln – Cather's college – he thinks of his teacher as Virgil, opening new worlds for Dante, but finds that, even as the classical landscape becomes vital to him, the literal landscape of his childhood refuses to give way to the literary:

> While I was in the very act of yearning toward the new forms that Cleric brought up before me, my mind plunged away from me, and I suddenly found myself thinking of the places and people of my own infinitesimal past. They stood out strengthened and simplified now, like the image of the plough against the sun. They were all I had for an answer to the new appeal.

The fusion of actual memory and of imagined world speaks to Burden from Virgil's *Georgics*:

> I propped my book open and stared listlessly at the page of the 'Georgics' where to-morrow's lesson began. It opened with the melancholy reflection that, in the lives of mortals, the best days are the first to flee. *'Optima dies . . . prima fugit.'* I turned back to the beginning of the third book, which we had read in class that morning. *'Primus ego in patriam meam . . . deducam Musas'*: 'for I shall be the first, if I live, to bring the Muse into my country'.

Gaston Cleric tells Burden that Virgil must have remembered writing that when he was dying, with the *Aeneid* still unfinished: 'Then his mind must have gone back to the perfect utterance of the "Georgics", where the pen was fitted to the matter as the plough is to the furrow.'[55] For Cather, the pen provides the picture-writing of the heroic moment, just as the plough traces pioneer history on the face of an untamed and reluctant land, in which, as she wrote of Wagner's *Tannhäuser*, 'the conquests of peace [are] dearer bought than those of war'.[56] Virgil tried in the *Georgics* to annex into the world of art, through the medium of the classical pastoral, the primitive struggle of a man cultivating his land. Cather was equally determined to make a space in art for the land itself, on which 'the record of the plow was insignificant, like the feeble scratches on stone left by prehistoric races, so indeterminate that they may, after all, be only the markings of glaciers, and not a record of human stirrings'.[57] The pioneer struggle with Nebraska claims the right to be told not because it symbolises human endurance, but because it expresses it, providing a literal manifestation instead of a literary metaphor. In the essays of Leslie Stephen and Alice Meynell the physical world responds to the human being, mirroring his spirit and answering his needs. This sublimely complacent view of geographical environment has been fostered at every turn by Christian allegory, and, despite Christianity's emphasis on humility, that appropriation of the physical environment has, as Pater argued, augmented man's sense of his own importance. He can imprint his image on the entire physical universe, which gives him a kind of godhead. Cather believed, as Woolf did, that the function of the artist must be to record not the harmonious but the discordant, the recalcitrant matter which seems unmalleable to art, or she will never cease to tread the long white road of literary cliché, a metaphor Woolf used to disparage the novels of George Moore (whom she found fascinating as a person) to David Garnett: 'I don't go with you all the way down the long smooth white undulating road of the novels.'[58] The writer must make her own way through the uncut grass.

II PIONEERS

Cather saw that children could cope with the struggles of pioneer life better than adults could because they create for themselves an imaginative medium out of what is available: cold mutton transubstantiates into red venison. But adults are less flexible. Steinbeck's *The Grapes of Wrath* begins with the women packing up to go west:

> The women sat among the doomed things, turning them over and looking past them and back. This book. My father had it. He liked a book. *Pilgrim's Progress*. Used to read it. Got his name in it. . . . Think we could get this china dog in? . . .
> How can we live without our lives? How will we know it's us without our past?[59]

In *My Ántonia* Mr Shimerda's violin marks his identity with the past, as do, in Wilder's books, Pa's fiddle, and Ma's china shepherdess, whom no one must touch but she. The shepherdess is never put out on her carved bracket until the Ingalls family are settled in a place. The moment when Pa can no longer play the fiddle because his hands are too swollen with the cold of the long winter is one of despair out of all proportion to the event itself: 'The worst thing that had happened was that Pa could not play the fiddle. If she had not asked him to play it, he might not have known that he could not do it.'[60] Cather had sketched Mr Shimerda's story in a tale called 'Peter' which was published in the Lincoln college magazine, in which a Czech violinist emigrated to Nebraska, taking his violin with him although he was no longer able to play it. His son insists on his selling the instrument, though Peter would rather die than do so, and in the end commits suicide.[61] Ántonia tells Jim about her father's playing in Bohemia:

> 'My papa sad for the old country. He not look good. He never

make music any more. At home he play violin all the time; for weddings and for dance. Here never. When I beg him for play, he shake his head no. Some days he take his violin out of his box and make with his fingers on the strings, like this, but never he make the music. He don't like this kawn-tree.'

'People who don't like this country ought to stay at home,' I said severely. 'We don't make them come here.'

In *Lark Rise to Candleford* Flora Thompson describes how her grandmother made her grandfather sell his violin because they needed money and how it seemed a violation of self-respect. Mr Shimerda is an educated man: 'Standing before them with his hand on Ántonia's shoulder, he talked in a low tone, and his daughter translated. He wanted us to know that they were not beggars in the old country; he made good wages, and his family were respected there.'[62] Without the things which have become inseparable from life itself, which create identity, living has no meaning.

Cather sympathised deeply with Mr Shimerda's plight. The artist's escape to the old world of European art was as vital to her development as it had been to Henry James's, though she returned to write about her native land and he did not. But she also understands Jim's tart comment. The only way to be a pioneer is to pioneer – to look forward, not back. When *O Pioneers!* opens Alexandra and Emil are looking towards the horizon: 'The road led southwest, toward the streak of pale, watery light that glimmered in the leaden sky. The light fell upon the two sad young faces that were turned mutely toward it: upon the eyes of the girl, who seemed to be looking with such anguished perplexity into the future; upon the sombre eyes of the boy, who seemed already to be looking into the past.' Alexandra realises the pioneer dream, where Emil wants only to get away from the land. Their fortunes are reflected in Cather's mode of writing, for Alexandra is the new creation while Emil remains a figure from the novel of tragic love, unconvincingly drawn. The pioneer, like the artist, must imagine the uncreated. Cather wrote of Alexandra: 'The history of every country begins in the heart of a man or a woman.'[63] The picture-writing of the plough, and the narrative which describes it, are almost the same thing: a vision. The pioneers have no time for romance any more than the artist can afford the glamour of genius, a perception which allies Cather to the Henry James of *Roderick Hudson*, in which the quiet plodding painter achieves results denied to the brilliant and pampered prodigy. Cather wrote: 'The business of an artist's life is not Bohemianism for or against, but ceaseless and unremitting labor.'[64] Cather believed that the artist shares a pioneer spirit natural to children. Jim looks back not on unremitting hardship, but on the 'whole adventure of our childhood'.

Both Cather and Wilder knew that the drive which impels the pioneer comes from the child's eagerness for what lies ahead, whether or not the pioneer *is*, in physical terms, still a child. The view of the mature being is nearly always that expressed by Robinson Crusoe's father to his restless son:

> He bid me observe . . . *that* the middle Station of Life was calculated for all kind of Vertues and all kinds of Enjoyments; that Peace and Plenty were the Hand-Maids of a middle Fortune . . . that this Way Men went silently and smoothly thro' the World, and comfortably out of it, not embarrass'd with the Labours of the Hands or of the Head.[65]

Willa Cather remarks smartly that this is the condition of most adults, as also of some children, and embodies their view of happiness. In *O Pioneers!* the Bergson boys have inherited none of their father's wish to look into the future: 'Like most of their neighbors, they were meant to follow in paths already marked out for them, not to break trails in a new country. A steady job, a few holidays, nothing to think about, and they would have been very happy. It was no fault of theirs that they had been dragged into the wilderness when they were little boys. A pioneer should have imagination, should be able to enjoy the idea of things more than the things themselves.'[66] Flora Thompson describes in *Lark Rise to Candleford* how the thought of going to Candleford entrances the children even more than the journey itself. When a man brings a honeycomb they wait for him to come again, 'for the hope was almost as sweet as the honey'.[67] A child enjoys everything in anticipation so that the actual event is dwarfed by the expectation of it. In *O Pioneers!* John Bergson's 'wandering, sad eyes . . . looked forward into the distance, as if they already beheld the New World'. Carl Linstrum, returning from the city to see the success Alexandra has made of her father's farm, remarks: 'I would never have believed it could be done. I'm disappointed in my own eye, in my imagination.'[68]

In Laura Ingalls Wilder's books the longing to go west is part of that childlike eagerness to realise the future. When the family have to leave their house on the prairie because the government have ordered the settlers out, the parents' disappointment is felt rather than named: 'Pa and Ma were still and silent on the wagon-seat, and Mary and Laura were quiet, too. But Laura felt all excited inside. You never know what will happen next, nor where you'll be tomorrow, when you are travelling in a covered wagon.'[69] In *By the Shores of Silver Lake* Laura's longing to go west almost provokes a family quarrel. Ma and Mary want to be settled and civilised but Pa and Laura long to move on:

All those golden autumn days the sky was full of wings. Wings beating low over the blue water of Silver Lake, wings beating high in the blue air far above it. . . .

The wings and the golden weather and the tang of the frost in the mornings made Laura want to go somewhere. She did not know where. She wanted only to go.

'Let's go West,' she said one night after supper. 'Pa, can't we go West when Uncle Henry does?' . . .

'Mercy, Laura!' Ma said. 'Whatever –' She could not go on.

'I know, little Half-pint,' said Pa, and his voice was very kind. 'You and I want to fly like the birds. But long ago I promised your Ma that you girls should go to school. You can't go to school and go West.'

Laura takes Carrie skating across Silver Lake. They see two enormous buffalo wolves; the same yearning envelops her: 'She felt herself a part of the wide land, of the far deep sky and the brilliant moonlight. She wanted to fly.'[70] Even the locusts share that instinct for moving on at last, when every green thing has been destroyed: 'That whole day long the grasshoppers walked west. All the next day they went on walking west. And all the third day they walked without stopping.'[71] The pioneering spirit copies a movement of nature. When it rains in *My Ántonia* 'one black cloud, no bigger than a little boat, drifted out into the clear space unattended, and kept moving westward'.[72] But nature has no spiritual destination: new Jerusalem or Delectable Mountains: 'Laura thought that little path went on for ever wandering on sunny grass and crossing friendly streams and always going around low hills to see what was on the other side. She knew it really must go to Mr Nelson's house, but it was a little path that did not want to stop anywhere. It wanted always to be going on.'[73] Pioneering is an end in itself, like art. It carries no burden of moral significance. The journey and its end are one and the same.

For Willa Cather that identification of travelling and arriving was one of the fascinations of Thomas Mann's *Tales of Jacob*, the first volume of the long novel, *Joseph and His Brethren*, which she reviewed when it appeared in English translation. She wrote of its felicitously slow pace:

> We are among a shepherd people; the story has almost the movement of grazing sheep. The characters live at that pace. Perhaps no one who has not lived among sheep can realize the rightness of the rhythm. A shepherd people is not driving towards anything. With them, truly, as Michelet said of quite another form of journeying, the end is nothing, the road is all. In fact, the road and the end are literally one.

Cather's novels of pioneer life, unlike Wilder's, begin when the journey is over, but it is *not* over, because going west is also surviving in, and settling the west. Cather saw that artistically Mann had the enormous advantage of telling a known tale: 'We are familiar with Mann's characters and their history, not only through Moses and the Prophets, but through Milton and Dante and Racine, Bach and Haydn and Handel, through painters and stone-cutters innumerable. We begin the book with the great imaginings and the great imaginators already in our minds.' His land is already written on, already Biblical country and not the raw material from which a country and its art are made. Cather's novels of pioneer life tapped that same root of Biblical history, as she was no doubt aware when she wrote of *Tales of Jacob*:

> The Bible countries along the Mediterranean shore were very familiar to most of us in our childhood. Whether we were born in New Hampshire or California, Palestine lay behind us. . . . It was in our language fixedly, indelibly. The effect of the King James translation of the Bible upon English prose has been repeated down through the generations, leaving its mark on the minds of all children who had any but the most sluggish emotional nature. . . . The Book of Genesis lies like a faded tapestry in the

consciousness of almost every individual who is more than forty years of age.[74]

The Philistinism of the translators of the New English Bible has now wiped that record as clean as if it had never existed.

Cather used the Old Testament not as metaphor, but as literal landscape. The promised land was the mid-West. 'Much have I travelled in the realms of gold' could never for her be a metaphor for reading, as it is for Keats. It could only mean the cornfields of the West. When Jim arrives at his grandfather's in *My Ántonia* he and Jake are summoned to family prayers; his grandfather reads the Book of Psalms: 'I was awed by his intonation of the word "Selah". "He shall choose our inheritance for us, the excellency of Jacob whom He loved. Selah." '[75] When Jim's grandparents set out for the Shimerdas' house after Mr Shimerda's suicide Jim describes them as looking Biblical. But the connection is primary, not secondary, analogy not metaphor, real inheritance in the wealth of the American cornfields, not spiritual inheritance in the Land of Beulah. The Israelites wanted their own country, not a country of the mind.

Exploration becomes metaphor when the world has been settled, as the journey was for Laura and Edmund in *Lark Rise to Candleford*: 'On the whole, they would rather not have known where they were bound for. They would have liked to be genuine explorers, like Livingstone in Africa; but as their destination had been decided for them, their exploring had to be confined to wayside wonders.'[76] Jim Burden, left in his grandfather's kitchen on the afternoon of Mr Shimerda's death, tries to read *Robinson Crusoe*, 'but his life on the island seemed dull compared with ours'. Far from supplying vicarious experience, or a dimension of living which is inaccessible to the child, the book has become redundant. The real world displaces the imagined one. There is no need to pretend to be pirates, explorers, invaders. Pioneer life includes all those adventures.

Furthermore, the power of the child's mind to transform his environment, even by the negative device of measuring fiction by fact and finding fiction wanting, makes it possible for him to see on the blank land something which is beyond physical hardship. Jim and Ántonia, unlike many of the adults around them, are able to reconcile the memories of the old world with the landscape of the new. Ántonia tells of the great forest full of game from which 'she and her mother used to steal wood on moonlight nights. There was a white hart that lived in that forest, and if anyone killed it, he would be hanged, she said.' When Jim kills the rattlesnake it becomes in retrospect a reluctant dragon, out of training for the fight: 'A snake of his size, in fighting trim, would be more than any boy could handle. So in reality it was a mock adventure; the game was fixed for me by chance, as it probably was for many a dragon-slayer.' White hart and snake become myth and make the land less raw. The same is true of the little grasshopper Antonia finds and shelters in her hair. When it sings rustily she tells Jim of 'an old beggar woman who went about selling herbs and roots she had dug up in the forest. If you took her in and gave her a warm place by the fire, she sang old songs to the children in a cracked voice, like this.' Mr Shimerda hears the insect and also remembers: 'He listened as if it were a beautiful sound.'[77] The story creates a medium in which the pioneers and the new land can acquire a past.

Stories of family history occupy for children a place poised between fiction and fact. Flora Thompson's mother in *Lark Rise to Candleford* tells a family story of the young man who shut his father up in a box and went to make his fortune in the Australian goldfields, but no one knew the end of the story although their mother had seen the box and heard the story for 'as long as she could remember'.[78] In both Cather's and Wilder's books the true story extends the raw present into a past era which is both real and mythical, truth and tale. When Mrs Shimerda gives Jim's grandmother dried mushrooms, they are not just mushrooms, but living relics of another world: 'They had been gathered, probably, in some deep Bohemian forest.' Peter and Pavel's Russian past is for Jim and Ántonia a recurring fiction which enhances their own lives: 'The story of the wedding party was never at an end. We did not tell Pavel's secret to anyone, but guarded it jealously – as if the wolves of the Ukraine had gathered that night long ago, and the wedding party been sacrificed, to give us a painful and peculiar pleasure. At night, before I went to sleep, I often found myself in a sledge drawn by three horses, dashing through a country that looked some-thing like Nebraska and something like Virginia.'[79] The stories of the old country in Cather's books civilise the new, giving it a place in an extended human consciousness, just as the stories of family life in Wilder's books allow the children access to other childhoods. Mary and Laura annex to themselves 'The Story of Grandpa and the Panther', and 'The Story of Grandpa's Sled and the Pig', which Pa tells them in *Little House in the Big Woods*. But in the same way the present also creates its stories – Pa confronting a bear over the honey tree, Ma banging another bear on its side and telling it to get over as though it were Sukey, their cow. For children, to live is to make a story about living, and this capacity provides a resource for combatting the hardship of the pioneer present which adults can only recapture with conscious effort.

The writer who comes nearest to blurring the distinction between remembered past and imagined story is William Mayne in *The Jersey Shore* (1973), a book which deals with a man who has come to the new world from the old. Benjamin Thatcher, in New Jersey, brought up in Osney Fen in Norfolk, one summer tells his grandchild Arthur the stories of his youth, not just what he remembers, but folk memories of Viking invasions, and children's games which play out those events. When the old man tells the story of the children drowned by the flood, both he and Arthur weep, but Arthur is not sure of its truth, any more than the reader is: 'It was to him that the old man talked, and it was to him that he handed on sight of things that had perhaps not ever happened. The man from the sea, for instance, he had almost witnessed with some inner eye, and certainly the old man had not seen him either. And today's story of the marsh had been shared in the same way, springing up from a memory they both shared but neither had experienced as an event.' When Benjamin describes the Fleetmen invading Osney Cold Fen only one child returns to the village, falling and dying within a few yards of it: 'The father of the dead boy picked him up as they passed, and that was the first blood they saw that day. . . . Arthur had come with increasing horror to this point. He did not want to see what came next, and he did not have to. There was an end to the pictures, to the sense of being there or of understanding the recollection or vision.'

Benjamin's narratives are released by the need to pass them on to the child. The past itself remains more inaccessible to him than it does to the listening boy:

'The Fleetmen,' said Arthur, startled suddenly by the memory of them and their boats, coming out of the eastern day. His eye had caught some sharp prows rising above the railway bank – ships might be drawn up – but it was only the posts of the railway signalling system, and he had often seen them before. Now he was to be haunted by them, he thought, as if they were ships and he had been at the place where they landed, half a world away in space and time. The old man had understood what he meant by his words, 'the Fleetmen'.

'Nothing of it came here with me,' he said. 'Nothing more than I tell you. There ain't nothing to be seen out here in this sand. Ghosts don't travel like that.'

At the centre of Benjamin's memories is that of the strange mythical ancestor of the Loving family, the dark visitant from the sea with the iron collar, forefather of Annie, who refuses to marry Benjamin:

'It can't be,' she said. 'We abide here, and folk bear with us, and we don't belong, and we look different, so dark we are, and we have to mind our ways, from when the first of us came like a captive', and 'twas then she showed me the chain, hung on the wall, old and thinned at the link ends. When that breaked, she said, they might be free. I said I would break it, but I knew it was no use, that time wasn't come.

Benjamin goes to America and marries Florence, who is dark like Annie. The Jersey shore, which harbours no ghosts of that old world, that sandy expanse on which the traces of Benjamin's past have been washed away as totally as the flood on Osney Fen washed the children away, and as the snow hid their graves, remains for Benjamin featureless as the sea of the untilled prairie was for Jim Burden or Mr Shimerda. The old man had left England in 1886. Wilder was born in 1867, and her books record the pioneering movements of the early seventies. When Benjamin Thatcher tells Arthur his age, on their last meeting, the boy from the mid-West 'realized that his grandfather was older than the town at home, older than the railway, older than the State he lived in, which had been a Territory then, or perhaps not even discovered'.

As an adult Arthur decides to go back to Osney Fen. He is a pilot in the Second World War and has to give his identity:

'Thatcher?' said the man, handing the papers back. 'That's more like an English name than what we'd, well, expect.'

'We thought we might expect someone coming from the sea to be like you, if you see what I mean,' said the other man.

'My grandfather,' said Art. 'He came from Osney.' . . .

Art went to the church first. The church was what came to his mind. He knew it was appropriate for a man from the sea, and he recalled now that Parson Ramage kept his dogs in it. He remembered too that the flood of the dream had filled it and he wanted to see whether it had happened.

It had happened. There was a mark on the walls, about a foot up from the ground.

The going-back is almost the piecing-together of the past which occurs in Alex Haley's *Roots*. The children stare at Arthur, and he thinks they have probably not seen anyone like him before. But he is wrong. He stops outside the Loving's house, and sees the chain that hangs on the door:

> The chain swung and rapped on the door for him. He gathered it in to himself, understanding every part of it. He remembered things his father had told him, things that his grandfather had perhaps not clearly known. His grandmother, Florence, the mother of his father, had been born a slave, in captivity. In the first years of her life she had known what chains like this, collars like this, were. Art was descended from slaves. The Lovings were descended from a slave. His grandmother had been freed by a war; the man from the sea by escape and shipwreck.

A girl opens the door and the moment of illumination for both man and reader is completed: 'Now he understood completely why Benjamin Thatcher had married someone born a slave. He saw that this beautiful girl had the same skin as himself, the same skin as his grandmother; that it was part of her beauty. He was himself captured by it too. He tried to put the chain down, but dropped one end of it. Somehow he pulled it in two, and a broken link fell separate to the floor.'[80]

William Mayne may have felt, as many readers do, the need to rewrite the ending of Kipling's story 'Cold Iron' in *Rewards and Fairies*, where the changeling child snaps the iron collar of the slave back on his neck and is doomed to follow that fortune for ever.[81] In the old world Kipling's story is bound by its own metaphors. In the new, human beings can write their own stories on the blank page of a land which is not yet territory. Mayne offers the story as Arthur's inheritance, just as Thomas Mann suggests that the stories told to the young Joseph 'create the stratified record upon which we set our feet, the ground beneath us'.[82] When Steinbeck's pioneers leave the old copy of *The Pilgrim's Progress* behind they may, like Defoe, leave behind the consolatory metaphor of the old world – the spiritual journey and the hope of heaven – but Bunyan's political message becomes part of their flesh-and-blood experience.

When Christian reaches the House Beautiful he is taken to the top floor and invited to view the prospect. Before him stretches 'a most pleasant Mountainous country' – a Bedford man's view of Paradise – which is called 'Immanuels Land: and it is common, said they, as this Hill is, to and for all Pilgrims'. Christian eventually reaches that country but it turns out that it belongs to 'the Lord of that Hill'. The sheep also belong to him: 'He laid down his life for them', explain the Shepherds. Although at first it seems as if the promise of radical community is not being fulfilled, it finally turns out that the sheep have been given rights over the Lord, indeed over his life, despite the fact that they and the mountains belong to him. The Lord and the land thus become one with the sheep and the shepherd, the wayfarer and the inhabitant, the journey and its end.

The question of who is master animates the most politically oriented confrontation in the book, which E. P. Thompson sees as the reason behind its adoption, in the late eighteenth and earlier nineteenth centuries, as the standard radical text of the working man. Apollyon claims Christian as his subject but Christian retorts:

> *Chr.* I was born indeed in your Dominions, but your service was hard, and your wages such as a man could not live on, *for the Wages of Sin is death*; therefore when I was come to years, I did as other considerate persons do, look out, if perhaps I might mend my self.
>
> *Apol:* There is no Prince that will thus lightly lose his Subjects; neither will I as yet lose thee.

The overridingly secular tone of that interchange has made it a blueprint for defiance of temporal authority: Jane Eyre standing up to Mrs Reed or proclaiming her equality with Mr Rochester. Christian is free to choose whom he will serve: 'To speak truth, I like his Service, his Wages, his Servants, his Government, his Company, and Countrey better than thine.'[83] The road is his, and Apollyon had better let him pass on his way. The road of the Christian life is the road of the Bedford preacher, free to choose his own metaphors for living and to demand proper wages. The Biblical text with its persistent metaphor almost seems out of place in the dialogue between Christian and Apollyon. It is not surprising that

Steinbeck's settlers had liked *The Pilgrim's Progress*, or that the literal American Amy March in *Little Women*, who could stand up against her class of hostile schoolmates if she had to, thought that it might be worth enquiring where the burden really lay.

The struggle for the pioneers is physical not spiritual. The enemy is at hand and un-Satanic, as Laura's Pa knows: 'Those sprouts are getting waist-high around the stumps in the wheat-field. A man just has to keep everlasting at it, or the woods'll take back the place.'[84] Compared with this reality, Crusoe's battles are child's play and his dominion over the island a victory hardly worth having: 'I had the Lives of all my Subjects at my absolute Command. I could hang, draw, give Liberty, and take it away, and no Rebels among all my Subjects.'[85] Bunyan might have commented, as Helen Burns does in *Jane Eyre*, when she reflects on the fate of Charles I: 'I thought what a pity it was that, with his integrity and conscientiousness, he could see no farther than the prerogatives of the crown. If he had but been able to look to the distance, and see how what they call the spirit of the age was tending.'[86] When the pioneers look to the distance, they see a land which belongs to everybody. Mrs Shimerda rebukes Lena for making up to a married man, but the girl retorts: 'I can't help it if he hangs around, and I can't order him off. It ain't my prairie.'[87] When Laura asks if the government will make the Indians go west, Pa replies:

'When white settlers come into a country, the Indians have to move on. . . . White people are going to settle all this country, and we get the best land because we get here first and take our pick. Now do you understand?'

'Yes, Pa,' Laura said. 'But, Pa, I thought this was Indian Territory. Won't it make the Indians mad to have to –.'

'No more questions, Laura,' Pa said, firmly. 'Go to sleep.'[88]

Laura Ingalls Wilder is too honest not to remember that the awkward basic question of human rights often comes from a child, who has yet to learn the adult art of evading the uncomfortable. Often the younger child is the more clear-sighted. When Pa tells Mary and Laura of the man who made a big door in his front door for the cat and a little one for the kitten, Mary begins to ask why the kitten couldn't go through the big door, and Laura interrupts: 'Because the big cat wouldn't let it.'[89]

The Fourth of July celebrations reinterpret for Laura Christian's confrontation with Apollyon: 'She thought: God is America's king. She thought: Americans won't obey any king on earth. Americans are free. That means they have to obey their own consciences. No king bosses Pa; he has to boss himself. Why (she thought), when I am a little older, Pa and Ma will stop telling me what to do, and there isn't anyone else who has a right to give me orders. . . . This is what it means to be free. It means, you have to be good. "Our father's God, author of liberty –." The laws of Nature and of Nature's God endow you with a right to life and liberty. Then you have to keep the laws of God, for God's law is the only thing that gives you a right to be free. Laura had not time then to think any further. Carrie was wondering why she stood so still, and Pa was saying, "This way girls! There's free lemonade." '[90] The country that belongs to the Pilgrims also belongs to God, but in the pioneer rewriting of Bunyan, lemonade is free as well as people. The promise of the land is not only freedom and territory, but also wealth. After the dust storm in *The Grapes of Wrath* the women still ask Bunyan's question: 'What'll we do?'[91] But they know what they will do: they will move on to a better place, not the land of the Promise, but more promising land – although in Steinbeck's novel this hope proves illusory.

When Carl Linstrum gazes over Alexandra's cornfields in *O Pioneers!* he is both astonished and disappointed by the fulfilment of a dream:

> I even think I liked the old country better. This is all very splendid in its way, but there was something about this country when it was a wild old beast that has haunted me all these years. Now, when I come back to all this milk and honey, I feel like the old German song, 'Wo bist du, wo bist du, mein geliebtest Land?'[92]

The adult mourns the loss of imaginative dimension when the dream becomes literal. In *On the Banks of Plum Creek*, when locusts have devoured the wheat and Pa has gone east to find work, Ma reads the Old Testament description of the plague of locusts:

> Ma read the promise that God made to good people, 'to bring them out of that land to a good land and a large, unto a land flowing with milk and honey'.
> 'Oh, where is that, Ma?' Mary asked, and Laura asked, 'How

can land flow with milk and honey?' She did not want to walk in milky, sticky honey.

Ma rested the big Bible on her knees and thought. Then she said, 'Well, your Pa thinks it will be right here in Minnesota.'

'How could it be?' Laura asked.

'Maybe it will be, if we stick it out,' said Ma. 'Well, Laura, if good milch cows were eating grass all over this land, they would give a great deal of milk, and then the land would be flowing with milk. Bees would get honey out of all the wild flowers that grow out of the land, and then the land would be flowing with honey.'

'Oh,' Laura said. 'I'm glad we wouldn't have to walk in it.'[93]

Lewis Carroll's Alice might have shared her disinclination. The poetic vision, which Ma translates into a literal one for the child's understanding, belongs to the adult art of the Old World. For both child and pioneer the promised land which is common to all pilgrims is not across the river of death, but across the Mississippi.

One of the earliest writers to resite Bunyan's vision in the literal American landscape was Frances Hodgson Burnett, in a book as different as anyone could conceive from *Little Lord Fauntleroy*, called *Two Little Pilgrims' Progress* (1895). The ten years which separate Burnett's two books demonstrate a change of atmosphere as sensational as that which marks the transition from the mournful interiors of *In the Closed Room* to the fresh air of *The Secret Garden*. *Two Little Pilgrims' Progress* was obviously aimed at an American readership, but, despite the fact that *Little Lord Fauntleroy* was doted on as much in the United States as in England, it is sobering for the English reader to perceive the much more bracing climate which surrounds the young American child in 1895, compared with his counterpart even in such a work as *The Golden Age*. Or is the difference just between Burnett and Grahame? If Burnett announced herself solidly as an English writer from an English background in *The Secret Garden*, she had declared roundly in 1895, as she perhaps did more covertly in 1911, that America had many ideas about the upbringing of children on which the Old World might profitably meditate.

The two children in the story decide, like the March girls in Alcott's book, to play at *The Pilgrim's Progress*, but it is more work than play. They earn enough money by helping out at their aunt's farm in Illinois to travel to the Chicago World Fair, a modern City Beautiful: 'They had never read the dear, old, worn *Pilgrim's*

Progress as they did in those days. . . . In it they seemed to find
parallels for everything.' The children in Burnett's story had created
new and more exciting adventures for Christian even before his
enterprises took shape from their own. When they reach the Fair, a
bystander observes: 'I'm blessed if they're not by themselves, . . .
That's Young America, and no mistake.' Robin remarks to his sister,
the more energetic of the two: 'Do you know what you said just now
about believing human beings could do *anything* if they set their
minds to it? Let's set our minds to it.' The book ends on a note as full
of New World energy as Colin Craven bursting through the door of
the garden in which he has grown strong:

> Every fairy story has a moral, and this has too. They are these:–
> The human creature is a strong thing – when it is a brave one.
> Nature never made a human hand without putting into it
> something to give.[94]

A little of this goes a good long way and begins to sound vaguely
familiar: love makes the world go round or is it everyone's minding
their own business? Nevertheless the spirit is that of both the
pioneer, and the child of the new century, Ellen Key's free being or
Bunyan's Christian recast in a secular mould.

Wilder and Cather are neither of them free from instructive aims.
Self-help, independence, physical hardiness are part of a utopian
vision which has Old-World roots. Flora Thompson's villagers still
know the art of being happy on little, which the pioneer practises
while dreaming of plenty. Sooner or later, there will be jam today.
The Ingalls family share values which made the factory hand, in
E. P. Thompson's words: 'the inheritor of Bunyan, of remembered
village rights, of notions of equality before the law, of craft
traditions'.[95] But the making of things, which in Morris's *News from
Nowhere* is a return to a vanished world of medieval community,
never acquires in Wilder's books the cultural significance of a lost
heritage, as it does in *My Ántonia*. When Fuchs makes Mr
Shimerda's coffin he handles the tools and the wood 'in an eager
beneficent way as if he were blessing them. He broke out now and
then into German hymns, as if this occupation brought back the old
times to him.'[96] Cather's evocation of a craft world derives from her
regret for the pioneer past and for the mechanised materialism
which has succeeded it. By contrast, Wilder, from an earlier
generation of pioneers, points out that Pa makes a door and nails

and planks for the floor, because there is no possibility of buying them. When he can buy them, not only is hard labour saved but the goods themselves are better quality. This is precisely true to childhood experience, where the bought dress is always more coveted than the home-made one, however beautiful the hand-stitching and however much love lies behind the work. Only the affluent society can look back nostalgically on some of the labour which Laura Ingalls Wilder describes, and she herself never does. When Pa is able to borrow a threshing machine, there is no sense that this threatens the dignity of human labour:

> Pa was very tired that night, but he was happy. He said to Ma:
> 'It would have taken Henry and Peterson and Grandpa and me a couple of weeks apiece to thresh as much grain with flails as that machine threshed today. We wouldn't have got as much wheat either, and it wouldn't have been as clean!'
> 'That machine's a great invention!' he said. 'Other folks can stick to old-fashioned ways if they want to, but I'm all for progress. It's a great age we're living in. As long as I raise wheat, I'm going to have a machine come and thresh it, if there's one anywhere in the neighbourhood.'[97]

In both Cather's and Wilder's books hard physical labour is brutal-ising not ennobling. Ma does not want Laura to work in the fields because only foreign women do that: 'Ma and her girls were Americans, above doing men's work.'[98] It is too modern a view to see Ma's discouragement of Laura's working outside as evidence of over-refinement.[99] Ma herself does a man's physical work because there is no one else to help Pa.

In the pioneer environment the great enemies are not despond and despair, although in Mr Shimerda's case those adversaries certainly mastered him. They are cold and hunger. Jim declares: 'I was convinced that man's strongest antagonist is the cold. I admired the cheerful zest with which grandmother went about keeping us warm and comfortable and well-fed.' Food and warmth are not metaphors for comfort and happiness – they remain the thing itself: 'Our lives centred around warmth and food and the return of the men at nightfall. I used to wonder, when they came in tired from the fields, their feet numb and their hands cracked and sore, how they could do all the chores so conscientiously. . . . When supper was over, it took them a long while to get the cold out of their bones.'

This is not the winter of Spenser's *Shepheardes Calender*, where the icicles hanging from the January boughs are Colin's tears for his cold love as much as for physical hardship, nor does Jim's perception of hardship parallel Hardy's evocation of the stony fields of Flintcomb Ash in *Tess of the d'Urbervilles*, where Tess's picking of turnips in the bitter cold creates an image of her desolation at Angel's desertion. The imagination in *My Antonia* can do nothing with the pioneer winter: 'The pale, cold light of the winter sunset did not beautify – it was like the light of truth itself. . . . The wind sprang up afresh, with a kind of bitter song, as if it said: "This is reality, whether you like it or not. All those frivolities of summer, the light and shadow, the living mask of green that trembled over everything, they were lies, and this is what was underneath. This is the truth." It was as if we were being punished for loving the loveliness of summer.'[100]

Wilder took a whole book to describe the seven-month-long winter, which had been foretold by the old Indian, and in which the town-dwellers almost starve. When Laura and Carrie rest after being almost lost on the open prairie, Laura 'could not imagine that Heaven was better than being where she was, slowly growing warm and comfortable, sipping the hot, sweet, ginger tea . . . and hearing the storm that could not touch them here'.[101] The moment is true to childhood, which does not separate mind and body. When Miss Temple brings toast and tea for Jane Eyre and Helen Burns, the comfort of affection is inseparable from the satisfaction of hunger, and Jane is dismayed to discern 'only a very small portion'.[102] In Wilder's book Laura's idea of heaven, in remaining rooted in physical comfort, conveys more directly than Cather's more mediated adult vision, that the pioneer must conquer the physical environment or be conquered by it.

Metaphors of spiritual struggle, which arise from adult meditations on physical duress, only develop when men and women have moved beyond the primary battle with the elements. For the child, as for the true pioneer in both Cather's and Wilder's books, hunger and despond are the same experience, registered indivisibly on mind and body.

III   DESIGN AND VISION

Cather's artistic problems all arose from compromises which she made with the traditions of the adult novel. When Laura Ingalls Wilder chose the children's book as the form for her memories of pioneer life,[103] she freed herself from the literary expectations which dogged Cather.

Willa Cather would have recognised the dilemma Mann identified for himself in *Tales of Jacob*: 'I do not conceal from myself the difficulty of writing about people who do not precisely know who they are.'[104] Cather was as anxious to move away from the individualised self as Virginia Woolf was. Alexandra in *O Pioneers!* has had no time to discover who she is: 'Her mind was a white book, with clear writing about weather and beasts and growing things.'[105]

The novel traditionally explores individual consciousness. Mann wrote of the people of Israel: 'It is highly significant that in those days there were no words for conceptions dealing with personality and individuality, other than such external ones as confession.' He demanded whether 'the notion that each person is himself and can be no other, is . . . anything more than a convention, which arbitrarily leaves out of account all the transitions which bind the individual consciousness to the general?'[106] In an essay on Katherine Mansfield, Cather claimed that every ego is always simultaneously 'greedily seeking [human relationships] and . . . pulling away from them'.[107] She herself wanted to escape from the inner dramas of Ibsen's plays quite as much as from the claustrophobic chambers of their enactment. As Alexandra gazes across her land 'she had a new consciousness of the country, felt almost a new relation to it. . . . Under the long shaggy ridges, she felt the future stirring.'[108] Cather's difficulty as author is that she is more interested in the shaggy ridges than she is in Alexandra herself. The land is the book's central consciousness, but this creates for the novelist problems of form.

Cather observed in 1932 in the Preface to *The Song of the Lark*: 'Success is never so interesting as a struggle – not even to the successful, not even to the most mercenary forms of ambition.'[109] *O Pioneers!* describes Alexandra's success to a degree which is disheartening to the reader. MacCabe has written that 'epic can be distinguished from classic realism in that there is no pressing necessity for an end',[110] but Cather in the early book has not trusted the epic progress of her story, which ends in the clichéd literary drama of human passion which she had been so determined to avoid. In *My Ántonia* the achieved pioneer vision is made more complex and interesting because the author explores simultaneously the grandfather's projection of a future dream, the present as it is, and Jim's memory of that dream:

It seemed as if we could hear the corn growing in the night; under the stars one caught a faint crackling in the dewy, heavy-odored cornfields where the feathered stalks stood juicy and green. . . . It took a clear, meditative eye like my grandfather's to foresee that they would enlarge and multiply until they would be, not the Shimerdas' cornfields, or Mr Bushy's, but the world's cornfields; that their yield would be one of the great economic facts, like the wheat crop of Russia, which underlie all the activities of men, in peace or war.

The enthusiasm is economic, as it must have been for Jacob when he bred an enormous flock for himself out of Laban's herd and bore it back to the land of his fathers. But the child's eye humanises the epic vision of literal wealth, representing the past as cyclical and recurrent. When Jim goes back to the old homestead at the end of the novel it is as if the whole book were beginning again: 'I had the sense of coming home to myself, and of having found out what a little circle man's experience is. For Ántonia and for me, this had been the road of Destiny; had taken us to these early accidents of fortune which predetermined for us all that we can ever be. Now I understood that the same road was to bring us together again. Whatever we had missed, we possessed together the precious, the incommunicable past.'[111] Gwen Raverat said that her own book of childhood recollections could be begun anywhere.[112] It was circular rather than linear, as Jacques Raverat wrote to Virginia Woolf of *Mrs Dalloway* (published seven years after Cather's *My Ántonia*), a book which can be read from middle to middle and retain perfect symmetry.

   The form of the novel nevertheless forces Cather – or she feels that it does – to imply more than the relationship between Jim and Ántonia can be made to contain. They are not 'together' in any adult sense: only in the remembered childhood which is still now and not then. The relationship is one of origins of consciousness and of Ántonia's symbolic relationship to the 'whole adventure of our childhood', not of individualised emotion. Cather succeeded almost too well in creating a group consciousness which remains more powerful in the book than that of either Jim or Ántonia as adults, and which remains tied to the land. Mr Shimerda's grave has in the end provided for both of them the picture writing on the blank land which transforms raw earth into living country:

The road from the north curved a little to the east just there, and the road from the west swung out a little to the south; so that the grave, with its tall red grass that was never mowed, was like a little island; and at twilight, under a new moon or the clear evening star, the dusty roads used to look like soft grey rivers flowing past it. I never came upon the place without emotion, and in all that country it was the spot most dear to me. I loved the dim superstition, the propitiatory intent, that had put the grave there; and still more I loved the spirit that could not carry out the sentence – the error from the surveyed lines, the clemency of the soft earth roads along which the home-coming wagons rattled after sunset. Never a tired driver passed the wooden cross, I am sure, without wishing well to the sleeper.[113]

The faint echo of *Wuthering Heights* is unmistakable: 'I lingered round them, under that benign sky; watched the moths fluttering among the heath and harebells; listened to the soft wind breathing through the grass; and wondered how any one could ever imagine unquiet slumbers for the sleepers in that quiet earth.'[114] Mr Shimerda's ghost humanises the empty land, just as the literary ghost gives that unsung grave a resting-place in the landscape of the mind. The moment demonstrates the circularity of Cather's design, for the recollection of the adult follows hard on the child's witnessing of the burial, which then recedes into the past, giving way to another present.

It is easier for Laura Ingalls Wilder to celebrate the unpeopled land because the child's vision lacks inherited metaphors. As Laura journeys further west into Dakota territory and grows older – each book marks a further stage not only in the development of the prairie but also in Laura's movement from small child to young adult – she senses that the prairie, even as it fills with settlers making a railroad, resists the pioneers:

There was almost no difference in the flowers and grasses. But there was something else here that was not anywhere else. It was an enormous stillness that made you feel still. And when you were still, you could feel great stillness coming closer. . . .

All their talking did not mean anything to the enormous silence of that prairie.

This is not the landscape of locality which enhances human dignity, but a vastness which the child is more willing to register because her own smallness is part of her identity. Cather sounds solemn when she describes Alexandra's kinship with the land. But when the Wilder family move out of their claim Laura is so ecstatic that, 'big girl as she was, [she] spread her arms wide to the wind and ran against it. She flung herself on the flowery grass and looked at the great blueness above her and the high, pearly clouds sailing in it.'[115] Having rolled like the horses to get rid of the sensation of harness, Laura leaps up, anxious that there is a grass stain on her dress. The option of doing what the animals do to express joy is still open to children, and this allows Wilder to clarify the relation between human beings and the land in a way which Cather, writing from an adult consciousness, cannot do.

Wilder realigns the species. In her books there are wild animals and wild men (wolves, buffaloes, bears, the fawns in the Big Woods, the creatures of the prairies, the wild birds, the muskrats; and Indians); and domesticated men and domesticated animals (the Ingalls family and the settlers, and the animals who form a vital part of their self-sufficient community: horses, the cow, Jack their watchdog and, later, the kitten – acquired after a mouse had bitten off some of Pa's hair in the night in order to make a nest). Somewhere between the two are the animals who impinge on their daily life: rabbits, prairie chickens, gophers, the badger Laura meets on the way to the creek pool. Pa hunts game for food, not for sport. When he sees the deer and her yearling fawn in the Big Woods he is unable to shoot them because they are so fearless and beautiful. But this is already a sign of a settled world: on the prairie animals cannot be viewed with a conservationist's eye, because life depends on successful hunting. When the family is forced to leave Indian territory the mockingbird sings, and Pa remarks: 'I've been thinking what fun the rabbits will have, eating the garden we planted.'[116] He hardly grudges the rabbit fun at his expense. He only intrudes on the animal kingdom in so far as he must in order to survive. When he has enough for the family to eat he orders Jack, their dog, to let a buck rabbit go, and he puts the surplus fish back into the creek. This economy contrasts with the elephant-hunting in Rider Haggard's *King Solomon's Mines* (1885), where the explorers lament that they have not killed the entire herd of elephants, despite the fact that they could only eat a small part of one. The ivory has to be buried in the sand because they do not know if they will ever return to retrieve it. In Wilder's books there is no place for wilful slaughter and plundering of the animal world, because in many ways – though not all – the pioneers depend on animals.

Pa has none of Crusoe's innate sense of man's superiority to beast. When Crusoe tells a story about a man and a bear, the story makes the bear ridiculous. When Pa tells one, the story makes Pa ridiculous.[117] In Wilder's book the human beings cannot afford to ignore the wisdom of animals, as they repeatedly do in Hardy's novels – Bathsheba's sheep in *Far from the Madding Crowd* take shelter from the oncoming storm while her haystack remains unprotected. When the prairie fire rages, Pa asks Ma what she would have done if it had come when he was in Independence: ' "We would have gone to the creek with the birds and the rabbits, of course," Ma said. All the wild things on the prairie had known what to do.' When Laura plays truant to the waterhole on Plum Creek she is stopped in her tracks by a strange animal which flattens itself before her on the path, and when she pokes it with a stick 'a frightful snarl came out of it. Its eyes sparkled mad, and fierce white teeth snapped almost on Laura's nose.'[118] She flies back to the dugout and Pa tells her it was a badger. In *The Long Winter* before the snows come Pa takes Laura to see the muskrat's house. He is struck by its being the heaviest built house that he has ever seen. The animals are prepared for the long winter, while the human beings are not. Laura is baffled by the muskrat's prescience:

'Pa, how can the muskrats know?' she asked.

'I don't know how they know,' Pa said. 'But they do. God tells them, I suppose.'

'Then why doesn't God tell us?' Laura wanted to know.

'Because,' said Pa, 'we're not animals. We're humans, and like it says in the Declaration of Independence, God created us free. That means we've got to take care of ourselves.'

Laura said faintly, 'I thought God takes care of us.'

'He does,' Pa said, 'so far as we do what's right. But He leaves it to us to do as we please. That's the difference between us and everything else in creation.'

'Can't muskrats do what they please?' Laura asked, amazed.

'No,' said Pa. 'I don't know why they can't, but you can see they can't. Look at that muskrat house. Muskrats have to build that kind of house. They always have and they always will. It's plain they can't build any other kind. But folks build all kinds of houses. A man can build any kind of house he can think of. So if his house doesn't keep out the weather, that's *his* look-out; he's free and independent.'

Animals are not free to choose their own ruin as Laura, though a child, is free to choose to drown in the waterhole, and would have done if the wild animal had not stopped her. The pioneer learns to know the animal world. Laura suffers acutely when the family moves to the town: 'Even if she could get over being afraid, she could not like strange people. She knew how animals would act, she understood what animals thought, but you could never be sure about people.'[119]

This closeness to animals is not allowed to become sentimental. The animals never acquire symbolic or mythical status. They are just animals. The wolves never stand for the human beings' emotions, as the wolves in the story of Russian Peter in *My Ántonia* come to symbolise Peter's guilt and the way in which it hounds him to death, just as the bridal couple were hounded by the actual beasts. Wilder's glittering moonpath, which leads her across the ice to where she sees the great buffalo wolf, is picture not parable. The beast remains free of the human being both physically and imaginatively. The wolves who run by Pa without attacking him are not fairy creatures sparing a good man's life, but animals who have just eaten and are out playing. If people drive the wolves out, they also are susceptible to being driven: 'Mr Edwards said he was going, too. He would not stay to be driven across the line like an ornery yellow hound.'[120] For a moment the settlers, threatened with the government's moving them on by force, become one with the wolves and Indians, driven from their own free land. There is nothing Ibsenish about any of Wilder's creatures. They remain solidly themselves, unliterary, literal beings on the literal land, free and independent of the human being as the land itself is free, and as Laura is free of Pa, and Pa of a king.

The children have a special relation with the domestic animals, who have names and identities, but, as in the case of Kipling's wolves, their identity is an animal one. The Christmas horses are beautiful, but remain David the bright one who can manage in the snow, and Sam the stupid one who cannot. Neither of them could ever be Black Beauty, with an inner life capable of criticising the adult world, any more than the children could conceivably become *ministering* children, metaphors for an adult view of pious childhood. When the cow is sold there is no childish lament for a petted quadruped: 'The gentle cow went meekly away with the rope around her long horns, and the calf frisked and jumped behind. There went all the milk and butter.' Jack, the watchdog, is a vital part of the Ingalls family because he is a good watchdog, not because he is a loving companion. When they think he has been drowned in the creek 'Pa did not whistle about his work as usual, and after a while he said, "And what we'll do in a wild country without a good watchdog I don't know." '[121] Jack is respected as a dog, not as dog capable of becoming human. He never acquires any of the character of Crusoe's Poll, that sociable bird who learned to talk. There are limits to what he can learn, and he never will learn that the Indians' trail belongs to Indians or that Mr Edwards is a neighbour coming to help Ma with her chores, and not an enemy. But he knows the things dogs can know: that there are wolves round the house and that Ma must stay in it, that he must find the wagon after he has been lost in the creek, that he must help Laura crawl across the floor to the water can, and that he is too old to go west when the family leaves Plum Creek.

The death of Jack marks the end of Laura's childhood, of that special time when an animal can be closer to a person than other human beings are, and, although Laura retains into adult life her love and trust of horses, the special relation with Jack can never be replaced, because it is a relation of dependence and equality. Laura now has others who depend on her to whom she must be the adult. This is the saddest moment in all the books. On that last night Laura reviews her whole life with Jack: 'Whenever Pa had gone away, Jack has always stayed with Laura to take care of her and the family. He was especially Laura's own dog.' She makes his bed ready for him, something she has neglected to do in the weariness following the scarlet fever which caused Mary's blindness: 'He stepped in and turned himself around once. He stopped to rest his stiff legs and slowly turned again. Jack always turned around three times before he lay down to sleep at night. He had done it when he was a young dog in the Big Woods, and he had done it in the grass under the wagon every night. It is a proper thing for dogs to do.' In the morning Jack is dead and they bury him:

> That morning Pa drove away in the rattling old wagon behind Aunt Docia's buggy. Jack was not standing beside Laura to watch Pa go. There was only emptiness to turn to instead of Jack's eyes looking up to say that he was there to take care of her.

Laura knew then that she was not a little girl any more. Now she was alone; she must take care of herself. When you must do that, then you do it and you are grown up. Laura was not very big, but she was almost thirteen years old, and no one was there to depend on. Pa and Jack had gone, and Ma needed help to take care of Mary and the little girls, and somehow to get them all safely to the West on a train.[122]

When Jack is gone there is no animal to stand between Laura and the adult world, where she too must be a watchdog.

The wild animals are realigned on the prairie with the Indians. When the Ingalls family has to move out of Indian territory, Pa stops at the creek to look back at the prairie:

As far as they could see, to the east and to the south and to the west, nothing was moving on all the vastness of the High Prairie. Only the green grass was rippling in the wind, and white clouds drifted in the high, clear sky.

'It's a great country, Caroline,' Pa said. 'But there will be wild Indians and wolves here for many a long day.'

The little log house and the little stable sat lonely in the stillness.

Only three times do the human beings unite across the barrier between wild and tame, once in *The Long Winter* when the old Indian warns the settlers that the winter will last for seven months, and once when Pa is hunting a panther, which he never tracks down:

One day in the woods he met an Indian. They stood in the wet, cold woods and looked at each other, and they could not talk because they did not know each other's words. But the Indian pointed to the panther's tracks, and he made motions with his gun to show Pa that he had killed that panther. He pointed to the tree-tops and to the ground, to show that he had shot it out of a tree. And he motioned to the sky, and west and east, to say that he had killed it the day before.

So that was all right. The panther was dead.

Laura asked if a panther would carry off a little papoose and kill and eat her, too, and Pa said yes. Probably that was why the Indian had killed that panther.

On the third occasion the Osage persuades the Indian tribes to leave. Laura, being nearer to animals, is also nearer to the Indians. She understands that both parents want to protect their children. She falls in love with the papoose and wants to follow it on the free road on its high-stepping pony. Their own life seems for once a form of coercion as well as an invasion of the rights of men and of animals.

The childish voice and the child's eye give the author both a vision uneducated by the preconceptions of the civilised world and a perspective of irony without which the American myth might become too strident. Children are never earnest in the way that adults are, which is why they became the centre of a late nineteenth-century attack on Victorian earnestness. The absence of a child's unconscious irony in the only book Wilder wrote from an adult's viewpoint – *The First Four Years* – is one reason why it is so unsuccessful. Wilder as a writer needs the child's vision.

When Pa and Ma decide to go west, Pa's idea of the prairie is almost of an Isaiah landscape: 'In the West the land was level, and there were no trees. The grass grew thick and high. There the wild animals wandered and fed as though they were in a pasture that stretched much farther than a man could see, and there were no settlers. Only Indians lived there.' The last sentence is completely deadpan: the child repeating what she hears the adult say, without foresight or hindsight. Yet in it lies the whole book, which deals with the conflict of men and Indians and men and wolves – those wild creatures who use the prairie as their pasture. In the event the reality of the prairie repudiates Isaiah: the lion does not lie down with the lamb. The irony in the confrontation of the literal truth with the literary vision is circumscribed within the child's eye view. When the Indians leave, a melancholy and elegiac mood descends on the prairie as if it had been robbed of its ancient rights: 'Ma said she didn't feel like doing anything, she was so let down. . . . [Laura] sat a long time on the doorstep, looking into the empty west where the Indians had gone. She seemed still to see waving feathers and black eyes and to hear the sound of ponies' feet.' The same mood is caught when Ma sings the song about Alfarata:

> So sang the Indian maid,
> Bright Alfarata,
> Where sweep the waters
> Of the blue Juniata.

Fleeting years have borne away
The voice of Alfarata,
Still flow the waters
Of the blue Juniata.[123]

In *My Ántonia* the Indians are already a memory, the ground marked
only by a faint circle where they used to ride. Jim observes that
'when the first light spray of snow lay over it, it came out with
wonderful distinctness, like strokes of Chinese white on canvas.
The old figure stirred me as it had never done before and seemed a
good omen for the winter.'[124] Cather's past is Wilder's present. The
Indians' displacement in Wilder's books is a price which the settlers
pay for the free land, for the dream of future wealth and
independence which makes the whole venture worthwhile: 'Pa told
them about all the seeds. . . . He said to Ma, "I tell you, Caroline,
when we begin getting crops off this rich land of ours, we'll be living
like kings." '[125] But the book ends with the rabbits living like kings.

The same ironic vision intrudes at the Thanksgiving dinner,
which celebrates not an Old-World victory over evil, but the
material conquest of physical hardship. The Ingalls family, having
bought their house on Plum Creek, are surprised that the previous
owner had sown so little wheat. The weather is fine and mild: the
settlers call it grasshopper weather:

If you caught a grasshopper and held him, and gently poked a
green blade of grass into his jaws, they nibbled it fast. They swiftly
nibbled in the whole grass blade, till the tip of it went into them
and was gone.

Thanksgiving dinner was good. Pa had shot a wild goose for it.
Ma had to stew the goose because there was no fire-place, and no
oven in the little stove. But she made dumplings in the gravy.
There were corn dodgers and mashed potatoes. There were butter
and milk, and stewed dried plums. And three grains of parched
corn lay beside each tin plate.

At the first Thanksgiving dinner the poor Pilgrims had had
nothing to eat but three parched grains of corn. Then the Indians
came and brought them turkeys, so the Pilgrims were thankful.

Now, after they had eaten their good, big Thanksgiving dinner,
Laura and Mary could eat their grains of corn and remember the
Pilgrims. Parched corn was good. It crackled and crunched, and
its taste was sweet and brown.

When Ma regrets that they are living in a dug-out – as Mrs Bergson in Cather's *O Pioneers!* refused to do – Pa promises her a good house next year: 'His eyes shone and his voice was like singing. "And good horses, and a buggy to boot! I'll take you riding, dressed up in silks! Think, Caroline – this level, rich land, not a stone or stump to contend with, and only three miles from a railroad! We can sell every grain of wheat we raise." '[126] When next year comes, the grasshoppers have eaten everything and laid their eggs in the earth. The disaster is physical. It leaves no burden in the mind, and the words which describe it are literal. When Ma reads from the Bible about the plague of locusts in Egypt, the Biblical account functions not as metaphor, but as shared experience, like reading someone else's diary about a time one has lived through.

The ironic perspective, which allows Wilder to undermine Pa's hopes without being sentimental, is possible because she is strict to the child's sense of the present. Nina Harling in *My Ántonia* thought that 'Christ was born in Bohemia a short time before the Shimerdas left that country.' Jim recalls that Grandfather 'read the chapters from Saint Matthew about the birth of Christ, and as we listened, it all seemed like something that had happened lately, and near at hand', but the perception of foreshortened time is an adult's, not a child's. In Wilder's books time moves with the children's growth, with the seasons, with the movement of the sun, but with hardly any concession to an awareness of a future already present in the writer's mind. When Jim Burden writes that the prairie spring was unlike anything he had experienced he uses a figure of speech: 'If I had been tossed down blindfold on that red prairie, I should have known that it was spring.'[127] But Wilder's account of summer is not placed by any parallel experiences in the child's mind:

Day after day was hotter than the day before. The wind was hot. 'As if it came out of an oven,' Ma said.

The grass was turning yellow. The whole world was rippling green and gold under the blazing sky.

At noon the wind died. No birds sang. Everything was so still that Laura could hear the squirrels chattering in the trees down by the creek. Suddenly black crows flew overhead, cawing their rough, sharp caws. Then everything was still again.

Ma said that this was midsummer.[128]

Wilder would never have written, as Jim Burden does, that 'the summer which was to change everything was coming nearer every day'.[129] Consciousness of time passing is measured by waiting: for Pa to come back, for the locusts to go, for the long winter to pass. A long day is one in which 'the sunshine had never moved so slowly on the floor as it did that day'.

There are only two moments when the adult Laura intrudes on the child's world, and then it is still with the voice of childhood. One is when the settlers believe they have caught the fever from eating water melons: 'No one knew, in those days, that fever 'n ague was malaria, and that some mosquitoes give it to people when they bite them.'[130] The other is when Grace is lost on the prairie, and the author suddenly allows herself a first-person pronoun: '[Laura] ran on and on. Grace must have gone this way. Maybe she chased a butterfly. She didn't go into Big Slough! She didn't climb the hill, she wasn't there. Oh, baby sister, I couldn't see you anywhere east or south on this hateful prairie.'[131] It is as if the intensity of that moment is still too much for the adult writer: it remains *now*, not in any way the incommunicable past which Jim shared with Ántonia. In consequence the communication between Laura Ingalls Wilder and the reader is more immediate than it is in Cather's books. Both author and reader survey the Ingalls children as Mr Shimerda looks at Jim: 'When his deep-seeing eyes rested on me, I felt as if he were looking far ahead into the future for me, down the road I would have to travel'.[132] In *Little Town on the Prairie* a lady sings in the church social that Time should turn back in its flight and 'Make me a child again, / Just for to-night';[133] Ma and the other ladies weep, but Laura does not. No authorial comment is offered; the reader hears the song with emotions in which adult sentiment coexists with childish detachment from it.

In this world there is none of Cather's perception of conflict between art and nature. Neither the child Laura nor the adult writer show any awareness of the artist's engaging with his material. Pa's fiddle-playing is not the last post of an Old-World culture, but the joyful response of a human being to the song of the lark, the title of Cather's next novel, in which the novelist is still trying to reconcile the singer and the soil. When Laura hears Pa's fiddle at night she thinks the stars are singing: 'The fiddle was still singing in the starlight. The night was full of music, and Laura was sure that part of it came from the great, bright stars swinging so low above the prairie.' The prairie is not a great empty waste. It has its own singers. Children listen to birds more readily than to music. Pa's fiddle has a life of its own which connects with the life of the prairie. It is as though the fiddle speaks from the civilised world to the wild one and creates harmony between them:

> When Pa's fiddle stopped, they could not hear Mr Edwards any more. Only the wind rustled in the prairie grasses. The big, yellow moon was sailing high overhead. The sky was so full of light that not one star twinkled in it, and all the prairie was a shadowy mellowness.
>
> Then from the woods by the creek a nightingale began to sing.
>
> Everything was silent, listening to the nightingale's song. The bird sang on and on. The cool wind moved over the prairie and the song was round and clear above the grasses' whispering. The sky was like a bowl of light overturned on the flat black land.
>
> The song ended. No one moved or spoke. Laura and Mary were quiet, Pa and Ma sat motionless. Only the wind stirred and the grasses sighed. Then Pa lifted the fiddle to his shoulder and softly touched the bow to the strings. A few notes fell like clear drops of water into the stillness. A pause, and Pa began to play the nightingale's song. The nightingale answered him. The nightingale began to sing again. It was singing with Pa's fiddle.
>
> When the strings were silent, the nightingale went on singing. The bird and the fiddle were talking to each other in the cool night under the moon.[134]

This is not the poet's nightingale which the monk heard in the woods, but a real nightingale, answering a real instrument held by a hand which tills the ground from which the bird picks worms. For both child and writer the literalness of the two is the condition of their concord.

IV   SOLIDITY AND THIN PAINT

Laura Ingalls Wilder could have written in a more 'literary' style if she had wished to do so. She was not, whatever one might like to believe, a writer who never blotted a word. Zochert records her saying in conversation that 'the use of words is of itself an interesting study. You will hardly believe the difference the use of one word rather than another will make until you begin to hunt for a word with just the right shade of meaning, just the right color for the picture you are painting in words. Had you thought that words have color? The only stupid thing about words is the spelling of them.'[135] The tone is plain, but the sentiments are those of Virginia Woolf, including the one on spelling. Cézanne wrote in a letter to Émile Bernard in 1904 that the artist 'must beware of the literary spirit which so often causes the painter to deviate from his true path – the concrete study of nature – to lose himself too long in intangible speculation'. He declared that 'the Louvre is a good book to consult but it must be only an intermediary. The real and immense study to be undertaken is the manifold picture of nature.'[136] Roger Fry protested against the tendency of painters to cultivate 'poetic' effects such as 'moonlight and mist': 'Such a landscape art is clearly more allied to literature than, let us say, the landscape of Rubens. For it depends mainly on the associated ideas of the things represented, although it has no doubt visual form insofar as the proportions and dispositions of the flat pattern are concerned.'[137] Willa Cather wrote in her journal in 1896, in terms which anticipate Fry and Woolf, and which recall Stevenson: 'Art is not thought or emotion, but expression, expression, always expression.'[138]

Laura Ingalls Wilder learnt to see the colour of words and to adhere to the literal, from having to describe the world for her blind sister Mary: 'On that dreadful morning when Mary could not see even the sunshine full in her eyes, Pa had said that Laura must see for her. He had said, "Your two eyes are quick enough, and your tongue, if you will use them for Mary." And Laura had promised. So she tried to be eyes for Mary, and it was seldom that Mary need ask her, "See out loud for me, Laura, please." ' But Mary has her own ideas about how this should be done:

'The road pushes against the grassy land and breaks off short. And that's the end of it,' said Laura.

'It can't be,' Mary objected. 'The road goes all the way to Silver Lake.'

'I know it does,' Laura answered.

'Well, then I don't think you ought to say things like that,' Mary told her gently. 'We should always be careful to say exactly what we mean.'

'I was saying what I meant,' Laura protested. But she could not explain. There were so many ways of seeing things and so many ways of saying them.[139]

Laura adopts Fry's principle, that you describe only what you see, whereas Mary wants her to say what she knows must be there: the end of the road. The younger child defies in the book itself the elder's vision. Wilder delights in observing that the wagon track ended in nothing at all, or that the path did not go anywhere. As early as 1887 Fry had remarked in his Fellowship dissertation that we 'always tend to represent things as *we know them to be* rather than as they *appear*'. In an unpublished lecture called 'Can't you see it?' (1928), he tried to persuade his listeners to rid themselves of their preconceptions about what they might see, both in life and in art.[140] Laura describes what she sees, but she is perfectly aware of her choice. Other people, Mary among them, would write in a more 'literary' way – according to Fry's definition of the term – depicting what they knew must be there rather than what the eye actually discerns.

As a consequence of the family circumstance of Mary's blindness, Wilder's writing approaches visual art, her books thus becoming part of an aesthetic which Cather herself wanted to embrace. Laura and Mary take a last walk before Mary goes to the blind-college at Iowa:

> They went walking past the stable and up the low hill beyond. The sun was sinking to rest, like a king, Laura thought, drawing the gorgeous curtains of his great bed around him. But Mary was not pleased by such fancies. So Laura said, 'The sun is sinking, Mary, into white down clouds that spread to the edge of the world. All the tops of them are crimson, and streaming down from the top of the sky are great gorgeous curtains of rose and gold with pearly edges. They are a great canopy over the whole prairie. The little streaks of sky between them are clear, pure green.'[141]

Although this description is more figurative than many in Wilder's books, the avoidance of the traditional literary metaphor 'like a king' comes from a sense of words as visual medium – signals of crimson and pure green. When Virginia Woolf first saw the still life by Cézanne which Maynard Keynes had bought, she was momentarily baffled:

> There are 6 apples in the Cézanne picture. What can 6 apples *not* be? I began to wonder. There's their relationship to each other &

their colour, & their solidity. . . . We carried it into the next room & Lord! how it showed up the pictures there, as if you put a real stone among sham ones; the canvas of the others seemed scraped with a thin layer of rather cheap paint. The apples positively got redder & rounder & greener.[142]

Fry claimed that the paucity of still-life paintings in British art came from a preference for the literary over the plastic. If one compares Wilder's descriptions with Maria Charlesworth's in *Ministering Children*, the cheap paint of the earlier writer's thin metaphors makes Wilder's prose look solid and authentic.

Wilder's writing contains no blessed rills of human sympathy flowing past aged feet, no sunbeams of love, rainbows of hope or stagnant pools of self, such as decorate the pages of *Ministering Children*. If Wilder noticed, as Cather did, that there were no fine flowers of sentiment in Defoe, it did not disturb her. Her rule for the description of feeling is the same as her rule for the visual landscape. She tells what she sees. When the government decide to turn the settlers out of Indian territory, Pa's 'face was very red and his eyes were like blue fire'. When the two Indians stinking of skunk leave the house taking the Ingallses' things with them, 'Ma sat down on the bed and hugged Laura and Mary tighter, and trembled. She looked sick.' The writer never inserts what the child Laura did not know at the moment of which she is speaking. When Mr Edwards comes for Christmas and the children have stockings after all, 'Pa shook Mr Edwards' hand, too, and shook it again. Pa and Ma and Mr Edwards acted as if they were almost crying, Laura didn't know why. So she gazed again at her beautiful presents.'[143] Laura paints a last sunset for Mary and her sister muses: 'I wonder if the sky and the sunsets are different in Iowa?', but Laura cannot offer her the reassurance an adult would: 'Laura did not know. They came slowly down the low hill. This was the end of their last walk together, or at least, their last walk for such a long time that it seemed forever.'[144] The passion for accurate observation makes it impossible to call any place the end of the road, or even the end of the book. It is all now because it can never be a long time ago.

Ma and Pa do not allow Laura and Mary to see more than a child should. Only twice does Ma cry, when Pa goes down the well to fetch Mr Scott after they have failed to use the precautionary candle, and when she and the children get the letter to say Pa is well, but emotion is contained in a language formulaic in simplicity: 'That was a dreadful day'; 'That was a terrible day'; 'That was a happy Christmas'. Ma's 'I declare!' and her exclaiming of her husband's name, 'Charles!', in different tones, tell more of what children know about adult feeling than any amount of literary language could. Perhaps no other writer could have settled a family on the Big Slough without occasionally finding that it was a Slough of Despond. But it never is.

When Ma makes cheese in *Little House in the Big Woods* Mary and Laura are allowed to eat some pieces:

> Ma laughed at them for eating green cheese.
>
> 'The moon is made of green cheese, some people say,' she told them.
>
> The new cheese did look like the round moon when it came up behind the trees. But it was not green; it was yellow, like the moon.
>
> 'It's green,' Ma said, 'because it isn't ripened yet. When it's cured and ripened, it won't be a green cheese.'
>
> 'Is the moon really made of green cheese?' Laura asked, and Ma laughed.
>
> 'I think people say that, because it looks like a green cheese,' she said. 'But appearances are deceiving.' Then while she wiped all the green cheeses and rubbed them with butter, she told them about the dead, cold moon that is like a little world on which nothing grows.[145]

Laura is interested in both the cheese and the moon, but she is also interested in the truth of their connection, which is alive when literal – the round cheese in her hand and the round yellow moon – but dead if it is only a 'poetic' metaphor. The tired metaphor creates its own little world where nothing grows, a place sterilised inside the artist's mind instead of fertilised by being outside it and free to be the living thing itself, the two separate entities of moon and cheese.

Virginia Woolf wrote in her diary that 'Yeats and Aldous agreed the other day that their great aim in writing is to avoid the "literary". Aldous said how extraordinary the "literary" fetish had been among the Victorians. Yeats said that he wanted only to use the words that real people say. That his change had come through writing plays. And I said, rashly, that all the same his meaning was very difficult. And what is "literary"?'[146] She thought she might put this question into a critical book, but that meanwhile she wanted to write 'On being despised'. The train of thought is evident. Roger Fry told her that she was inclined to 'poetise' her creations and that this had spoilt *The Waves*. She recorded that it was the most useful criticism she had ever had, inserting it into Roger Fry's biography although she did not identify herself as the person criticised.[147] With her usual hypersensitivity, she felt that the enunciation of the male aesthetic showed contempt for her own work, and with her customary capacity to fight back she demanded, in tones her great-aunt Julia Cameron used for the question 'what is focus?': 'What is literary?'[148]

Willa Cather declared of Tolstoy's novels that 'the clothes, the dishes, the haunting interiors of those old Moscow houses, are always so much a part of the emotions of the people that they are perfectly synthesized; they seem to exist, not so much in the author's mind, as in the emotional penumbra of the characters themselves. When it is fused like this, literalness ceases to be literalness – it is merely part of the experience.'[149] Woolf would have agreed. She praised *War and Peace* for 'its directness, its realism'. Comparing Joyce with Tolstoy she remarked: 'I feel that myriads of tiny bullets pepper one and spatter one; but one does not get one deadly wound straight in the face – as from Tolstoy, for instance; but it is entirely absurd to compare him with Tolstoy.' She recorded in her diary that T. S. Eliot told her that Joyce 'is a purely literary writer. He is founded upon Walter Pater with a dash of Newman. . . . He thought that Joyce did completely what he meant to do. But he did not think that he gave a new insight into human nature – said nothing new like Tolstoy. . . . Indeed, he said, this new method of giving the psychology proves to my mind that it doesn't work. It doesn't tell as much as some casual glance from outside often tells.'[150] Eliot and Woolf disagree about the value of the 'literary', the poet, to the novelist's implied scorn, rating the 'literary' aspects of Joyce higher than the 'human' ones.

Charlotte Yonge declared that, unlike the merely literary compositions of other children's writers, *Alice* injected into the traditional fairy tale a dose of solidity, of the literal rather than the literary. Ruskin's *King of the Golden River* is by comparison a literary fairy tale. But Ruskin as art critic was well aware of the problem of speciousness. He wrote of Raphael: 'A dim sense of impossibility attaches itself to the graceful emptiness of the representation; we feel instinctively that the painted Christ and painted apostle are not beings that ever did or could exist; and this fatal sense of fair fabulousness, and well-composed impossibility, steals gradually from the picture into the history, until we find ourselves reading St. Mark or St. Luke with the same admiring, but uninterested, incredulity, with which we contemplate Raphael.' [151] That fair fabulousness hovers over the representation of the child in *Eric, Or Little by Little* and other such works. Walter de la Mare's first book of poems, *Songs of Childhood* (1902), sounds fictitious compared with Stevenson's *A Child's Garden of Verses*. When the child, in 'The Child in the Story goes to Bed', summons his nurse, his language would not bear translation into a real nursery:

> I prythee, Nurse, come smooth my hair,
>   And prythee, Nurse, unloose my shoe,
> And trimly turn my silken sheet
>   Upon my quilt of gentle blue. [152]

The poet works up his archaisms. There is no hint here of the undercutting of sentiment evident in Thomas Hood's 'A Parental Ode to my Son', in which the child's escapades interrupt the adult 'poetic' text. In Hood's poem the literal intrudes on the literary text, making it impossible for the reader to take its sentiments seriously.

In a short story called 'Novelty and Romancement' – his own misreading of the words 'Roman cement' – Lewis Carroll juxtaposes the literal and the literary:

> I have risen with the lark – 'day's sweet harbinger' – (once, certainly, if not oftener), with the aid of a patent alarm, and have gone forth at that unseemly hour, much to the astonishment of the housemaid cleaning the door steps, to 'brush with hasty steps the dewy lawn', and have witnessed the golden dawn with eyes yet half-closed in sleep. . . .
>
> I have wandered in the solemn woods at night, and bent me o'er the moss-grown fountain, to lave in its crystal stream my tangled locks and fevered brow. (What though I was laid up with a severe cold in consequence, and that my hair was out of curl for a week? Do paltry considerations such as these, I ask, affect the poetry of the incident?) [153]

The 'literary' language is undermined by the facts of experience: the alarm clock, the housemaid cleaning the steps, the frightful cold and the straight hair as the consequence of bathing in the fountain. The carnivalesque aspect of the piece does not come from the intertextual relationship of two kinds of discourse,[154] but from the juxtaposition of discourse with the objects it describes, the irreconcilability of the outer world with the world of words. Carroll presupposes the reader's instant recognition of disjunction between what is described and the mode of describing it.

This disjunction is celebrated in E. Nesbit's books and grew partly from Carroll's influence and partly from experience – her own childhood recognition that a real shepherdess was a different being from a literary one.[155] Jacqueline Rose claims that 'realism in children's writing cannot be opposed to what is "literary" or truly "aesthetic", once it is seen that realism does not refer just to the content of what is described but to a way of presenting it to the reader'.[156] But Nesbit believed that the choices between different kinds of language were as available to a children's writer as to a writer for adults. Her first book of adult short stories, *The Literary Sense* (1903), deals with adults trapped in the linguistic modes of the books they have read. She would have agreed with Bernard in *The Waves* that 'it is curious how, at every crisis, some phrase which does not fit insists upon coming to the rescue – the penalty of living in an old civilization with a notebook'.[157] Zangwill declared in the *Pall Mall Magazine* that 'it is, in fact, impossible for us moderns, educated in a long literary tradition, to live our lives as naturally and naïvely as the unlettered of today, and the people of the pre-literary geological epoch'.[158]

Nesbit's interest lies in the book not as moral guide but as a way of making children experience language. Robert, in *Five Children and It*, finds himself the victim of a wish made by the others that they should be besieged in a castle, which leaves him stranded outside the walls among the enemy:

'By my halidom,' said one, 'a brave varlet this!'
   Robert felt pleased at being *called* brave, and somehow it made him *feel* brave. He passed over the 'varlet'. It was the way people talked in historical romances for the young, he knew, and it was evidently not meant for rudeness. He only hoped he would be able to understand what they said to him. He had not been always able quite to follow the conversations in the historical romances for the young.
   'His garb is strange,' said the other. 'Some outlandish treachery, belike.'

'Say, lad, what brings thee hither?'

Robert knew this meant, 'Now then, youngster, what are you up to here, eh?' – so he said:

'If you please, I want to go home.'

'Go, then!' said the man in the longest boots: 'none hindereth, and nought lets us to follow. Zooks!' he added in a cautious undertone, 'I misdoubt me but he beareth tidings to the besieged.'

'Where dwellest thou, young knave?' inquired the man with the largest steel-cap.

'Over there,' said Robert; and directly he had said it he knew he ought to have said 'Yonder!' [159]

The strange disjunctions of language anticipate Daisy Ashford's *The Young Visiters* (1919). The narrative depends on the reader's acceptance of a blatant authorial interposing of literary language upon a text which claims by contrast its own authenticity. Nesbit's unreal worlds are as fabulously unreal as Carroll's Unicorn, but they are offered to the reader solidified by the children's belief in them.

Nesbit's children themselves see their ordinary activities through the spectacles of books. When they rescue the high-born babe, the language suggests Scott's *Guy Mannering* embroidered by a childish hand:

'I expect they stole the titled heir at dead of night, and they've been travelling hot-foot ever since, so now they're sleeping the sleep of exhaustedness,' Alice said. 'What a heart-rending scene when the patrician mother wakes in the morning and finds the infant aristocrat isn't in bed with his mamma.'

Eventually the baby is restored to his distraught parent having caused the children far more trouble by crying loudly all the time than they would have expected. Oswald concludes: 'If Oswald is ever married – I suppose he must be some day – he will have ten nurses to each baby. Eight is not enough. We know that because we tried, and the whole eight of us were not enough for the needs of that deserted infant who was not so extra high-born after all.' The literary reading of experience proved its own fabulousness.

The art of narration always hinges for Oswald on a choice between the 'literary' and the literal:

Let me to my narrating. I hope you will like it. I am going to try to

write it a different way, like the books they give you for a prize at a
girls' school – I mean a 'young ladies' school', of course – not a
high school. High schools are not nearly so silly as some other
kinds. Here goes:–
'"Ah me!" sighed a slender maiden of twelve summers,
removing her elegant hat and passing her tapery fingers lightly
through her fair tresses, "how sad it is – is it not? – to see
able-bodied youths and young ladies wasting the precious
summer hours in idleness and luxury."
'The maiden frowned reproachingly, but yet with earnest
gentleness, at the group of youths and maidens who sat beneath
an umbragipeaous beech tree and ate black currants.
'"Dear brothers and sisters," the blushing girl went on, "could
we not, even now, at the eleventh hour, turn to account these
wasted lives of ours, and seek some occupation at once improving
and agreeable?"
'"I do not quite follow your meaning, dear sister," replied the
cleverest of her brothers, on whose brow – '
It's no use. I can't write like these books. I wonder how the
books' authors can keep it up.
What really happened was that we were all eating black
currants in the orchard, out of a cabbage leaf, and Alice said –
'I say, look here, let's do something. It's simply silly to waste a
day like this. It's just on eleven. Come on!'
And Oswald said, 'Where to?'[160]

These alternatives are equally available to Orlando, who 'now
preferred the heroic and pompous; next the plain and simple; now
the vale of Tempe; then the fields of Kent or Cornwall; and could
not decide whether he was the divinest genius or the greatest fool in
the world'.[161] Wordsworth and Defoe, John Bunyan and Willa
Cather, Lewis Carroll and Laura Ingalls Wilder, Frances Hodgson
Burnett and D. H. Lawrence, Catherine Sinclair and George Eliot all
face the same choices. The difference after *Alice* is that the reader is
awakened to the fact that she is being practised upon by that chooser
of words, the supposedly knowing author: who hovers over her
hero as Woolf does in *Jacob's Room*, 'endowing Jacob Flanders with
all sorts of qualities he had not at all – for though, certainly, he sat
talking to Bonamy, half of what he said was too dull to repeat'.[162]
The reader here wants to write in the margin not 'How like life', but
'Yes, Jacob is dull, how nice that you saw it too: what shall we do

about it?' The answer which hangs in the air between author and reader is: don't let him become an Olympian.

Oswald recognises that writing and reading constitute an alliance within language: 'I hope this is not very dull to read about. I know it was jolly good fun to do.' He aims to educate the reader not in how to live, but in how to write: 'A great glorious glow of goodness gladdened (those all go together and are called alliteration) our hearts when we saw our own tramp coming down the road.' At one point he leaves a note in the text as if the printer had hurried him to press: 'H. O. spoke suddenly. He is the sort of person who rushes in where angels fear to tread, as Denny says (say what sort of person that is).' He likes the page to look right:

> (We thought we could make the Andes out of hurdles and things, and so we could have but for what always happens. (This is the unexpected. (This is a saying Father told me – but I see I am three deep in brackets so I will close them before I get into any more).).).[163]

Nesbit intends Oswald's professionalism as a writer to be measured against the amateurishness which Charlotte Yonge despised in many children's books, and particularly in the pious ones.

For Nesbit, language mirrors the mind that uses it. Denny's acquisition of boy's slang is approved by Oswald because it manifests a new independence of spirit. Words depict accurately the speaker's ethical colour. When the Bastables pretend to rescue Lord Tottenham from the dog Oswald calls out:

> 'Dicky, we must rescue this good old man.'
> Lord Tottenham roared in his fury, 'Good old man be – something or othered. Call the dog off!'
> Then Noel said, 'Haste, ere yet it be too late.'

Only when their victim confronts them with their own trickery do they see that the literary language disguises literal meanness: 'I never felt so cheap in all my life.'[164] Even the unpredictability of words bears witness to the truthfulness of the pen:

> We made two expeditions to discover the source of the Nile (or the North Pole), and owing to their habit of sticking together and doing dull and praiseable things, like sewing, and helping with

the cooking, and taking invalid delicacies to the poor and indignant, Daisy and Dora were wholly out of it both times.[165]

The poor and indigent would have been the orthodox reading, but Bettelheim has shown, as Freud had also done, that words can create their own forms of subversion.[166]

The revolt of Nesbit and her generation which heralds the modernism of Virginia Woolf and her contemporaries is against writing which claims morality while despising art. When Nesbit's children ape a 'literary' style, they expose the compromises and hypocrisies not only of the book, but of the world which produces and sanctions it.

So what exactly does the confrontation between the literary and the literal imply? Carroll had suggested that the literary meant a quick round up of the good, the true and the beautiful with a dash of Romantic language. Board of Education and Government circulars, issued in 1910 and 1912, implied, as Jacqueline Rose points out, that there are vital distinctions to be drawn between the literal which relates to experience, and the literary, which constitutes the language of 'literature'. Rose argues that the identifying of these two kinds of language embodied cultural assumptions about the class status of the learning child: elementary English versus cultured English.[167] Rock of Ages, cleft for me, as Jacob Flanders sings sitting on a rock off the Scilly Isles.[168]

In the draft version of the (second) essay which Woolf wrote on *Robinson Crusoe*, at the time when she was beginning *To the Lighthouse*, she suggested that the adult reader's pleasure in Crusoe's activities is 'to find all our sense of what is true miraculously freshened & sharpened, so that we are . . . like children ~~again taking natural objects~~ enjoying life literally'.[169] She goes on to speak of Defoe's 'literal & ferocious simplicity'. In the published essay she sketches the literary expectations aroused by the idea of a desert island. She had noted in a letter that she was reading *The Tempest* to compare with the novel, but in the final version of the *Crusoe* essay the comparison remains a subconcious one: 'Before we open the book we have perhaps vaguely sketched out the kind of pleasure we expect it to give us. We read; and we are rudely contradicted on every page. There are no sunsets and no sunrises; there is no solitude and no soul. There is, on the contrary, staring us full in the face nothing but a large earthenware pot.' She concludes: 'Thus Defoe, by reiterating that nothing but a plain earthenware pot stands in the foreground, persuades us to see remote islands and the solitudes of the human soul. By believing fixedly in the solidity of the pot and its earthiness, he has subdued every other element to his design.'[170] The question of solid reality against a background of literary expectations, which animated Roger Fry's art criticism, was in her mind just as she embarked on *To the Lighthouse*, in which both literary and artistic expectations are flouted. The lighthouse is not a symbol and the journey is not an allegorical one, any more than James and Mrs Ramsay, represented as a purple triangle, are what Williams Bankes expects from a traditional artistic representation of mother and child. Woolf argues that in Defoe's novel the contemplation of the literal contains all that the watcher need know about the literary.

At the beginning of 'The Reluctant Dragon' in *Dream Days* Grahame's boy narrator draws a parallel between Defoe and Wordsworth:

> Footprints in the snow have been unfailing provokers of sentiment ever since snow was first a white wonder in this drab-coloured world of ours. In a poetry-book presented to one of us by an aunt, there was a poem by one Wordsworth, in which they stood out strongly – with a picture all to themselves too – but we didn't think very highly either of the poem or the sentiment. Footprints in the sand, now, were quite another matter, and we grasped Crusoe's attitude of mind much more easily than Wordsworth's.[171]

Both are literary footprints because they are created in a language world – the world of the book. But whereas the Wordsworth snow tracks seem to belong in a book, like the dragon in Nesbit's 'The Book of Beasts', that footprint in the sand steps out of the page to alarm the reader as much as it first alarmed Robinson Crusoe.

So close the Wordsworth just for now, because it probably will have something to say about fields of sleep, or was it sheep? Is that a sheep in the boat, or is it Mr Ramsay in a bark? And is he barking, or is he only quoting poetry? Is that a real lighthouse, or is it a man of genius, or is it a line down the middle of a picture, or is it a word? Because, in the end, the difference between the literal and the literary, as Alice could have told you if Humpty Dumpty hadn't been so certain that words can mean anything you want them to, is something to do with meaning what you say and saying what you mean, or not doing those things. And if you don't stop conducting imaginary orchestras, and feather like mad, you'll catch a crab and the ball will unwind and the stocking will never be finished.

Notes

CHAPTER 1: CHILDREN'S BOOKS, CHILDHOOD AND MODERNISM

1 *Characteristics of French Art* (London, 1932). The original lectures are graphically described in Virginia Woolf's diary for Saturday, 13 February 1932: 'I break off from my plain duty which is to read the Anatomy of the World, to record Roger's lecture: last night. Roger rather cadaverous in white waistcoat. A vast sheet. Pictures passing. He takes his stick. Gets into trouble with the lanternists. Is completely at his ease. Elucidates unravels with fascinating ease & subtlety this quality & that: investigates (with his stick) opposing diagonals: emphasises the immediate & instantaneous in French art. Here a Queen about to fling out her fingers: here a mother "turning to look at something & losing herself in pensive & tender reverie, while her child struggles to look the other way, & she restrains it, unconsciously, with perfect ease & control" ' – *The Diary of Virginia Woolf*, ed. Anne Olivier Bell and Andrew McNeillie (Harmondsworth, 1982) iv.76.

2 When *The Wind in the Willows* was reviewed in the *TLS* on 22 October 1908 (p. 362), the reviewer suggested that the new book, which contained 'the materials for an English "Uncle Remus" . . . without the animating spirit', was perhaps intended 'to send readers [for the hundredth time] to its deathless forerunners – to "The Golden Age" and "Dream Days".' Virginia Woolf's unsigned review of E. M. Forster's *A Room with a View* appeared in the *TLS* just below this one on the same page, creating a juxtaposition which, if curious to a modern reader for whom the reputation of *The Wind in the Willows* has totally eclipsed that of Grahame's earlier books, shows the esteem in which *The Golden Age* and *Dream Days* were held earlier in the century.

3 *Alice's Adventures in Wonderland* was published by Macmillan in 1865 but withdrawn because Carroll and Tenniel were dissatisfied with the printing – Martin Gardner, *The Annotated Alice* (Harmondsworth, 1960) p. 347. The book was reissued in 1866. It was followed by *Through the Looking-Glass and What Alice Found There* (Macmillan, 1871). In this study I have adopted the practice of Roger Fry and of many Victorian as well as modern writers of referring to the first book as *Alice in Wonderland*. All quotations are from Gardner, *The Annotated Alice*. Page references, prefixed *AW* for *Alice in Wonderland* and *L-G* for *Through the Looking-Glass*, are given in parentheses following quotations.

4 Stuart Dodgson Collingwood, *The Life and Letters of Lewis Carroll* (London, 1898) p. 107, notes: 'So recently as July, 1898, the *Pall Mall*

Gazette conducted an inquiry into the popularity of children's books. "The verdict is so natural that it will surprise no normal person. The winner is 'Alice in Wonderland'. . . . With the exception of Shakespeare's plays, very few, if any, books are so frequently quoted in the daily Press as the two 'Alices.' " '

5　Virginia Woolf, 'Lewis Carroll', *The Moment and Other Essays* (London, 1947) pp. 70–1.

6　*The Diary of Virginia Woolf*, ii.135.

7　*The Letters of Virginia Woolf*, ed. Nigel Nicolson and Joanne Trautmann (London, 1975–80) iv.128–9; Frances Spalding, *Roger Fry* (London, 1980) pp. 145, 246–7, 261. Professor Quentin Bell wrote to the author: 'I am pretty sure that the Stephen children had both the Alice books. I have no hard evidence.' He thought that the nickname 'the White Knight' was used 'long before that celebrated party' (letter to the author, 10 Aug. 1985).

8　Woolf, 'Lewis Carroll', *The Moment*, p. 70.

9　Virginia Woolf, *A Writer's Diary*, ed. Leonard Woolf (London, 1975) pp. 360, 359, 120.

10　Peter Coveney, *The Image of Childhood* (Harmondsworth, 1967) p. 314.

11　*The Diary of Virginia Woolf*, iv.322: 'No doubt Proust could say what I mean – that great writer whom I cannot read when I'm correcting, so persuasive is he. He makes it seem easy to write well; which only means that one is slipping along on borrowed skates' (18 Nov. 1924). Five months later she wrote: 'He will I suppose both influence me & make me out of temper with every sentence of my own' (8 Apr. 1925).

12　Roger Fry, *Reflections on British Painting* (London, 1934) p. 107. The late Mrs Pamela Diamand, daughter of Roger Fry, said in a recorded conversation with the author, now in the King's College archive, that a very old copy of *Alice in Wonderland* was among the Fry children's books.

13　Roger Fry, 'The Seicento', *Transformations* (London, 1926) p. 126, wrote: 'In this matter of the arts we suffer from every form of verbal misfortune. To begin with, the application of art and artist almost exclusively to the art of painting, when artist should be a word of general application to any one who constructs with a view to esthetic satisfaction. . . . Goodness knows the writers are badly off enough, but at least they have some rough classification of those who use words; they can talk of a poet, an essayist, a novelist, a critic, a précis-writer, and so forth.' In this book the word 'art' refers equally to the arts of writing and of painting.

14　Jacqueline Rose, *The Case of Peter Pan or the Impossibility of Children's Fiction* (London, 1984) pp. 142–3.

15　To explain this phenomenon is to venture beyond the field of purely literary enquiry. Rose urges that children's books should not be considered as a self-contained genre developing exclusively in relation to other children's books or other literary works. The same plea has been made for the study of modernism by Lothar Hönnighausen in ' "Point of View" and its Background in Intellectual History', *Comparative Criticism*, 2 (Cambridge, 1980) 152: 'The problem occupying many of us at the present time is to define categories and areas which enable a process of mediation between the social and literary spheres to take place.'

16 Max Beerbohm, 'The Child Barrie', *Saturday Review*, 7 Jan. 1905, pp. 13–14.
17 Peter Green, *Kenneth Grahame, 1859–1932* (London, 1959) p. 161.
18 Max Beerbohm, 'Pantomime for Children', *Saturday Review*, 14 Jan. 1905, p. 45.
19 Alice Woods, review of James Sully, *Studies of Childhood* (London, 1895), in *Mind*, 5, n.s., no. 18 (Apr. 1896) 256.
20 Ed Block, 'Evolutionary Psychology and Aesthetics: *The Cornhill Magazine* 1875–1880', *Journal of the History of Ideas*, XLV, no. 3 (July–Sep. 1984) 465–75, analyses connections between the writings of Sully and Stevenson. In *The Letters of Virginia Woolf*, I.356, 501, Woolf notes that Sully liked her critical writing, and declared that she would write to tell him of her engagement. She did not always feel so genial, however, complaining in her diary on 3 April 1905 of a Professor Lee who bore a somewhat watered-down resemblance to both Sully and another of her father's friends identified by the initials 'C.B.' – possibly Charles Booth – and who bored her to extinction (Diary, Xmas 1904–27 May 1905, p. 94, Berg Collection). She was at the time on board ship to Spain.
21 James Sully, 'The Child in Recent English Literature', *Fortnightly Review*, 67, n.s., no. 61 (Feb. 1897) 218–28.
22 Ellen Key, *The Century of the Child* (New York and London, 1909) p. 185.
23 Coveney, *The Image of Childhood*, p. 280.
24 *Autobiography of Friedrich Froebel*, tr. Emilie Michaelis and H. Kealey Moore (London, 1886) pp. 54–5.
25 Michel Foucault, *The Order of Things: An Archaeology of the Human Sciences*, tr. from the French (London, 1970).
26 Baroness Marenholtz-Bülow, *Child and Child-Nature*, tr. Alice M. Christie (London, 1879) p. 43.
27 Friedrich Froebel, *Mutter- Und Kose-Lieder*, tr. F. and E. Lord, quoted in E. R. Murray, *Froebel as a Pioneer in Modern Psychology* (London, 1914) p. 207.
28 Murray, *Froebel as a Pioneer in Modern Psychology*, pp. 209, 205.
29 F. J. Harvey Darton, *Children's Books in England*, ed. Brian Alderson (Cambridge, 1982 [1st edn 1932]) p. 314.
30 Baroness Marenholtz-Bülow, *Woman's Educational Mission: Being an Explanation of Frederick Froebel's System of Infant Gardens*, tr. Elizabeth, Countess Krockow von Wickerode (London, 1855).
31 Sigmund Freud, 'Totem and Taboo' (1913 [1912–13]), *The Standard Edition of the Works of Sigmund Freud*, tr. James Strachey (Hogarth Press, 1965) XIII.127. All quotations from Freud's works are from this edition, hereafter referred to as *SE*.
32 Friedrich Froebel, *The Education of Human Nature*, in *Froebel's Chief Writings on Education*, tr. by S. S. Fletcher and J. Welton (London, 1912) pp. 32, 23.
33 Murray, *Froebel as a Pioneer in Modern Psychology*, pp. 68–9, 73–5.
34 F. H. Hayward, *The Educational Ideas of Pestalozzi and Froebel* (London, 1904) p. 61, notes that Froebel's distinctive contribution to Pestalozzi lay in his pioneering of education of the very young child through play.

35 Friedrich Froebel, *Pedagogics of the Kindergarten*, tr. Josephine Jarvis, quoted in Murray, *Froebel as a Pioneer in Modern Psychology*, pp. 203–4, 171, 243.
36 Marenholtz-Bülow, *Women's Educational Mission*, pp. 26, 32.
37 Murray, *Froebel as a Pioneer in Modern Psychology*, pp. 102, 199, 202, draws attention to Cooke's prominence as a supporter of Froebel's ideas. His position as Vanessa Bell's first art-master is noted in Frances Spalding, *Vanessa Bell* (London, 1983) p. 17, where the author refers both to his connection with Froebel and to that with Ruskin in the 1850s through the Working Men's College. Cooke contributed articles on Froebel's thought to the Froebel journal *Child Life* (see below, n. 116).
38 The late Mrs Pamela Diamand said that she and her brother were cared for by a Froebel-trained nurse whose principle seemed to be not to teach at all, which is perhaps a classic case of the parent's reacting against his own education (Fry complained about the love of facts in his Quaker home) and giving his children the exact opposite. Mrs Diamand would have preferred some formal instruction (recorded conversation, King's College archive).
39 Marenholtz-Bülow, *Child and Child-Nature*, pp. 30, 56, 32.
40 *Virginia Woolf, The Waves: the two holograph drafts*, transcribed and edited J. W. Graham (London, 1976) pp. 749, 747.
41 Professor Quentin Bell wrote to the author: 'Vanessa remembered Ebenezer Cooke with affection and I asked her about his teachings, but all that she could say was that E. C. pointed out that there was colour in highlights and she thought this an acute and interesting observation.' He added that as children he and his brother and sister were given colours and encouraged to draw and paint as much as they pleased but that 'the work I brought home from my preparatory school produced exclamations of horror and injunctions to disregard my teacher'. Froebel believed that children were given far too much instruction and should be allowed to find things out for themselves (see above, n. 38).
42 Virginia Woolf, *The Voyage Out* (Hogarth Press, 1975) p. 361.
43 Marenholtz-Bülow, *Child and Child-Nature*, p. 64.
44 Walter Pater, *Plato and Platonism*, *The Works of Walter Pater* (London, 1901) vi.269. All references to Walter Pater's writings are to this edition. Hönnighausen, ' "Point of view" and its Background in Intellectual History', *Comparative Criticism*, 2.154, 158, draws attention to Pater's significance in the development of modernism.
45 Pater, 'The Child in the House', *Miscellaneous Studies, Works*, viii.173, 185–6. The reference to Proust is to *Swann's Way*, vol. i of *A la recherche du temps perdu*, tr. C. K. Scott Moncrieff and Terence Kilmartin, as *The Remembrance of Things Past*, pp. 150–60.
46 William James, *The Principles of Psychology* (London, 1890) i.254, wrote of the progress made by Galton and Huxley in 'exploding the ridiculous theory of Hume and Berkeley that we can have no images but of perfectly definite things. Another [step] is made in the overthrow of the equally ridiculous notion that, whilst simple objective qualities are revealed to our knowledge in subjective feelings, relations are not.'
47 Marenholtz-Bülow, *Child and Child-Nature*, p. 58.

48 Sully, *Studies of Childhood*, p. 4. Herbert Speigelberg, *The Phenomenological Movement*, I (The Hague, 1960) 36, 27, describes the 'two major divisions' of phenomenology as 'descriptive psychology and genetic psychology', as set forth in Brentano's lectures for 1888–9.

49 Roger Fry, 'On the Laws of Phenomenology and their Application to Greek Painting', Fry Papers, King's College, Cambridge.

50 Marenholtz-Bülow, *Child and Child-Nature*, p. 156.

51 Husserl, one of the earliest phenomenologists, acknowledged his debt to William James. Spiegelberg, *The Phenomenological Movement*, I.67, 113, records that James visited Carl Stumpf in Prague in October 1882: 'Husserl himself told Dorian Cairns in 1931 that it had been Stumpf who had referred him first to James's *Psychology*.' Husserl refers twice in an article written in 1894 to James's chapter 'The Stream of Thought' and specifically to his doctrine of 'fringes'. Hegel's *Phenomenology of Mind* was, according to Spiegelberg, less influential in Germany than in France, and Murray states that Froebel only knew Hegel's work at second hand and did not admire it (*Froebel as a Pioneer in Modern Psychology*, p. 205).

52 Sully, *Studies of Childhood*, p. 7.

53 Henri Bergson, *Time and Free-Will* tr. F. L. Pogson (London, 1910) p. 8. This is a translation of Bergson's *Essai sur les données immédiates de la conscience*, first published in 1889 but composed during 1883–7. It contains Bergson's celebrated theory of simultaneity, which accounts for the specificity of the English title compared with the original French. Throughout this book Bergson's work will be referred to by this English title.

54 William James, *Essays in Radical Empiricism* (London, 1912) p. 20.

55 The *Lilliput Lectures* by Matthew Browne [William Brighty Rands] were originally published in *Good Words for the Young*. In 'Art and Arts' (Lilliput Lecture v), *Good Words for the Young*, III (May 1869) 316, a child, having watched her brother playing at Robinson Crusoe, enquires:

> 'Papa, what is Art?'
> And Papa made answer:
> 'Art, dear, is make-believe.'
> 'Then, Papa, I suppose Tom was an Artist, when he made-believe he was Robinson Crusoe in the garden?' said the little girl.

Darton, *Children's Books in England*, p. 281, contains biographical information about the author, William Brighty Rands, who wrote under several pseudonyms, but was probably best known for the *Lilliput Lectures* (1871) and their companion volumes, *Lilliput Levee* (1864) and *Lilliput Legends* (1872). Stevenson's discussion of *Robinson Crusoe* and children's love of imitation in 'Child's Play' may have owed something to Browne's lecture, but he is clearer about the differences between a child's make-believe and creative art. It is worth noting that when Freud observed in 'Creative Writers and Day-Dreaming' (1908 [1907]), *SE*, IX. 141–54, that 'every child at play behaves like a creative writer, in that he creates a world of his own', and that this is paralleled in the writer's fantasy world, those ideas had been common currency for a long time.

284 *Notes to pages 14–18*

56 Roger Fry, 'Some Aspects of Chinese Art', *Transformations* (London, 1926) p. 81.
57 Woolf, *A Writer's Diary*, p. 137.
58 José Ortega y Gasset, *The Modern Theme* (London, 1931) pp. 81, 82, originally presented as lectures in 1921–2, the year Fry and Vanessa Bell were both in Spain.
59 Pater, 'Wordsworth', *Appreciations, Works*, v.55.
60 'On Simple and Sentimental Poetry', *Schiller's Essays Aesthetical and Philosophical*, tr. from the German (London, 1875) p. 266. I have used the translation from this edition, although some readers would prefer 'naïve' to 'simple', as conveying Schiller's meaning more accurately.
61 Virginia Woolf, *The Waves* (Hogarth Press, 1980) p. 196.
62 Kenneth Grahame, *The Golden Age* (London, 1915) pp. 193–4.
63 Thomas Traherne, *Centuries of Meditation* (Oxford, 1960) p. 14.
64 Linda Pollock, *Forgotten Children* (Cambridge, 1983) p. 140.
65 Marenholtz-Bülow, *Child and Child-Nature*, p. 42.
66 C. W. Kimmins, 'The Child as the Director of the Parent's Education', *Child Life*, III (Apr. 1901) 166.
67 Review of Charlotte Perkins (Stetson) Gillman, *Concerning Children*, *Child Life*, III (July 1901) 166.
68 Kate Greenaway, *Little Folks Painting Book* (London, 1879) p. 64.
69 'Reflections and Remarks on Human Life', *The Works of Robert Louis Stevenson* (Edinburgh, 1898) Appendix, p. 27.
70 Paul Levy, *Moore: G. E. Moore and the Cambridge Apostles* (Oxford, 1981) p. 113.
71 Roger Fry, 'Shall We Obey?', and letter to Lady Fry, dated by Dr Michael Halls 13 Nov. 1887, both in Fry Papers, King's College, Cambridge.
72 Kenneth Grahame in conversation, quoted in Green, *Kenneth Grahame*, p. 302.
73 'Peter Pan', *Child Life*, VII (16 Apr. 1905) 103.
74 In the Diary which Virginia Woolf kept from Xmas 1904 to 27 May 1905 she noted Galton's *Heredity* in the list of books that she had read that year (Berg Collection).
75 Leslie Stephen, 'Robert Louis Stevenson', *Studies of a Biographer*, IV (London, 1902) 209–10.
76 Brian Crozier, 'Notions of Childhood in London Theatre, 1880–1905' (unpublished PhD thesis, Cambridge, 1981) pp. 152–4, 171.
77 Key, *The Century of the Child*, p. 26.
78 'Our Outlook', *The Child*, I (Oct. 1910) 1.
79 Marenholtz-Bülow, *Child and Child-Nature*, p. 24.
80 Martin Hoyles (ed.), *Changing Childhood* (London, 1979) p. 11, quotes one of his contributors, Shulamith Firestone: 'We will be unable to speak of the liberation of women without also discussing the liberation of children, and vice versa.' This was published in 1979, exactly a hundred years after Marenholtz-Bülow's *Child and Child-Nature*.
81 Nigel Middleton, 'The Education Act of 1870 as the Start of the Modern Conception of the Child', *British Journal of Educational Studies*, XVIII, no. 2 (June 1970) 166–79.
82 Johanna Spyri, *Heidi* (London, 1950) pp. 270–1, 280–5 and *passim*.

83 J. A. and Olive Banks, *Feminism and Family Planning in Victorian England* (Liverpool, 1964) pp. 88, 92–3.

84 Michael Holroyd, *Lytton Strachey* (London, 1967) 1.16; the photograph faces p. 88.

85 Edward Westermarck, *The Origin and Development of Moral Ideas* (London, 1906) 1.618.

86 Lloyd DeMause (ed.), *The History of Childhood* (London, 1976) p. 6.

87 George Henry Payne, *The Child in Human Progress* (London, 1916) pp. 3, 6.

88 Coveney, *The Image of Childhood*, p. 241.

89 Payne, *The Child in Human Progress*, p. 8.

90 Peter Fuller, 'Uncovering Childhood', in Hoyles (ed.), *Changing Childhood*, p. 98.

91 Philippe Ariès, *Centuries of Childhood*, tr. Robert Baldick (Harmondsworth, 1973) p. 36: 'No one thought of keeping a picture of a child if that child had either lived to grow to manhood or had died in infancy.' The fact that Ariès' thesis has been widely attacked by historians does not diminish its significance in opening up the history of childhood for investigation. *See* below, n. 114.

92 *The Complete Works of Lewis Carroll* (London, 1914) pp. 981–2. All quotations from Carroll's verse and incidental prose are from this edition. 'Hiawatha's Photography' was one of Carroll's contributions to the journal *The Train* (Dec. 1859), the paper for which he first used the pseudonym Lewis Carroll, which its editor chose from among four alternatives. See Lewis Carroll, *For the Train* (London, 1856–7) pp. xiv, xv.

93 Ogden Nash, *Custard and Company* (Harmondsworth, 1979) pp. 58–9.

94 Roger Fry, 'Plastic Colour', *Transformations* (London, 1926) pp. 217–18.

95 Roger Fry, 'The Artist's Vision', *Vision and Design* (London, 1920) p. 48. In 'Some Questions in Aesthetics' (1926), *Transformations*, pp. 19–21, Fry replied to I. A. Richards' criticism of his insistence on the purely formal in art in *Principles of Literary Criticism* (1924).

96 Key, *The Century of the Child*, p. 8. Roger Fry lamented Cézanne's refusal in later life to study from nude models. See *Characteristics of French Art*, p. 90; *Reflections on British Painting*, pp. 40–1, 147; *Cézanne: A Study of his Development* (London, 1932) pp. 8, 29.

97 George Melly, 'Jokes About Modern Art', in George Melly and J. R. Glaves-Smith, *A Child of Six Could Do It* (London, 1973) pp. 62, 9–10. Spalding, *Roger Fry*, p. 139, suggests that 'the public saw a hidden violence in those revolutionary paintings and related it to a general unrest'.

98 Fry, 'London Sculptors and Sculptures', *Transformations*, p. 144, and 'Retrospect', *Vision and Design*, p. 290.

99 *The Letters of Virginia Woolf*, 1.440.

100 Fry, 'Vincent Van Gogh', *Transformations*, pp. 178, 183, 186.

101 Fry, 'On Some Modern Drawings', *Transformations*, p. 204; 'Negro Sculpture', *Vision and Design*, pp. 93–4; *Reflections on British Painting*, pp. 134–5.

102 Fry, 'An Essay in Aesthetics', *Vision and Design*, p. 20, and 'Vincent Van Gogh', *Transformations*, pp. 181, 183.
103 Fry, 'Claude', *Vision and Design*, p. 222; *Cézanne*, p. 14.
104 Virginia Woolf, *Roger Fry* (London, 1940) pp. 179–80; Spalding, *Roger Fry*, pp. 212–13.
105 Roger Fry, 'Children's Drawings' (1917), Fry Papers, King's College, Cambridge. Robert Louis Stevenson had also planned to write on 'Child Art' for W. E. Henley's shortlived journal *The Magazine of Art*, but although Henley wrote to him on 26 October 1881 that 'the Child Art is a good idea', the project came to nothing (Stevenson Collection, Beinecke Library).
106 Fry, *Cézanne*, p. 88. For Fry's admiration of Wilfrid Trotter's book, *Instincts of the Herd in Peace and War* (London, 1916), see Woolf, *Roger Fry*, p. 202, as also for Fry's interest in psychology.
107 Fry, 'Art and Socialism' and 'Art and Life', *Vision and Design*, pp. 57–8, 15.
108 Fry, 'Some Questions in Aesthetics', *Transformations*, p. 3; *Cézanne*, pp. 1, 75, 42, 2; 'Seurat', *Transformations*, p. 201; *Reflections on British Painting*, p. 123. Fry was particularly interested in Milton's place in the debate about thought and feeling. He observed that in the poet's work 'sensuality is always veiled with learning and . . . austere theology is often clothed in sensuous imagery' (*Characteristics of French Art*, p. 35). He wrote to Goldsworthy Lowes Dickinson of his admiration for Milton's radical views on divorce. 'And to think that the B[ritish] P[ublic] swallow Milton as a type of Puritan straitlaced virtue and never see what he really was' (letter dated 24 Feb. 1889, Fry Papers, King's College, Cambridge). Valuable insight is provided into Fry's influence on Woolf by J. K. Johnstone, *The Bloomsbury Group: A Study of E. M. Forster, Lytton Strachey, Virginia Woolf and their Circle* (New York, 1954), and Jean Guiguet, *Virginia Woolf and her Works*, tr. Jean Stewart (London, 1965).
109 M. C. Bradbrook, 'Notes on the Style of Mrs Woolf', *Scrutiny*, I, no. 1 (May 1932) 37. Woolf wrote in her diary: 'What ought I to feel & say & do when Miss B. devotes an article in *Scrutiny* to attacking me. She is young, Cambridge, ardent. And she said I'm a very bad writer. Now I think the thing to do is to note the pith of what is said – that I don't think – then to use the little kick of energy which opposition supplies to be more vigorously oneself' (*The Diary of Virginia Woolf*, IV.101).
110 Freud, 'A Difficulty in the Path of Psycho-analysis' (1917), *SE*, XVII.140.
111 Marenholtz-Bülow, *Child and Child-Nature*, p. 142.
112 Stephen Kern, 'Freud and the Discovery of Child Sexuality', *History of Childhood Quarterly*, I, no. 1 (Summer 1973) 122, 136–7.
113 Julia Kristeva, 'Place Names', *Desire in Language* (New York, 1980) p. 271.
114 Similar objections have been made to Ariès' locating of changed attitudes to children in the late eighteenth century. Pollock, *Forgotten Children*, p. 10, protests against giving too much prominence to Rousseau: 'How could *one* writer have such an influence?' For other

evaluations of Ariès's work see Lloyd DeMause (ed.), *The History of Childhood*; Hoyles (ed.), *Changing Childhood*.

115 Jean-Jacques Rousseau, *Emilius or A Treatise of Education*, tr. from the French (Edinburgh, 1763) i.148, ii.125–9.

116 Ebenezer Cooke, 'Is Development from Within? Did Froebel's Conception of Development differ from Darwin's?' *Child Life*, vi (Oct. 1904) 185–92; vii (Jan. 1905) 19.

117 Froebel, *Pedagogics of the Kindergarten*, p. 36, quoted in Murray, *Froebel as a Pioneer of Modern Psychology*, p. 156: 'What the little one has up to this time directly felt so often by the touch of the mother's breast – union and separation – it now perceives outwardly in an object which can be grasped and clasped.' See D. W. Winnicott, *Playing and Reality* (London, 1971), for a comparable analysis of the soft toy as mediator (Froebel's word) between the child's relation with his mother and his relation with the outside world.

118 Fuller, 'Uncovering Childhood', in Hoyles (ed.), *Changing Childhood*, p. 96.

119 Norman O. Brown, *Life Against Death: The Psychoanalytic Meaning of History* (London, 1959) p. 26.

120 Michel Foucault, *The History of Sexuality*, tr. Robert Hurley (London, 1978) p. 99.

121 See Elizabeth Wright, *Psychoanalytic Criticism* (London, 1984) p. 161, for this reading of Foucault's argument.

122 Leo Tolstoy, *Childhood, Boyhood, Youth*, tr. Isabel F. Hapgood (London, 1889) p. 34.

123 The earlier version is from *Childhood and Youth*, tr. Melwida von Meysenbug (London, 1862) p. 43. The child Nikolai had previously described to his elder brother his passion for Sonya, and had been offended by the older boy's scorn and insistence on kissing, which the young child thought 'absurd' (1862), 'nonsense' (1889) and 'stupid' (1964), the latter word perfectly translating a child's contempt for a sexuality for which he is not ready. The 1964 translation is by Rosemary Edmonds for Penguin and will be used for all further references in this book to *Childhood, Boyhood, Youth*.

124 Freud, 'Delusions and Dreams in Jensen's *Gradiva*' (1907 [1906]), *SE*, ix.8, 54: 'In their knowledge of the mind they are far in advance of us everyday people, for they drew upon sources which we have not yet opened for science.'

125 E. M. Field, *The Child and His Book* (London, 1891) p. 8; Sully, 'The Child in Recent English Literature', *Fortnightly Review*, 67, n.s. 61 (Feb. 1897) 226.

126 Catherine Ponton Slater, 'Story-Book Children', *Child Life*, vii (Jan. 1905) 26–8.

127 Ann Thwaite, *Waiting for the Party: The Life of Frances Hodgson Burnett 1849–1924* (London, 1974) p. 95, notes that *Heidi* and *Treasure Island* were listed as best-selling novels in 1884, *A Child's Garden of Verses* and *Huckleberry Finn* in 1885, *Little Lord Fauntleroy*, *King Solomon's Mines* and *War and Peace* in 1886. *The Golden Age* and *Dream Days* were both written for adults, as were Kipling's *Puck of Pook's Hill* and *Rewards and Fairies*.

In terms of the argument of this book, these works are discussed as 'children's books' because adults would now consider them, with the possible exception of *Huckleberry Finn*, to be books which literate children (however small a number of persons that might be) rather than literate adults, would read. The problems of this category, admirably set out by Jacqueline Rose in *The Case of Peter Pan* are discussed at various points in this work. Historically the distinction between children's books and books for adults is by no means a hard-and-fast one. *The Pilgrim's Progress* and *Robinson Crusoe* were both intended originally for adults but quickly appropriated by adults for children's reading.

128 In this book Virginia Woolf is always referred to by that name whether or not the reference is to the period in which she used it, on the grounds that it is a professional not a married name and that this practice makes less complicated reading.

129 Virginia Woolf, Diary, Xmas 1904–27 May 1905, p. 25 (Berg Collection).

130 J. M. Barrie, *Peter Pan, or The Boy Who Would Not Grow Up, The Plays of J. M. Barrie* (London, 1928) pp. xi–xii. The Stephen family were very friendly with the Barries. In the 1897 Notebook Virginia records going with Stella to enquire after Mrs Barrie and her children (1 Mar. 1897), and remarks four days later that Sylvia had lent her three books (Notebook for 1897, Berg Collection).

131 Rose, in *The Case of Peter Pan*, an otherwise penetrating study of Barrie's authorial ambivalence, ignores the impact of the flying on a child audience.

132 Israel Zangwill, 'Without Prejudice', *Pall Mall Magazine*, ix (May–Aug. 1896) 154. Zangwill was a close friend of Frances Hodgson Burnett – Marghanita Laski, *Mrs Ewing, Mrs Molesworth and Mrs Hodgson Burnett* (London, 1950) p. 76 – but he was too judicious a critic to allow himself to be blinded by friendship. Sidney Colvin wrote to Stevenson on 1 December 1893, sending him 'the new Pall Mall Gaz Mag. with the first chapter of Meredith's story. Remarks on RLS by a not quite untalented fat Jew called Zangwill' (Stevenson Collection, Beinecke Library). Zangwill's witty and astringent column in the *Pall Mall Magazine* from 1893 to 1896 shows him to be quite capable of dealing with the anti-Semitism which he encountered in some circles. *Without Prejudice* was published in book form in 1896.

133 Henry James, 'Robert Louis Stevenson', *Century Magazine*, Apr. 1888, in Janet Adam Smith (ed.), *Henry James and Robert Louis Stevenson* (London, 1948) p. 157.

134 Dorothy Richardson, *March Moonlight*, vol. iv of *Pilgrimage* (London, 1967) 514.

135 Slater, 'Story-Book Children', *Child Life*, vii (Jan. 1905) 26–8.

136 D. H. Lawrence, *Sons and Lovers* (Harmondsworth, 1983) pp. 23–5, 44.

137 Barrie, *Peter Pan*, p. 103.

138 Virginia Woolf, 'Madame de Sévigné', *The Death of the Moth* (London, 1942) p. 37; Proust, *Within a Budding Grove, The Remembrance of Things Past*, ii.701–3.

139 L. E. Jones, *A Victorian Boyhood* (London, 1955) pp. 27, 140.

140 *The Diary of Virginia Woolf*, iii.95.

141 Rose, *The Case of Peter Pan*, pp. 10–13, 32.

142 Fuller, 'Uncovering Childhood', in Hoyles (ed.), *Changing Childhood*, p. 104.

143 Darton, *Children's Books in England*, p. 301, sees in the children's books by Grahame, Kipling and Nesbit a continuation of the revolutionary impulse set in motion by the *Alice* Books.

144 Field,*The Child and His Book*, pp. 1–2. Like Roger Fry, Field held that '*The Crofton Boys* [Harriet Martineau, 1841], *Alice in Wonderland*, and *The Rose and the Ring* detach themselves from the general mass' of children's books (p. 6).

145 Zangwill, 'Without Prejudice', *Pall Mall Magazine*, v (Jan.–Apr. 1895) 177. Zangwill was praising Joseph Jacobs' new edition of Aesop's fables for Macmillan, together with his 'More Celtic Fairy Tales'. Mentioning by way of comparison Andrew Lang's 'The Yellow Fairy Book', Zangwill remarked that Lang's book sounded like 'a nursery counterpart of "The Yellow Book".'

146 Sully, *Studies of Childhood*, pp. 2, 27.

147 DeMause (ed.), *The History of Childhood*, pp. 4, 14.

148 Robert Gittings, *Young Thomas Hardy* (London, 1975) pp. 32–3, describes the hanging of a woman on 9 August 1856, which fascinated the sixteen-year-old Hardy.

149 Heather Glen, *Vision and Disenchantment: Blake's Songs and Wordsworth's Lyrical Ballads* (Cambridge, 1983) p. 145.

150 Flora Thompson, *Lark Rise to Candleford* (Oxford, 1945) p. 253. 'Brenda' was the pseudonym of Mrs G. Castle Smith.

151 James Sully, *Outlines of Psychology* (London, 1884) pp. 219–21.

152 Arthur Waugh, 'Reticence', *Yellow Book*, i (Jan. 1894) 212.

153 Havelock Ellis, *From Rousseau to Proust* (London, 1936) p. 16.

154 'Literature of Childhood', *London and Westminster Review*, xxxiii, no. 2 (1839) 137–8.

155 'Children's Literature', *London Review*, xiii (Jan. 1860) 470–2, 484, 486.

156 E. L. M., 'Lewis Carroll, the Children's Writer', *Child Life*, iii (Jan. 1901) 95.

157 Henry James, *What Maisie Knew* (New York, 1909) p. 10.

158 Harry Levin, '*Wonderland* Revisited', in Robert Phillips (ed.), *Aspects of Alice* (London, 1972) p. 179, points out that Walter de la Mare first drew the parallel between *What Maisie Knew* and *Alice in Wonderland* in his centenary biography of Carroll in 1932.

159 William Empson, *Some Versions of Pastoral* (London, 1935) p. 208.

160 Darton, *Children's Books in England*, p. 260.

161 Brian Alderson, Preface to Darton, *Children's Books in England*, p. xiii.

162 *The Diary of Virginia Woolf*, iv.337, 103.

163 George Boas, *The Cult of Childhood* (London, 1966) p. 9.

164 René Wellek, 'Literary Criticism and Philosophy', *Scrutiny*, v (Mar. 1937) 376.

165 Quoted in Stephen, 'Robert Louis Stevenson', *Studies of a Biographer*, iv.216.

166 J. A. Hammerton, *Stevensoniana* (Edinburgh, 1907) p. 1.

167 Jenni Calder, *RLS: A Life Study* (London, 1980) p. 51. J. H. Lockhart,

Memoirs of the Life of Sir Walter Scott, Bart. (Edinburgh, 1939) IV. 180–237. The diary is entitled 'Voyage in the Lighthouse Yacht to Nova Zembla, and the Lord knows where'. The Bell Rock was the first port of call.

168 *The Letters of Virginia Woolf*, I.49.

169 Lyndall Gordon, *Virginia Woolf: A Writer's Life* (Oxford, 1984) p. 13, from the unpublished source, 'The Hyde Park Gate News'.

170 In an entry in the Notebook for 1897 (Berg Collection), under 31 Jan. 1897, Virginia recorded that she had stayed in bed till ten o'clock, and had then gone to read Lockhart with her father, which had taken up the rest of the morning, and which she enjoyed more each time they read the book. The fact that she read Lockhart with Leslie Stephen makes it more likely that she knew Robert Louis Stevenson's account, because of the professional connection between the two men on the *Cornhill*, the journal which enjoyed in England a reputation comparable to that of *Scribner's Magazine* in the United States. Stevenson claimed that Scott spent much of the voyage quoting under his breath, as Mr Ramsay does in *To the Lighthouse*, and Robert Stevenson senior recalls that at one point the novelist 'quietly pocketed a skull' (p. 499). Mr Ramsay is reading Scott, one of Leslie Stephen's favourite novelists, in *To the Lighthouse*. Indeed, Professor Quentin Bell remarks that the only work he recollected Virginia Woolf's reading to him and his brother when they were children was the first chapter of *Waverley* (letter to the author).

171 Robert Louis Stevenson, 'Scott's Voyage in the Lighthouse Yacht', *Scribner's Magazine* (Oct. 1883) pp. 493–4.

172 Woolf, *A Writer's Diary*, p. 76.

173 F. G. Kilton, 'A Visit to the Eddystone Lighthouse', *Strand Magazine*, IV (July–Dec. 1892) 340–51.

CHAPTER 2: THE VOICE OF THE AUTHOR

1 Erich Auerbach, *Mimesis: The Representation of Reality in Western Literature*, tr. Willard R. Trask (Princeton, NJ, 1953) p. 531. Cf. James Naremore, *The World without a Self* (New Haven, Conn., and London, 1973) pp. 13–14, 123.

2 William Makepeace Thackeray, *Vanity Fair* (London, 1864) p. 878. Leslie Stephen, recalling his dead wife for his children in his *Mausoleum Book*, wrote: 'It seemed to me at the time that she had accepted sorrow as her lifelong partner' – *Sir Leslie Stephen's Mausoleum Book*, ed. Alan Bell (Oxford, 1977) p. 41.

3 Virginia Woolf, *To the Lighthouse* (Hogarth Press, 1982) p. 277. This point is discussed further in David Lodge, *The Modes of Modern Writing* (London, 1977) pp. 177–88.

4 David Lodge, *The Novelist at the Crossroads* (London, 1971) p. 119; Colin MacCabe, *James Joyce and the Revolution of the Word* (London, 1978) p. 27.

5 Quoted in Phillips (ed.) *Aspects of Alice*, p. xxii: 'Still, you know, words mean more than we mean to express when we use them; so a whole

book ought to mean a great deal more than the writer means. So whatever good meanings are in the book, I'm glad to accept as the meaning of the book.'

6 Roland Barthes, 'The Death of the Author', *Image Music Text*, tr. Stephen Heath (London, 1977) p. 147.

7 [Elizabeth Rigby], 'Children's Books', *Quarterly Review*, LXXIV (June 1844) 7–8.

8 Quoted in M. Nancy Cutt, *Mrs Sherwood and her Books for Children* (London, 1974) p. 67.

9 Elizabeth Turner, *The Daisy, or Cautionary Stories in Verse* (London, 1807), and *The Cowslip, or More Cautionary Stories in Verse* (London, 1811); Hilaire Belloc, *Cautionary Tales for Children* (London, 1908). Belloc's volume may have owed some of its inspiration to Stevenson's *Moral Emblems* composed for his stepson, Lloyd Osborne, who printed them on his own printing-press with Stevenson's woodcuts:

> Mark, printed on the opposite page,
> The unfortunate effects of rage.
> A man (who might be you or me)
> Hunts another into the sea.
> Poor soul, his unreflecting act
> His future joys will much contract;
> And he will spoil his evening toddy
> By dwelling on that mangled body.

Moral Emblems (Davos-Platz, 1881), bound into *The Works of Robert Louis Stevenson*, XIV. The booklet was not published before this edition in 1898, so that Belloc's *The Bad Child's Book of Beasts* (1896) which preceded the *Cautionary Tales for Children* was an altogether independent production. Janet Adam Smith points out in her edition of Robert Louis Stevenson's *Collected Poems* (London, 1950) p. 560, that a copy of Isaac Watts's *Songs Divine and Moral for the Use of Young Children* (1715) was among Stevenson's childhood books, as was the case for many of his generation. When Virginia Woolf wrote her 'Warboys' diary in 1899 she took particular delight in gluing her own manuscript pages onto an ancient copy of Isaac Watts's *Logic, or the Use of Right Reason With a Variety of Rules to Guard Against Error in the Affairs of Religion and Human Life as Well as in the Sciences* (London, 1786), observing in the process that she would not have desecrated any other book in this way but that no one could lament the loss of Watts's work (Warboys Diary, 4 Aug.–23 Sep. 1889, Berg Collection).

10 Robert Louis Stevenson, 'Random Memories', *Across the Plains* (London, 1982) p. 178.

11 Elisabeth Jay, *The Religion of the Heart: Anglican Evangelicalism and the Nineteenth-Century Novel* (Oxford, 1979) p. 12.

12 Charlotte Yonge, 'Didactic Fiction', 'Children's Literature of the Last Century', *Macmillan's Magazine*, XX (May–Oct 1869) 309.

13 Field, *The Child and His Book*, p. 203.

14 Mark Twain [Samuel Langhorne Clemens], *The Adventures of Huckleberry*

Finn (London, 1884) p. 154. The book was first published in London in 1884 and in New York the following year.

15 C. Day Lewis, *The Buried Day*, quoted in Geoffrey Trease, *Tales out of School* (London, 1964) p. 28.

16 'Children's Literature', *London Review*, xiii (Jan 1860) 495–6.

17 Thomas Day, *The History of Sandford and Merton* (London, 1783–9) Preface and i.295.

18 Marilyn Butler, *Jane Austen and the War of Ideas* (Oxford, 1975) p. 85, notes that several of Jane Austen's predecessors linked the words 'pride and prejudice', and refers to a correspondence in the *TLS*, 29 Dec. 1961, p. 929, and 26 Jan. 1962, p. 57. The second letter mentions Fanny Burney's use of the words in *Cecilia* (1782), but it is more likely that Day drew on the source mentioned by the first correspondent, namely, Gibbon's *Decline and Fall of the Roman Empire*, i.41, in which the author speaks of the slaves 'whom pride and prejudice almost disdained to number among the human species'. All of these sources would have been available to Jane Austen.

19 Day, *Sandford and Merton*, ii.238–9; Jane Austen, *Pride and Prejudice* (Oxford, 1967) pp. 48, 25, 100.

20 E. Nesbit, *The Wouldbegoods* (London, 1902) pp. 140, 143.

21 'Children's Literature', *London Review*, xiii.495–6.

22 Maria Louisa Charlesworth, *Ministering Children* (London, 1854) p. 147. The book was reprinted in 1899 as well as many other times. Brian Alderson notes that it was reprinted again as late as 1930. The first episode of *The Wouldbegoods*, which parodies Charlesworth's book, appeared in the *Pall Mall Magazine* in July 1900.

23 Mary Martha Sherwood, *The Little Woodman and his Dog Caesar* (Wellington, N.Z., 1828) p. 87, reproduced facsimile in Cutt, *Mrs Sherwood and her Books for Children*.

24 Edward Lear, *A Book of Nonsense* (1863) title page.

25 Brenda [Mrs G. Castle Smith], *Froggy's Little Brother* (London, 1875) p. 158.

26 Nesbit, *The Wouldbegoods*, p. 32.

27 F. W. Farrar, *Eric, Or Little by Little* (London, 1928 [1858]) p. 82.

28 Charlesworth, *Ministering Children*, p. 170.

29 'Children's Books', *Quarterly Review*, lxxiv.10.

30 John Bunyan, *The Pilgrim's Progress* (Old Woking, 1978) pp. 14, 25–7, 39, 41, 43, 45, and 'The Author's Apology for his Book', p. 1.

31 Charlotte M. Yonge, *The Daisy Chain or Aspirations, A Family Chronicle* (London, 1856) p. 61.

32 John R. Knott, Jr, 'Bunyan's Gospel Day: A Reading of *The Pilgrim's Progress*' (1973), in Roger Sharrock (ed.), *Bunyan, The Pilgrim's Progress: A Casebook* (London, 1976) pp. 224–5.

33 Anna Barbauld and John Aiken, *Evenings at Home*, i (London, 1794) 90–1. Mrs Barbauld and John Aiken were sister and brother.

34 Roger Fry wrote to his mother from Cambridge in 1886 that he had enjoyed reading his father's lecture on the travelling student, but 'might he [the student] not sometimes enjoy himself without learning facts?' Writing to Lowes Dickinson in Rome the following year Fry remarked:

'You have not profitted [*sic*] much by my father's description of the ideal tourist with Ordnance survey map – geological hammer – Hooker's British Flora – Parker's handbook of Gothic architecture &c. &c.' (Fry Papers, King's College, Cambridge). This letter was brought to my attention by Dr Michael Halls.

35 Charles Kingsley, 'Madam How and Why', *Good Words for the Young*, I (Jan. 1868) 9. The series was issued as a book in 1870.

36 Jean Ingelow, 'Nineteen Hundred and Seventy-Two', *Good Words for the Young*, IV (Feb. 1872) 186.

37 H. B. Tristram, 'The Spider and its Webs', *Good Words for the Young*, II (Feb. 1869) 186.

38 E. B. White, *Charlotte's Web* (New York, 1952) p. 41.

39 Louisa M. Alcott, *Little Women* (London, 1910) p. 19.

40 Freud, 'Jokes and their Relation to the Unconscious' (1905), *SE*, VIII.120.

41 Edgar Allan Poe, review of Nathaniel Hawthorne, *Twice-Told Tales*, *Godey's Lady's Book* (Mar. 1846), in Eric Warner and Graham Hough (eds), *Strangeness and Beauty, An Anthology of Aesthetic Criticism 1840–1910* (Cambridge, 1983) I.153–4.

42 George Eliot, *The Mill on the Floss* (Edinburgh and London, 1875) p. 12.

43 Nesbit, *The Wouldbegoods*, pp. 29, 231. Although Mr Greatheart in the second part of *The Pilgrim's Progress* does provide a hero figure, it is the figure of Christian in the first part who has become the centre of the cultural myth.

44 Robert Bridges, 'Bunyan's *Pilgrim's Progress*' (1905), in Sharrock (ed.), *The Pilgrim's Progress: A Casebook*, pp. 110–11, 114.

45 Sir Charles Firth, Introduction to *The Pilgrim's Progress* (1898), in Sharrock (ed.), *The Pilgrim's Progress: A Casebook*, p. 81.

46 Flora Thompson, *Lark Rise to Candleford*, p. 359.

47 Samuel Butler, *The Way of All Flesh* (London, 1903) p. 115.

48 Yonge, 'Didactic Fiction', 'Children's Literature of the Last Century' *Macmillan's Magazine*, XX (May–Oct.) 310. This was the second of three articles on children's literature which Yonge wrote for *Macmillan's Magazine* in 1869.

49 Yonge, *The Daisy Chain*, pp. 95, viii, 60, 25. Gillian Avery, *Nineteenth Century Children* (London, 1965) pp. 113–15, argues that Yonge's books opened up for discussion the whole question of a child's implicit obedience to its parents.

50 'Portraits of Celebrities', *Strand Magazine*, II (July–Dec. 1891) 479.

51 Letter to Miss M. E. Christie, 8 Dec. 1896, in Christabel Coleridge, *Charlotte Mary Yonge: Her Life and Letters* (London, 1903) p. 338.

52 Coleridge, *Charlotte Mary Yonge*, p. 311.

53 Catherine Sinclair, *Holiday House* (London, 1885) p. ix.

54 Yonge, 'Class Literature of the Last Thirty Years', 'Children's Literature of the Last Century', *Macmillan's Magazine*, XX.449–52.

55 'Literature of Childhood', *London and Westminster Review*, XXXIII, no. 2, 142–3, 145–6.

56 Key, *The Century of the Child*, pp. 305, 302.

57 Gwen Raverat, *Period Piece* (London, 1952) p. 280.

58 E. M. Forster, *Virginia Woolf* (New York, 1942) p. 12, originally delivered as the Clark Lectures in 1941.
59 Avery, *Nineteenth-Century Children*, p. 17.
60 Yonge, *The Daisy Chain*, pp. 7–8.
61 Quoted in Ellen Moers, *Literary Women* (New York, 1977) pp. 32–3.
62 *The George Eliot Letters*, ed. Gordon S. Haight, v (London and New Haven, Conn., 1956) 444.
63 Gordon S. Haight, *George Eliot* (Oxford, 1968) pp. 344, 420, 385, notes that George Eliot and Lewes were reading *The Daisy Chain* in Florence in 1861. The novelist probably began brooding on *Middlemarch* as early as 1866.
64 Nesbit, *The Wouldbegoods*, p. 221.
65 Zangwill, 'Without Prejudice', *Pall Mall Magazine*, v (Jan.–Apr. 1895) 691.
66 Goldsworthy Lowes Dickinson to Roger Fry, 7 Aug. 1887, Fry Papers, King's College, Cambridge.
67 Phyllis Greenacre, 'The Childhood of the Artist: Libidinal Phase Development and Giftedness' (1957), 'The Relation of the Impostor to the Artist' (1958), 'The Family Romance of the Artist' (1958), 'Woman as Artist' (1960), in *Emotional Growth: Psychoanalytic Studies of the Gifted*, ii (New York, 1971) 498–591 and *passim*.
68 John Demos, 'Developmental Perspectives on the History of Childhood', *Journal of Interdisciplinary History*, ii, no. 2 (Autumn 1971) 327.
69 Virginia Woolf, 'Mr. Bennett and Mrs. Brown', *The Captain's Death Bed* (Hogarth Press, 1950) p. 110.

CHAPTER 3: VIRGINIA WOOLF AND THE IRREVERENT GENERATION

1 Quoted in Laski, *Mrs Ewing, Mrs Molesworth and Mrs Hodgson Burnett*, pp. 37, 29–33.
2 Lewis Carroll, 'An Easter Greeting to Every Child Who Loves "Alice" ', *Alice's Adventures Under Ground* (London, 1886) p. 94.
3 Woolf, *The Voyage Out*, pp. 22–3. The walrus is a late addition to *The Voyage Out*. An earlier typescript draft makes Helen's speech more strident, but omits the walrus: 'I would rather my daughter told lies than believed in God; only they come to the same thing' (*The Voyage Out*, earlier typescript, p. 30, Berg Collection). *See also Melymbrosia*, ed. Louise A. DeSalvo (New York, 1982). This follows Woolf's practice in the process of revision of making her novels funnier, more outrageous but less directly polemical (see Ch. 4, nn. 58 and 60).
4 Humphrey Carpenter, *Secret Gardens: A Study of the Golden Age of Children's Literature* (London, 1985) p. 66. Chapter 3 of Carpenter's book, pp. 50–66, is entitled '*Alice in Wonderland* and the Mockery of God'. The present chapter was in draft form when I read Carpenter's original and

stimulating discussion, which, although I disagree with its interpretation of Carroll, contributes to an understanding of the radical redirection of writing for children in the late nineteenth century.

5 Lewis Carroll, 'My Fairy', *The Complete Works of Lewis Carroll*, p. 700. This was the earliest poem Carroll published. For further discussion of it see p. 166.

6 Carpenter cites this argument about Carroll's insecure faith from Elizabeth Sewell, *The Field of Nonsense* (London, 1952).

7 Raverat, *Period Piece*, pp. 213, 210, 219. Raverat adds: 'Now I could read *The Daisy Chain*, or *The Wide Wide World* [E. Wetherell, pseudonym of Susan Warner], and just take the religion as the queer habits of those sorts of people, exactly as if I were reading a story about Mohammedans or Chinese.'

8 Fry, 'Emotion in Art', *Transformations*, pp. 59–60.

9 Quoted in Kathleen Blake, *Play, Games and Sport: The Literary Works of Lewis Carroll* (Ithaca, NY, 1974) p. 11.

10 Sinclair, *Holiday House*, Preface, pp. vi, v, vii.

11 Alderson, Appendix to Darton, *Children's Books in England*, p. 317, points out that although the Religious Tract Society, founded in the early 1800s, was 'motivated by extra-trade considerations; nevertheless, by its very efficiency in employing printers and devising a distribution network it was behaving in a way that would be followed by commercial publishers later on.'

12 J. A. Sutherland, *Victorian Novelists and Publishers* (London, 1976) p. 75.

13 Darton, *Children's Books in England*, p. 320.

14 Rose, *The Case of Peter Pan*, p. 105.

15 Sutherland, *Victorian Novelists and Publishers*, p. 39, points out that 'novels in volumes were given a new impetus by the price reductions of the 1890s'. In a review of Henry James's new volume of short stories, *The Real Thing*, published in 1893, Zangwill praised the novelist for condensing into one volume material which a hack novelist would have expanded into three, and concludes with a recipe:

MUDIE MEASURE

Ten lines make one page;
Ten pages make one point;
Two points make one chapter;
Five chapters make one episode;
Two episodes make one volume;
Three volumes make one tired.

'Without Prejudice', *Pall Mall Magazine*, i (May–Oct. 1893) 442.

16 Doris Langley Moore, *E. Nesbit* (London, 1967) pp. 15, 206.

17 Hilaire Belloc, *Complete Verse* (London, 1970) p. 53.

18 Quoted in Laski, *Mrs Ewing, Mrs Molesworth and Mrs Hodgson Burnett*, p. 53.

19 E. Nesbit, *The Story of the Treasure Seekers* (London, 1899) p. 18.

20 Quoted in Geoffrey Trease, *Tales Out of School* (London, 1964) p. 23.

21 Avery, *Nineteenth Century Children*, p. 153.
22 Carpenter, *Secret Gardens*, p. 104.
23 Mary Howitt, *The Children's Year* (London, 1847), Preface. Avery, *Nineteenth Century Children*, p. 80, names Howitt as one of the first writers for children who opposed didacticism in children's books.
24 Key, *The Century of the Child*, p. 140: 'The most frequent as well as the most dangerous of the mistakes made in handling children is that people do not remember how they felt themselves at a similar age.'
25 Carpenter's argument for Richard Jefferies' *Bevis* (1882) as a pioneering work underestimates the influence of *Tom Sawyer* on children's books, as does his picture of American children's fiction as a one-line descent from Louisa M. Alcott (*Secret Gardens*, pp. x, 97).
26 Samuel Rutherford Crockett, *The Surprising Adventures of Sir Toady Lion* (London, 1897) pp. 206–7.
27 In a letter to Lytton Strachey urging him to write a novel, Woolf declared: 'Plots don't matter, and as for passion and style and immorality, what more do you want?' (*The Letters of Virginia Woolf*, I.370).
28 Crockett, *Sir Toady Lion*, pp. 4, 354.
29 Mark Twain, *The Adventures of Tom Sawyer* (Hartford, Conn., 1876) p. 38.
30 Lewis Carroll, 'Brother and Sister', *The Complete Works of Lewis Carroll*, pp. 702–3.
31 E. Nesbit, 'My Schooldays', *Girl's Own Paper*, XVIII (Oct. 1896) 29 (the first of twelve articles which appeared monthly in this paper between 1896 and 1897); *The Story of the Treasure Seekers*, p. 258.
32 Eliot, *The Mill on the Floss*, p. 56.
33 Walter de la Mare, *Early One Morning in the Spring: Chapters on Children and on Childhood as is revealed in particular Early Memories and in Early Writings* (London, 1935) p. xviii. See also Edward Blishen (ed.), *The Thorny Paradise: Writers on Writing for Children* (Harmondsworth, 1975), especially C. Walter Hodges, 'Children? What Children?': 'If in every child there is an adult trying to get out, equally in every adult there is a child trying to get back' (p. 57).
34 Glen, *Vision and Disenchantment: Blake's Songs and Wordsworth's Lyrical Ballads*, p. 20.
35 Virginia Woolf, 'How Should One Read a Book?', *The Common Reader II* (London, 1980) p. 259. The draft of this essay is in the same notebook as *To the Lighthouse*. See Virginia Woolf, *To the Lighthouse: the original holograph draft*, ed. Susan Dick (Toronto and Buffalo, 1982) p. 56.
36 C. S. Lewis, 'On Three Ways of Writing for Children', *Of This and Other Worlds*, ed. Walter Hooper (London, 1982) p. 70.
37 Twain, *The Adventures of Tom Sawyer*, p. 32; cf. Brenda, *Froggy's Little Brother*, p. 154, at the death of Benny. The author cries: 'Little children, pray for that Presence – pray that Jesus may come and abide with you, then you can never be very lonely, or very sad!'
38 Zangwill, 'Without Prejudice', *Pall Mall Magazine*, VI (May–Aug. 1895) 476. Cf. Hugh Crago, 'Cultural Categories and the Criticism of Children's Literature', *Signal*, no. 30 (Sep. 1979) 140–50, for a contemporary repudiation of the critical third-person.

39 Twain, *The Adventures of Huckleberry Finn*, p. 345.
40 See, for example, a letter from Mrs L. N. Fairchild to Stevenson (undated) in which the author writes of her contempt of Kipling, and her admiration for Tolstoy, Flaubert and Conrad, which she obviously believes Stevenson to share. She continues: 'I am just through with reading Treasure Island again, having read it aloud alas! to my youngest boy. To be sure the rest all stopped what they were doing to listen. But you can't imagine what it is to unfold John Silver to a new mind! To have conceived him can hardly be much better' (Stevenson Collection, Beinecke Library).
41 Stephen, 'Robert Louis Stevenson', *Studies of a Biographer*, IV.219, 233.
42 S. L. Clemens [Mark Twain] to Robert Louis Stevenson, 3 June 1893, and Charles Webster to Charles Baxter, 17 July 1893, with reference to a letter from Stevenson, Stevenson Collection, Beinecke Library. However, in 'My First Book: *Treasure Island*', *The Idler*, Aug. 1894, pp. 6–10, Stevenson acknowledged debts to *Robinson Crusoe*, *Masterman Ready*, Kingsley's *At Last* and Washington Irving's *Tales of a Traveller*, stating that his indebtedness to Irving embarrassed him.
43 Andrew Lang to W. E. Henley (undated), Stevenson Collection, Beinecke Library.
44 Zangwill, 'Without Prejudice', *Pall Mall Magazine*, VI (May–Aug. 1895) 477.
45 Woolf, *The Voyage Out*, pp. 27, 10, 98, 84, 180, 82, 242, 253, 262.
46 Virginia Woolf, 'The Patron and the Crocus', *The Common Reader I* (Hogarth Press, 1984) p. 207.
47 Woolf, *A Writer's Diary*, pp. 120–1, 97, 135. Cf. T. S. Eliot, 'Tradition and the Individual Talent', *The Sacred Wood* (London, 1920) pp. 52–3: 'Poetry is not a turning loose of emotion, but an escape from emotion; it is not the expression of personality, but an escape from personality.'
48 Zangwill, 'Without Prejudice'. *Pall Mall Magazine* II (May–Oct. 1893) 442.
49 Woolf, *A Writer's Diary*, pp. 188, 216–17, 285. In 'How It Strikes a Contemporary', *The Common Reader I*, p. 238, Woolf wrote: 'To believe that your impressions hold good for others is to be released from the cramp and confinement of personality. It is to be free, as Scott was free, to explore with a vigour which still holds us spellbound the whole world of adventure and romance.'
50 James, *The Principles of Psychology*, 1.254.
51 Cf. Naremore, *The World Without a Self*, p. 13.
52 Théophile Gautier, Preface to *Mademoiselle de Maupin*, in Warner and Hough (eds), *Strangeness and Beauty: An Anthology of Aesthetic Criticism 1840–1910*, I.161.
53 Susan M. Coolidge, *What Katy Did* (Harmondsworth, 1963) p. 33.
54 Twain, *The Adventures of Tom Sawyer*, p. 138.
55 William James, *The Will to Believe* (London, 1897) p. 43.
56 Woolf, 'George Eliot', *The Common Reader I*, p. 171.
57 Woolf, *A Writer's Diary*, pp. 151, 132.
58 Edmund Gosse, *Father and Son* (London, 1929) pp. 154–5.
59 Butler, *The Way of All Flesh*, pp. 190, 128.

60 Quoted in Ann Thwaite, *Edmund Gosse: a literary landscape 1849–1928* (London, 1984) p. 436.
61 Brenda, *Froggy's Little Brother*, p. 64.
62 Woolf, 'Mr. Bennett and Mrs. Brown', *The Captain's Death Bed*, p. 92; *The Letters of Virginia Woolf*, III.242, 254.
63 Yonge, 'Class Literature of the Last Thirty Years', 'Children's Literature of the Last Century', *Macmillan's Magazine*, xx.452.
64 Levin, '*Wonderland* Revisited', in Phillips (ed.), *Aspects of Alice*, p. 180.
65 Woolf, *Roger Fry*, p. 242.
66 Woolf, *A Writer's Diary*, p. 134.
67 Vanessa Bell, *Notes on Virginia's Childhood*, ed. Richard J. Schaubeck, Jr (New York, 1974). In a letter to the author, dated 13 Dec. 1985, Professor Quentin Bell questions the accuracy of Vanessa's story, and recalls a different version recounted by Virginia in a letter to Ethel Smyth, in which the teacher asked her the meaning of Christmas, and she replied that it 'celebrated the crucifixion of our Lord'.
68 Quentin Bell, *Virginia Woolf* (London, 1973) I.59.
69 Vanessa Bell, *Notes on Virginia's Childhood*.
70 Zangwill, 'Without Prejudice', *Pall Mall Magazine*, IV (Sep.–Dec. 1894) 525.
71 Fry to his mother, 9 Oct. 1878, Fry Papers, King's College, Cambridge.
72 Frank Whitehead, A. C. Capey, Wendy Maddren and Alan Wellings, *Children and Their Books* (London, 1977) pp. 227–30.
73 John Rowe Townsend, *Written for Children* (London, 1965) p. 108. Hugh Brogan, *The Life of Arthur Ransome* (London, 1984) p. 46, notes Ransome's admiration for Nesbit – whose children also escape parental control – and names him 'her successor'.
74 Grahame, *The Golden Age*, p. 231. Grahame owed both his title and his narrator's lament – '*Et in Arcadia ego* – I certainly did once inhabit Arcady' (p. 8) – to Stevenson's *Fragment of an Autobiography*: 'That was my golden age: *et ego in Arcadia vixi*' (quoted in Janet Adam Smith (ed.), *Robert Louis Stevenson: Collected Poems*, p. 552).
75 Freud, 'Jokes and their Relation to the Unconscious' (1905), *SE*, VIII.184.
76 Grahame, *The Golden Age*, pp. 59, 27, 7.
77 Woolf, *The Voyage Out*, pp. 10–11, 59.
78 Yonge, *The Daisy Chain*, p. 73.
79 Edward Lear, 'The Seven Parents', *Nonsense Songs and Stories* (London, 1894) pp. 135–6.
80 Woolf, *Roger Fry*, p. 245.
81 John Ruskin, *Modern Painters*, II, part III, section 1 (Orpington, 1888 [1846]) 36.
82 Virginia Woolf, 'The Mark on the Wall', *A Haunted House* (Hogarth Press, 1978) p. 44.
83 Nesbit, 'My Schooldays', *Girl's Own Paper*, XVIII (Aug. 1897) 711.
84 Woolf, 'The Mark on the Wall', *A Haunted House*, p. 43.
85 Woolf, 'How Should One Read a Book?' *The Common Reader I*, p. 258.
86 Woolf, *The Waves*, p. 43.
87 Carroll, 'Lays of Mystery, Imagination, and Humour', no. 1: 'The Palace of Humbug', *The Complete Works of Lewis Carroll*, pp. 725–7.

88 Woolf, *A Writer's Diary*, p. 351.
89 Woolf, 'Lord Macaulay', *The Common Reader I*, p. 95. Her criticism is of Macaulay's essay on Addison. His *History* had in 1897 aroused her enthusiasm (Notebook for 1897, Berg Collection).
90 Letter to Roger Fry, *The Letters of Virginia Woolf*, ii.283.
91 Woolf, *The Voyage Out*, p. 35.
92 Woolf, 'George Eliot', *The Common Reader I*, p. 163.
93 Woolf, *A Writer's Diary*, p. 57.
94 Virginia Woolf, *Orlando* (Hogarth Press, 1928) pp. 275, 240–1.
95 Virginia Woolf, *Night and Day* (Hogarth Press, 1977) p. 30.
96 Quentin Bell, *Virginia Woolf*, i.1–10.
97 Woolf, *Night and Day*, p. 30.
98 Woolf, *Orlando*, p. 188.
99 Fry, 'Fra Bartolommeo', *Transformations*, p. 82. Spalding, *Roger Fry*, p. 252, states that Helen Anrep urged Fry to write this essay for the new volume, which would mean that it post-dated *The Common Reader I* by one year. Virginia Woolf implies (probably mistakenly) in *Roger Fry*, p. 100, that it was an early essay for the *Athenaeum*.
100 Woolf, 'Laetitia Pilkington: Lives of the Obscure', *The Common Reader I*, p. 119.
101 Woolf, *Night and Day*, pp. 33–5. The portrait of Mrs Hilbery was based on Annie Ritchie (*née* Thackeray, sister of Leslie Stephen's first wife), of whom Stephen wrote in the *Mausoleum Book*: 'Partly from a want of proper focusing, partly from her desire to put things picturesquely and consequent reluctance to give the proper detail of commonplace fact, her books were often hard to follow' (*Sir Leslie Stephen's Mausoleum Book*, ed. Alan Bell, p. 16). In a letter written in 1919 to C. P. Sanger, Woolf admitted that 'there are touches of Lady Ritchie in Mrs Hilbery; but in writing one gets more and more away from the reality, and Mrs Hilbery became to me quite different from any one in the flesh' (*The Letters of Virginia Woolf*, ii.406). But in 1921 in a different mood she wrote to Vanessa: 'My only triumph is that the Ritchies are furious with me for Mrs Hilbery' (*The Letters of Virginia Woolf*, ii.474).
102 Raverat, *Period Piece*, p. 125.
103 Tristram Powell, Preface to Julia Margaret Cameron, *Victorian Photographs of Famous Men and Women*, with introductions by Virginia Woolf and Roger Fry (London, 1973) p. 10.
104 Fry, Introduction to Cameron, *Victorian Photographs*, p. 24.
105 Powell, Preface to Cameron, *Victorian Photographs*, p. 10.
106 Fry, Introduction to Cameron, *Victorian Photographs*, p. 24. Fry wrote that 'it was by an exact sense of how to make use of all these accidents that these astonishing results were secured'.
107 Quoted in Helmut Gernsheim, *Julia Margaret Cameron* (London, 1975) p. 70. Virginia Woolf wrote a riotous comedy on her great-aunt's establishment, called *Freshwater* (*see* pp. 158–9, 206).
108 Alvin Langden Coburn, 'The Future of Pictorial Photography 1916', in Beaumont Newhall (ed.), *Photography: Essays and Images* (London, 1980) p. 205.
109 Proust, *Swann's Way*, *The Remembrance of Things Past*, i.426.

110 Powell, Preface to Cameron, *Victorian Photographs*, p. 10.
111 Theodore Meyer Greene, *The Arts and the Art of Criticism* (Princeton, NJ, 1940) p. 296.
112 Alain Robbe-Grillet, *Snapshots and Towards a New Novel*, tr. Barbara Wright (London, 1965) p. 92.
113 Stuart Collingwood, ' "Before Alice" – The Boyhood of Lewis Carroll', *Strand Magazine*, xvi (July–Dec. 1898) 616.
114 Woolf, *The Waves*, p. 132.
115 Woolf, *To the Lighthouse*, pp. 84–5, 87.
116 Woolf, *Orlando*, p. 260.
117 Grahame, 'Miscellanies', quoted in Green, *Kenneth Grahame*, p. 239.
118 Woolf, *Night and Day*, p. 37.
119 Robert Louis Stevenson, 'Victor Hugo's Romances', *Familiar Studies of Men and Books* (London, 1882) p. 8. This essay was significant in Stevenson's career because it was the first to be published by Leslie Stephen in the *Cornhill Magazine*. Stephen wrote an extremely encouraging and judicious letter of criticism to Stevenson when he accepted the essay in 1874, observing: 'I think very highly of the promise shown in your writings and therefore think it worth while to write more fully than I can often do to contributors' (15 May 1874, Stevenson Collection, Beinecke Library). Two years later he urged Stevenson to try his hand at a novel, expressing his longing to find 'a Walter Scott or Dickens or even a Miss Brontë or G. Eliot. Somehow the coming man or woman has not yet been revealed' (7 June 1876, Stevenson Collection, Beinecke Library). That person in the end turned out to be Hardy, not Stevenson, much as Stephen admired *Treasure Island* (see p. 160), a book which came into being partly as a result of his sympathetic urging of the young author, a role which shows Leslie Stephen at his most admirable.
120 Woolf, *A Writer's Diary*, p. 42.
121 Stevenson, 'Victor Hugo's Romances', *Familiar Studies of Men and Books*, p. 11.
122 Woolf, *Orlando*, pp. 137, 30–1.
123 Zangwill, 'Without Prejudice', *Pall Mall Magazine*, x (Sep.–Dec. 1896) 450. Zangwill declared that there could be no such thing as photographic realism: 'For not only is a single day irreproducible unselected in fiction, even a single moment is too complex for the purposes of art. For there is not only going on the main stream of consciousness, but all sorts of sidestreams and subcurrents, and in your most dramatic dialogues with lovers or your enemies, all sorts of irrelevant memories keep flashing through your mind: your tooth may ache a little, and you are perhaps wondering whether your necktie is straight.' Zangwill may have read William James's *The Principles of Psychology* (1890), but it is interesting to see these ideas expressed in a popular journal with wide circulation.
124 Zangwill, 'Without Prejudice', *Pall Mall Magazine*, ix (May–Aug. 1896) 156.
125 Rudyard Kipling, *Stalky & Co.* (London, 1982) pp. 162–3.
126 Farrar, *Eric, Or Little by Little*, p. 81.

127 *The Letters of Virginia Woolf*, I.31.
128 M. A. Titmarsh [W. M. Thackeray], *The Kickleburys on the Rhine* (London, 1851) p. 78.
129 E. Nesbit, *The Railway Children* (London, 1906) p. 58.
130 Quoted in Geoffrey Tillotson, *A View of Victorian Literature* (Oxford, 1978) p. 164.
131 Woolf, *The Voyage Out*, pp. 67, 62–3. Woolf wrote in 'How It Strikes a Contemporary', *The Common Reader I*, p. 237: 'Undoubtedly there is a dullness in great books. There is an unabashed tranquillity in page after page of Wordsworth and Scott and Miss Austen which is sedative to the verge of somnolence.' Richard Dalloway snores after a very small dose of *Persuasion*: ' "Triumph!" Clarissa whispered at the end of a sentence.'
132 Carroll, 'The Hunting of the Snark', *The Complete Works of Lewis Carroll*, pp. 684, 689.
133 Woolf, *The Waves*, p. 42.
134 Nesbit, *The Story of the Treasure Seekers*, p. 11.
135 Nesbit, *The Wouldbegoods*, p. 156.
136 Nesbit, *The Story of the Treasure Seekers*, p. 222.
137 Woolf, *To the Lighthouse*, p. 257. In *Sir Leslie Stephen's Mausoleum Book*, ed. Alan Bell, p. 57, Stephen misquotes one of Shakespeare's sonnets (sonnet 71) which may have given Woolf the idea for the reading of another sonnet (98) in *To the Lighthouse*, pp. 186–7, where it is not, however, misquoted.
138 See p. 308 n38.
139 Woolf, *Orlando*, p. 243.
140 Nesbit, *The Wouldbegoods*, p. 46.
141 Green, *Kenneth Grahame*, pp. 61–2.
142 Joel Chandler Harris, *Uncle Remus and his Legends of the Old Plantation* (London, 1883) p. 187.
143 Carpenter, *Secret Gardens*, provides a facsimile of this letter (plate 16), but does not mention its reference to *Uncle Remus*, or Harris's influence on Grahame, although he does state that A. A. Milne was brought up on the stories (p. 202) and suggests, rather improbably, that Beatrix Potter was also influenced by them (p. 144). Generally, Carpenter underestimates the influence of American writing on children's books of this period.
144 Woolf, 'How It Strikes a Contemporary', *The Common Reader I*, p. 239.
145 L. Frank Baum, *The Wizard of Oz* (London, 1984) pp. 113–14.

CHAPTER 4: DEATH

1 Virginia Woolf, 'A Sketch of the Past' (1939), *Moments of Being*, ed. Jeanne Schulkind (Sussex, 1976) p. 95.
2 Woolf, 'Reminiscences', (begun in 1907), *Moments of Being*, p. 40.
3 Woolf, 'A Sketch of the Past', *Moments of Being*, p. 92.
4 John Carey, *John Donne: Life, Mind and Art* (London, 1981) p. 214.

5 Francis Bacon, *Essays* (London, 1937) pp. 9–11.
6 Woolf, 'Montaigne', *The Common Reader I*, p. 60.
7 Woolf, *A Writer's Diary*, p. 72.
8 'That to Philosophize, is to Learne How to Die', *The Essayes of Michael Lord of Montaigne*, tr. John Florio (London, 1928) I.80, 84.
9 Quoted in Woolf, *Roger Fry*, p. 242.
10 Woolf, 'A Sketch of the Past', *Moments of Being*, p. 95.
11 Gosse, *Father and Son*, pp. 72–3. Philippe Ariès, *Western Attitudes toward Death*, tr. Patricia M. Ranum (London, 1976) p. 38 and *passim*, discusses 'the role played by the dying man himself in the ceremonies surrounding his own death'.
12 Woolf, 'A Sketch of the Past', *Moments of Being*, p. 94.
13 Virginia Woolf, *The Years* (Hogarth Press, 1979) pp. 47–9.
14 Woolf, *A Writer's Diary*, pp. 223–4.
15 Tolstoy, *Childhood*, tr. Edmonds, p. 93. The Hogarth Press published translations of many of Tolstoy's works. Virginia Woolf studied Russian with Koteliansky and collaborated with him on various translations, among them *Tolstoi's Love Letters*, published by the Hogarth Press in 1923 (*The Letters of Virginia Woolf*, II.516, 573). Tolstoy was younger than the child Nikolai when his mother died: indeed the screaming baby seems nearer to a recollection of his own terror at his mother's death-bed than the older boy's meditations do. *See* Henri Troyat, *Tolstoy*, tr. Nancy Amphoux (Harmondsworth, 1970) p. 24.
16 Woolf, *The Voyage Out*, p. 33, and *Melymbrosia*, p. 8, ch. 3. On Monday, 5 May 1919, Woolf wrote in her diary: 'The day mother died twenty something years ago. The smell of wreaths in the hall is always in the first flowers still; without remembering the day I was thinking of her, as I often do – as good a memorial as one could wish' (*The Diary of Virginia Woolf*, I.269). One of the most striking revisions relating to Rachel's dead mother in *The Voyage Out* occurs early in the earlier typescript draft when Clarissa and Helen meditate on the pain of leaving their children behind, provoking an instant reaction from Rachel: 'The tears suddenly rushed to Rachel's eyes. "They might know I've no mother" she said; and left them abruptly for her music' (typescript draft of *The Voyage Out*, Berg Collection). In the final version the moment has been toned down by being put into indirect speech: 'Rachel was indignant with the prosperous matrons, who made her feel outside their world and motherless, and turning back, she left them abruptly' (p. 60).
17 Tolstoy, *Childhood*, tr. Edmonds, pp. 95–6.
18 Tolstoy, *Boyhood*, tr. Edmonds, pp. 166–7.
19 Montaigne, 'That to Philosophize, is to Learne How to Die', *Essayes*, I.91.
20 Ortega y Gasset, *The Modern Theme*, p. 75.
21 Montaigne, 'Of Judging of Others Death', *Essayes*, II,328.
22 Willa Cather, *My Ántonia* (London, 1980) pp. 100–1, 107, 116–17, 115.
23 Woolf, *To the Lighthouse*, p. 199. The brackets and precise form of the sentence narrating Mrs Ramsay's death are not in the original draft in the Berg Collection – another example of Woolf's wish in revision to make her books more startling or outrageous to the reader.
24 'Child's Play', *Good Words*, 6 (1865) 732.

25 Kenneth Grahame (ed.), *The Cambridge Book of Poetry for Children* (Cambridge, 1932) p. xiv. This edition (the first was in 1916), appeared in 1932 just after Grahame's death, with woodcuts by Gwen Raverat.
26 Walter de la Mare, *Early One Morning*, pp. 550, 73–4.
27 Woolf, *Orlando*, pp. 207, 219.
28 Freud, 'Thoughts for the Times on War and Death' (1915), *SE*, xiv.289.
29 Thwaite, *Waiting for the Party: The Life of Frances Hodgson Burnett 1849–1924*, p. 4.
30 See Winnicott, *Playing and Reality*, for a discussion of children's devotion to soft toys.
31 Margaret Gatty, *Aunt Sally's Life* (London, 1865) p. 3 (reprinted from *Aunt Judy's Letters*).
32 Rumer Godden, *The Dolls' House* (London, 1947) p. 9.
33 Penelope Lively, *A Stitch in Time* (London, 1976) p. 65.
34 Mary Louisa Molesworth, *The Cuckoo Clock* (London, 1967), pp. 73–4. Molesworth's earlier book *Tell Me a Story* (1874) contains a more conventional death scene in the tale 'Good-night, Winnie'.
35 Twain, *The Adventures of Tom Sawyer*, pp. 146–7.
36 Twain, *The Adventures of Huckleberry Finn*, pp. 272–4.
37 Frances Hodgson Burnett, *The Secret Garden* (London, 1971) p. 119.
38 Montaigne, 'Of Judging of Others Death', *Essayes*, ii.327.
39 Burnett, *The Secret Garden*, pp. 119, 104.
40 Frances Hodgson Burnett, *In the Closed Room* (London, 1904), p. 82.
41 Burnett, *The Secret Garden*, pp. 120, 9.
42 Gertrude Jekyll, a friend of Violet Dickinson's, is mentioned in Woolf's letter to Dickinson, 12 April [1907], *The Letters of Virginia Woolf*, i.291. Jekyll's wonderful book *Children and Gardens*, based on the garden she had as a child, and giving children instruction on gardening, was published in 1908. The pictures in it may have given Burnett some ideas for *The Secret Garden*, published three years later. *See* pp. 199 and 201. 'The Selfish Giant' is one of the stories in Wilde's collection *The Happy Prince and Other Stories* (London, 1888).
43 Lawrence, *Sons and Lovers*, pp. 173–6.
44 Burnett, *The Secret Garden*, p. 240.
45 Quoted in Thwaite, *Waiting for the Party: The Life of Frances Hodgson Burnett 1849–1924*, pp. 205, 136.
46 Twain, *The Adventures of Huckleberry Finn*, pp. 154–5.
47 Both works were re-issued in the first decade of the twentieth century in a delightful illustrated series called 'Grandmother's Favourites'. *The Fairchild Family* was edited in 1913 by Lady Strachey, mother of Lytton, who explained that she had omitted the passages in which Sherwood indulged in 'a morbid insistence on death in its most terrible forms as a precursor of hell . . . although the religious teaching on which the work is based has been retained in its milder and more tolerant form'. She also omitted the prayers and hymns.
48 Nesbit, *The Story of the Treasure Seekers*, pp. 4, 181–3.
49 Quoted in George H. Pollock, 'On Siblings, Childhood Sibling Loss and Creativity', *Annual of Psychoanalysis*, vi (1978) 480. Woolf was reading De Quincey during the year that she was writing *To the Lighthouse*. The

novel was begun in January 1926 and she wrote to Edward Sackville West in February: 'I've been looking at de Quincey.' Her essay on De Quincey, 'Impassioned Prose', appeared in the *TLS* on 16 September 1926. In July she had mentioned the article to Vita Sackville West and added: 'My God Vita, if you happen to know do wire whats the essential difference between prose and poetry' (*The Letters of Virginia Woolf*, III.240, 276n., 281).

50 Martin Grotjahn, *Beyond Laughter* (New York, 1957) pp. 235–6, observes alongside many penetrating remarks about *Alice in Wonderland*, that 'education by laughter has not yet been tried in earnest. It would encourage irreverence and lead to a spirit of democracy in the next generation to an extent for which we are not yet prepared.'

51 Woolf, *A Writer's Diary*, pp. 297, 122.

52 *The Letters of Virginia Woolf*, I.271.

53 Quoted in Richard N. Coe, *When the Grass Was Taller: Autobiography and the Experience of Childhood* (New Haven, Conn., and London, 1984) p. 208.

54 John Bayley's paper 'Diminishment of Consciousness: A Paradox in the Art of Virginia Woolf', given at the Virginia Woolf centenary conference at Fitzwilliam College in 1982, and now published in Eric Warner (ed.), *Virginia Woolf: A Centenary Tribute* (London, 1984) pp. 69–82, has influenced my thinking about all Virginia Woolf's novels, as well as about the one he discussed, *The Voyage Out*.

55 Freud, 'Thoughts for the Times on War and Death' (1915), *SE*, XIV.291.

56 Flora Thompson, *Lark Rise to Candleford*, p. 274. See my article, 'The Child's Eye and the Adult's Voice: Flora Thompson's *Lark Rise to Candleford*', *Review of English Studies*, n.s. XXXV, no. 137 (Feb. 1984) 61.

57 Harris, *Uncle Remus*, p. 95.

58 Zangwill, 'Without Prejudice', *Pall Mall Magazine*, VIII (Jan.–Apr. 1896) 333.

59 Belloc, *Cautionary Tales for Children*, p. 102.

60 Woolf, 'The Patron and the Crocus', *The Common Reader I*, pp. 208–9.

61 *Mrs Dalloway* deserves discussion in this context but I have omitted it because it does not deal with a child's consciousness as *The Voyage Out*, *Jacob's Room* and *To the Lighthouse*, as well as, of course, *The Waves*, may be said to do – at least in part. The question of death and survival in Woolf's novels has been interestingly discussed in a recent study which appeared after I had written this section; *see* Garrett Stewart's *Death Sentences: Styles of Dying in British Fiction* (Cambridge, Mass., 1984).

62 Gordon, *Virginia Woolf: A Writer's Life*, p. 99.

63 Woolf, *The Voyage Out*, pp. 259, 371, 416, 431, 441, 458. Gordon, *Virginia Woolf: A Writer's Life*, p. 282, points out that Woolf's suicide note to Leonard echoed Rachel's 'no two people have ever been so happy as we have been'. Rachel Vinrace might also be seen as one of the line of children which Carpenter traces from Tom in *The Water-Babies* to *Peter Pan*, who drown but do not die; Virginia Woolf's own death by drowning herself, like that of Michael Llewellyn Davies, might be considered in this context.

64 Virginia Woolf, *Jacob's Room* (Hogarth Press, 1980) p. 5. The opening

pages of the novel show Woolf particularly interested in using words for effects from painting, as in the reiteration of points of colour, particularly red and black. On p. 37 she mentions both Rossetti and Van Gogh. On the first page of the draft (in the Berg Collection) of *To the Lighthouse* Woolf wrote, on separate consecutive lines:

What then is the medium through which we regard human beings? Tears.

65 Henry James, *Roderick Hudson* (New York, 1960 [1875]), Preface, pp. 18–19. Christina Light appears again in *The Princess Casamassima*.
66 Auerbach, *Mimesis*, p. 532.
67 Woolf, *To the Lighthouse*, pp. 12, 157, 94–5, 98–9.
68 Woolf, *To the Lighthouse*, holograph draft, pp. 147, 149 (Berg Collection).
69 Woolf, *To the Lighthouse*, pp. 172–3, 188–9. In Molesworth's *An Enchanted Garden* the fairy caretaker 'knits' stories (p. 42).
70 Woolf, *To the Lighthouse*, holograph draft, pp. 7, 1 (Berg Collection).
71 Woolf, *To the Lighthouse*, p. 169.
72 Woolf, *To the Lighthouse*, holograph draft, p. 5 (Berg Collection).
73 Woolf, *A Writer's Diary*, p. 360.
74 Woolf, 'A Sketch of the Past', *Moments of Being*, pp. 80–1.
75 Woolf, *A Writer's Diary*, pp. 107, 138.
76 E. Nesbit, 'The Book of Beasts', *Strand Magazine*, XVII (Jan.–June 1899) 346–54. This was the first of a group of stories called *The Seven Dragons*, probably inspired by Kenneth Grahame's 'The Reluctant Dragon', which was published in 1899 in *Dream Days*.
77 Woolf, 'The String Quartet', *The Haunted House*, p. 31.
78 *The Letters of Virginia Woolf*, I.129–40. Gordon, *Virginia Woolf: A Writer's Life*, pp. 17–27, emphasises Woolf's closeness to Leslie Stephen and her resemblance to him in character.

CHAPTER 5: THE MEDIUM OF ART

1 In the *Catalogue of Books from the Library of Leonard and Virginia Woolf*, Monk's House Catalogue, *Section VI*: 'Books with notes and reference to text on end pages in the hand of LW,' p. 9, are entries for both *The Adventures of Huckleberry Finn* (1925), and *The Adventures of Tom Sawyer* (1924). *Huckleberry Finn* was well-known in the circles in which the Woolfs moved; Gwen Raverat quotes it in *Period Piece* (see p. 209). Woolf recorded, in her notes on Roger Fry's correspondence, Fry's admiration for Twain when he met him in New York; but she left out of the biography that 'he [Twain] has the courage to speak out for what is honest and humane' (Berg Collection). Neither Woolf's essay 'American Fiction' in the *Saturday Review of Literature* (New York, 1925), nor the piece which she published in *Hearst's International combined with Cosmopolitan* in April 1938 (typescript in the Berg Collection) mentions *Huckleberry Finn*, although the later essay does describe the effect of

James Fenimore Cooper's *The Last of the Mohicans* – a Bastable favourite – on the reader's scalp.

2 See Naremore, *The World Without a Self*, pp. 151–89 for an illuminating discussion of language in *The Waves*.

3 Sully, *Outlines of Psychology*, pp. 255–6, writes: 'It is difficult for us at first to conceive that a child could ever have had a succession of unlike experiences and not instantly referred these to their positions in the time-order as before or after. Yet there is every reason to think that the knowledge of time is a late acquisition. In its developed form the representation of events in their temporal order is attained much later than that of objects in their spatial or local order. The genesis of the former is intimately connected with the process of reproductive imagination, whereas the origin of the latter is connected with that of sense-perception. Children attain very clear ideas about the position of objects in space, the relations of near and far, inside and outside, &c., before they have any definite ideas about the succession and duration of events. Thus a child of three and a-half year, who had a very precise knowledge of the relative situations of the several localities visited in his walks, showed that he had no representations answering to the terms "this week", "last week", and still tended to think of "yesterday" as an undefined past.'

Jean Piaget substantially reiterated Sully's views in 1947 in *The Child's Conception of Time*, tr. A. J. Pomerans (London, 1969) pp. 39–48 *passim*, especially in his reinforcement of the argument that for many children 'age is equated with size, so that age differences can be annulled or reversed by growth in height', and that 'duration is at first confused with the path traversed – thus all children at stage I define age by size'. Piaget makes connections between Einstein's theory of relativity, first published in 1905, and children's primitive capacity to register speed and distance before they can relate them to the passage of time: 'Relativistic time is therefore simply an extension, to the case of very great velocities, and quite particularly to the velocity of light, of a principle that applies at the humblest level in the construction of physical and psychological time, a principle that, as we saw, lies at the root of the time conceptions of very young children' (pp. 275–6).

4 Woolf, 'A Sketch of the Past', *Moments of Being*, pp. 67, 66. The article Woolf wrote on De Quincey, of which a fragment exists in the draft notebook of *To the Lighthouse*, suggests that she was influenced by De Quincey both in that novel and in *The Waves*. She admired his 'Autobiographic Sketches' and observed of his recollections of his own childhood: 'A serene and lovely light lies over the whole of that distant prospect of his childhood. The house, the fields, the garden, even the neighbouring town of Manchester, all seem to exist, but far away on some island separated from us by a veil of blue. On this background, where no detail is accurately rendered, the little group of children and parents, the little island of home and garden, are all distinctly visible, and yet as if they moved and had their being behind a veil. . . . Of facts, we learn scarcely anything. One has been told what De Quincey wished us to know; and even that has been chosen for the sake of some

adventitious quality – as that it fitted in here, or was the right colour to go there – never for its truth.' If this sounds like Lily Briscoe's method of representing Mrs Ramsay and James, Woolf's identification of De Quincey's special mode of writing, which is neither poetry nor prose, leads her to a question which looks forward to her own method in *The Waves*. She spoke of De Quincey's 'echoes and fragments' which 'shifted the values of familiar things. . . . And this he did in prose, which makes us wonder whether, then, it is quite so limited as critics say, and ask further whether the prose writer, the novelist, might not capture fuller and finer truths than are now his aim if he ventured into those shadowy regions where De Quincey has been before him' ('Impassioned Prose', *TLS*, 16 Sep. 1926, pp. 601–2).

5 Woolf, *The Waves*, pp. 5–6.
6 See p. 11. Of the seven notebooks, now in the Berg Collection, containing the drafts of *The Waves*, the first three represent the first draft. The revision of the manuscript begins in the middle of notebook 4 and is dated 13 June 1930. The author sets out a plan which contains the note about the globe (reminiscent of her own idea of 'a picture that was globular' in 'A Sketch of the Past') and suggests nine chapters, of which the final one is called 'Books & sensation' (p. 79). The plan which follows two days later on 15 June 1930 (quoted on p. 11) makes no chapter divisions and stresses sensations, omitting any reference to books.
7 Woolf, *The Waves*, pp. 6–7.
8 Sully, *Outlines of Psychology*, p. 285.
9 Laura Ingalls Wilder, *Little House in the Big Woods*, (Harmondsworth, 1963) pp. 19, 39, 61, 69, 51.
10 Woolf, *A Writer's Diary*, p. 159.
11 William James, 'The Stream of Thought', *The Principles of Psychology*, I.243.
12 Woolf, *The Waves*, pp. 7–8.
13 Sully, *Outlines of Psychology*, p. 266: 'It is only as memory is developed in this distinct and complete form that there arises a clear consciousness of personal identity, that is to say an idea of permanent self continuing to exist in spite of the numberless changes of its daily experience. Since the consciousness or knowledge of self thus presupposes a considerable development of representative power, it is attained much later than a knowledge of external things.'
14 William James, 'The Perception of Time', *The Principles of Psychology*, I.605.
15 Woolf, *The Waves*, p. 15.
16 Bergson, *Time and Free-Will*, pp. 130–9, 162–5, 122, 171. See Guiguet, *Virginia Woolf and her Works*, and Hermione Lee, *The Novels of Virginia Woolf* (London, 1977), for discussion of the possible influence of Bergson on Woolf. She herself in 1932 denied having read his works: 'I may say I have never read Bergson and have only a very amateurish knowledge of Freud and the psychoanalysts; I have made no study of them' (*The Letters of Virginia Woolf*, v.91). Bergson's thought could have reached her through William James's work, and through Roger Fry.
17 William James, *The Principles of Psychology*, I.260.

18 Quoted in Wild, *The Radical Empiricism of William James*, p. 45.
19 William James, *The Principles of Psychology*, I.277.
20 Woolf, 'Modern Fiction', *The Common Reader I*, p. 150.
21 Woolf, *A Writer's Diary*, p. 171.
22 Woolf, 'The Art of Fiction', *The Moment*, pp. 89–93.
23 Quoted in Spalding, *Roger Fry*, p. 212.
24 Robert Louis Stevenson, 'On Style in Literature', *Contemporary Review Advertiser*, Apr. 1885, pp. 549–51, 543.
25 Virginia Woolf, *Freshwater, A Comedy*, ed. Lucio P. Ruotolo (New York and London, 1978) p. 66.
26 *The Letters of Virginia Woolf*, II.571.
27 Pater, 'An Essay on Style', *Appreciations, Works*, v.17.
28 Woolf, *A Writer's Diary*, p. 57.
29 Stephen, 'Robert Louis Stevenson', *Studies of a Biographer*, IV.213.
30 *The Letters of Virginia Woolf*, III.201. When Miss Case taught her Greek Woolf sensed, alongside her admiration and affection for her tutor, great differences in their attitudes to literature, which she defined in a sketch in one of her early notebooks as an inability to read purely for pleasure without searching for meanings, morals, and instructions about how to live (holograph notebook, 30 June–Oct. 1903, Berg Collection). Her irritation over *Mrs Dalloway* stemmed from Miss Case's attempt, which Woolf challenges in the letter quoted in the text, to 'separate expression from thought in an imaginative work'. She wrote in her diary: 'Odd how I'm haunted by that damned criticism of Janet Case's "it's all dressing . . . technique. (Mrs Dalloway). The C.R. [Common Reader] has substance" ' (*The Diary of Virginia Woolf*, III.109). The outburst against Stevenson arises partly from her feeling that he deserves that censure and that she herself does not.
31 Woolf, holograph draft of '*Robinson Crusoe*' (*The Common Reader II*) in notebook containing *To the Lighthouse*, I.83 (Berg Collection).
32 Leslie Stephen to Robert Louis Stevenson, 2 Jan. 1984 (Stevenson Collection, Beinecke Library).
33 Noel Annan, *Leslie Stephen* (London, 1984), p. 109. See Virginia's note on Leslie Stephen in Frederic William Maitland, *The Life and Letters of Leslie Stephen* (London, 1906), p. 474.
34 Woolf, Diary, Xmas 1904 – 27 May 1905, p. 72 (Berg Collection).
35 Woolf, 'Cornwall' diary, 11 Aug. – 14 Sep. [1905] (Berg Collection).
36 Woolf, *A Writer's Diary*, p. 101.
37 Stevenson, 'Random Memories', *Across the Plains*, pp. 189–92.
38 Woolf, *Orlando*, pp. 163, 160, 157–8. Leonard Woolf records, in the fourth volume of his autobiography, T. S. Eliot's request for criticism of *Ash Wednesday*: '[Virginia] told Tom that he had got into the habit of ending lines with a present participle; he had done it with great effect at the beginning of *The Waste Land*, and he was doing it again in this poem. She thought he should beware of it becoming a habit. Tom said that she was quite right and that what she said was very useful.' Leonard Woolf then reproduces the two versions:

The printed version is:

Here are the years that walk between, bearing
Away the fiddles and the flutes, restoring
One who moves in the time between sleep and waking, wearing ...

In the original typescript the three lines read:

Here are the years that walk between, bearing
Away the fiddles and the flutes, restoring
One who walks between season and season, wearing ...

Leonard Woolf, *Autobiography*, IV: *Downhill All the Way: 1919–39* (Hogarth Press, 1967) p. 110. See p. 109 for Woolf's parody of the '-ing' termination in *Orlando*, which was finished before she had read 'Ash Wednesday' in the summer of 1928, but in which she may have had in mind Eliot's predisposition towards the present participle.

39 Saussure's *Course in General Linguistics* was published in 1915.
40 Woolf, *The Waves*, p. 35.
41 Robert Louis Stevenson, 'Child's Play', *Virginibus Puerisque and Other Papers* (London, 1881) p. 226.
42 Woolf, *The Waves*, pp. 21–2, 11, 17–18.
43 Nesbit, *The Wouldbegoods*, p. 3.
44 Woolf, *The Waves*, pp. 25, 11, 15, 50–1, 82. This analysis was written before I read Naremore's parallel account of the children's language in *The World Without a Self*.
45 Woolf, *A Writer's Diary*, p. 165.
46 Woolf, *The Waves*, pp. 69, 84, 95, 49, 26, 28.
47 Gordon, *Virginia Woolf: A Writer's Life*, p. 228, points out that 'the foreign origins of Leonard Woolf crack through Louis's Australian veneer'.
48 Woolf, *The Waves*, pp. 50, 154, 17, 167.
49 Carrol, 'My Fairy', p. 700.
50 Molesworth, *The Cuckoo Clock*, p. 83.
51 Virginia Woolf, *Flush: A Biography*, (London, 1933), pp. 63, 110.
52 Woolf, *Orlando*, p. 212.
53 Woolf, *A Writer's Diary*, p. 315.
54 Virginia Woolf, 'Women and Fiction', *Granite and Rainbow* (London, 1958) pp. 145–6.
55 Rudyard Kipling, 'Gloriana,' *Rewards and Fairies* (London, 1983) p. 38.
56 Woolf, *The Waves*, pp. 198–9, 28. One of the poems in Stevenson's 'Songs of Travel', *The Works of Robert Louis Stevenson* (Edinburgh, 1898) XIV.290, adopts the same image:

> Bright is the ring of words
>   When the right man rings them
> Fair the fall of songs
>   When the singer sings them.

57 Woolf, 'Modern Fiction', *The Common Reader I*, pp. 149–50.
58 Kipling, *Rewards and Fairies*, pp. 175–6.

59 Woolf, 'Reading', *The Captain's Death Bed*, p. 17. Both Woolf and Kipling may have drawn inspiration for Queen Elizabeth from Mandell Creighton's *Queen Elizabeth* (Edinburgh, 1896), which Virginia was given for her birthday on 25 January 1897 (Notebook, 3 Jan. 1897 – 1 Jan. 1898, Berg Collection). Creighton stresses the Queen's theatricality, and recounts the story of her rebuke to Robert Cecil before her death: 'Little man, little man, if your father had lived, you durst not have said so much, but you know I must die, and that makes you presumptuous' (p. 195). Virginia recalled the irony of 'must die' (followed by 'is "must" a word to be addressed to princes?') in *Orlando*, and perhaps in the emphasis on 'must' in *The Waves*. Although the Notebook declares Creighton's book to be as gorgeous as its subject – it is very large with beautiful reproductions – Woolf's evocation of Elizabeth as fantastically jewelled and strutting suggests Kipling's figure as much as Creighton's.

60 Kipling, *Rewards and Fairies*, p. 49.

61 Avrom Fleishman, *The English Historical Novel: Walter Scott to Virginia Woolf* (Baltimore, 1971) pp. 235–6, suggests that Kipling's two books *Puck of Pook's Hill* (1906) and *Rewards and Fairies* (1910) offered a new and fragmented vision of the past which looks forward to *Between the Acts*.

62 Stevenson, 'Random Memories', *Across the Plains*, pp. 189–92.

63 Woolf, *A Writer's Diary*, pp. 142–3. On the title page of the first draft of the novel, dated 2 July 1929, she set out the following alternatives:

> The Moths
> or the life of anybody
> life in general
> or ⎰ *Moments of Being*
> or ⎱ *The Waves*

On the next page she still called the novel 'The Moths or the life of anybody' but followed the title with the four seasons to mark the different stages in the book (holograph draft of *The Waves*, Berg Collection);.

64 Woolf, *The Waves*, p. 12.

65 Woolf, *A Writer's Diary*, p. 145.

66 Woolf, *The Waves*, pp. 202–3.

67 Ortega y Gasset, *The Modern Theme*, p. 144. Woolf repudiated the Utopian direction of some modern fiction in 'Mr. Bennett and Mrs. Brown', *The Captain's Death Bed*, p. 100: 'There are no Mrs. Browns in Utopia. Indeed, I do not think that Mr. Wells, in his passion to make her what she ought to be, would waste a thought upon her as she is'.

68 Søren Kierkegaard, *Either/Or*, quoted in Adi Shmuëli, *Kierkegaard and Consciousness*, tr. Naomi Handelman (Princeton, NJ, 1971) pp. 177–84.

69 Quoted in Spalding, *Roger Fry*, p. 259.

70 Wild, *The Radical Empiricism of William James*, p. 16.

71 William James, *The Principles of Psychology*, I.264–5n.

72 Woolf, 'A Sketch of the Past', *Moments of Being*, p. 7.

73 Woolf, *The Waves*, pp. 27, 103, 183.

74 Woolf, *The Waves*, p. 189.
75 Woolf, *Kew Gardens*, decorated by Vanessa Bell (Hogarth Press, 1927): 'That ponderous woman looked through the pattern of falling words at the flowers standing cool, firm, and upright in the earth, with a curious expression. . . . She stood there letting the words fall over her, swaying the top part of her body slowly backwards and forwards, looking at the flowers.'
76 *The Letters of Virginia Woolf*, II.450.
77 Fry, 'The Artist's Vision', *Vision and Design*, p. 51.
78 Fry, *Cézanne*, pp. 58–9.
79 Woolf, *To the Lighthouse*, pp. 319, 276.
80 John Bayley, 'Diminishment of Consciousness: A Paradox in the Art of Virginia Woolf', in Warner (ed.), *Virginia Woolf: A Centenary Tribute*, p. 81, shows how 'the bildungsroman is disowned and exploited' in *The Voyage Out*.
81 Gordon, *Virginia Woolf: A Writer's Life*, p. 14, relates 'The Window' to Woolf's account in the 'Cornwall' diary (1905) of the Stephen children's visit to Talland House, although they did not in fact look through the window but only through the hedge.
82 Helen Gardner, *The Composition of Four Quartets* (London, 1978), p. 39. I owe this reference to Dr J. C. Rathmell.
83 T. S. Eliot, *Four Quartets* (London, 1944) p. 7.
84 Woolf, *A Writer's Diary*, pp. 142, 136, 163–4.
85 Fry, *Cézanne*, p. 78.
86 Woolf, *Roger Fry*, p. 213.
87 Woolf, *A Writer's Diary*, p. 220.
88 Woolf, *The Waves*, p. 169.
89 Woolf, *Roger Fry*, p. 186.
90 Woolf, *A Writer's Diary*, pp. 69, 208.
91 Woolf, *The Waves*, p. 17; based on an incident described in 'A Sketch of the Past', *Moments of Being*, p. 71, concerning the suicide of Mr Valpy: 'The next thing I remember is being in the garden at night and walking on the path by the apple tree. It seemed to me that the apple tree was connected with the horror of Mr Valpy's suicide. I could not pass it. I stood there looking at the grey-green creases of the bark – it was a moonlight night – in a trance of horror.'
92 Woolf, *The Waves*, pp. 105, 109, 114.
93 Shmuëli, *Kierkegaard and Consciousness*, p. 188.
94 Woolf, *The Waves*, p. 188.
95 Ortega y Gasset, *The Modern Theme*, p. 45.
96 Woolf, *A Writer's Diary*, p. 345.
97 Woolf, *The Waves*, p. 187.
98 Grahame, *Dream Days*, p. 85.
99 Kenneth Grahame, 'The Inner Ear', *Yellow Book*, v (Apr. 1895) 74.
100 Woolf, *The Waves*, p. 28.
101 Woolf, *A Writer's Diary*, p. 162.
102 Woolf, *The Waves*, p. 209.
103 Woolf, Notebook, 3 Jan. 1897–1 Jan. 1898 (Berg Collection).
104 Woolf, *The Waves*, pp. 171, 210–11.

105 Woolf, *A Writer's Diary*, p. 169.

CHAPTER 6: MAKING SPACE FOR A CHILD

1 Woolf, *A Writer's Diary*, p. 156.
2 Woolf, 'Mr. Bennett and Mrs. Brown', *The Captain's Death Bed*, pp. 106, 103, 97.
3 Robert Louis Stevenson, 'A Note on Realism', *Magazine of Art*, Nov. 1883, pp. 28, 26. He commented that the fashion for factual description in novels 'has led to the works which now amaze us on a railway journey'.
4 Quoted in Janet Adam Smith (ed.), *Henry James and Robert Louis Stevenson* (London, 1948) p. 23.
5 Woolf, Diary, Florence, Apr. 1909, p. 86 (Berg Collection).
6 Stevenson, 'A Note on Realism', *Magazine of Art*, Nov. 1883, p. 26.
7 Woolf, *Orlando*, p. 70.
8 Stevenson, 'Child's Play', *Virginibus Puerisque and Other Papers*, pp. 241–2.
9 Woolf, *A Writer's Diary*, p. 126.
10 Nesbit, *The Story of the Treasure Seekers*, p. 196.
11 Stevenson, 'Child's Play', *Virginibus Puerisque and Other Papers*, p. 243.
12 Oscar Wilde, *The Decay of Lying* (London, 1891) p. 51.
13 E. Nesbit, *The Story of the Amulet* (London, 1905) p. 130.
14 Kipling, *Rewards and Fairies*, p. 51.
15 Woolf, *The Waves*, p. 54.
16 E. Nesbit, *Five Children and It* (London, 1902), p. 6.
17 Woolf, *Orlando*, p. 270.
18 Henry Hall, 'A Submarine Boat', *Strand Magazine*, xv (Jan.–June 1898) 705.
19 Flora Thompson, *Lark Rise to Candleford*, p. 305.
20 *The Letters of Virginia Woolf*, I.328, 331. In Nesbit's *The Wouldbegoods*, p. 184, the high-born babe who cries all the time reminds the Bastables of Alice and the baby who turned into a pig.
21 Stevenson, 'Child's Play', *Virginibus Puerisque and Other Papers*, p. 243.
22 J. R. R. Tolkien, *Tree and Leaf* (London, 1964) pp. 43–4.
23 Grahame, 'The Reluctant Dragon', *Dream Days*, p. 160.
24 'Dragons and Dragon-Slayers', by the Author of 'The Hotel of Petit St Jean', *Good Words*, II (1870) 275.
25 Woolf, *To the Lighthouse*, p. 13.
26 Grahame, 'The Reluctant Dragon', *Dream Days*, pp. 178–9, 192.
27 Kenneth Grahame, Introduction to *One Hundred Fables of Aesop*, quoted in Green, *Kenneth Grahame*, p. 7.
28 Woolf, *Orlando*, pp. 245–6.
29 Ralph Waldo Emerson, *Journals*, quoted in Wolfgang Schivelbusch, *The Railway Journey: Trains and Travel in the 19th Century*, tr. Anselm Hollo (Oxford, 1980) p. 57.
30 Stevenson, 'From a Railway Carriage', *A Child's Garden of Verses*, p. 8.

31 Written in August 1837, quoted in Schivelbusch, *The Railway Journey*, p. 59.
32 Nesbit, *The Railway Children*, pp. 50–1, 245–6.
33 Woolf, *The Waves*, pp. 22, 47.
34 Ingelow, 'Nineteen Hundred and Seventy-Two', *Good Words for the Young*, IV.64.
35 Zangwill, 'Without Prejudice', *Pall Mall Magazine*, VII (Sep.–Dec. 1895) 154.
36 Grahame, *The Golden Age*, pp. 173–83.
37 Woolf, *A Writer's Diary*, p. 123.
38 Woolf, *The Voyage Out*, p. 142.
39 Woolf, 'A Sketch of the Past', *Moments of Being*, p. 71.
40 Woolf, *The Waves*, p. 8.
41 Burnett, *The Secret Garden*, p. 202.
42 Marenholtz-Bülow, *Child and Child-Nature*, p. 32.
43 Stevenson, 'My Kingdom', *A Child's Garden of Verses*, p. 85.
44 Grahame, *Dream Days*, p. 49.
45 Kipling, *Rewards and Fairies*, p. 31.
46 Burnett, *The Secret Garden*, p. 82.
47 Philippa Pearce, *Tom's Midnight Garden* (London, 1958) p. 81. *See* also Lesley Aers' article 'The Treatment of Time in Four Children's Books', *Children's Literature in Education*, no. 2 (July 1970) 69–81.
48 Molesworth, *The Cuckoo Clock*, p. 165.
49 Burnett, *The Secret Garden*, p. 202.
50 Nesbit, *The Story of the Amulet*, pp. 155, 246, 304.
51 George Orwell, *The Road to Wigan Pier* (Harmondsworth, 1962) pp. 108–9.
52 Moore, *E. Nesbit* (London, 1967) pp. 15, 206.
53 Stevenson, 'Travel', *A Child's Garden of Verses*, pp. 18–19. In the notebook in which Stevenson drafted many of the poems for *A Child's Garden of Verses*, 'Travel' begins:

> O I should like to rise and go
> And wander on my feet
> Where all the golden apples grow
> And things are nice to eat.

It is only eight lines in all. In the first version of Stevenson's collection, which was set up for press as *Penny Whistles* (1883) but never published, the poem was still only eight lines, and it was not until 1885, when the poems appeared as *A Child's Garden of Verses*, that the forty-six-line version, from which the quotation in the text is taken, appeared. See George L. McKay, *A Stevenson Library: Catalogue of Writings by and about R. L. Stevenson formed by E. J. Beinecke* (New Haven, Conn., 1951–69) p. 2030. The first four lines in the published version read:

> I should like to rise and go
> Where the golden apples grow;
> Where below another sky
> Parrot islands anchored lie.

It is interesting in view of Yeats's echo of the first line in 'The Lake Isle of Innisfree' that Stevenson wrote to the poet in 1894 expressing his admiration for that poem and received this reply:

> I need hardly tell you that your praise of 'The Lake Isle of Innisfree' has given me great pleasure. After all it is the liking or disliking of one's fellow craftsmen, especially of those who have attained the perfect expression one does but grope for, which urges one to to [sic] work – else were it best to dream our dreams in silence.
>
> My grandfather a very passionate old retired sailor – quite the reverse of literary – read 'Treasure Island' upon his death-bed with infinite satisfaction. It is the only work I ever heard of him reading. I wonder at this voice, which while delighting studious & cloistered spirits, can hush with admiration such as he, much as I wonder at that voice which stilled the waves of old.

The notebook containing the draft poems, and Yeats's letter, dated 14 October 1894, are both in the Stevenson Collection, Beinecke Library. Stevenson's letter to Yeats is published in *The Letters of Robert Louis Stevenson to his Family and Friends*, ed. Sidney Colvin (New York, 1899) II.388. If Yeats's letter seems to a modern reader both bardic and extravagant, it nevertheless suggests the high esteem in which Stevenson's work was held in the 1890s.

54 Nesbit, *The Story of the Amulet*, pp. 176, 195–6.
55 E. Nesbit, *Harding's Luck* (London, 1909) pp. 1, 221–2.
56 Woolf, *The Voyage Out*, pp. 45–6.
57 Woolf, *Melymbrosia*, ed. Louise A. DeSalvo, pp. xxxvi–xxxix.
58 Mitchell A. Leaska, 'Virginia Woolf's *The Voyage Out*: Character Deduction and the Function of Ambiguity', *Virginia Woolf Quarterly*, I (Winter 1973) 36, notes Woolf's tendency when revising her novels to make them less explicit.
59 Nesbit, *Harding's Luck*, pp. 280–1.
60 Woolf, *Freshwater*, p. 14. This interchange comes in the later version of the play, which was performed in 1935, and illustrates Woolf's practice of making her jokes more outrageous in revision. Another example in *Freshwater* is in a discussion of Craig's house in Gordon Square. When he announces that it is in WC1, Watts exclaims: 'Young man, have a care, have a care. Ladies are present.' ('WC' was the shorthand the Stephen family used for the lavatory). But on a different level of discourse it is noticeable how late in the revising-process Woolf decided to make Clarissa deliver her wonderful howler about her passion for the *Antigone* and how many Clytemnestras she had known (p. 46). In the typescript draft of *The Voyage Out* now in the Berg Collection, the play is still the *Agamemnon* (p. 63). *See* Ch. 3, n. 3, for a further example of this tendency in revising manuscripts.

The interest of young children in the questions discussed in this section is observed in Gareth Matthews, *Philosophy and the Young Child* (Cambridge, Mass., 1980) p. 23.

61 Wild, *The Radical Empiricism of William James*, p. 172, quotes James's statement that the present is 'an altogether ideal abstraction . . . that is never realised in the world of sense where we live and act'.

62 Gardner, *The Annotated Alice*, pp. 264, 276: 'Students of *Finnegans Wake* do not have to be reminded that Humpty Dumpty is one of that book's basic symbols: the great cosmic egg whose fall, like the drunken fall of Finnegan, suggests the fall of Lucifer and the fall of man.'

63 Virginia Woolf, 'Freudian Fiction', *TLS*, 25 Mar. 1920, p. 199.

64 Wilhelm Jensen, *Runic Rocks: A North-Sea Idyll*, tr. Marianne E. Suckling (London, 1895) preface (by G. Fiedler) pp. vii, viii, xiv. The island referred to in this story is probably Juist. Jensen studied in Munich. Other works referred to in this discussion are *Gradiva*, in *Delusion and Dream and Gradiva*, tr. Helen M. Downey (London, 1917); *Fair Isle: A Tale in Verse*, tr. from the German by a Shetlander (Kirkwall, 1881); and Freud, 'Delusions and Dreams in Jensen's *Gradiva*' (1907 [1906]), *SE*, IX.

65 Key, *The Century of the Child*, pp. 29–30.

66 Allon White, ' "L'éclatement du sujet": The Theoretical Work of Julia Kristeva' (Centre for Contemporary Cultural Studies, University of Birmingham, SP.49, 1977) p. 5.

67 Freud, *Civilization and Its Discontents* (1930 [1929]), *SE*, XXI.70.

68 Woolf, *A Writer's Diary*, p. 79, records of the composition of *Mrs Dalloway*: 'I remember the night at Rodmell when I decided to give it up, because I found Clarissa in some way tinselly. Then I invented her memories'.

69 Raverat, *Period Piece*, p. 216, quoting from *The Adventures of Huckleberry Finn*, p. 346.

70 Twain, *The Adventures of Huckleberry Finn*, pp. 135–41.

71 Trotter, *Instincts of the Herd*, pp. 40–1.

72 Twain, *The Adventures of Huckleberry Finn*, pp. 320–1.

73 Henry James, *What Maisie Knew*, pp. 230, 32. In 'The Art of Fiction' James queried Stevenson's view of what constituted a 'story' in terms which suggest the fictional ground of *What Maisie Knew*: 'I call *Treasure Island* delightful because it appears to me to have succeeded wonderfully in what it attempts; and I venture to bestow no epithet upon *Chérie* [M. Edmond de Goncourt], which strikes me as having failed in what it attempts – that is, in tracing the development of the moral consciousness of a child. But one of these productions strikes me as exactly as much of a novel as the other, and as having a "story" quite as much. The moral consciousness of a child is as much a part of life as the islands of the Spanish Main. . . . For myself . . . the picture of the child's experience has the advantage that I can at successive steps . . . say Yes or No, as it may be, to what the artist puts before me. I have been a child, but I have never been on a quest for buried treasure, and it is a simple accident that with M. de Goncourt I should have for the most part to say No. With George Eliot, when she painted that country, I always said Yes.' When Stevenson answered this essay in 'A Humble Remonstrance', *Longman's Magazine*, Dec. 1884, he protested that 'there never was a child (unless Master James) but has hunted gold, and been a pirate, and a military commander, and a bandit of the mountains'. Both essays are

reproduced in Janet Adam Smith (ed.), *Henry James and Robert Louis Stevenson*, pp. 80–1, 94.

74 Russell Hoban, *The Mouse and His Child* (Harmondsworth, 1976) p. 17. The theme of both physical and emotional space is central to Hoban's book:

> 'But what *is* a territory?' asked the mouse child again.
> 'A territory is your place,' said the drummer boy. 'It's where everything smells right. . . .'
> The father walked in silence as a wave of shame swept over him. *What chance has anybody got without a territory!* he repeated to himself and knew the little shrew was right. What chance had they indeed! (pp. 52–3).

75 Payne, *The Child in Human Progress*, p. 3.
76 Quoted in Green, *Kenneth Grahame*, p. 35.
77 Frances Hodgson Burnett, *A Little Princess* (Harmondsworth, 1961) p. 109. The story was originally published, with another tale, as *Sara Crewe*, in *Sara Crewe and Editha's Burglar* (London, 1888). The passage quoted here is in the original version, (p. 39), but Ermengarde there proves incapable of entering the story and Sara is contemptuous of her. Burnett made Sara more sympathetic in the later version, perhaps because of the popularity of the 1902 dramatised version, entitled *A Little Princess*.
78 Woolf, *The Waves*, p. 27.
79 Burnett, *A Little Princess*, p. 47.
80 Virginia Woolf, *A Room of One's Own* (Hogarth Press, 1929) p. 11.
81 Fry, 'An Essay in Aesthetics', *Vision and Design*, p. 23.
82 Ted Hughes, 'Myth and Education', in G. Fox (ed.), *Writers, Critics and Children: Articles from Children's Literature in Education* (London, 1976) pp. 80, 87, 82.
83 Flora Thompson, *Lark Rise to Candleford*, p. 273. See Dusinberre, 'The Child's Eye and the Adult's Voice: Flora Thompson's *Lark Rise to Candleford*', *Review of English Studies*, n.s. xxv.65.
84 Henry James, 'The Art of Fiction', Janet Adam Smith (ed.), *Henry James and Robert Louis Stevenson*, p. 76.
85 Freud, 'Creative Writers and Day-Dreaming', (1908 [1907]), *SE*, ix.143–4.
86 Nesbit, *The Wouldbegoods*, p. 68.
87 Sully, *Studies of Childhood*, pp. 53–4.
88 Nesbit, *The Phoenix and the Carpet*, p. 212.
89 Sinclair, *Holiday House*, pp. 39–40, 45–7; Eliot, *The Mill on the Floss*, pp. 54–5.
90 Stevenson, *A Child's Garden of Verses*, p. 136. Janet Adam Smith (ed.), *Robert Louis Stevenson: Collected Poems*, p. 549, notes that 'Stevenson began writing these verses at Braemar in 1881, when his mother showed him Kate Greenaway's *Birthday Book for Children* with text by Mrs Sale Barker.'

91 Gaston Bachelard, *The Poetics of Reverie*, tr. David Russell (New York, 1969) p. 122.
92 Gosse, *Father and Son*, p. 47.
93 Thwaite, *Edmund Gosse*, p. 34, points out that the time in question only lasted for six weeks.
94 Quoted in Bachelard, *The Poetics of Reverie*, p. 129.
95 Alison Uttley, *A Traveller in Time* (Harmondsworth, 1977) Foreword and pp. 131, 241.
96 Kenneth Grahame, 'The Iniquity of Oblivion', *Yellow Book*, I (1894) 194–5.
97 Uttley, *A Traveller in Time*, p. 286.
98 Thompson, *Lark Rise to Candleford*, p. 85.
99 Thomas Mann, *Tales of Jacob*, vol. I of *Joseph and His Brethren*, tr. H. T. Lowe-Porter (London, 1934–45) p. 25: 'What concerns us here is not calculable time. Rather it is time's abrogation and dissolution in the alternation of tradition and prophecy, which lends to the phrase "once upon a time" its double sense of past and future and therewith its burden of potential present. Here the idea of reincarnation has its roots. . . . It was not until three thousand years later that men began disputing as to whether the Eucharist "was" or only "signified" the body of the Sacrifice; but even such highly supererogatory discussions as these cannot alter the fact that the essence of the mystery is and remains the timeless present.'
100 Wilder, *Little House in the Big Woods*, p. 137.
101 Grahame, 'The Roman Road', *The Golden Age*, p. 170 (first published in the *Yellow Book*, II).
102 Nesbit, *The Wouldbegoods*, pp. 244, 330.
103 Woolf, *The Waves*, p. 153. The great South Sea Island traveller, apart from Nesbit's children, was Stevenson, who ended his days in Samoa.
104 Bachelard, *The Poetics of Reverie*, p. 123.
105 Stevenson, 'The Lantern-Bearers', *Across the Plains*, pp. 219, 220. James wrote to Stevenson on 15 April 1892 that he liked that essay (Janet Adam Smith (ed.), *Henry James and Robert Louis Stevenson*, p. 195).
106 Woolf, *Orlando*, p. 292.

CHAPTER 7: THE LITERARY AND THE LITERAL

1 Carroll, 'Poeta Fit, non Nascitur', *The Complete Works of Lewis Carroll*, p. 791.
2 Carroll, 'Upon the Lonely Moor', *The Complete Works of Lewis Carroll*, pp. 727–30.
3 Raverat, *Period Piece*, p. 132.
4 Woolf, *Roger Fry*, p. 190.
5 Bergson, *Time and Free-Will*, p. 162.
6 Levin, '*Wonderland* Revisited', in Phillips (ed.), *Aspects of Alice*, p. 192.
7 Brian Alderson pointed out to the author that the 'rock of ages' was 'an actual rock in Burrington Combe (Somerset) where the "poet" [A. M. Toplady] sheltered and became inspired to metaphor!'

8 Woolf, *To the Lighthouse*, p. 13.
9 Annan, *Leslie Stephen*, pp. 126–9. The biographer rightly draws attention, as does Lyndall Gordon in her recent life of the novelist, to the close likenesses between Stephen and Virginia, which are particularly apparent in Stephen's comments on books and writing. His letters to his wife (now in the Berg Collection) show an affectionate, open-hearted nature which takes pleasure in recounting his children's doings even when they were very small. Annan gives a harsh picture of Stephen's relation to Laura, child of his marriage to Minny Thackeray, who proved to be mentally deficient. It is not true that he felt no affection for the child. (Annan, *Leslie Stephen*, p. 122). His letters are full of his feeling for her, which he wishes were less in that it would make her situation less agonising for him. When Virginia Woolf went through her father's letters in order to help Maitland with his biography she wrote that 'the history of Laura is really the most tragic thing in his life I think; and one that one can hardly describe in the life. The letters are full of her' (*The Letters of Virginia Woolf*, 1.164). Woolf's own feeling for her father after his death became so intense and was so stimulated by her experience of reading his letters that she suffered in the summer of 1904 another severe mental breakdown. She wrote to Violet Dickinson in March of that year: 'I know that I wasn't really wrong; it had to be – but I cant bear to think of his loneliness, and that I might have helped, and didn't. If he had only lived I could have made up. I think he just knew how much I cared, and the happy time was just beginning – and now it is all over. That is what seems so cruel. If I could only tell him once – but its no use writing it. But we have been very happy together' (*The Letters of Virginia Woolf*, 1.136).
10 Letter to Robert Louis Stevenson, 24 Feb. 1876 (Stevenson Collection, Beinecke Library).
11 Stephen, 'In Praise of Walking', *Studies of a Biographer*, III.280, 285, 257, 259.
12 Woolf, *To the Lighthouse*, pp. 237–8.
13 Arnold Kettle, 'The Precursors of Defoe: Puritanism and the Rise of the Novel', in B. S. Benedikz (ed.), *On the Novel* (London, 1971) pp. 210–11.
14 Rosemary Freeman, *English Emblem Books* (London, 1948), p. 2.
15 Margery Fisher, *Intent Upon Reading* (Leicester, 1961) p. 16.
16 Quoted in Green, *Kenneth Grahame*, p. 226.
17 Woolf, 'A Sketch of the Past', *Moments of Being*, p. 110.
18 Woolf, Diary, 'An Excursion to Greece', beginning 14 Sep. [1906], p. 46 (Berg Collection).
19 Woolf, *A Writer's Diary*, p. 100.
20 Cather, *My Ántonia*, Introduction.
21 Willa Cather, Journal, 12 Apr. 1896, in *The Kingdom of Art: Willa Cather's First Principles and Critical Statements 1893–1962*, ed. Bernice Slote (Lincoln, Nebr., 1966) p. 337: 'So many boys' books are written for little Lord Fauntleroys who are supposed to spend their youth dreaming in their nurseries. . . . The whole category of child literature is largely a farce anyway. . . . If a boy will read Bunyan and Goldsmith in his youth, say when he is ten years old, it signifies much; . . . If he reads Louisa

Alcott or some kindred spirit it signifies nothing. Who are these writers of child literature anyway? Generally people who have ingloriously failed in every other line of authorship.' In the *Courier*, 2 Nov. 1895, *The Kingdom of Art*, ed. Slote, p. 232, Cather wrote of Stevenson: 'We owe him so much, that great master of pure romance. . . . Romance is the highest form of fiction and it will never desert us.' Woolf, *Orlando*, p. 128, rewrites Jane Austen's 'Let other pens dwell on guilt and misery.'

22 David Daiches, *Willa Cather* (Ithaca, NY, 1951) pp. 24, 44.
23 Willa Cather, 'On *Shadows on the Rock*' and 'On *Death Comes to the Archbishop*', *On Writing* (New York, 1968) pp. 16, 79.
24 Daiches, *Willa Cather*, p. 139.
25 Cather, 'On *Death Comes to the Archbishop*', *On Writing*, p. 10.
26 Quoted in Daiches, *Willa Cather*, p. 16.
27 Rosa Ann Moore: 'The *Little House* Books: "Rose Colored Classics"', *Children's Literature*, v (1976) 12; 'Laura Ingalls Wilder's Orange Notebooks and the Art of the *Little House* Books', *Children's Literature*, iv (1975) 118.
28 Cather, 'My First Novels', *On Writing*, p. 96.
29 Isabelle Jan, *On Children's Literature*, tr. from the French, ed. Catherine Storr (London, 1973) p. 119.
30 Laura Ingalls Wilder, *The First Four Years* (Guildford, 1973), p. 87.
31 Edgar Allan Poe, *Marginalia*, in Daniel Defoe, *Robinson Crusoe*, ed. Michael Shinagel (New York, 1975) p. 291.
32 Defoe, *Robinson Crusoe*, p. 259.
33 Cather, Preface to Defoe's *The Fortunate Mistress*, *On Writing*, p. 76.
34 Defoe, *Robinson Crusoe*, p. 261.
35 Charles Lamb, 'On Defoe's Novels', in Defoe, *Robinson Crusoe*, p. 290.
36 Charlotte Brontë, *Jane Eyre* (Oxford, 1969), p. 20.
37 Raverat, *Period Piece*, p. 114.
38 Woolf, 'Defoe', *The Common Reader* I, p. 86.
39 Wilde, *The Decay of Lying*, pp. 43–4.
40 Pater, 'Wordsworth', in *Appreciations*, *Works*, v.45, 48–50.
41 Alice Meynell, *The Spirit of the Place and Other Essays* (London, 1898) p. 3.
42 Grahame, 'The Roman Road', *The Golden Age*, p. 166.
43 Thomas Hardy, *The Return of the Native* (London, 1972) p. 8.
44 Brontë, *Jane Eyre*, p. 101.
45 Cather, *My Ántonia*, pp. 7–8.
46 Woolf, 'American Fiction', *The Moment*, p. 104.
47 Wilder, *Little House in the Big Woods*, p. 7.
48 Cather, *My Ántonia*, p. 15.
49 Laura Ingalls Wilder, *Little House on the Prairie* (Harmondsworth, 1964) pp. 23–4.
50 Cather, *O Pioneers!*, (London, 1913) pp. 15, 19.
51 Cather, 'My First Novels', *On Writing*, pp. 94, 92.
52 Cather, 'Sarah Orne Jewett', *Not under Forty* (London, 1936) pp. 101–2, 88.
53 Cather, *My Ántonia*, Introduction.
54 Cather, 'On *Death Comes to the Archbishop*', *On Writing*, p. 12.

55 Cather, *My Ántonia*, pp. 245, 262–4.
56 Cather, 'A Wagner Matinée', quoted in Daiches, *Willa Cather*, p. 148.
57 Cather, *O Pioneers!*, p. 20.
58 *The Letters of Virginia Woolf*, IV.32.
59 John Steinbeck, *The Grapes of Wrath* (New York, 1939) p. 120.
60 Laura Ingalls Wilder, *The Long Winter* (Harmondsworth, 1968) p. 181.
61 Daiches, *Willa Cather*, pp. 3–4.
62 Cather, *My Ántonia*, pp. 89, 76; Flora Thompson, *Lark Rise to Candleford*, pp. 92–3.
63 Cather, *O Pioneers!*, pp. 14, 65.
64 Cather, Journal, 5 Apr. 1896, *The Kingdom of Art*, ed. Slote, p. 413.
65 Defoe, *Robinson Crusoe*, p. 6.
66 Cather, *O Pioneers!*, p. 48.
67 Flora Thompson, *Lark Rise to Candleford*, p. 88.
68 Cather, *O Pioneers!*, p. 118.
69 Wilder, *Little House on the Prairie*, pp. 216–17.
70 Wilder, *By the Shores of Silver Lake* (Harmondsworth, 1967) pp. 97, 126.
71 Wilder, *On the Banks of Plum Creek* (Harmondsworth, 1965) p. 171.
72 Cather, *My Ántonia*, p. 139.
73 Wilder, *On the Banks of Plum Creek*, p. 87.
74 Cather, 'Joseph and His Brethren', *Not under Forty*, pp. 112, 115.
75 Cather, *My Ántonia*, p. 13.
76 Flora Thompson, *Lark Rise to Candleford*, p. 344.
77 Cather, *My Ántonia*, pp. 100, 102, 49–50, 39, 42.
78 Flora Thompson, *Lark Rise to Candleford*, p. 275.
79 Cather, *My Ántonia*, pp. 79, 61.
80 William Mayne, *The Jersey Shore* (Harmondsworth, 1976) pp. 108, 76, 77–8, 54, 123, 140–1, 142. Peter Hunt, 'The Mayne Game: An Experiment in Response', *Signal*, no. 28 (Jan 1979) 20, describes readers' criticisms of the book's sexlessness, which recall Strachey's complaint about *To the Lighthouse*.
81 Kipling, 'Cold Iron', *Rewards and Fairies*, p. 23. Brian Alderson draws my attention to the fact that Mayne agreed to rewrite the ending of *The Jersey Shore* for the American edition, leaving out 'the "slavery" implications'.
82 Thomas Mann, *Tales of Jacob: Joseph and His Brethren*, I.179.
83 Bunyan, *The Pilgrim's Progress*, pp. 188–9, 94–6; E. P. Thompson, *The Making of the English Working Class* (London, 1963) p. 53. Michael Wheeler, *The Art of Allusion in the Victorian Novel* (London, 1979) pp. 36–43, analyses Charlotte Brontë's use of *The Pilgrim's Progress* as a parallel text in *Jane Eyre*.
84 Wilder, *Little House in the Big Woods*, p. 112.
85 Defoe, *Robinson Crusoe*, p. 188.
86 Brontë, *Jane Eyre*, p. 64.
87 Cather, *My Ántonia*, p. 169.
88 Wilder, *Little House on the Prairie*, p. 158.
89 Wilder, *Little House in the Big Woods*, p. 18.
90 Wilder, *Little Town on the Prairie* (Harmondsworth, 1969) p. 60.
91 Steinbeck, *The Grapes of Wrath*, p. 6.
92 Cather, *O Pioneers!*, p. 118.

93 Wilder, *On the Banks of Plum Creek*, p. 143.
94 Frances Hodgson Burnett, *Two Little Pilgrims' Progress: A Story of the City Beautiful* (London, 1895) pp. 70, 28, 91, 61, 215.
95 E. P. Thompson, *The Making of the English Working Class*, p. 194.
96 Cather, *My Ántonia*, p. 110.
97 Wilder, *Little House in the Big Woods*, pp. 131–2.
98 Wilder, *The Long Winter*, p. 10.
99 Moore, 'Laura Ingalls Wilder's Orange Notebooks and the Art of the *Little House* Books', *Children's Literature*, IV.115–16, shows that Wilder's revisions of her original drafts had the effect of making Ma more refined and less robust mentally than she was in the notebooks: 'Often her responses are so altered that she appears almost suspiciously pious and refined, when one suspects that a good deal of gusto, zest for life, and a large degree of tolerance were more likely tools for survival in her kind of life.' But, rather than being an error of aesthetic judgement, Wilder's revisions, by insisting on Ma's distance from life at its most basic level of subsistence, highlight her importance as the guardian of civilised living.
100 Cather, *My Ántonia*, pp. 27, 66, 173.
101 Wilder, *The Long Winter*, pp. 76–7.
102 Brontë, *Jane Eyre*, p. 84.
103 Moore, 'The *Little House* Books: "Rose Colored Classics"', *Children's Literature*, V (1976) 12, notes that Rose Wilder advised her mother against the children's book form, on the grounds that it would not sell.
104 Mann, *Tales of Jacob: Joseph and His Brethren*, I.117.
105 Cather, *O Pioneers!*, p. 3.
106 Mann, *Tales of Jacob: Joseph and His Brethren*, I.112–13.
107 Cather, 'Katherine Mansfield', *Not under Forty*, p. 154.
108 Cather, *O Pioneers!*, p. 17.
109 Quoted in Daiches, *Willa Cather*, p. 36.
110 MacCabe, *James Joyce and the Revolution of the Word*, p. 61.
111 Cather, *My Ántonia*, pp. 137, 371–2.
112 Raverat, *Period Piece*, Preface: 'This is a circular book. It does not begin at the beginning and go on to the end; it is all going on at the same time, sticking out like the spokes of a wheel from the hub, which is me.' Jacques Raverat's letter to Woolf is discussed in Quentin Bell, *Virginia Woolf*, II.106–7.
113 Cather, *My Ántonia*, pp. 118–19.
114 Emily Brontë, *Wuthering Heights* (Oxford, 1931) p. 385.
115 Wilder, *By the Shores of Silver Lake*, pp. 49, 206.
116 Wilder, *Little House on the Prairie*, pp. 7, 220.
117 Defoe, *Robinson Crusoe*, pp. 227–30; Wilder, *Little House in the Big Woods*, pp. 66–9.
118 Wilder, *Little House on the Prairie*, p. 188; *On the Banks of Plum Creek*, p. 25.
119 Wilder, *The Long Winter*, pp. 15–17, 59.
120 Wilder, *Little House on the Prairie*, pp. 68, 211.
121 Wilder, *Little House on the Prairie*, pp. 24, 212.
122 Wilder, *By the Shores of Silver Lake*, pp. 14–16.
123 Wilder, *Little House on the Prairie*, pp. 216, 174, 8, 207, 157, 58.

124 Cather, *My Ántonia*, p. 62.
125 Wilder, *Little House on the Prairie*, p. 18.
126 Wilder, *On the Banks of Plum Creek*, pp. 59–60.
127 Cather, *My Ántonia*, pp. 176, 84, 120.
128 Wilder, *Little House on the Prairie*, p. 117.
129 Cather, *My Ántonia*, p. 193.
130 Wilder, *Little House on the Prairie*, pp. 200, 134.
131 Wilder, *By the Shores of Silver Lake*, p. 212.
132 Cather, *My Ántonia*, p. 87.
133 Wilder, *Little Town on the Prairie*, p. 164.
134 Wilder, *Little House on the Prairie*, pp. 40, 51–2.
135 Donald Zochert, *Laura: The Life of Laura Ingalls Wilder* (Chicago, 1976) p. 235.
136 Paul Cézanne, *Letters*, ed. John Rewald (Oxford, 1976) p. 302.
137 Fry, *Reflections on British Painting*, pp. 116–17.
138 Cather, Journal, 1 Mar 1896, *The Kingdom of Art*, ed. Slote, p. 417.
139 Wilder, *By the Shores of Silver Lake*, pp. 22,47.
140 Roger Fry, 'On the Laws of Phenomenology and their Application to Greek Painting' (unpublished Fellowship dissertation) and 'Can't You See It?' (1928), both in Fry Papers, King's College, Cambridge.
141 Wilder, *Little Town on the Prairie*, p. 85.
142 *The Diary of Virginia Woolf*, I.140. Curiously enough, there are seven apples in this picture, which is on loan to the Fitzwilliam Museum, Cambridge.
143 Wilder, *Little House on the Prairie*, pp. 210, 98, 167.
144 Wilder, *Little Town on the Prairie*, p. 85.
145 Wilder, *Little House in the Big Woods*, p. 111.
146 Woolf, *A Writer's Diary*, p. 236.
147 Woolf, *A Writer's Diary*, p. 311; *Roger Fry*, p. 209: ' "Poetisation", making things out more interesting than they really are, that imposition of the writer's personality for which there is no exact critical term, was another sin that he discovered in the work of another friend.'
148 Woolf, *A Writer's Diary*, p. 168.
149 Cather, 'The Novel Demeublé,' *On Writing*, pp. 39–40.
150 Woolf, *A Writer's Diary*, pp. 327, 49–51.
151 Ruskin, *Modern Painters*, III, pt IV, 56–7.
152 Walter Ramal [Walter de la Mare], 'The Child in the Story Goes to Bed', *Songs of Childhood* (London, 1902) p. 94. Humphrey Carpenter, *The Oxford Companion to Children's Literature* (Oxford and New York, 1984) pp. 490–1, notes that this was de la Mare's first collection of poems, and that, although they were inspired by the birth of the poet's own children, his publisher, Longman, thought them 'over the heads of children'.
153 Carroll, 'Novelty and Romancement', *The Complete Works of Lewis Carroll*, pp. 974–5.
154 Kristeva, *Desire in Language*, pp. 70–1.
155 Nesbit, 'My Schooldays', *Girl's Own Paper*, XVIII (Apr. 1897) 436: 'I looked, but such a sight had no charms for me. Where was my flowered-silk, Watteau-hatted maiden? Where was her crook with the

pink ribbons on it? And as for the king's son, his horse could never have ridden up this steep hillside. It was a disenchanted world where I stood gazing sadly at a wrinkle-faced old woman in a blue woollen petticoat. . . . Like Mrs Overtheway, I had looked for pink roses, and found only *feuilles mortes*.' The *'feuilles mortes'* represent the child's disappointment in the once beautiful Mrs Moss in Mrs Ewing's story *Mrs Overtheway's Remembrances* (1869).

156 Rose, *The Case of Peter Pan*, p. 65.
157 Woolf, *The Waves*, p. 131.
158 Zangwill, 'Without Prejudice', *Pall Mall Magazine*, ix (May–Aug. 1896) 156.
159 Nesbit, *Five Children and It*, pp. 159–60.
160 Nesbit, *The Wouldbegoods*, pp. 171, 189, 146–7.
161 Woolf, *Orlando*, p. 77.
162 Woolf, *Jacob's Room*, p. 72.
163 Nesbit, *The Wouldbegoods*, pp. 14, 252, 222, 316, 133.
164 Nesbit, *The Story of the Treasure Seekers*, pp. 160–1. *See* Rosemary Jackson, *Fantasy: The Literature of Subversion* (London and New York, 1981) p. 84: 'The fantastic draws attention to difficulties of representation and to conventions of literary discourse.'
165 Nesbit, *The Wouldbegoods*, p. 145.
166 Bruno Bettelheim and Karen Zelan, *On Learning to Read: The Child's Fascination with Meaning* (London, 1981) pp. 50–3, 71, 90–4, 118–20.
167 Rose, *The Case of Peter Pan*, pp. 118–19.
168 Woolf, *Jacob's Room*, p. 50.
169 Woolf, holograph draft of *'Robinson Crusoe'* in notebook containing *To the Lighthouse*, i. 83 (Berg Collection).
170 Virginia Woolf, *'Robinson Crusoe'*, *The Common Reader II*, pp. 54, 58. The essay was originally published in the *Nation & Athenaeum*, 6 Feb. 1926; Woolf wrote to Vita Sackville West on 7 January 1926: 'I read some of the Tempest, to compare with Defoe.' Two days later she wrote again: 'I'm so furious: I was to begin that wretched novel *To the Lighthouse* today, and now bed and tea and toast and the usual insipidity.' (*The Letters of Virginia Woolf*, iii.226–7.)
171 Grahame, *Dream Days*, p. 149.

Select Bibliography

Note. Dates in square brackets are dates of first edition, where that is not the edition cited.

Aers, Lesley, 'The Treatment of Time in Four Children's Books', *Children's Literature in Education*, no. 2 (July 1970) 69–81.

Alcott, Louisa M., *Little Women* (London, 1910 [1868]).

Annan, Noel, *Leslie Stephen* (London, 1984).

Ariès, Philippe, *Centuries of Childhood*, tr. Robert Baldick (London, 1969).

——, *Western Attitudes toward Death*, tr. Patricia M. Ranum (London, 1976).

Ashford, Daisy, *The Young Visiters* (London, 1963 [1919]).

Avery, Gillian, *Nineteenth Century Children* (London, 1965).

Auerbach, Erich, *Mimesis: The Representation of Reality in Western Literature*, tr. Willard R. Trask (Princeton, NJ, 1953).

Austen, Jane, *Pride and Prejudice* (Oxford, 1967 [1813]).

Babenroth, A. C., *English Childhood: Wordsworth's Treatment of Childhood in the Light of English Poetry from Prior to Crabbe* (New York, 1922).

Bachelard, Gaston, *The Poetics of Reverie*, tr. Daniel Russell (New York, 1969).

Banks, J. A. and Olive, *Feminism and Family Planning in Victorian England* (Liverpool, 1964).

Barbauld, Anna and Aiken, John, *Evenings at Home* (London, 1794).

Barrie, J. M., *Peter Pan, or The Boy Who Would Not Grow Up, The Plays of J. M. Barrie* (London, 1928).

——, *The Little White Bird* (London, 1902).

Barthes, Roland, *Image Music Text*, tr. Stephen Heath (London, 1977).

Battiscombe, Georgina and Laski, Marghanita (eds), *A Chaplet for Charlotte Yonge* (London, 1965).

Baum, Alwin L., 'Carroll's *Alices*: The Semiotics of Paradox', *American Imago*, 34 (Spring 1977) 86–108.

Baum, L. Frank, *The Wizard of Oz* (London, 1984 [1902]).

Beer, Gillian, *Darwin's Plots* (London, 1983).

Beerbohm, Max, 'The Child Barrie' and 'Pantomime for Children', *Saturday Review*, 7 and 14 Jan. 1905.

Bell, Quentin, *Virginia Woolf* (London, 1973).

Bell, Vanessa, *Notes on Virginia's Childhood*, ed. Richard J. Schaubeck, Jr (New York, 1924).

Belloc, Hilaire, *Complete Verse* (London, 1970).

——, *The Bad Child's Book of Beasts* (London, 1923 [1896]).

——, *Cautionary Tales for Children* (London, 1908).

Benedikz, B. S. (ed.), *On the Novel* (London, 1971).

Bergson, Henri, *Time and Free-Will*, tr. F. L. Pogson (London, 1910) from *Essai sur les données immédiates de la conscience* (Paris, 1889).

Bettelheim, Bruno and Zelan, Karen, *On Learning to Read: The Child's Fascination with Meaning* (London, 1981).

Blake, Kathleen, *Play, Games and Sport: The Literary Works of Lewis Carroll* (Ithaca, NY, 1974).

Blishen, Edward (ed.), *The Thorny Paradise: Writers on Writing for Children* (Harmondsworth, 1975).

Block, Ed, 'Evolutionary Psychology and Aesthetics: The Cornhill Magazine 1875–1880', *Journal of the History of Ideas*, XLV (July–Sep. 1984) 465–75.

Boas, George, *The Cult of Childhood* (London, 1966).

Brenda [Mrs G. Castle Smith], *Froggy's Little Brother* (London, 1875).

Brogan, Hugh, *The Life of Arthur Ransome* (London, 1984).

Brontë, Charlotte, *Jane Eyre* (Oxford, 1969 [1847]).

Brontë, Emily, *Wuthering Heights* (Oxford, 1931 [1847]).

Brown, Norman O., *Life Against Death: The Psychoanalytic Meaning of History* (London, 1959).

Browne, Matthew, [William Brighty Rands], *Lilliput Lectures*, in *Good Words for the Young*, 1869.

Bunyan, John, *The Pilgrim's Progress* (Old Woking, 1978 [facsimile of 1678 edn]).

Burnett, Frances Hodgson, *Little Lord Fauntleroy* (Harmondsworth, 1974 [1885]).

——, *Sara Crewe and Editha's Burglar* (London, 1888).

——, *A Little Princess* (Harmondsworth, 1961 [1905]).

——, *The One I Knew Best of All* (London, 1893).

——, *Two Little Pilgrims' Progress: A Story of the City Beautiful* (London, 1895).

——, *How Fauntleroy Occurred* (London, 1894).

——, *In the Closed Room* (London, 1904).

——, *The Secret Garden* (London, 1971 [1911]).

Butler, Marilyn, *Maria Edgeworth: A Literary Biography* (Oxford, 1972).

——, *Jane Austen and the War of Ideas* (Oxford, 1975).

Butler, Samuel, *The Way of All Flesh* (London, 1903).

Calder, Jenni, *RLS: A Life Study* (London, 1980).

Carey, John, *John Donne: Life, Mind and Art* (London, 1981).

Carpenter, Humphrey, *Secret Gardens: A Study of the Golden Age of Children's Literature* (London, 1985).

—— and Prichard, Mari, *The Oxford Companion to Children's Literature* (Oxford and New York, 1984).

Carroll, Lewis, [Charles Lutwidge Dodgson], *Alice's Adventures in Wonderland* (London, 1865).

——, *Through the Looking-Glass, and What Alice Found There* (London, 1871).

——, *Alice's Adventures Under Ground* (London, 1886).

——, *For the Train* (London, 1856–7).

——, *The Complete Works of Lewis Carroll* (London, 1914).

——, *The Annotated Alice*, ed. Martin Gardner (Harmondsworth, 1960).

Cather, Willa, *O Pioneers!* (London, 1913).

——, *My Ántonia* (London, 1980 [1918]).

——, *Not Under Forty* (London, 1936).

——, *The Kingdom of Art: Willa Cather's First Principles and Critical Statements 1893–1962*, ed. Bernice Slote (Lincoln, Nebr., 1966).

——, *On Writing*, (New York, 1968).

Cézanne, Paul, *Letters*, ed. John Rewald (Oxford, 1976).

Charlesworth, Maria Louisa, *Ministering Children* (London, 1854).

'Children's Books', *Quarterly Review*, LXXIV (June 1844) 1–26.

'Children's Literature', *London Review*, XIII (Jan. 1860) 469–500.

The Child's Own Book (London, 1870).

Coe, Richard N., *When the Grass Was Taller: Autobiography and the Experience of Childhood* (New Haven, Conn., and London, 1984).

Coke, V. D. (ed.), *One hundred years of photographic history: essays in honour of Beaumont Newhall* (Albuquerque, 1975).

Coleridge, Christabel, *Charlotte Mary Yonge: Her Life and Letters* (London, 1903).

Collingwood, Stuart Dodgson, *The Life and Letters of Lewis Carroll* (London, 1898).

Cook, Elizabeth, *The Ordinary and the Fabulous* (Cambridge, 1969).

Cooke, Ebenezer, 'Is Development from Within? Did Froebel's Conception of Development Differ from Darwin's?', *Child Life*, VI (15 Oct. 1904) 185–92; VII (16 Jan. 1905) 14–23.

Coolidge, Susan, *What Katy Did* (Harmondsworth, 1963 [1872]).

Coveney, Peter, *The Image of Childhood* (Harmondsworth, 1967).

Crago, Hugh, 'Cultural Categories and the Criticism of Children's Literature', *Signal*, no. 30 (Sep. 1979) 140–50.

Crockett, Samuel Rutherford, *The Surprising Adventures of Sir Toady Lion* (London, 1897).

——, *Sir Toady Crusoe* (London, 1905).

Crouch, Marcus, *The Nesbit Tradition* (London, 1972).

Crozier, Brian, 'Notions of Childhood in London Theatre, 1880–1905' (unpublished PhD thesis, Cambridge, 1981).

Cutt, M. Nancy, *Mrs Sherwood and her Books for Children* (London, 1974).

Daiches, David, *Willa Cather* (Ithaca, NY, 1951).

Darton, F. J. Harvey, *Children's Books in England*, ed. Brian Alderson (Cambridge, 1982 [1932]).

Darwin, Charles, 'Biographical Sketch of an Infant', *Mind*, 2 (July 1877) 285–94.

Day, Thomas, *The History of Sandford and Merton* (London, 1783–9).

Defoe, Daniel, *Robinson Crusoe*, ed. Michael Shinagel (New York, 1975 [1719]).

de la Mare, Walter, *Songs of Childhood* (London, 1902). [Published under pseudonym 'Walter Ramal'.]

——, *Early One Morning in the Spring: Chapters on Children and on Childhood as is Revealed in Particular Early Memories and in Early Writings* (London, 1935).

——, *Memory and Other Poems* (London, 1938).

DeMause, Lloyd (ed.), *The History of Childhood* (London, 1976).

Dusinberre, Juliet, 'The Child's Eye and the Adult's Voice: Flora Thompson's *Lark Rise to Candleford*', *Review of English Studies*, n.s. XXXV, no. 137 (Feb. 1984) 61–70.

Eliot, George, *The Mill on the Floss* (Edinburgh, 1875 [1860]).

——, *The George Eliot Letters*, ed. Gordon S. Haight (London and New Haven, Conn., 1956–78).

Eliot, T. S., *Four Quartets* (London, 1944).

——, 'Tradition and the Individual Talent', *The Sacred Wood* (London, 1920).

Ellis, Havelock, *From Rousseau to Proust* (London, 1936).

E. L. M., 'Lewis Carroll, the Children's Writer', *Child Life*, III (Jan. 1901) 93–6.

Empson, William, *Some Versions of Pastoral* (Cambridge, 1935).

Ewing, Juliana Horatia, *Mrs Overtheway's Remembrances* (London, 1925 [1869]).

Farrar, F. W., *Eric, Or Little by Little* (London, 1928 [1858]).

Field, E. M., *The Child and His Book* (London, 1891).

Fisher, Margery, *Intent Upon Reading* (Leicester, 1961).

Fleishman, Avrom, *The English Historical Novel: Walter Scott to Virginia Woolf* (Baltimore, 1971).

——, 'Woolf and McTaggart', *English Literary History*, 36 (Dec. 1969) 719–38.

Forster, E. M., *Aspects of the Novel* (London, 1927).

——, *A Room with a View* (London, 1908).

——, *Virginia Woolf* (New York, 1942).

Foucault, Michel, *The Order of Things: An Archaeology of the Human Sciences*, tr. from the French (London, 1970).

——, *The History of Sexuality*, tr. Robert Hurley (London, 1978).

Fox, G. (ed.), *Writers, Critics and Children: Articles from Children's Literature in Education* (London, 1976).

Freeman, Rosemary, *English Emblem Books* (London, 1948).

Freud, Sigmund, *Standard Edition of the Works of Sigmund Freud*, tr. James Strachey, 21 vols (Hogarth Press, 1978).

Froebel, Friedrich, *Autobiography*, tr. Emilie Michaelis and H. Kealey Moore (London, 1886).

——, *Froebel's Chief Writings on Education*, ed. S. S. F. Fletcher and J. Welton (London, 1912).

Fry, Roger, *Vision and Design* (London, 1920).

——, *Transformations* (London, 1926).

——, *Characteristics of French Art* (London, 1932).

——, *Cézanne* (London, 1932).

——, *Reflections on British Painting* (London, 1934).

——, *Last Lectures* (Cambridge, 1939).

Gardner, Helen, *The Composition of Four Quartets* (London, 1978).

Gaskell, Elizabeth, *North and South* (Harmondsworth, 1970 [1854–5]).

Gatty, Margaret, *Aunt Sally's Life* (London, 1865).

Gernsheim, Helmut, *Lewis Carroll: Photographer* (London, 1949).

——, *Julia Margaret Cameron* (London, 1975).

Glen, Heather, *Vision and Disenchantment: Blake's Songs and Wordsworth's Lyrical Ballads* (Cambridge, 1983).

Godden, Rumer, *The Dolls' House* (London, 1947).

Gordon, Lyndall, *Virginia Woolf: A Writer's Life* (Oxford, 1984).

Gosse, Edmund, *Father and Son* (London, 1929 [1907]).

Grahame, Kenneth, *Pagan Papers* (London, 1894).

——, *The Golden Age* (London, 1915 [1895]).
——, *Dream Days* (London, 1899).
——, *The Wind in the Willows* (London, 1908).
—— (ed.), *The Cambridge Book of Poetry for Children* (Cambridge, 1932 [1916]).
Green, Peter, *Kenneth Grahame, 1859–1932* (London, 1959).
Greenacre, Phyllis, *Emotional Growth: Psychoanalytic Studies of the Gifted and a Great Variety of Other Individuals*, ii (New York, 1971).
Greenaway, Kate, *Book of Games* (London, 1889).
——, *Under the Window: Pictures and Rhymes for Children* (London, 1879).
——, *Little Folks Painting Book* (London, 1879).
——, *Marigold Garden* (London, 1885).
——, *Kate Greenaway's Alphabet* (London, 1885).
——, *Mother Goose or the Old Nursery Rhymes* (London, 1881).
——, *A Apple Pie* (London, 1886).
Greene, Theodore Meyer, *The Arts and the Art of Criticism* (Princeton, NJ, 1940).
Grotjahn, Martin, *Beyond Laughter* (New York, 1957).
Guiguet, Jean, *Virginia Woolf and her Works*, tr. Jean Stewart (Hogarth Press, 1965).
Haggard, H. Rider, *King Solomon's Mines* (Harmondsworth, 1979 [1885]).
Haight, Gordon S., *George Eliot* (Oxford, 1968).
Hammerton, J. A., *Stevensoniana* (Edinburgh, 1907).
Hardy, Thomas, *The Return of the Native* (London, 1972 [1878]).
——, *Tess of the d'Urbervilles* (London, 1967 [1891]).
——, *Far from the Madding Crowd* (London, 1974 [1874]).
Harris, Joel Chandler, *Uncle Remus and his Legends of the Old Plantation* (London, 1881).
Hatch, Beatrice, 'Lewis Carroll', *Strand Magazine*, xv (Jan.–June 1898) 413–23.
Hayward, F. H., *The Educational Ideas of Pestalozzi and Froebel* (London, 1904).
Hoban, Russell, *The Mouse and His Child* (Harmondsworth, 1976).
Holroyd, Michael, *Lytton Strachey* (London, 1968).
Hönnighausen, Lothar, ' "Point of view" and its Background in Intellectual History', *Comparative Criticism*, 2 (Cambridge, 1980) 151–66.
Hough, Graham, *The Last Romantics* (London, 1949).
——, *Image and Experience: Studies in a Literary Revolution* (London, 1960).
Howitt, Mary, *The Children's Year* (London, 1847).
——, *The Spider and the Fly* (London, 1939), repr. from *Sketches of Natural History* (London, 1834).
Hoyles, Martin (ed.), *Changing Childhood* (London, 1979).
Hunt, Peter, 'Criticism and Children's Literature', *Signal*, no. 15 (Sep. 1974) 117–30.
——, 'The Mayne Game: An Experiment in Response', *Signal*, no. 28 (Jan. 1979) 9–25.
Husserl, Edmund, *The Phenomenology of Time-Consciousness*, ed. Martin Heidegger, tr. James S. Churchill (Bloomington, Ind., and London, 1966).
Jackson, Rosemary, *Fantasy: The Literature of Subversion* (London and New York, 1981).

James, Henry, *What Maisie Knew* (New York, 1909 [1897]).
——, *Roderick Hudson* (New York, 1960 [1875]).
——, *The Portrait of a Lady* (Harmondsworth, 1974 [1881]).
——, *The Real Thing and Other Tales* (London, 1893).
James, William, *The Principles of Psychology* (London, 1890).
——, *Essays in Radical Empiricism* (London, 1912).
——, *The Will to Believe* (London, 1897).
Jan, Isabelle, *On Children's Literature*, tr. and ed. Catherine Storr (London, 1973).
Jay, Elisabeth, *The Religion of the Heart: Anglican Evangelicalism and the Nineteenth-Century Novel* (Oxford, 1979).
Jefferies, Richard, *Bevis* (London, 1891 [1882]).
Jekyll, Gertrude, *Children and Gardens* (London, 1908).
Jensen, Wilhelm, *Delusion and Dream and Gradiva*, tr. Helen M. Downey (London, 1917).
——, *Fair Isle: A Tale in Verse*, tr. from the German by a Shetlander (Kirkwall, 1881).
——, *Runic Rocks, A North-Sea Idyll*, tr. Marianne E. Suckling (London, 1895).
Johnstone, J. K., *The Bloomsbury Group: A Study of E. M. Forster, Lytton Strachey, Virginia Woolf and their Circle* (New York, 1954).
Jones, L. E., *A Victorian Boyhood* (London, 1955).
Kern, Stephen, 'Freud and the Discovery of Child Sexuality', *History of Childhood Quarterly*, I (Summer 1973) 117–41.
Key, Ellen, *The Century of the Child* (New York and London, 1909).
Kimmins, C. W., 'The Child as the Director of the Parent's Education', *Child Life*, III (July 1901) 128–34.
Kingsley, Charles, *The Water-Babies* (London, 1863).
——, 'Madam How and Why', *Good Words for the Young*, IV (Feb. 1869); regular contributions later collected into a book, *Madam How and Lady Why* (London, 1870).
Kipling, Rudyard, *The Jungle Book* (London, 1894).
——, *The Second Jungle Book* (London, 1895).
——, *Stalky & Co.* (London, 1982 [1899]).
——, *Just So Stories for Little Children* (London, 1902).
——, *Puck of Pook's Hill* (London, 1924 [1906]).
——, *Rewards and Fairies* (London, 1983 [1910]).
Kirkpatrick, B. J., *A Bibliography of Virginia Woolf*, 3rd ed. (Oxford, 1980).
Kristeva, Julia, *Desire in Language*, tr. Thomas Gora, Alice Jardine and Leon S. Roudiez (New York, 1980).
Laski, Marghanita, *Mrs Ewing, Mrs Molesworth and Mrs Hodgson Burnett* (London, 1950).
Lawrence, D. H., *Sons and Lovers* (Harmondsworth, 1983 [1913]).
Lear, Edward, *A Book of Nonsense* (London, 1863 [1846]).
——, *Nonsense Botany and Nonsense Alphabets* (London, 1870).
——, *Nonsense Songs and Stories* (London, 1894).
Leaska, Mitchell A., *Virginia Woolf's Lighthouse: A Study in Critical Method* (London, 1970).
——, 'Virginia Woolf's *The Voyage Out*: Character Deduction and the Function of Ambiguity', *Virginia Woolf Quarterly*, I (Winter 1973) 18–41.

Lee, Hermione, *The Novels of Virginia Woolf* (London, 1977).
Leeson, Robert, *Children's Books and Class Society, past and present* (Writers and Readers Publishing Co-operative, 1977).
Lehmann, John F., *Lewis Carroll and the Spirit of Nonsense* (Nottingham, 1972).
Levy, Paul, *Moore: G. E. Moore and the Cambridge Apostles* (Oxford, 1981).
Lewis, C. S., *Of This and Other Worlds*, ed. Walter Hooper (London, 1982).
'Literature of Childhood', *London and Westminster Review*, xxxiii, no. 2 (1839) 137–62.
Lively, Penelope, *A Stitch in Time* (London, 1976).
Lockhart, J. H., *Memoirs of the Life of Sir Walter Scott, Bart.* (Edinburgh, 1839).
Lodge, David, *The Novelist at the Crossroads* (London, 1971).
——, *The Modes of Modern Writing* (London, 1977).
Lombroso, Cesare, *The Man of Genius* (London, 1891).
Long, Michael, *Marvell, Nabokov, Childhood and Arcadia* (Oxford, 1984).
MacCabe, Colin, *James Joyce and the Revolution of the Word* (London, 1978).
McKay, George L., *A Stevenson Library: Catalogue of a Collection of Writings by and about R. L. Stevenson formed by E. J. Beinecke* (New Haven, Conn., 1951–69).
Manlove, C. N., *The Impulse of Fantasy Literature* (London, 1983).
Mann, Thomas, *Joseph and His Brethren*, tr. H. T. Lowe-Porter (London, 1934–45).
Marenholtz-Bülow, Baroness, *Child and Child-Nature*, tr. Alice M. Christie (London, 1879).
——, *Woman's Educational Mission: Being an Explanation of Frederick Froebel's System of Infant Gardens*, tr. Elizabeth, Countess Krockow von Wickerode (London, 1855).
Martineau, Harriet, *The Crofton Boys*, vol. iv of *The Playfellow* (London, 1841).
Melly, George, and Glaves-Smith, J. R., *A Child of Six Could Do It* (London, 1973).
Molesworth, Mary Louisa, *Tell me a Story* (London, 1875).
——, *Carrots* (London, 1876).
——, *The Cuckoo Clock* (London, 1877).
——, *The Tapestry Room* (London, 1879).
——, *The Adventures of Herr Baby* (London, 1881).
——, *An Enchanted Garden* (London, 1892).
Montaigne, Michel de, *The Essayes of Michael Lord of Montaigne*, tr. John Florio (London, 1928).
Montgomery, Florence, *Misunderstood* (London, 1869).
Moore, Doris Langley, *E. Nesbit* (London, 1967).
Moore, Rosa Ann, 'Laura Ingalls Wilder's Orange Notebooks and the Art of the *Little House* Books', *Children's Literature*, iv (1975) 105–19.
——, 'The *Little House* Books: "Rose-Colored Classics"', *Children's Literature*, v (1976) 7–16.
Morris, William, *News from Nowhere* (London, 1892 [1873]).
Murray, E. R., *Froebel as a Pioneer in Modern Psychology* (London, 1914).
Naremore, James, *The World Without a Self* (New Haven, Conn., and London, 1973).

Nash, Ogden, *Custard and Company* (Harmondsworth, 1979).
Nesbit, E., *The Story of the Treasure Seekers* (London, 1899).
——, *The Wouldbegoods* (London, 1902 [1901]).
——, *The Book of Dragons* (London, 1901).
——, *Five Children and It* (London, 1902).
——, *The Phoenix and the Carpet* (London, 1905 [1904]).
——, *The Story of the Amulet* (London, 1906 [1905]).
——, *The Railway Children* (London, 1906).
——, *The House of Arden*, (London, 1908).
——, *Harding's Luck* (London, 1909).
——, 'My Schooldays', *Girl's Own Paper*, xviii (Oct. 1896–Aug. 1897).
——, *The Literary Sense* (London, 1903).
Newhall, Beaumont (ed.), *Photography: Essays & Images* (London, 1980).
Orwell, George, *The Road to Wigan Pier* (Harmondsworth, 1962 [1937]).
Ortega y Gasset, José, *The Modern Theme*, tr. James Cleugh (London, 1931).
Pater, Walter, *The Works of Walter Pater* (London, 1900).
Payne, George Henry, *The Child in Human Progress* (New York and London, 1916).
Pearce, Philippa, *Tom's Midnight Garden* (London, 1958).
Phillips, Robert (ed.), *Aspects of Alice* (London, 1972).
Piaget, Jean, *Play, Dreams and Imitation in Childhood* (London, 1951).
——, *The Child's Conception of Time*, tr. A. J. Pomerans (London, 1969 [1947]).
Pickering, Samuel F., Jr, *John Locke and Children's Books in Eighteenth-Century England* (Knoxville, Tenn., 1981).
Plumb, J. H., 'The New World of Children in Eighteenth-Century England', *Past and Present*, 67 (May 1975) 64–93.
Pollock, George H., 'On Siblings, Childhood Sibling Loss and Creativity', *Annual of Psychoanalysis*, vi (1978) 443–81.
Pollock, Linda, *Forgotten Children* (Cambridge, 1983).
Proust, Marcel, *The Remembrance of Things Past*, tr. C. K. Scott Moncrieff and Terence Kilmartin (Harmondsworth, 1981).
Raverat, Gwen, *Period Piece* (London, 1952).
Rees, David, 'The Novels of Philippa Pearce', *Children's Literature in Education*, 4 (Mar. 1971) 40–53.
——, *Painted Desert, Green Shade* (Boston, Mass., 1984).
Richardson, Dorothy, *Pilgrimage* (London, 1967 [1915–35]).
Richardson, Joanna, *Edward Lear* (London, 1965). Writers and their Work, No. 184.
Robbe-Grillet, Alain, *Snapshots and Towards a New Novel*, tr. Barbara Wright (London, 1965).
Rose, Jacqueline, *The Case of Peter Pan or the Impossibility of Children's Fiction* (London, 1984).
Rousseau, Jean-Jacques, *Emilius or A Treatise of Education*, tr. from the French (Edinburgh, 1763).
Ruskin, John, *Modern Painters* (Orpington, 1888).
Saussure, Ferdinand de, *Course in General Linguistics*, ed. Charles Bally and Albert Sechchaye, tr. Wade Baskin (London, 1974 [1915]).
Schiller, Friedrich, *Schiller's Essays Aesthetical and Philosophical*, tr. from the German (London, 1875).

Schivelbusch, Wolfgang, *The Railway Journey: Trains and Travel in the 19th Century*, tr. Anselm Hollo (Oxford, 1980).

Sewell, Elizabeth, *The Field of Nonsense* (London, 1952).

Sharrock, Roger (ed.), *Bunyan, The Pilgrim's Progress: A Casebook* (London, 1976).

Sherover, Charles M., *Heidegger, Kant and Time* (Bloomington, Ind. 1971).

Sherwood, Mary Martha, *The History of the Fairchild Family* (London, 1841 [1818]).

——, The Fairchild Family, re-told by Jeanie Lang, *Grandmother's Favourites* (London and Edinburgh [1908]).

——, *The Fairchild Family*, ed. Lady Strachey (London, 1913).

Shmuëli, Adi, *Kierkegaard and Consciousness*, tr. Naomi Handelman (Princeton, NJ, 1971).

Sinclair, Catherine, *Holiday House* (London, 1885 [1839]).

——, *Holiday House*, retold by Olive Allen (London, 1908).

Slater, Catherine Ponton, 'Story-Book Children', *Child Life*, VII (Jan. 1905) 26–8.

Smith, Janet Adam (ed.), *Henry James and Robert Louis Stevenson* (London, 1948).

Spalding, Francis, *Roger Fry* (London, 1980).

——, *Vanessa Bell* (London, 1983).

Spiegelberg, Herbert, *The Phenomenological Movement* (The Hague, 1960).

Spyri, Johanna, *Heidi* (London, 1950 [1881]).

Steinbeck, John, *The Grapes of Wrath* (New York, 1939).

Stephen, Leslie, *Studies of a Biographer*, 4 vols (London, 1902).

——, *Sir Leslie Stephen's Mausoleum Book*, ed. Alan Bell (Oxford, 1977).

Stevenson, Robert Louis, *The Works of Robert Louis Stevenson* (Edinburgh, 1898).

——, *Robert Louis Stevenson: Collected Poems*, ed. Janet Adam Smith (London, 1950).

——, *Treasure Island* (London, 1885 [1883]).

——, *Kidnapped: being Memoirs of the Adventures of David Balfour* (London, 1886).

——, *A Child's Garden of Verses*, illustrated by Charles Robinson (London, 1896 [1st edn, not illustrated, 1885]).

——, *Virginibus Puerisque and Other Papers* (London, 1881).

——, *Familiar Studies of Men and Books* (London, 1882).

——, *Across the Plains* (London, 1892).

——, *An Apology for Idlers and Other Essays* (Portland, Maine, 1905).

——, *Poems by R. L. Stevenson, hitherto unpublished*, ed. George S. Hellman and William P. Trent (Boston, Mass., 1921).

——, *Stevenson's Workshop*, ed. William P. Trent (Boston, Mass., 1921).

——, *The Letters of Robert Louis Stevenson to his family and friends*, ed. Sidney Colvin (New York, 1899).

Stewart, Garrett, *Death Sentences: Styles of Dying in British Fiction* (Cambridge, Mass., 1984).

Strachey, Lytton, *Eminent Victorians* (London, 1918).

Sully, James, *Sensation and Intuition: Studies in Psychology and Aesthetics* (London, 1874).

———, Outlines of Psychology (London, 1884).
———, Studies of Childhood (London, 1895).
———, Children's Ways (London, 1897).
———, 'The Child in Recent English Literature', Fortnightly Review, 67, n.s. 61 (Feb. 1897) 218–28.
Sutherland, J. A., Victorian Novelists and Publishers (London, 1976).
'M. Taine on the Acquisition of Language by Children', Revue Philosophique, 1 (Jan 1876), tr. in Mind, 2 (Apr. 1877) 252–9.
Thackeray, William Makepeace, The Rose and the Ring (New York, 1947 [1855]).
———, [under pseudonym 'M. A. Titmarsh'], The Kickleburys on the Rhine (London, 1851 [1850]).
———, Vanity Fair (London, 1864 [1847]).
Thwaite, Ann, Waiting for the Party: The Life of Frances Hodgson Burnett 1849–1924 (London, 1974).
———, Edmund Gosse: a literary landscape 1849–1928 (London, 1984).
Thompson, E. P., The Making of the English Working Class (London, 1963).
Thompson, Flora, Lark Rise to Candleford (Oxford, 1945).
Tillotson, Geoffrey, A View of Victorian Literature (Oxford, 1978).
Tolkien, J. R. R., Tree and Leaf (London, 1964).
Tolstoy, Leo, Childhood and Youth, tr. Melwida von Meysenbug (London, 1862).
———, Childhood, Boyhood, Youth, tr. Isabel F. Hapgood (London, 1889).
———, Childhood, Boyhood, Youth, tr. Rosemary Edmonds (Harmondsworth, 1964).
Townsend, John Rowe, Written for Children (London, 1965).
———, A Sense of Story (London, 1971).
Trease, Geoffrey, Tales Out of School (London, 1964).
Trotter, Wilfrid, Instincts of the Herd In Peace and War (London, 1916).
Troyat, Henri, Tolstoy, tr. Nancy Amphoux (Harmondsworth, 1970).
Turner, Elizabeth, The Daisy, or Cautionary Stories in Verse (London, 1807).
———, The Cowslip, or More Cautionary Stories in Verse (London, 1811).
Twain, Mark [Samuel Langhorne Clemens], The Adventures of Tom Sawyer (London, 1876).
———, The Adventures of Huckleberry Finn (London, 1884).
Uttley, Alison, A Traveller in Time (Harmondsworth, 1978 [1939]).
Warner, Eric and Hough, Graham (eds), Strangeness and Beauty: An Anthology of Aesthetic Criticism 1840–1910 (Cambridge, 1983).
Warner, Eric (ed.), Virginia Woolf: A Centenary Tribute (London, 1984).
Watts, Isaac, Divine Songs, attempted in easy language for the use of children (London, 1971 [1715]).
Wells, H. G., The Time Machine (Harmondsworth, 1966 [1895]).
Westermarck, Edward, The History of Human Marriage (London, 1891).
———, The Origin and Development of Moral Ideas (London, 1906).
Wheeler, Michael, The Art of Allusion in the Victorian Novel (London, 1979).
White, Allon, '"L'éclatement du sujet": The Theoretical Work of Julia Kristeva' (Centre for Contemporary Studies, University of Birmingham, SP.49, 1977).
White, E. B., Charlotte's Web (New York, 1952).

Whitehead, Frank, Capey, A. C., Maddren, Wendy and Wellings, Alan, *Children and Their Books* (London, 1977).

Wild, John, *The Radical Empiricism of William James* (New York, 1969).

Wilde, Oscar, *The Happy Prince and Other Stories* (Harmondsworth, 1962 [1888]).

——, *The Decay of Lying* (London, 1891).

Wilder, Laura Ingalls, *Little House in the Big Woods* (Harmondsworth, 1963 [1932]).

——, *Little House on the Prairie* (Harmondsworth, 1964 [1935]).

——, *On the Banks of Plum Creek* (Harmondsworth, 1965 [1937]).

——, *By the Shores of Silver Lake* (Harmondsworth, 1978 [1934]).

——, *The Long Winter* (Harmondsworth, 1968 [1940]).

——, *Little Town on the Prairie* (Harmondsworth, 1969 [1941]).

——, *Those Happy Golden Years* (Harmondsworth, 1970 [1943]).

——, *Farmer Boy* (Harmondsworth, 1972 [1933]).

——, *The First Four Years* (Guildford, 1973 [1971]).

Winnicott, D. W., *Playing and Reality* (London, 1971).

Woolf, Leonard, *Autobiography* (Hogarth Press), I: *Sowing, 1880–1904* (1960); II: *Growing, 1904–1911* (1977); III: *Beginning Again, 1911–1918* (1978); IV: *Downhill All the Way, 1919–1939* (1967), V: *The Journey not the Arrival Matters, 1939–1969* (1969).

Woolf, Virginia, *The Voyage Out* (Hogarth Press, 1975) [1915]).

——, *Night and Day* (Hogarth Press, 1977 [1919]).

——, *Jacob's Room* (Hogarth Press, 1980 [1922]).

——, *Mrs Dalloway* (Hogarth Press, 1925).

——, *To the Lighthouse* (Hogarth Press, 1982 [1927]).

——, *Orlando* (Hogarth Press, 1928).

——, *A Room of One's Own* (Hogarth Press, 1929 [1928]).

——, *The Waves* (Hogarth Press, 1980 [1932]).

——, *Flush* (Hogarth Press, 1933).

——, *The Years* (Hogarth Press, 1979 [1937]).

——, *Between the Acts* (Hogarth Press, 1941).

——, *Roger Fry: A Biography* (Harmondsworth, 1979 [1940]).

—— and Woolf, Leonard, *Two Stories* (Hogarth Press, 1917).

——, *Mr. Bennett and Mrs. Brown* (Hogarth Press, 1924).

——, *Kew Gardens*, decorated by Vanessa Bell (Hogarth Press, 1927 [1919]).

——, *The Common Reader I* (Hogarth Press, 1984 [1925]).

——, *The Common Reader II* (Hogarth Press, 1980 [1932]).

——, *The Death of the Moth* (Hogarth Press, 1942).

——, *The Moment and Other Essays* (Hogarth Press, 1947).

——, *A Haunted House* (Hogarth Press, 1978 [1944]).

——, *The Captain's Death Bed* (Hogarth Press, 1950).

——, *Granite and Rainbow* (Hogarth Press, 1958).

——, *Moments of Being*, ed. Jeanne Schulkind (Sussex, 1976).

——, *The Diary of Virginia Woolf*, ed. Anne Olivier Bell and Andrew McNeillie (Hogarth Press, 1977–84).

——, *A Writer's Diary*, ed. Leonard Woolf (Hogarth Press, 1975).

——, *The Letters of Virginia Woolf*, ed. Nigel Nicolson and Joanne Trautmann (Hogarth Press, 1975–80).

———, *Freshwater, A Comedy*, ed. Lucio P. Ruotolo (New York and London, 1978).

———, *Melymbrosia*, ed. Louise DeSalvo (New York, 1982).

———, *To the Lighthouse: the original holograph draft*, ed. Susan Dick (Toronto and Buffalo, 1982).

———, *Virginia Woolf, The Waves*: The two holograph drafts transcribed and edited J. W. Graham (London, 1976).

Wright, Elizabeth, *Psychoanalytic Criticism* (London, 1984).

Wordsworth, William, *The Complete Poetical Works* (London, 1950).

Yeats, W. B., *Reveries over Childhood and Youth* (Churchtown, Dundrum, 1915).

Yonge, Charlotte Mary, *The Daisy Chain or Aspirations, A Family Chronicle* (London, 1856).

———, *A Book of Golden Deeds* (London and Cambridge, 1864).

———, 'Children's Literature of the Last Century', *Macmillan's Magazine*, xx (May–Oct. 1869) 229–37, 302–10, 448–56.

Zangwill, Israel, 'Without Prejudice', *Pall Mall Magazine*, 1893–6.

Zochert, Donald, *Laura: The Life of Laura Ingalls Wilder* (Chicago, 1976).

UNPUBLISHED MATERIALS

Roger Fry Papers, King's College, Cambridge.

Robert Louis Stevenson Collection, the General Collection, Beinecke Rare Book and Manuscript Library, Yale University.

Virginia Woolf papers, Henry W. and Albert A. Berg Collection of English and American Literature, New York Public Library.

Taped conversation between Mrs Pamela Diamand and Juliet Dusinberre, King's College, Cambridge.

Index

Index